The Wolf in a Suit

The 7 Secrets Inside Relationship Abuse

Fairy Tales and Truths for Women, Community and Professionals

Anita Bentata

First published by Busybird Publishing 2016
Copyright © 2016 Anita Bentata
Print ISBN: 978-0-9946156-5-7
Ebook ISBN: 978-0-9946156-6-4

Anita Bentata has asserted her right under the Copyright, Designs and Patents Act 1988 to be identified as the author of this work. The information in this book is based on the author's experiences and opinions. The publisher specifically disclaims responsibility for any adverse consequences, which may result from use of the information contained herein. Permission to use information has been sought by the author. Any breaches will be rectified in further editions of the book.

All rights reserved. No part of this publication may be reproduced, stored in or introduced into a retrieval system, or transmitted in any form, or by any means (electronic, mechanical, photocopying, recording or otherwise) without the prior written permission of the author. Any person who does any unauthorised act in relation to this publication may be liable to criminal prosecution and civil claims for damages. Enquiries should be made through the publisher.

Cover image: Kev Howlett, Busybird Publishing
Cover design: Busybird Publishing
Illustrator: Jessica Hall
Layout and typesetting: Busybird Publishing

Busybird Publishing
PO Box 855
Eltham Victoria
Australia 3095
www.busybird.com.au

Testimonials

'The world thought I had the perfect life and the perfect family. No one knew the truth behind closed doors. The family violence was unnamable for me and without a doubt, you helped me to recognise and name it. I remember the great sense of relief to hear you call it 'violence' – like finally, there was someone in the world that could confirm that what happened was wrong.

'The safe space that you created and held for me, your openness in sharing some of your own experiences (which built on the trust and your patience and skill), knowing when I needed a moment (or several) in silence or some kind of intervention to ease my distress – all of this helped me with identifying and naming the violence I experienced and working through it to be free from it.

'I finally feel like I am enough! And that's a mighty victory for me! 'Thank you' will never, ever cut it.'
    Lisa G, Client

'Knowing that Anita is a psychotherapist and a specialist in the field of DV, I saw her for a number of sessions to deal with, and heal, my distress about a troubled relationship with a sibling.

'Anita was amazing. She very quickly and succinctly clarified the dynamic including domestic violence, which made an enormous difference for me. I was able to dissolve the self-blame I hadn't even realised I was carrying, come to terms with the reality of the relationship, and minimise my contact. I am now very much at peace.'
    Anonymous Female Client

'Anita's professional supervision bridged the gap between what I found lacking from my university experience and what I needed to develop to feel sufficiently equipped in my private practice. Anita takes a nuanced approach to the inherently complex question of what each individual needs from therapy. She detected Family Violence issues that I might not have otherwise found, and taught me how to remain open, curious and trusting of my new skills. Anita has a wealth of experience and a dedication to her work that far surpasses any other I've come in contact with.'
    Alex Spartels

'I wanted to work with someone who could hear of my culture, background and the story of my life so far. I very much appreciated [Anita's] ability to listen, connect the dots and ask questions that created greater awareness for me, and also challenged me to think about my relationship and the subtle family violence (FV) aspects.

'As a man, emotional abuse in a relationship is, I think, a taboo issue. [She] helped me talked about it in safety and 'stood by me' as I unpacked six years of abuse, emotional violence, my coping strategies and how I ended up where I am today. Labelling it made a big difference. Just the fact that [she] pieced together the toxicity in the relationship in the last few years – and also confirming to me that it was not all my fault – helped me get stronger and made me feel as though I mattered again.

'[Anita] always went back to my values, beliefs and limitations and challenged which ones were real and which my excuses to strive off emotional abuse. [Anita] helped me realise that as a man, it was okay to hurt and find ways forward by accepting me as who I am.'
Anonymous Male Client

'I have a history of family violence. My father was physically violent to my mother. I was unhappy in my marriage and had tried to leave but found it difficult to make the break. Anita helped me clarify feelings, which were hazy and unclear.

'Anita helped me acknowledge, recognise and confirm that I was in an abusive relationship, which enabled me to feel independent in my choice to leave the abuser after a twenty-seven year marriage. I now feel at peace from my past.'
Cristina Zambon, Client

'Working with Anita Bentata to create her Keynote was incredibly exciting. Anita has a depth of compassion, experience, training and genius in presenting her material to embrace the wider social context and provide truly positive solutions and understandings. She also addresses the possibilities for resolution and transformation for personal trauma. She is a superb educator and passionately connected to being of service with her work. Anita walks her talk. Her authenticity, combined with her constructive insights are a blessing to this subject. I would recommend that she speak to any audience, intimate or vast with her work.'
Dominique Oyston, Keynote coach and speaking specialist, The Speaking Coach for Conscious Women

'As a psychotherapist I wanted to learn how best to support and help heal clients who have been victims of family violence. Anita's workshop provided all of that and more. She presented the information in a clear and concise manner, and her compassion, experience and expertise shone through. I left with more confidence and an enhanced ability to work with my clients affected by family violence.'
Irene E. Speiser, Psychotherapist August, 2015

'I have been working with Anita on her upcoming book, *The Wolf in a Suit: 7 Steps Out Of Violence*. Anita's story is very relevant in a day when domestic violence is on the cusp of being talked about more freely. Her book will open up the conversation and save many women from a life of fear, sadness and despair. Busybird Publishing is very honoured to have been chosen to work on the book with Anita and we look forward to watching her make a big difference to people's lives.'
Blaise van Hecke, Director at Busybird Publishing

'Anita has been an inspiration to work with. Her new way of thinking, brought to a problem that is so common in our society is a breath of fresh air. She is creative, determined and passionate about the cause. Anita continues to change many women's lives from being a survivor to thriving and excelling in their new lives. Thank you for allowing me to help you bring out *The Wolf in a Suit to reality*.'
Natasa Denman – Founder of Ultimate 48 Hour Author

'Anita, I want to thank you for your beautiful message to everybody. I already owe this group so much. For me, connecting with a bunch of women who get it, meant so so much! As I understand it not feeling seen and heard is a big part of what was done to us. I only know I met some beautiful and inspiring women who really got it! For me that was so important and so healing. I really want to catch up with everybody again. I felt deeply connected with you all from just the one session I was able to get to. Anita you are a lovely person with a terrific vision. Your efforts with this group have already helped me more than you know.'
Anonymous, from Anita's 370+ member Women Starting Again group

'I walked away today feeling affirmed, excited and empowered ... already!'
Anonymous, from Anita's 370+ member Women Starting Again group

'I find your book extremely thorough and thought-provoking. I really love how you've discussed all of the issues in the context of the reinterpreted fairy stories. I'm loving the way you're weaving the fairy stories into your book ... [The Cinderella, Anger] chapter was particularly very well presented and really enlightening. Thank you for sharing your wisdom!
  Richard Burian, Language and E-book publishing Specialist

'An amazing woman, teacher and mentor – words would never do justice to how much I would recommend working with Anita!'
  J. S Client

A guide to reading

Read the Introduction

You may then be ready to dive in and read *The Wolf in a Suit* from cover to cover.

If you are not, and want to take a piece at a time, here is a suggested guide.

To read my story:

Read Chapters 1-6

To read about: What is abuse, the types of abuse and the difference between abuse and conflict, read Chapter 7

To read about: Family, Culture, History, Religion, read Chapter 8

To read about: Love, False Love and the hooks, which make it hard to leave, read Chapter 9

To read about: Anger, Power, Assertion, Aggression and Passivity, read Chapter 10

To read about: Hope and the Cycle of Violence, read Chapter 11

To read about: Stress, Women's unique stress response, read Chapter 12

No matter what order you read the rest of the book, for Closure, Read about Healing and reclaiming your feminine instinct, Chapter 13

And then read the Afterword for closure.

Dedication

To *my daughters,*
my heartbeat, my flesh, my pride and joy.
For your innocence and your wisdom.
For opening me to love, power and no more secrets.

~

Kaalii and Andrew Cargill
My Soul Centred Psychotherapy teachers and supervisors
who brought me back to life
from the twisted depths of hell.

~

For the women in the Making Choices and Creating Connections groups,
I keep my promise
to explain to the world why women stay.

~

For my maternal grandmother, Matylda Engelman
Author of Journey Without End and End of the Journey
Nana, the journey continues.

~

For me
For never, ever, ever giving up.

Contents

Introduction: Who is Telling Tales? ... i

Part 1: Fairy Tale or Nightmare? ... 1
   Chapter 1:   The Little Red Riding Hood Effect ... 3
   Chapter 2:   In the Wolf's Belly ... 25
   Chapter 3:   The Woodcutter Within ... 45
   Chapter 4:   The Snarling Wolf ... 63
   Chapter 5:   Changing Paths ... 91
   Chapter 6:   Where are Mother and Father? ... 139

Part 2: The Real World ... 175
   Chapter 7:   Rumpelstiltskin ... 177
   Chapter 8:   The Handless Maiden ... 209
   Chapter 9:   Bluebeard's Seduction ... 255
   Chapter 10: Banished Lilith ... 303
   Chapter 11: The Little Match Girl ... 355
   Chapter 12: The Red Shoes ... 385
   Chapter 13: Vasilisa the Queen ... 423

Afterword ... 473

Resources ... 481

Meet Anita ... 487

Offer 1 ... 491
Offer 2 ... 493
Offer 3 ... 496
Offer 4 ... 499

Acknowledgements ... 503

References and Further Reading ... 507

Notes ... 517

Introduction: Who is Telling Tales?

I remember when my lawyer asked me to write out everything that had happened while it was still fresh in my mind. I could feel shame and stupidity running through me as I sat alone with the whole catastrophe. No one was able to bear the whole, including me, and the hole lay gaping within me.

I would sit at my sister's computer, as I did not possess my own. Day after day, I'd play catch-up and type years of memories. Sobbing silently at the painful memories so I did not disturb my children in the next room. Sobbing in despair over how the words were so inadequate in portraying the depth of what had happened.

How could I translate being frozen in fear? The unpredictable and violent actions; those icy, cruel looks that made me flinch mid-motion; those cold words thrown like knives; the heavy, thick fear coating every particle of air and every cell in my being. He was a walking reminder of all the threats and punishment that had been and were yet to come. My isolation. Pinned against the wall, dragged on the ground. How would anyone understand what got me here? How could I? After all, aren't we all taught right from wrong as a child?

Knowing right from wrong and ending up in abuse – is a big gap. At times, don't we all fall into gaps? Gaps from overwhelm, or we don't want to upset someone. Gaps because we don't know how to be with uncomfortable feelings; difficult experiences and helplessness.

We have lost touch with the art of living. We are superimposed with elite ideals and bombarded with technology and marketing. We don't want to feel out of control and reveal the 'mess' – that we don't know what to do. We don't want anyone to fall to pieces. We don't want to reject anyone or be rejected, shamed or ridiculed. We don't want to be wrong or 'weak'.

So we leave gaps in our sentences, deleting important details. Gaps in our feelings, leaving out certain feelings and information. Gaps in our actions, invisibly interrupted by discomfort from taking the 'right' action. Some important pieces in the puzzle are left to slide underground. Maybe more often than is helpful in our relationships and in our sense of self, connections and choices.

Misunderstandings, misperceptions, miscommunication and confusion creep in.

There are two faces of confusion. There is destructive confusion, which arises from trauma and overwhelm – it inhibits us and keeps us in limbo. There is also healthy confusion, which allows us to pause, reflect, notice more and ask questions. It enables us to check and re-test our reality to gain a deeper clarity and understanding.

If we stay with a certainty that what we know is the absolute 'all', then there is no confusion, but there is also no growth. Confusion becomes necessary to allow us to question and become curious. Confusion creates the space for change and curiosity. Curiosity allows new information to come in.

If we just stay with the old way of perceiving or engaging with our experiences, we remain unquestioning of the old. There is no crack or pathway for the new to come into our awareness. We are fixed in our orientation. Confusion creates cracks, which let some light in.

I imagine you can think of instances where you were convinced you knew the whole truth, but then some time later realised that there is more to 'it' then you realised. Pause now for a minute and think of an instance in your life that was without question, but later your perception or understanding changed. Perhaps a time when hindsight brought new information to an old awareness. It could be about a person you met, or that saturated fats are bad for you.

We need confusion to destabilise the old way and allow uncertainty to open up space for questions and new possibilities to arise. We also need emotional muscle to allow questions and curiosity about this confusion.

I think there is too much destructive confusion and overwhelm in our society. Too many fixed, black and white views. Too much reductionist thinking. Too much of an attempt to stay in control through blame or power. Too much control over life and death, such as keeping people alive when their body would die if left alone (I am not talking about leaving people in pain), by war, gun laws and terrorism. Narrow answers bring narrow solutions and are not lasting. This narrow blinkered focus to find the quick and 'magic solution'; dissecting details down to find the 'gene', the chemical or the 'answer' in an effort to save the whole, loses the bigger context, information and meaning.

We need healthy confusion to identify and clear the rubbish out of the way. We need to develop emotional muscle to match our intellectual muscle, so we can open up to the whole and bear the confusion. Emotional muscle to open up to vulnerability, shame and the unknown – and ownership of our reality and our experience. We need to know that our heart can bear our wounds.

For this reality check to take place, we need effective internal resources and support, as well as external resources and support. A social tribe and community that sees and provides both space and ways of being with the whole of our experience. We need ritual and honour for what we go through.

When we go through a horrific experience, we need rituals to contain it and provide a structure to process the event. Rituals, such as we have for death, are also needed for episodes of our life. Our pain needs to be shared in our community space through rituals. We need to not be alone. Together we can be with the largeness of life.

People are afraid to be with the whole of their experience. People deny the feeling of what is happening for a range of reasons: traumatic response, shame, lack of skills or support, fear of rejection and isolation, emotional pain – and we need to do something about this. Urgently.

We come face to face with people every day who are denying what is happening with their feelings or life in general. We can see evidence of this with the epidemic of anxiety, depression, addictions of all sorts, disconnection from a full landscape of feelings and emotions, and of course in domestic violence.

Don't we teach children to own their mistakes, bear the consequences and develop emotional muscle to face what they have done? We do this so they learn, grow and mature: we don't want them to blame and deny. Don't we do this because we want our children to become decent adults and develop consciousness and responsibility? Are we walking the talk and modelling what we ask of children? Have we turned into the kind of adults we don't want to be? Are we acting as if things are okay, offloading the blame and shame? Are we big enough to face the music and create a community that we are proud of?

I believe we are at a crossroad. Either our society becomes divided, with adults and organisations that are big bullies and want someone else to take the blame and maintain a distorted reality; or we become mature adults, grounded in the whole, with creative and constructive skills and resources. We need a map based on solid theory, which contains, processes and heals. Some pockets of society have knowledge of this map. We need emotional muscle to experiment and try new things out of our comfort zone so this new old map can spread.

We need the capacity to metabolise our unthinkable thoughts, unbearable feelings, toxic shame and incorrect actions. We do currently have the potential to support and change individual, family, social and legal systems. This is happening in pockets around communities, but we need global change to benefit as a whole.

This book is here to help bridge between the old and the new; to create mindful, creative confusion and conversations about abuse in the family and relationships. To serve the bigger truth. To help stir questions and awareness. To further understandings about this web of silence, secrecy and shame which modern society has continued to weave from our history into the new day. We need to look at the foundations of society: people and power. After all, when we strip back the context of family violence in relationships and violence in all other settings, it is all about individual power being taken over by a select few.

This has all been going on for so long that disconnection has become 'normal'. These gaps and cracks mean we all speak with deletions and split from the whole story. It is a social and cultural norm. We speak of our ideal as if we live it, but we don't. We speak about the ideal as if we have a right to have the ideal, that life is being 'unfair' and 'unjust' when life is, in reality, 'the full catastrophe'. Light and darkness. We want life to be like a fairy tale, but it isn't. Life isn't the fairy tale dream.

In my life I have had to work hard to dissolve this idealised longing, wishing pattern within me. It has been tough going. Hopes are so enticing. They are based on ideals that seem so enchanting. The wound of hope and ideals is that they are bound in waiting and longing for what is idealised or desired to be bestowed. *Hope leaves us waiting to be taken care of, instead of taking ownership of our dreams or reality.* What are you hoping and longing for? How are you telling yourself or those around you a 'fairy tale' and ignoring or denying part of what is real?

When you have experienced suffering, you automatically long for the opposite. When you experience wrongs, you know how it 'should' be. But in reality these 'ideal' longings and hopes often become bewitching, and are actually destructive if we hold to their perfection – leading us to 'righteousness' and 'over-entitlement' instead of them being a beacon to take action. The ideals and hopes are not based on the reality that we face

– the imperfection of humanity – and they do not help us metabolise these imperfections, but rather feed a desire to escape from our reality.

These kinds of dreams are not in context with the reality of life, nor are they constructive wishes. They are not dreams that have seeds in reality, which have the potential to lead to positive change. Remember, I am not speaking from black and white, absolute, reductionist thinking that wipes out all hope and wishes. I am talking about a specific kind of hope and wishes.

This orientation of hope and wishes holds deletions, and is a mismatch with reality. Ideal hope creates a helplessness – a longing and wishing that prevents you being able to fully stand on positive and confident ground, and going for what you can develop. This mismatch leaves us vulnerable prey for people who have fixed ideals or a distorted image of reality. *A perfect fit: we can't bear reality, and they offer us a 'reality', albeit a fantasy reality, where we can be taken care of.* Little Red Riding Hood and the Wolf. Even the actions of the mother and the absent father in the story collude with this ideal fantasy reality; all you need to know about, is to be kind and there is nothing that will get you. A fairy tale, yet we can see the gaps that are not filled – and how Little Red Riding Hood falls in the gaps, unable to navigate the real world.

I want a world where we can engage with ourselves and others in creative fullness. I want the world to be a better place than what I was born into. I want you to live and breathe emotional courage and resiliency. To be with the whole.

Let's face it, life is not a fairy tale or the Garden of Eden. Even the Garden of Eden could not last and had its light and dark. Life is made up of the good and the bad, night and day, joy and sorrow, winter and summer, life and death. The full life cycle.

Yet there is a place for fairy tales. What? Aren't I contradicting what I just said?

Let's think about the fairy tales we read as children. They are not idealised wishes and hopes. They all have wonder and horror, good and bad. These stories serve a purpose and embody real life dynamics that we need to wake up to, but we have inadvertently tended to dismiss – dynamics that are very real in our day-to-day life. Dynamics about people and life's challenges. The dismissal of these real life dynamics is a bit like when we drive and become so used to driving that we don't see the streets that we pass; or that train track that we live beside and how we no longer hear the train every twenty minutes; or how we turn the radio on and don't even hear it playing. What is in your life that you have tuned out?

I'm going to tell you lots of fairy tales in *The Wolf in a Suit*. We will begin with Little Red Riding Hood, which will be familiar to you in some kind of way, but perhaps not in the way I retell it. I will tell you some fairy tales that may not be as familiar to you, but they each shed more light on meaningful connections and the inner dynamics and shadows that are often present in relationships. After all, each and every relationship has dynamics that are also familiar to abusive relationships.

All relationships involve the self and the other, along with some challenges around control, stress, conflict, love, anger, boundaries, power and even hate. All these dynamics affect relationships, and all relationships affect our inner self as well as our outer lives. So the information and stories I tell are valuable to anyone who is in any kind of relationship – either with yourself, a partner, someone in your family, even a boss in your workplace.

Given this book is about abuse – a very heavy, sad and horrific topic – I find fairy tales allows us to look within, through a soulful lens. They allow us to go beyond the external facts, the broken bones and the wounded sense of self. Don't get me wrong, the facts are important and we talk about this in depth in Part 2 of *The Wolf in a Suit*. But I want to focus on facts that are not as commonly connected to or understood in the context of abuse.

Fairy tales allow us the opportunity to become witness to dynamics. There is less need to defend these dynamics when the story is not about us. Hearing a story allows us to receive information, clarity and insight about a dynamic; from here we can become curious, experimenting and reflecting on our own experience and truth. We can take in the dynamic in a non-threatening way.

Fairy tales can remind us that we are more than a survivor or a perpetrator. We are part of a family, a society, a history that has played a part in shaping us and contributed to who we are. Fairy tales can reassure us that we are not alone and remind us that these things are not just happening now, as these stories are old and retell tales of what we as humans keep struggling with. Let's awaken to our real life and not just that of our advanced technological mind.

We are more than the modern society's mode of being a thinking machine.

We have depth and layers, a conscious and an unconscious. A mind and a body. An inner and outer. We are more than the evolved society or the individuated person. We are an individual within a society. Isn't it time we be with the whole? Where the individual can, in their wholeness, be accepted in society – and society can include and value the individual. We have evolved enough that the tribe does not need to kill off the individual who is different from the rest of the tribe.

I want to bring the *unconscious and the body* into the conversation of abuse. Our current conversation is disembodied, disembowelled. The solution requires us to be with the mind and the body, the conscious and the unconscious, the inner and the outer. After all, science tells us that it is not the conscious brain that determines our decisions and impulses. We have been focusing on the conscious, as that can feel comfortable, contained and knowable. But the answers are in the darkness of the unconscious, impulses and the body.

Factual words cannot capture the fullness of what has happened. I remember the despair when I wrote in my diary what was happening in the relationship and in the many years following, going through court to protect my children. I was writing facts, but facts don't paint the full picture. The courts didn't want the full picture, but the facts don't give you the smell in the air. Isn't the full picture inclusive of the atmosphere? Doesn't the atmosphere shape our behaviours and choices?

Whether we are in our old school room, the library, the theatre or the football stadium, each place has an atmosphere. This atmosphere is created from the people and their actions. Each teacher in each classroom is different and has their own influence, even if they're all doing the same thing in each classroom. If we just described the seat arrangement and the event, but not the wave of effect from and between the people, there is a huge chunk missing.

Fairy tales can help us connect to our soulful and magical depths, the subtle layers that are not necessarily fully grasped or made real through everyday words which just speak of the outer world and its facts. Our language is peppered with metaphors and symbology to describe the atmosphere of experiences of life beyond the rational word: the abyss, being quiet as a mouse, a heart of stone, life is a rollercoaster, love is battlefield, the elephant in the room, the sacred cow …

We need a language, which describes a greater fullness of the experience.

Metaphors and symbology describe this and need to be valued as providing real and true meaning. By losing access to the language of our unconscious and our dreaming night self, we can easily become lost in the fast external pace and stressful survival elements of life and lose our soul. We can lose solace and become depressed. Let us be part of the age of awakening to the real, full life.

Life and fairy tales are about 'this *and* that'. Life is full of opposites. Life is not about 'this *or* that'. The mode of 'this *and* that' is a feminine quality. It is inclusive and attends to the big picture. 'This *or* that' is a more masculine attribute: black and white, discerning, about details. I am not implying 'feminine = good' and 'masculine = bad'. Not at all. We all have feminine and masculine qualities and attributes within each of us, regardless of our gender. The feminine and masculine within each of us needs the other, as each expresses part of the whole.

The feminine can be said to be about feelings, inclusiveness, the body, the unconscious, symbols, art, relating, connections, music and 'being'. This is typically spoken of as the right brain.

The masculine can be said to be about the mind, conscious thinking, words, numbers, details, sequences, dissecting, compartmentalising, mathematics, analysing and action. This is typically understood to be the left brain.

I speak of the two parts of the whole as feminine and masculine rather than 'left' or 'right' for the following reason. We have become a society, which values the left brain's 'masculine' attributes and devalues the knowledge and power of the right brain, the 'feminine' orientation. Yet when we talk about the brain, we automatically would know that we need a left and right brain to be wholly functioning. We can't just be left brain, can we? We are more comfortable being with the 'right brain' and 'left brain' labelling than for our society to acknowledge, reflect, allow and know that the whole is only complete when both the feminine and masculine attributes are engaged.

Both the feminine and masculine are valuable to access, express, and learn from and be informed by in each aspect of our life, events and relationships. Both the feminine and masculine are essential in all contexts of life and are at risk of being polarised and held hostage in relationship with an abuser.

We need the feminine and masculine. *We need to think about our feelings and feel about our thinking.* How can we truly connect to our whole brain, our whole body, our whole experience if we only perceive and understand from one lens? We need both. We need this *and* that.

'This' is my personal story. 'That' is the context of theories about abuse. 'This' is also fairy tales. We learn and absorb through more than one lens. This book is about many stories in the context of abuse. These stories include fairy tales, the mind and the body, the conscious and the unconscious, the individual in the family, the family in society – all in an attempt to include the whole of the human psyche and its surroundings.

The purpose of my book is to tell the whole story and link the pieces together. Something can only be filed away if all the pieces are together. If you have a folder on your computer but some of the files for the folder are on the desktop or a USB drive, then that folder can't be filed away. Not until all the files are in the one folder can there be completion. Let's do some real naming so we can do some gathering, filing and resolution.

***

The Wolf in a Suit is not about casting all men as evil. This book is not about blaming or shaming anyone, including my family. My purpose for telling my story is speaking about what is unspoken. We need to speak about the unbearable feelings and unthinkable thoughts to get out of the confusion and integrate the new into the old, so we don't keep repeating the cycle and looping like an eternal nightmare.

The purpose to telling my uncensored story is not to shock you or talk about certain people in a bad light. I invite you inside a real life, behind the closed doors: the truth about abuse, beyond shame and secrets, so you can really get a picture of what life is like. I invite you to notice the impactful actions, and also what doesn't take place but creates equal (if not greater) impact. Notice how it is to allow the honest, raw, unexaggerated depth of detail to create a picture of what living in abuse is really and truly like. Notice your responses – if you have an internal voice saying, 'No, she is exaggerating,' or, 'No, that is an unusual experience, that doesn't happen in my world …'

My uncensored story does not include every single detail. This is to protect some privacy for myself, my children and everyone I write about – including the Wolf. I speak of him as the Wolf because I speak of the archetype possessing the man. I am not speaking of the man's essence. I am not judging. I am naming to tell a clear story.

Open yourself to read my uncensored story. To feel, hear and sense the actions and impact, rather than getting caught in facts, egos or protecting statuses. I want people to be able to rise above the need to defend their worst face. *Do we want to keep protecting what is wrong and lacking, or do we want to become the adults we teach our children to be?*

***

This story is for anyone who wants to understand what it's like to live in family violence. This story is for anyone who wants to understand about relationship abuse. If you don't know what abuse really is, in all its fullness, you will have gaps in being able to protect your friend, your future self, your client, your children – or you may be in abuse to some degree now and not realise.

Our society is still not comfortable with acknowledging abuse. So many women and men do not realise until after they left the relationship that they were living with abuse. Our society does not regard the full spectrum of abuse as being 'real', which leaves people confused, in conflict and immobilised. Society still asks the question, 'Why doesn't she leave?' because society still does not accept the full spectrum of abuse and so cannot get the full impact on how abuse shapes and limits any individual.

I tell my story because it is my story, through my eyes. It is not for me to tell another's story; and despite my years of therapy something was incomplete. My story exists and has a rightful place. I needed to speak it publicly; for my sake, for all women, for our children's sakes and for society to become more involved in picking up the pieces and creating change.

Everyone's story of abuse deserves to exist, and to be recognised and responded to as required. There needs to be room in the world for all the stories. After all, these are not just 'stories'; these are people. We are real people with real lives. We are your sister, daughter, mother, grandmother, girlfriend, wife. How can we not make space for people and their stories? We need more survivor stories and wisdom influencing social policy and procedures in how to address this epidemic.

If I tell my story with censorship, deletions, secrets and excuses, then how can you ever really understand what abuse is like? If we keep protecting what is wrong, how can our society address the shame or have an opportunity to repair and fill those gaps?

When healthy shame and accountability is not resting where it belongs, it rests on those more vulnerable. We need to become clear about the difference between mindless blame and shame that is used to control, deny and maintain power, and healthy shame and accountability. Shame and blame are enacted by perpetrators not taking responsible action, and also by a society not enforcing consequences on perpetrators. This kind of blame and shame has no generative context to a bigger picture of mind, body and social growth and has no follow-through for reparation or healing.

There is a necessity in naming, holding accountability and bearing healthy shame that is inevitable for healthy and inclusive change and action to take place. This type of naming and accountability may be mislabelled as 'blaming' and 'shaming'. However, naming should not be suffocated just because individuals and society feel healthy or toxic shame at the lack of appropriate response when naming taking place. We need a society that can respond to and differentiate between healthy shame and toxic shame. Otherwise, we are repeating the pattern of abuse and remaining silent, walking on eggshells as a group, so that the perpetrator is not made to feel bad and defend and backlash out of shame – but also so society does not feel bad and expend a backlash defence out of shame. It is really important to understand these differences.

Those who don't have the power to push back are currently bearing the shame that is not theirs to bear. I want everything to be in its rightful place. Let people hold their own egos and seek out services to assist with their own process to negotiate healthy or toxic shame or guilt, rather than burdening the vulnerable. If they can't, let us build a society that holds those not accountable in a tighter boundary, even if they can own their accountability, rather than let the most silent or least aggressive one be dumped with the blame, shame and guilt. Let us make sure that shame and ego do not get in the way of returning to the bigger picture of a healthy, functional society. We need to be open to a generative way of addressing abuse in the family, relational and social systems.

This is my story of how I lived with the good and the bad aspects of fairy tales and life, and how I travelled from being censored to becoming uncensored. Being with the good and the bad, the named and the unnamed, the comfortable and the uncomfortable, the conscious and the unconscious, the mind and the body, the individual and the group – this brings in the whole. So the print on this page can be more than ink and patterns. Here is my personal and professional story, laid bare. My pain and my transformation.

I have seen these fairy tales within me also echoed in clients – the ideals, wishes and hopes that trapped me in my personal story. As a professional I unwrap the fairy tales and misguided hopes. I can be with that in me (and others) the innocent Little Red Riding Hood, as I draw on my internal Woodcutter to protect her from the tricksters out in the wild … those Wolves that are waiting for the unsuspecting.

***

Given that I am a female and my true experience was with the perpetrator being male, I have written this book from that perspective. After all, I can only do justice to my story. However, everything that I write can be reversed, and it can also be applied to same sex relationships. In my twenty-plus years of professional experience I have worked with women living in partner abuse, as well as men being victimised by partner abuse. I have worked with heterosexual and same-sex relationship abuse.

We all know something of the experience of walking on eggshells at some point in our lives. The experience of being betrayed, or of not feeling confident or safe enough to speak out. Perhaps we stay silent rather than stand by someone who is at risk, because of some sense of risk of repercussions to ourselves or to the other. We don't speak at the time, feel bad about it and don't speak about it later. It all becomes too hard or too much. *The Wolf in a Suit* is here to support anyone in their journey to be with the whole and not walk on eggshells.

***

The Wolf in a Suit is a book for all women, for all men and for anyone – professionals, friends or family members – who hold some concern about their own past or for someone in their lives. This book is for women who have been (or still are) living in family and partner violence. This book is for women who feel isolated and overwhelmed and not sure what to do or what is next. This book is for anyone who wants to protect or prevent anyone from being in any kind of toxic relationship.

The Wolf in a Suit is also written for any professional who, through their work, meet with women who have a possibility of living with abuse that may have been missed – women who are stressed, women who have health problems. This includes psychiatrists, psychotherapists, counsellors, doctors, nurses and various health professionals. There are many links between abuse and emotional, physical and mental health. This book is also a valuable resource for police, lawyers and mediators to understand and get the inside story on the issue – both when it is spoken, and when it is there but unspoken. There are ways to bring the story out when the person feels accepted, believed and understood without putting words into someone's experience.

The Wolf in a Suit can be read by anyone who wants to understand and use this information to make a difference in their community.

I want more for you than to just 'be aware' or 'understand'. I want you to be able to receive a map that holds practical steps to navigate the way through. To have access to practical advice and information for women struggling with past or present family/relationship abuse, and advice for professionals, family and friends on how to increase their identification of abuse and effective action.

***

The seed to write this book first came about in the nineties, when I was running domestic violence groups in the counselling agency where I was first employed as a counsellor.

The women participating felt comfortable with me, partially because they knew I wasn't just a therapist – that I had lived through the same abuses as them. There was a sisterhood between us. The women spoke from their heart, asking me to be their voice, to tell the story of why we stay. They bestowed a trust in me to share their stories and voices, and dispel the myths and judgements about why women stay. I hope I have honoured and adequately answered their request.

Why write this book now? This abuse happened over twenty years ago. I am free and safe now. My children are free and safe.

I found as I edged closer to turning fifty that the whisperings to write this book were getting louder and louder. I did not want my desire to write to stay just that, a desire. I wanted this book to become a reality, to have a life of its own; to inform the gaps in the current conversation about abuse. I didn't want my pain to remain as resentment at the lack in our social and family system towards women and children in crisis. I did not want my dream to remain unlived, and for these important pieces unable to reach a wider group of people beyond my immediate contact.

I have been waiting to write this book for over twenty years. The opportunity has opened up now that my children are adults and parents themselves. My children have the mature depth of understanding that comes from their lives and their deep primal urge to protect their own children. With their permission, it is now okay for me to present our story.

Even though abuse in the home is becoming more and more visible in media and social awareness, it is still a mystery to the larger society. Society often blames women for not seeing the abuse and leaving, yet many times society also does not see the telltale signs of abuse. There is a shared difficulty to see what is there and how to respond. I want to contribute in speaking up and addressing these gaps. I wanted to leave a legacy, a contribution to changes within the community and society.

I want all those years and moments of trauma, suffering and helplessness to contribute to a positive change beyond my own personal growth. To share the effects of how the abuses shaped and influenced me and my children, with the intention of our pain becoming part of a healing process for ourselves and others. Of course, I don't share all of my children's stories, out of respect for them and their life stories. But I write what I can of what is most relevant, to assist you to understand the impact on our reality. I write so you understand that truth is more shocking than fiction and to encourage you to believe what appears unthinkable. I write so you can understand emotional abuse and not just physical abuse. So you can recognise abuse is not logical. Abuse is unthinkable.

I also wrote this book because of the anger that is still present in me. I became aware of this anger every time I heard something about abuse in the news and observed the lack of handling or appropriate enquiring that is still evident in the response and reports. This anger sits within my deep disappointment and grief towards our culture, our society, the gaps in the legal and policing system, the gaps in the family system and the gaps in my own family. Despite our advanced capabilities as a civilisation, we hold a significant social deficit in communication and the emotional muscle to hear and speak.

My anger motivates me to participate in clearing the cobwebs from misperceptions and myths that continue to prevail when someone is caught inside family and partner abuse. Those misperceptions and judgements do not recognise the complexities in being stuck. Those accusations about, 'But what did you do? After all, it takes two,' or 'Why did you stay?' whilst the man is let off the hook. Why are we not asking, 'Why did he target a woman?' Why did he persist to abuse and not find someone or something to help him stop and change? How come he could 'lose control' with her, but not lose control with his boss or best friend? How come when he 'lost control' her belongings or pets were destroyed and not his?

The question, 'Why does she stay?' is still not clearly understood in our society. I want to take you through my personal story and then unpack further awareness that developed through my twenty-plus years of professional experience and my own long, personal, therapeutic journey. This way, we can move beyond the old questions, and ask questions about him – and about the society that stays silent, and does not recognise emotional and psychological abuse as 'criminal'. A society that believes physical and sexual abuse is criminal and our inner world is less important creates a degraded society.

I want you to truly understand and recognise why women get caught in the first place: why women don't leave or they keep returning, and how our society and family are part of the 'why'.

In my opinion, these questions about *why* she gets caught, *why* she doesn't leave, *why* she stays, *why* she returns are all very different and important questions. But really, why are other questions not considered important? *Why* do the men abuse, and *why* don't they stop? *Why* does society not step in? *Why* do we have a system that relies on proof when abuse happens behind closed doors? *Why* can't we explore a more accurate and broader concept of proof? *Why* is a child's word asked for but then not listened to? *Why* is the natural and developmental way a child communicates, predominantly through behaviour, not taken as evidence? *Why* are we not more inclusive of all the evidence and material that is available, which is not currently valued in the legal system?

Why are these questions not loud and present, or louder, in our conversations? Why do we presume that a woman *should* know before she *can* know? Who is able to put up their hand and say truthfully that in their life they have always been able to leave before something worse happened – whether it is a 'bad' habit, addiction, job or something else? Who is able to say they never overstayed and tried longer for the possibility of a happier outcome? How many people have said they didn't leave that job that was killing their soul because they couldn't afford the risk of the unknown, of not having financial security?

Why are women in abuse expected to be more able to get out of the clutches of something destructive than anyone else? Don't most people have something they can relate to, that they succumb to?

The Wolf in a Suit is about those binds of secrecy and abuse that remain hidden in the home. In writing this book I came to understand the act of walking on eggshells in far more detail then I thought possible. I already knew about the secrecy and shame when living in abuse and no one becomes involved. There is a further trauma of walking on eggshells through the court and police system in an effort to be believed and making sure you don't come across as a 'revengeful, spiteful woman who has no 'proof' so she must be lying'. Most abuse happens 'behind closed doors' – perhaps because he 'knows' he is doing the wrong thing.

There is a reinforced belief that only one of the two differing stories can be acknowledged. That the story is only 'real' when witnessed by another. I wanted to write a book to explain why we need to listen to and believe one person's story, and not insult them by claiming that it is only valid if another can speak of or see it.

In writing *The Wolf in a Suit*, I came to realise more about the layers of walking on eggshells beyond the survivor's experience – that society walks on eggshells too. I had lived through family abuse and neglect, knowing it through experience while 'asleep' and later knowing it through 'becoming awake' and later intimately knowing it through naming and unpacking what happened. This unpacking led me to realise the many layers of society also walking on eggshells. I was blown away how pervasive walking on eggshells is through society. Denial: 'It's none of my business.' Toxic shame, overwhelm, white lies, excuses, blame and more. Start to look for it around you. Is it there? We need the broad focus, not just the narrow focus, to address the whole.

Even when I could not consciously name it, I felt and knew the unnameable experience of being abused. It felt wrong and kept me walking on eggshells on a daily basis, year in, year out because no one beyond me (personally or socially) acknowledged the full reality of abuse. I knew the experience of being behind closed doors, people around me acting as if no boundaries were broken, keeping secrets due to overwhelm, fear and confusion and with the clear messages, verbal and non-verbal, not to betray another of their blinded and blinkered view of themselves. When no one around you acknowledges reality, it is hard to be the one to make a fuss or trust the reality you feel.

When I escaped and went through court, I became aware of how the legal system was another form of abuse that denied my reality, because it was my word against his. There is abuse through our system still on so many levels. I started to become curious about why this societal power, denial and controlling abuse is not shifting when people do not want abuse in society.

In recent times I came to realise more about how friends and families also walk on eggshells around people they have concerns about. Our society doesn't teach how to navigate the Wolves. Far too often, the Wolves are running the show.

As a society, people don't know how to bring up concerns, uncertain if it is 'any of my business' or whether to trust the concerns that they have as being valid. It leaves many people walking on eggshells, in case speaking up would mean a backlash on their friendship or on the relationship of the person they are concerned about. It is understandable. It is uncomfortable to talk about abuse or toxic relationships but staying silent is not the solution.

This is not a comfortable conversation, let alone to know what to say or do when you're only receiving bits of information. A part of me automatically pipes up now to say that even if you don't know what to say or do, you can name some version of this – 'I don't know what to say right now but it seems like something is not right. How does it seem to you?' I wish someone had been able to name what I could not and open a door to enable me to come back to life. I wish someone had tried and not given up. There is no perfect conversation or outcome but there is a better way than what is currently happening.

In writing about my experience with the police and court system, and the failures that I experienced in the lack of protection for me and my children, I came to realise that maybe even the police and the legal system also walk on eggshells. This pattern of abuse in the relationship, in families, is also in our legal system. Not in exactly the same way, and I don't want to let them off the hook in their part of being accountable in their role, but the pattern of violence and denying reality is even bigger than just in the relationship.

This is not to excuse the system, but to consider the bigger picture. After all, every system is made up of people and everyone comes from a family. So if everyone comes from a family and one in three women experience abuse in their lifetime, then maybe there is a large percentage of people in the entire system denying or minimising abuse to defend against their own family or ancestral story.

The statistic of one in three women having experienced physical violence means abuse is happening in almost every family, doesn't it? What about the presence of emotional abuse, the precursor to all violence? What about all the Wolves who create damage purely through psychological and emotional abuse? What does this mean for our perception of a stable, functional and healthy society? How does this awareness impact the health and choices of the tribe ... if we truly absorb the reality of how prevalent abuse is?

What would happen if as a society, we really recognised these failures? Stop and think of the amount of perpetrators everywhere who deny their own behaviours and patterns of control, hurting and punishing others over and over again, day in and day out, year in and year out. Stop and think about our 'functional' society that allows these perpetrators to abuse the vulnerable. How many schoolteachers, doctors, nurses and police officers are helpless to a system that does not identify or intervene appropriately? Sure, we will always miss some perpetrators, but we have the ability to change the degree so that fewer people slip through the system – so that we restrain many more perpetrators and protect many more vulnerable women, children and men.

What would happen to society if perceptions about masculinity and patriarchy were more actively deconstructed? So much of our way of schooling, farming, 'work', war, politics and law is based on patriarchy and has become disconnected from rhythms, cycles, instinct and nature. What would happen to society if perceptions about femininity were significantly reconstructed? If women's knowledge about the body, life and power were incorporated and visible in all the areas of work, law, politics, war, schooling and farming and all areas of life? Is the broader societal level of walking on eggshells in place to avoid the challenges and changes these questions bring, rather than shaking up the system of power and the society's perception of men, women and how our society really is structured?

These are important concepts to question and explore, but let us return to the personal face of abuse.

Abuse is still so misunderstood, yet accommodated. When we connect all the pieces and know the full extent of all the types of abuse, and how our habits and society are involved in maintaining the pattern of abuse, then maybe then we can turn a corner. I believe we have an allergic reaction to being affected, hurt and vulnerable. We deny another person's experience so we don't open the door to personal pain that we don't want to re-experience and don't know what to do about. What you deny in yourself, you deny in another.

What if instead of denying ourselves and others, we include and allow? We are so fortunate today to have access to therapies that don't just talk, but gently and effectively release trauma from the body, as well as therapies that support the neural pathways which became interrupted and disconnected due to overwhelm. What if we saw therapy as part of the ongoing process of growing as a human – evolving, transforming and identifying this growth as a personal strength, instead of the stigma of having something wrong?

After all, we regularly service our cars, knowing that by being on the road they will inevitably be affected and need checking and restoring to their optimal condition. Why do we ignore how our own system runs, instead running ourselves into the ground on so many levels? We run our busy lives in reaction, in a survival mode, instead of being the powerful, creative beings we are.

There are so many reasons why I wanted to write this book. Most abuse is emotional and mental, unrecognised by the system despite often being the forerunner to physical and sexual abuse. Emotional and mental abuse is much more prevalent. Depression, addiction, suicide, ill health and poor social connections are all associated with emotional and psychological abuse.

Often the media focuses on physical and sexual abuse, while the other forms fall through the cracks as if they do not exist. Yet everyone who has been abused will emphasise the deep harm of emotional and psychological abuse and its harm on the self and identity. These types of abuses are far more damaging on every level: mental health, emotional health, future relationships, future employment, physical health, being able to trust yourself and others again and living a full life. Emotional and mental abuse falls through the cracks, yet these methods of psychological and emotional torture, as well as isolation, are used in war and considered war crimes. It is not just physical and sexual abuse impacting and wounding women, children and men. We need to recognise the full spectrum of abuse.

While we are talking about secrets, omissions and myths: family violence isn't just happening in lower socioeconomic circumstances. It doesn't always involve drugs. Let's not excuse the abuse as a symptom of alcohol – not everyone who drinks to excess is violent or abusive. Not everyone who has a mental illness is abusive. Abuse happens in every suburb and across all ages and socioeconomic backgrounds. In my teenage years, I remember my boyfriend and I driving to an older relative's home in a wealthy suburb to help her secretly leave her abusive husband.

I want everyone to understand the real-life experience and deep wounds from attacks on the sense of self through all the types of abuses, many of which are still not fully recognised. I tell my story of abuse in Part 1, and in Part 2 I describe all the types of abuse for you to gain a greater understanding towards how I see the layers and challenges in what maintains our whole society and individual immobilisation. There are probably more types of abuse than you realise. I describe in detail about the non-physical abuses and how they still impact on the physical body. Part 2 of my book is where I outline my professional understandings – offering key insights, information and suggestions with specific steps outlined towards the end of each chapter on how to integrate the material contained in each chapter.

I suggest different ways of taking this information and making meaningful use of it in your own personal process – either as a woman who has or is currently experiencing family violence, or as a professional to become more aware of vulnerable women, men and children trapped inside family violence.

Please remember, if you are in an unsafe situation and you are reading this book, you may want to leave your copy at a friend's home and read it while there or access the ebook to read.

I break down all the complex layers involved with abuse in the home, in easy and clear ways. These complex layers intermingle and confuse the mental, physical, biological and neurological layers of self, leaving those vulnerable in states of survival and shell-shock. When practitioners and society do not know all the complex layers, assistance is severely limited.

Understanding the complex layers, and the impact of abuse on all the different parts and systems that shape you (or another), is really important to be able to address the complexity and confusion that is wrapped up in abuse. Looking at and processing is about being able to look at all the parts and how they connect as a whole.

***

Each of us is 'one' person, yet we can have many selves within that are residual from different stages and events in our life. Each mind and body holds many systems working within, each one separate yet connected. Each layer of the human psyche is in part integrating or managing the information of our experiences, each sub-system in its own ways.

We need each part of our system communicating to each other about all the different facets of what our senses absorb. It's important to not block these communication pathways, so we can get the whole picture and therefore be in an optimal place to work out where to go from here. When these communications are congruent we have energy, flow, clarity and power – but when our selves are in conflict about our experience and how to be in the world, we have collapse, procrastination and self-sabotage.

Perhaps someone has denied something of your reality, your feelings or needs at some point in your life, and you did not feel equipped to oppose their aggression or vehemence. None of us are immune from the impact of repetitive intimidation, threats, humiliation and other kinds of abuses – whether in our family home, school, workplace or when living in a war-zone. When repetitive, unpredictable 'power and control' over another becomes an ongoing, persistent pattern, the physical and the emotional self is tainted, affecting the whole psyche.

Living through and writing about *The Wolf in a Suit* shaped and changed my life. It is shocking to realise that in Australia in 2016, there are still one in three women that are or have been in an abusive relationship. I believe the real number to be higher. Not everybody discloses or reports abuse and not everyone realises they are living with abuse. When society or those around us don't recognise all the abuses, it is hard to recognise that what we are being inflicted with is abuse. Abuse has become normal.

One of the disturbing concerns for me is that physical or sexual violence is considered criminal, yet all the other abuses are not identified as criminal offences, so abuse continues to permeate through our society. Power, control and denial of another's reality are not the exception. It is commonplace. Even criminal offences of physical and sexual abuse are not recognised as often as they occur.

On average one woman is being killed each week in Australia. Children are present in one out of every three violence cases reported. Studies show that even when abuse is not directed at children, their health, relationships and identity are impacted – for life.

When we can acknowledge the emotional forms of abuse, and not just physical and sexual abuses, we optimise our society's chances to be healthy and preventative, responding earlier in the progression of violence.

I have gone to court more times than I would like, for myself and for my clients. I guide clients through intervention order applications to help protect them in legal proceedings. I find it necessary to advocate for clients through their legal process, as the shame and fear they possess when they go to court can make it difficult to name their reality and ask for what they really need. When you have spent time minimising the abuse to cope and survive, it is a challenge to enter a system, which requires you not to minimise the abuse to be fully protected. Often there is a double bind of needing to tell your reality and not minimise, yet you are in a system, which does not accept your reality – or you may see yourself through the eyes of a perceived social filter that you must be exaggerating or you are being revengeful. It is also a shocking reality to realise that it is you in this situation – one that you never imagined would be part of your story. It becomes doubly difficult when the people in the system you interact with cannot hear your story and actually try to change it.

I recall one time sitting with a client and the court registrar to write up the interim intervention order. I had to request the registrar go back about five times to make corrections to the notes she had taken from my client's account. The registrar continued to minimise the account and write using deletions, creating an inaccurate account which misrepresented the degree of abuse in the client's situation. I found it shocking to still have to do this in 2014.

It is clear to me that there is still a great need for professionals to become more conscious of the details of and impact from family violence, and develop a focus to support people as they accurately record their situation. It is evident there is still a great need for services and supports to be proactive towards a client's needs and challenges: one, because often the client is not familiar with the system and so can find it difficult and overwhelming to name what is necessary; and two, it can be a challenge to overcome their shame, fear, self-blame, shock and guilt from being in this situation.

I have spoken with more clients than I would like about helping address the self-blame and guilt set up from abuse. I want my clients to feel supported by a society that acknowledges their right to be themselves and to be safe on all levels – mentally, physically and emotionally. I want to be part of creating a positive and powerful change in how we look at and address family violence. I want my grandchildren and other children to grow up free from secrets and abuse. I want to stop the abuses being passed down the family lines. I want women and men to feel secure and safe in their identity, their psyche, their relationships, and in their right to be different and their own person. I want to support members of society who want to be part of the change to respond when someone is trapped, or helpless or overwhelmed.

***

The Wolf in a Suit is talking about the 'elephant in the room'. That thing that people don't want to talk about. Elephants have also been my favourite animal for as long as I can remember. When I was a child, I had an elephant toy. When I was in overwhelm, isolated and scared I knew my elephant was there. It was soft and was nothing like where I lived. My elephant was a comfort to me. It belonged to another place. It was as if my elephant contained the innocent, little me, giving that part of me protection and safety by living outside of me.

As a child, I remember reading a story about elephants: *Elephant Adventure*, by Willard Price. I loved his whole series. I read about their size and strength and yet how they can be so very gentle. I remember reading about this contrast and my love for elephants was cemented. I loved and wished for so many qualities of elephants and their social structure.

Elephant herds are small, social and led by the matriarch. The male comes to mate but does not live with the herd. I am not meaning to imply men and women should live separately, but maybe there can be more permission for everyone to live as they choose without the social pressure to meet, marry/live together, and have babies. In the elephant kingdom, there is room for the female to hold power – not power over, but shared power. The male doesn't have to be dominating and take up so much space. All the females in a herd share and look after the young as needed, including feeding and adopting other young elephants. Family and social connection is very important for elephants, with the herd holding very close bonds.

I wish my family, including the extended family, had had that flow of support rather than act like everything was normal when it wasn't. I think our modern society has lost some important supports in focusing on individual advancement, leaving gaps in family support. When the other female elephants can be available to be there for the young and share as a team or sisterhood, the whole tribe benefits.

Elephants are affectionate and have an incredible memory with a rich emotional life, expressing playfulness and also joy, grief, anger, depression and trauma responses. Has our focus on success, image and technological advancement left us with a narrow palette of feelings?

As we begin this journey and speak of the elephant in the room, I want your deep, emotional self to have the space to come home to you. I want you to be able to know in every cell of your being – not just your conscious, rational mind – that it's not your fault and that you're not alone. It's not your fault if you didn't speak up for someone you love or if you got caught by the Wolf. You are part of a bigger picture that left you doing the best you could at that time.

I want you to know: change is possible now, no matter how long ago the abuse was or if it went on for a long time. I want you to know you can be part of the change, so history does not continue to repeat itself. Whether you are now healing your past, so future generations are free to have greater choices; or you are a practitioner, family member or friend; you can be part of a ripple effect.

Part 1:
Fairy Tale or Nightmare?

Chapter 1:
The Little Red Riding Hood Effect

Little Red Riding Hood

Once upon a time, there lived an innocent, pretty girl who was loved by her mother. Her grandmother loved her so much that she made her a beautiful red cape.

One day Little Red Riding Hood's mother gave her a basket of food and said, 'Go and visit your grandmother as I think she may be unwell.'

Little Red Riding Hood dutifully left to follow the path to the village beyond the forest where her grandmother lived. A Wolf sees her and wants to eat her, but the Woodcutters are nearby so the Wolf just starts talking to her, acting friendly and curious, and asks where she is going.

Little Red Riding Hood does not know that the Wolf is dangerous. She politely tells the Wolf where she is going and why. The Wolf acts as if he also wants to visit her grandmother and entices her into a game to see who gets there first. The Wolf takes a shortcut. By the time Little Red Riding Hood arrives at her grandmother's house, the Wolf has eaten the grandmother.

Little Red Riding Hood knocks on the door. She hears the Wolf's voice, disguised as her grandmother, beckon her in and she feels scared. Usually Little Red Riding Hood enjoys visiting her grandmother and she is uncomfortable that she doesn't want to go in today. She wants to go home but she convinces herself that the reason her grandmother's voice sounds strange is because she is unwell.

Little Red Riding Hood enters the house. The Wolf asks her to get in bed with 'her'. As Little Red Riding Hood gets undressed, she tells the Wolf what big arms, legs, ears and eyes 'she' has. The Wolf has an answer for everything. When Little Red Riding Hood comments on 'her' big teeth, the Wolf eats her up.

Adapted from Tales From Mother Goose *(Perrault 1697).*

I can tell my story because I no longer live with the Wolf. I made a promise to myself after I left the Wolf: I'd take back my life. I promised myself that I would not keep toxic secrets to myself, which involve others and impacted my reality and my safety. No more secrets even after I leave, so that the shame, fear and even righteous anger about the Wolf do not keep me trapped in the past. No more control over my thoughts, feelings and actions – that control leads to secrets and inhibits the healing flow. No more secrets that inhibit healing and withhold necessary knowledge. No more minimising. No more censoring. No more protecting others at the cost of the innocent and vulnerable.

My story begins with Little Red Riding Hood. Is Little Red Riding Hood in you too? I want to open you up to becoming curious to discover what your story is. My story won't be your story – but the more I tell my story to others, the more I hear other women say that they share important parts of my story. I get surprised sometimes, as I can have that funny thought that no one has the same story as me, and the fear that people won't understand what happened to me. That I am an oddity. Yet I discover women saying, 'Yes, that happened to me too.'

Even though our stories are similar, they are also different. Everyone is unique and yet everyone is so similar. Let's discover together our shared chapters and discover more about your own story. We are different in being able to get angry or not being able to. The Wolves we met are different in what they show of themselves and how they control.

This is my story. I love saying these words! This is my story. I hope you can gain comfort and validation from searching, discovering and listening for your own story that is within you. The words, 'This is my story,' are so comforting and validating to me. Say the words aloud to yourself and feel what they offer you.

I want to begin by telling you my version of the original story of Little Red Riding Hood and what I call the Little Red Riding Hood Effect. Listen with your inner ears, your inner eyes, your inner senses, so that you can hear this story in a way you may not have heard it told before. Listen to the story as it was meant to be told, before it became diluted and was taken away from its original intention and message.

Little Red Riding Hood is told by her mother to go visit her grandmother and bring her some food. She's not told anything other than to stick to the path and to just go and do the 'right' thing, the nice thing: take care of someone else.

She's not told that she may come across Wolves out there. She is not told that Wolves are tricksters and can appear friendly and nice. She is not taught how to see the warning signs of a trickster. She is not taught the options to take if she meets a Wolf. She is not taught that not everyone does the 'right' thing. She's not told how to navigate those situations when others are not reasonable, right or fair. She is not taught that being fair, understanding or assertive does not work with Wolves. She is not taught that the world is not always a fair place, even though we try to live that way. She is not given a choice or given the option to oppose – to say, 'No, this is too much for me. I don't want to go look after Grandmother.'

In this tale, there is no father present to teach her how to be in the world. He is absent. There is silence and a gap in the lack of masculine energy acting as a protector in Little Red Riding Hood's life in this stage of the tale. Maybe in reality father is present, but not present in the safe, warm, embodied way a child developmentally needs.

The Woodcutter becomes available as a protector in the crisis situation later in the story. The fact the Woodcutter comes late highlights the lack of our society's awareness or preventative approach. Notice, that the Woodcutter is a transitory figure; he is not a constant in her life. While Little Red Riding Hood is growing up and learning, she needs a constancy of reflection, reinforcement and permission on how to be safe in the world. This is the role of mother *and* father.

The mother is asking Little Red Riding Hood to go to another village and through the woods, and yet she doesn't give Little Red Riding Hood any option or tools to navigate the risks within the woods.

Is she asking too much of her daughter at too young an age, where she is not equipped or taught how to handle this challenge? Is she hurrying up her child's innocence, prompting her to grow up too fast? Is she asking her daughter to fill the gap that should be her own task?

Why isn't the mother doing this task? Is she blind to the dangers, and so can't pass on the ways to navigate the world on to her daughter? Does the mother have her own history of abuse that leaves her immobilised or silent, passing on the submissiveness instilled by her own life? Is there no one around who sees these impositions and unrealistic expectations? Is there no one to step in to bridge and protect? Where is the mother's awareness of Little Red Riding Hood's capability (or hesitation) to do this big task? We will go into even deeper layers about these questions throughout Part 2, The Real World.

The Wolf knows where the Woodcutter is, so he makes sure to come in when there is a gap – an opportune moment when the innocent is left exposed, vulnerable, unprotected and ill-equipped to recognise or respond to any threat. Innocence can only be innocence when there is protection (adult presence, Woodcutter). *Innocence without protection becomes naivety.* Where do we open up gaps and leave doors unlocked within ourselves for Wolves to come in? Where do we contribute to gaps in our children's psyches?

The Woodcutter is the one who has his eyes and ears open (for wolves and falling trees) and can take action. The Woodcutter can cut through. Are we taught to develop our inner Woodcutter? Who models this and teaches these protective ways of instinct and healthy aggression – using strength to create and protect? Who bestows this healthy aggression on girls and women?

Wolves know how to be charming and present well, otherwise they wouldn't get away with their wiles. Little Red Riding Hood is not taught how to see the tricks and becomes easy prey to be tricked by the Wolf. Little girls are taught to be pleasing and seek the approval of others. This is the Little Red Riding Hood Effect. Little girls are not encouraged to point out the gaps in others. Little girls are encouraged to 'look after' dolls, parents and others.

When Little Red Riding Hood arrives at her grandmother's house, she knocks on the door. Her instincts let her know that something is not right, but instead of listening to her inner self and possibly disappointing her mother and grandmother, she follows what she was told and gets eaten up.

She has been taught well to follow others rather than herself. She doesn't have the emotional muscle to bear the risk of a disappointed mother. She doesn't have the emotional muscle to allow herself to take a risk with the intention of taking care of herself, even if it means at times she may get it wrong.

Isn't it better to get it wrong sometimes? You can learn and grow and develop your own point of reference, rather than listening to others and having your point of reference in limbo, outside of you and unable to affect your reality.

Little Red Riding Hood didn't receive the emotional and mental permission and acceptance from her own parents to follow her own gut. Whether she is right or wrong is irrelevant. Mistakes need to be allowed in the effort to take care of yourself. She doesn't get the opportunity to follow, learn and find 'rightness' and 'wrongness' from her own choices. She doesn't get to discover the signals that lead her to knowing what is right and wrong in her reality. She is taught to be obedient.

Listening to and allowing the 'yes' and 'no' signals of our children is, after all, a more challenging journey to allow in our children. We tend to quell our child's energy if we don't have access to our own fullness of trusting ourselves and forming our own path of *yes, no* and our mistakes. We tend to dampen our child's energy if we are taken over by our work or other drives; which does not place our own well-being or our child's as priority. If we sacrifice ourselves to outer expectations and are dislocated from our own centre, we may unconsciously steer our children away from their own energised, true centre.

Little Red Riding Hood doesn't have her inner senses and instincts developed, and so she is swallowed up in the ultimate trick of the Wolf's 'conviction' that his big teeth are not harmful to her. I know what it is like to let someone else's conviction be bigger than my quiet inner knowing. I learnt the hard way that bigger and loud does not equal right. Quiet and little can hold truth and power.

We know Little Red Riding Hood gets caught and swallowed up by the Wolf. She gets tricked. She's not well prepared. There's no masculine principle providing assistance and teachings about how to navigate the real world. Maybe in real life, father is there but he too is a Wolf. She is just encouraged by the feminine principle to be 'nice' and do the 'right thing' by another. There is real danger when girls are not given permission to access their masculine attributes, just as it is dangerous when boys are not given permission to access their feminine principles.

There is a real danger when we are taught that the reference point on what is right is completely outside us. There is real danger when we are taught that the reference point of what is right is all about niceness and does not include healthy aggression. A mother cat will admonish her kitten if it goes near the curb of the road. There is a good fierceness that is life-protective and life-enhancing.

***

That Little Red Riding Hood was me. I'd learnt really well from my childhood how to be nice. Don't show anger. Don't feel anger. Don't even recognise my own anger.

I knew how to give the family smile. I was taught to follow rules. I was taught that the reference point was my mother and father and their reality. I was taught that the reference point did not include my reality. 'Be fair' – but fairness was about the other person's needs and was not what was fair by me.

I did not grow up with the space and permission to have individual experiences. In many ways my parents were also limited in their own experience, being victim to their own family history and significant life events. The difference here is I am now speaking of the child's experience. Adults have power and choices that children don't have. Just as Wolves have more power and choices compared to Little Red Riding Hood who is under threat of harm or survival and without an income or choices.

In many ways I was given a message as a child, verbally and non-verbally: don't rock the boat. Accept the unacceptable. Act as if what is not normal is okay. The boundaries were skewed.

There seemed no interest, encouragement or conversation from either parent to discover who I was, how my day was or to give space for me to show and be who I was. There seemed no interest or encouragement for me to engage with my parents based on my natural, unique, spontaneous self. I did not gain the experience of being liked for me. I learnt how to be liked for how I could make them feel better. So I did not get the flow-on effect to like myself. I was not equipped to be in the world. I was not equipped to handle conflict, challenges, uncomfortable feelings or how to stand strong in opposition or be different.

I grew up scared of everything. There was no room in my system to push back as I was always on the edge of terror. This was my original blueprint and it led to how I got caught.

So here is my Little Red Riding Hood story and about how the Wolf found me and swallowed me. I tell my story through the eyes of the child in me and the wounded young woman I was. This is my truth.

***

I was a very quiet child – blonde, petite and with green eyes. I learnt to keep quiet to please my parents and not get in the way. One of four girls, the second youngest.

My parents weren't managing their lives together well at all. They weren't managing their lives as individuals well either. They were both in their own world full of loss, emotional pain, and disappointment. Putting on brave faces. They were not happy and were so self-absorbed in their own story of survival and emotional pain that I grew up feeling invisible, non-existent and unimportant.

I fell through the cracks. Home was not home. It was cold and lonely. Words were harsh or impersonal. Rules were flying everywhere, nothing made sense and there were no shared realities. My sisters and I played together. Quietly. I read a lot.

It was as if I knew that I couldn't be my full self. Spontaneity and the shrieks of a child's playfulness were not included. We played dutifully and quietly. Reading. Writing. Contained games. We didn't talk about our parents or what was going on. It was like a shared secret that we didn't know we shared.

I didn't have friends at school. My memory of kindergarten is of the day of the school photographs. It was a sunny day. I could feel the sun on my hair and my skin. It felt good but I could also feel the coolness of the shadows. I stood alone. No one wanted me. I did not know how to include myself.

In primary school, I remember being chased and ridiculed. Constantly. I'd try to hide in the library and classroom to get away from the bullies. I had no friends. I was teased. I couldn't eat my lunch; it would swirl around in my mouth turning into mush, and trying to swallow it would almost make me vomit. I would try and find my younger sister and her friend to play with them, but I couldn't ask my little sister to save me every day.

I remember telling my mother one day that I was being teased. She said for me to say back to them, 'Well …' and if they said more, to say, 'Wishing well.' I know … it doesn't make sense. It would be funny, if it weren't so tragic for both of us. Trapped in our pain of being in the world. She didn't know how to navigate the world herself.

Every now and then I would quietly pipe up about the bullying. She probably never realised that the bullying never stopped. She would write me a note to request I stay in the classroom over recess and lunch, but back then my parents and the school did nothing to address my daily tormenting and alienation. I felt shameful and alone, cast out from all the children.

I recall a single conversation with my father where he actually asked about me. Which of the two high schools would I choose? I was looking forward to going to a different school from the children from my primary school peers. I could start again. No one knew me there. It was a private school too. Maybe things would be different from the public school system. I made friends with a girl on Orientation Day and we spent some time together over the school holidays before the year began. School started and I made friends with another girl who went on the same public bus as me.

A few weeks into school, and school life sorts out who is popular and who is not. I was alone again. But I was used to this. I would take the crumbs of what was good. My bus friend would talk to me on the bus to school and going home, and at school I was alone. My other friend just forgot about me as she clicked with the other 'popular' girls. So life continued to reinforce the endurance of being unseen, forgettable and not likeable. I enjoyed the small crumbs of goodness that came my way and didn't complain about being dropped like an object. I was used to being an object. Without even realising at the time, I made out to myself that the small crumbs were better and bigger than they were, as I disconnected from the pain and rejection. This helped me cope and get through each day.

When I was sixteen, my parents divorced. It was a relief – the pressure living with their difficult relationship was heavy and created a cold and uncomfortable, family atmosphere. This relief accompanied a wonderful opportunity that comes in teenage years. An opportunity where surges of energy erupt and life giving attitudes that may have been dormant burst through. And I finally found a friend at school.

It was a hot summer's day, near the beach. I was sitting in the cool shade of the milk bar's concrete step with my friend, having a break from the intense heat, ice creams in hand. Here I saw this quiet, good-looking young man in front of me with some of his friends.

One week after meeting him, I left home to be with this sensitive guy who I really connected to. I was in bliss. My parents objected to me leaving school and home but the combination of my teenage energy awakening, my parents' divorce and my sister standing up for me won. My sister told them how at sixteen I could do what I wanted, that by law they couldn't force me to stay – so couldn't they just help me?

There was no help or conversation; their help was just telling me not to go. There was no conversation to enquire what had happened at school and why I didn't want to stay. There was no conversation about what I wanted for myself in the world and help to find a career. There was no conversation on how to help me. It was him and me, alone in the world.

It was wonderful to leave home and school – two places of not belonging. I wasn't leaving school because of the studies. I could do that, except for maths! I had tried and tried but I could not work out what to study and what future direction was calling me. Neither school nor my parents were interested in helping me set my path. I was miserable and lost. I just needed to get away and choose my own life.

In meeting my man, I was in bliss because for the first time in my life I had a direction. I was not alone. Someone was aware of my existence and wanted me in their life. Life felt good. It was exciting times. All I wanted was to be seen and wanted – I didn't care about a career or anything else. I was starved for love and attention. I was craving to be loved and touched and seen. He was my world.

There was no celebration or mentoring from my parents on this important transition of leaving home. There was no bundle of blankets or crockery for me to have in starting up my own home. No photos or childhood books to take with me. There were no kind words of encouragement. Why would I have thought leaving home would be any different to the years growing up?

All I remember is my mother telling me shortly afterwards that men need sex and if they don't get it they'll be angry. It's a need, she said, like eating and sleep and they have to have it – and the unspoken message was that it was my duty to give it.

So I left school and we set up our own home. It felt good to finally have a home. I loved creating new recipes to cook for him. I got a job – yay! After working a week at a supermarket, I couldn't do that job for some reason. I made some mistakes. The boss gently suggested I was not in the right job. I left and began working at a city takeaway place. I remember sitting in the train watching the sun rise as I had to start early. It felt exciting and fun. This time I was not able to work fast enough. More kind words and I left after a week.

I found the job for me: office junior. I liked where I was working. It was quiet with not too much personal interaction. I could put everything in order and balance accounts. My fingers became quick at calculating and I would fly through the numbers. I was a diligent worker and pretty soon I would finish my work and help other people with their jobs. I was appreciated. I felt free for the first time in my life. I felt in charge of my own life at last.

We created a simple home. Just us two against the world. He too felt alone in the world and was escaping a tough and abusive childhood. We would cook and eat good, wholesome food, nourished too by the feeling of being soul mates. Life was simple. Work, going to Victorian market for our food, cooking, movies at home, listening to music, visiting his sister, going out on drives to the beach and bush. This was our social life …

Life was also simple because I was so used to not being heard that I remember thinking of what I was going to say to him, but then not saying it. It was as if as soon as I thought it, there was no need to speak. I was so used to no one being interested in me and my thoughts that the thoughts just dissolved.

From the day we met, we were together. Never a day apart until the very end and never a harsh word between us until the end. Maybe being good at keeping quiet helped.

I wanted to give him whatever he wanted so he could be free the way I wanted to be free. So I supported him on my wage while he stayed at home to live his dream of being an artist. He was a very gifted painter and artist. I bought him an easel and oil paints. I wanted him to live his dream. Unfortunately his introversion or fears of being in the world got in the way of exhibiting his creative talent and beautiful skills to the world. After about a year, he returned to work that he hated.

We spoke briefly about having a child, at some point. Nearly three years passed. We agreed I would stop taking the pill.

I fell pregnant at nineteen. I was delighted. I felt joy and such a connection to my baby. As she grew in my belly, I grew in confidence to be able to speak up and protect her, to love her in a way that I felt I hadn't been. She was dependent on me. She needed me.

My days consisted of feeding or cooking for my daughter, going out for walks to the park and beach with her, taking her to playgroup, reading to her, playing with her – doing all the things that for me were paramount to be a 'good mother'. I was giving my daughter what I had not received: attention, love, support, connection and the space to develop skills and good feelings of being in her body and feeling good to be in the world.

I would feel guilty if I was not playing with her and giving her attention. I had experienced so much deprivation that I wanted her to feel seen and supported, to experience the world as a fun and good place every second of her waking life. This ruled my day and my life.

As my strength and confidence grew, my relationship began to fall apart. He had quit his job when I became pregnant and withdrew into himself. He didn't want to share the wonder of our pregnancy. When she kicked, he said it looked like there was an alien in my belly. He didn't want to share the wonder of being a parent with me. Despite not working, I had to remind him to include her in his life. He became fully absorbed with his hobby of model trains, shut away in the spare room.

He had admitted his fear that he would become like his own father: extremely violent. This was despite the fact that in the six years we were together, he was never violent. I had tried to do everything possible to draw him out, connect to him and include him. But he was locked away in a world of his own.

I tried and tried for nearly three years. My worries were increasing. I could see that despite nearly three years of trying to reach him, his withdrawn solitude and our separate lives in the one home were affecting not only me, but now also our precious daughter. I didn't want her to see her parents living separate lives. I did not want her to think this was a normal relationship. I didn't want her to miss out on having a normal childhood. I wanted her to have what I didn't have and experience the benefits of two parents engaging healthily and interacting.

It felt wrong but after three years of trying, there seemed nothing I could do to change things. I was alone again, even though he was living with me. I couldn't bear the thought of again living with someone and still being alone. I wanted more for my daughter and having her motivated me to want to protect her from a cold, empty and disconnected home.

I left with my daughter and stayed with my sister and brother-in-law to work out what I was going to do next. I was apprehensive. A few years earlier, I had briefly left the relationship, for the seeds of the same reason. He sent me orchids – my favourite flower. We began dating again and thought we would try again. We spoke about having a baby. Choosing to go off the pill to become pregnant was just after we decided to give it another go. The pregnancy was part of the honeymoon stage of starting again. Maybe we thought a baby would fill the gap between us.

When I left the first time, he had reacted strongly to the news. I had come home from work one day after telling him I was going to leave and opened my wardrobe to find my new, best clothes cut to shreds with the scissors lying on top. I froze in fear. I didn't know what he would do next. This was so unpredictable and out of the norm.

In hindsight, the only other warning sign of this kind of behaviour in the relationship was that if I did anything outside of being with him, like on the rare occasion I would hang out briefly with the girls at work, he was always angry when I returned. In the six years we were together I never developed a social life. I was used to not having friends and the repercussion wasn't worth it. I didn't want him to be displeased with me.

We had a very small world. Just him and me, and now I was breaking that up ...

On leaving this time, he reacted again. Though he had not been willing to address what was not working in our relationship when I was with him, he now spoke of how much the planned separation was affecting him, telling me how much weight he had lost.

On the day I left, he hid my car keys. I waited. Finally able to leave, in the weeks and months that followed, I would notice his car tailing me. I was receiving phone calls and silence. So was my mother. I was uneasy. He felt alone in the world and was saying and doing unpredictable things. He changed the way he dressed and did his hair. He was acting strange and buying presents for our little girl that were almost as if he was courting her. It was weird. He was no longer the person I knew. He was desperate and alone. I didn't know how to make my world feel safe, pleasant and secure. I was alone again. I just wished he had been willing to connect with me and our girl or get some help.

Conversations floated through my mind from when we were together. Conversations about him feeling estranged from and disappointed with his family, whom he saw as dysfunctional. Other than being with me, he had felt alone in the world. I was fearful that this despair would lead him to do something more unpredictable then the last time I left. That this time it would be worse, as this time our split was permanent.

Though he had not showed much connection with our daughter and had been absorbed with his model train set, not working and spending money on his trains, here I was now taking her away. He was angry with me and complaining about his rights as a father. I was scared he would take our daughter and leave Australia, as he had nothing holding him here.

He was behaving erratically, dressing differently and treating our two-year-old daughter with so many seemingly inappropriate gifts. This continued for quite a while. My world was uncertain and I did not know how to make these things out of my control feel more negotiable.

I had grown up so alone with no support that I was just used to not speaking to anyone about what was bothering me. I continued in my very self-reliant, solitary way, focusing on the daily needs of my daughter and not on the bigger picture. I was used to coping by staying with the daily expectations and nothing more. Unconscious to any whispers of what I needed or what was bothering me.

Two and a half months after leaving, it was New Year's Eve. I felt like everyone was going to be with someone and I was going to be alone, other than with my little girl. Being alone was my biggest threat. I was filled with fear. When I was alone, the things my mother had said to me would come back and I was terrified. My sister and brother-in-law invited me to come with them to a party, so I came with my daughter just to be around people.

That is where I met him. The Wolf in a Suit. Or more truthfully, he found me. Little Red Riding Hood, who knew all the nice things to say, but couldn't negotiate his obsession with getting me.

That night at the party, he would follow me from room to room. I couldn't say, 'Go away,' when he came over. I'd been taught not to say no or get angry. So I spoke very politely and amicably, as we had been taught. I didn't want to talk with him or see him. I didn't like the look of him. I would go to another room at the party, but he'd follow me. Even when I went into a private room to breastfeed my daughter to sleep, he walked in.

The Little Red Riding Hood in me couldn't object to his crossing my boundary, even when he intruded on my very private space while breastfeeding. If only the uncensored, disowned part of me had been free to say, 'Just fuck off. Leave me alone. I am not interested in talking with you or seeing your face. Just fuck off and leave me be.' Maybe if I had made myself 'unattractive' that way, he would have got the message. He clearly couldn't take a subtle message. He was in his own delusional world of what was going on.

But I was silent and he persisted. He kept following me around the party. I was so timid and quiet and occupied with looking after my little girl, I just wanted him to go away. I wished he could just read my mind and leave me alone. But he didn't. He wanted my phone number and because I had learnt that you don't say no to people, I gave it to him.

I hoped that if my brother-in-law was a friend of his brother, whose party I was at, he must be not that bad. Without a word, I handed my trust over to my brother-in-law who didn't even realise I had given him this trusted role.

The Wolf kept ringing me to meet up. He tried to be really helpful. He offered me his car to help me move out from my sister's when I found a place for my daughter and me. I was touched. I wasn't used to someone trying to help me. I barely knew him and he was offering me his car. Wow, that was generous. He trusted me. No one had ever supported or trusted me before. The Wolf gave me his pager number so I could contact him 24/7, any time of day.

The combination of offering me 24/7 support, along with my unspoken and irrational sense of hope and faith in my brother-in-law's friendship connection, meant the first hook was cemented. I'd never had someone be that available to me – *for* me. He would look at me with his clear, blue eyes, so confident and seemingly present. He must be good and nice with such nice eyes. Being able to look me in the eye in that direct kind of way. My ex had never been able to make eye contact. This was the total opposite and so my young naive self thought it must be right, as it was the opposite to what had not worked. Again, a belief founded on nothing substantial, just more hope. In Part 2, 'The Real World', I will take you through many layers about hooks and hope.

I was so disengaged from my own instincts that I couldn't trust my aversion of him to be stronger than his persistence. Combined with my terror of being alone and not being able to talk to anyone, I was caught. My aversion stayed a quiet niggle that I tried to ignore because I did not know how to get away. It was as if I fabricated beliefs about his character, based on his eyes or loaning me his car, that were not accurate. It was as if I had to convince myself that things were okay because I didn't know how or what to do to get away.

From early life, I had developed an automatic and involuntary ability to switch off my small, quiet, instinctual voice. I didn't have a coherent identity.

I was lost to me. Deep down, I wanted some guidance from somewhere. I cried inside the secret, solitude of me. I was so used to no one being there that I did not have any awareness to reach out. There was no one reaching out to me in my lost place. It may sound strange but I did not know how to reach out. I couldn't find guidance. I was disconnected, overwhelmed and scared. My familiar fear kept me frozen.

It's just like looking on a map – if you don't know (who you are) where you are, how can you make any decisions on where to go? You are lost. When you are full of fear, it is hard to talk or think clearly. I didn't know how to think. Have you ever had those times of fear or being lost driving in a new suburb, when you feel so disorientated that you don't know what direction to go? Imagine that happening and not ending, because there is no map out.

If every cell in your body does not know you deserve more, or that it is possible to have more, and you don't know clearly where you want to go or what to do, you have no markers to determine which street to go down and which street to avoid. So I just stayed in my little circle of existence, loving my girl. I didn't know what else to do and I didn't have anyone to talk to except my little girl.

This is hard to admit, but at that time of leaving, I wanted my little two-year-old, in her innocence, to be able to tell me what to do. I trusted her more than anyone in the world. She was not yet tainted by the world and seemed closer to the divine in her natural instinctual self. I hoped that she would have the responses to guide me to make the best decisions.

I had met a different man before I met the Wolf, but it was early days and he went away to find work interstate. I had felt a connection with him and there had been magic there. But he was willing to leave without asking me to come. I felt devastated and rejected when his love for his music career became more important than me. So again, hope and fear were leading me astray. Hope didn't want me to stay with the unbearable fear of being alone and rejected. I couldn't trust myself and I, like Little Red Riding Hood's mother, was placing too much on my child.

My hope again was based on unrealistic wishes and unrealistic feedback. I wanted to be guided by whether she looked happy, to let me know if what I was doing was right. But she was too young. At her young age, she could not negotiate the tricks and complexities of people, so around the Wolf she was subdued and knew how to be pleasing to him. Deep down, I knew her silence was not a good one. I could see her face change. He took charge and she, like me, followed his rules. I could not rely on feedback from her. I was lost and struggling.

I will never forget the day he came to visit me and we were walking down the street. I felt this sinking feeling in my heart. I had tried so many times to not let him in my life but he ignored my subtle signals. After all, he couldn't read my mind. I felt this internal collapse: I can't escape. It must be my spiritual task to love this man. There's something good in everyone, isn't there?

This echoed the messages I'd received in childhood in different ways from both my parents: spirituality and religion were my parents' centre. I received the message that religion and spirituality were more important than noticing my own needs and experience. I did not know how to reject the Wolf. I surrendered to his advances. I did not know how to navigate when the Wolf was unrelenting and 'charming'. I wasn't allowed to own some of those skills that the Wolf owns.

I had a long-standing fear of the world and of being alone. This fear consumed me growing up. I used to wake up screaming from nightmares. As a child, I would constantly check behind me, no matter where I was. I would be walking to school with my sister and check behind. I would be standing in my bedroom and check all around me. I was terrified of the dark, of the shadows. I was terrified to have a shower. I would ask my younger sister to wait in the bathroom with me, which she would do. I was haunted going to the toilet. I was constantly terrified, expecting to be attacked.

This terror never left me alone. Even when I left home, I was still not free of the terror of being alone.

So when the Wolf helped me by letting me borrow his car to move into my new home, what happened next was like a tsunami. I was so disconnected and naive I did not expect what happened when I unlocked the door to my new home, my little girl by my side. I was so used to acting as if everything was okay.

I walked into my new little home with my little girl, and my longstanding fear and terror of being alone totally swallowed me up. In that moment, I felt the biggest wave of terror I had ever experienced. I couldn't breathe. I couldn't go on. I was frozen in panic. I couldn't get out of this house quick enough. I couldn't remain in the rental that I had just gotten the keys for. Outwardly, I kept pretending that everything was okay for my little girl but inside I was a mess. Thirty minutes after arriving, while running the bath for my daughter, I rang him and said, 'Help, come and get me, I can't do this.' He was available and he came over. Immediately.

The pervasive habits of not being rude or offending people were so strong that when he continued to want so much of me, I couldn't tell him to go away. After all, he was the only one interested in me and wanted to help me. He saved me from the tsunami of terror. It feels unthinkable but my fear of the danger of being alone was more powerful than my aversion to him. It was as if *when he did something nice for me, I was obligated and committed to him.*

I still didn't want to be with him, but the fear of being alone was bigger than anything. At that time, I had no choice. The Wolf's persistence, along with my unbearable fear, made the next step decided. I had no choice. My fear of the world was bigger than my aversion of him in that moment.

No one had taught me how to be anything other than Little Red Riding Hood and as my fear overrode everything I had no option. My terror of being alone was the biggest thing. It destroyed me.

So this is how I met the Wolf. This is my story of Little Red Riding Hood. This is how I got swallowed up and began living in the Wolf's belly. This is how it came to pass that no one heard or saw what was going on. This is how it was when no one stepped in and asked me questions. It left me feeling that this life was normal. Maybe even that no one loved me enough to notice me. I did not want to disturb anyone with my needs when they were not reaching out to me. I did not feel loved or lovable.

***

As I tell you my story, you may recognise some aspects of yourself, your friend or your client. My story is my story, and it's really okay and understandable that some details may not be like your story or their story. However, there will be some themes, dynamics, limiting behaviours, expectations or beliefs that are familiar for you. Perhaps you recognise the lack of support, the internal collapse, the hopes or fears, and not having that strength of spirit that won't give up until you find the support you need. Or maybe it is one of those hooks that pulls you in and overrides your quiet voice, your doubts – not feeling worthy, believing your needs are too much, feeling too demanding or too needy.

As you work your way through this book, have a notebook beside you – just for your connections. Write down the responses, insights, questions and memories that come to mind about your current situation or the past, about your parents and siblings, and so on. Listen to the still, quiet voice. Sometimes things had to be muted, because it wasn't okay to notice your inner knowings. Those inner knowings that may have challenged someone who could not tolerate being challenged and would not allow their own gaps to be reflected. Someone who needed you to reflect that they are doing all the right things. Sometimes wisdom is held in the quiet voice because it wasn't given permission to speak louder and be heard, or because if it were shown you would be rejected, punished or shamed.

As you read this book, listen to those doubts or disbeliefs; just make note of them without making them right or wrong. This will develop a healthy witness and keep the door open to new insights and connections.

You can begin to become curious about the spoken and unspoken attitudes and beliefs you developed from what you grew up in. Those beliefs about anger, power, love, dating and boundaries. About being female, being male – being you. Start to be curious if Little Red Riding Hood lived at your house – who was the Woodcutter and where was the Wolf? Who was absent? Who was asleep? Who was overburdened with more than they could bear for their age or stage of life?

Reflect on your childhood years, your teenage years, and your young adult years. Reflect on your parents' influences on you and other significant people. What were the rules or limits that you swallowed, that your younger self did not have the skills, capacity, independence or power to dispute? What were the unbearable feelings and unthinkable thoughts that you had to avoid at all costs to not rock the boat in your family? Who was allowed to rock the boat? What happened if you or someone else rocked the boat? What did you learn about those occurrences, so you didn't experience what they did?

What did you need to do to stay connected to your parents, given that you were dependent and powerless as a child? What needed to go underground or become minimised, denied or deleted so as to prevent rejection, humiliation, shame, isolation, judgement, punishment or abandonment? Or maybe, what did you need to do so your parent(s) didn't fall apart?

What did you need to sacrifice for you to fit in? How did hope structure your choices, beliefs, feelings and behaviours?

Most families have wounds and gaps. If we can't recognise our own and our family wounds, we are destined to have difficulty seeing others. If we are blind to some states as being unbearable feelings and unthinkable thoughts, we will find ways to silence those states in other people (family, friends, clients). We live in a society of gaps and unmet needs, of aches and pain of not being seen. We tend to find crutches to fill those places we prefer not to feel or think about. Co-dependent relationships, food, drugs, shopping, plastic surgery, computer games, Facebook …

Chapter 2:
In the Wolf's Belly

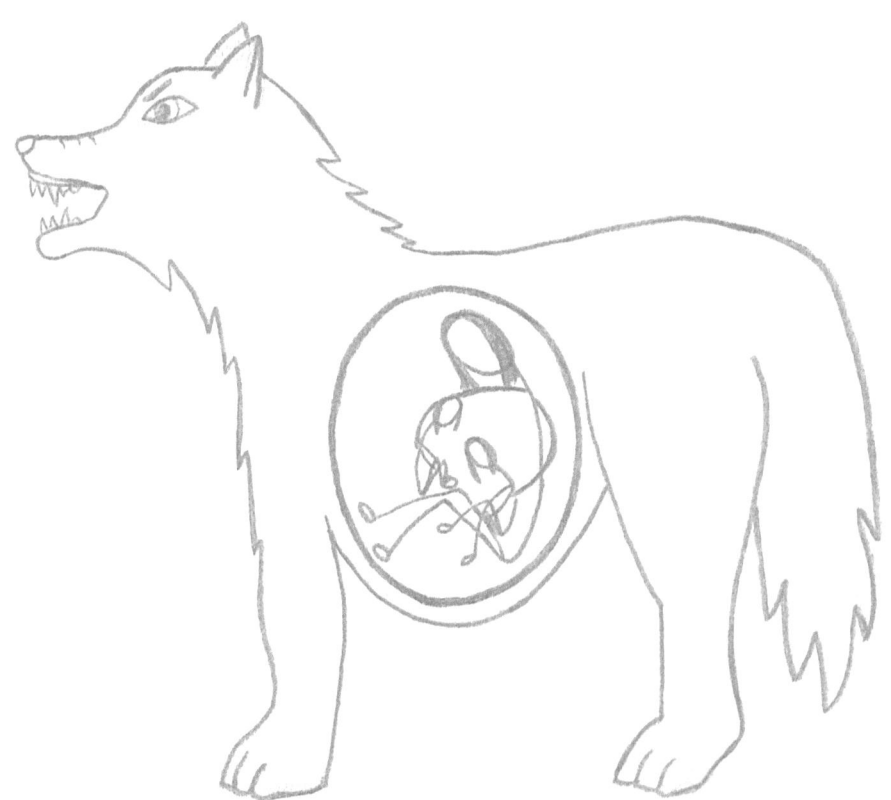

Little Red Cap

Little Red Cap was named this way because her grandmother loved Little Red Cap so much she made her a special red cap to wear. Everyone loved Little Red Cap.

One day Little Red Cap's mother sent her to visit her grandmother, who was unwell. Little Red Cap was given food and wine to take and was told to leave early before the heat, stay on the path, be quiet, walk pleasantly and take care not to break the bottle, as well as making sure to speak and behave pleasantly and don't look in the corners when she got there.

Little Red Cap promises to follow the instructions and leaves. A Wolf meets her on the path. She doesn't know the Wolf is dangerous. He walks with her and she answers all his questions. He suggests she not be so serious and enjoy the sights and sounds in nature.

Little Red Cap enjoys the invitation to play. The Wolf sneaks away and goes to her grandmother's house, where he eats the Grandmother up and dresses up as her.

Little Red Cap suddenly remembers her Grandmother and goes back on the path. She feels uneasy as she gets close to the house, which is unusual for her as she loves visiting her grandmother. She calls out, 'Good morning!' and ignores the bad feeling, stepping into the silent bedroom.

Little Red Cap thinks her grandmother looks strange. She comments on her big ears, hands and teeth. The Wolf eats her and falls asleep.

A Huntsman walking outside hears loud snoring. When he enters he decides not to shoot and instead to open the Wolf with the grandmother's scissors, in case there is someone inside. Little Red Cap and Grandmother come out. Little Red Cap finds some stones to put in the Wolf's belly and with help they sew him up. The Wolf wakes up. When he moves to stand, the weight of the stones make him fall and he dies.

Little Red Cap decides she will always do as she is told, stay on the path and not go into the woods. The Huntsman is happy to have the Wolf's skin and the grandmother enjoys her cake and wine.

Adapted from Children's and Household Tales *(Grimm 1812)*

Little Red Riding Hood was in the Wolf's belly, along with her grandmother. Helpless and waiting. Alive but with no tools to get out. Like me. The wound of Little Red Riding Hood passed through the mother's line. My mother was wounded and could not teach me, and no one else stepped in to give me tools.

Little Red Riding Hood is taught to be 'proper', obedient and told not to look in corners. She is shaped to be naive and 'asleep' to her wild instinctual feminine self; the one who has the life skills to negotiate the world. The wild, instinctual feminine self is grounded within her body and the earth; to her creative life force, her passion and timeless knowings. She owns her separateness and her connections, her sensuality and her sexuality. She owns her power and is able to access her fierceness to protect her and the vulnerable.

Patriarchy restricts the whole feminine expression to only express aspects of the feminine energy: her giving, caring, light and mothering self. Now she is at risk of being attacked and ravaged to suit the degraded masculine. Even her sexuality is changed to please the patriarchal vision, rather than her own wild expression. When the fierce feminine energy is not available, she is incomplete. Disempowered. Like me. Like many women.

When Little Red Riding Hood is told not to look in corners, she is basically being told not to ask questions. She has been told not to see the full picture of what is going – she is being shaped by the degraded masculine to see what others want her to see, and not the reality of what she sees. She is shaped to lose her curiosity, instinct, opposition, darkness and power.

This is what the degraded masculine requires. The degraded masculine is not in relationship with the fullness of the feminine aspect. The degraded masculine is patriarchy, which wants to take over and control.

The degraded masculine does not recognise the healthy masculine can remain potent and powerful when serving the wild, healthy feminine and the creative spirit within the self. This serving of the feminine by the masculine is called for within every man and woman.

Chapter 2: In the Wolf's Belly

Little Red Riding Hood has been swallowed up by the degraded, persecutory aspects of masculine energy and meets her grandmother inside the Wolf. The ancestral line of the disempowered feminine swallowed by the patriarchal, degraded masculine.

If the mother is silent and wounded and Grandmother is in the Wolf's belly, where does Little Red Riding Hood learn the Wild Woman skills to navigate life? Where is the powerful wise women community to teach women to oppose and to feel firm in their inner power, no matter whether people believe her or not? Where is the community support for her to be powerful rather than being seen or degraded in the way the patriarchal world sees powerful women – as 'having balls' or 'a bitch'?

I was swallowed up inside the Wolf's belly. I tried to focus on the positive and minimise what I was overwhelmed with. 'I was not looking in the corner of the room'. I noticed his nice eyes and that he was interested in me. I didn't act on my noticing I wasn't interested in him. I was taken in by the story of 'how big his eyes and ears were' instead of what was bothering me that felt unnamable. I felt relieved I wasn't alone. He was in some ways opposite to my ex. He was social, could make eye contact, was ambitious and wanted a family. He said he loved children. How could he be bad for me? Again, my hope (along with his story of his 'big eyes were all the better to see me with') took all this and twisted it to mean something positive – that this show was true and he was good. After all, these were all great signs, weren't they? I tried to rationalise these into logical points but they never felt solid or comforting. As I had been taught to ignore my wild self and feelings, my fears were not valued as holding important information worth acting upon. I put my hope in the Wolf instead of where it needed to be – in me and the world.

The thin veil of what appeared good was not enough. In living with him, I very quickly became trapped and isolated in something that was bigger than me. I had no car, no money and there was no concerned or caring other reaching out to me, seeing me and wondering how I was.

I was used to being on my own in my life, tolerating despair, neglect and harshness. I was good at enduring, but in those early days I would cry secretly when he was out. I was locked inside learnt helplessness. I knew I was sad but I had no embodied sense of being able to take charge and take action. Remember, I was always terrified. The world was not a welcoming place for me. I had no way of knowing what the steps were that I needed or that I could have support.

I desperately wanted to leave, but to go where? I felt blank and full of terror. I had no solid sense of where I could live and feed myself without my panic shattering me. The world was a scary place for me and now I had a little girl to look after. No money and no one having a real conversation with me. My last attempt had failed and there was no way I was going to open the door to that fear of being alone again. I was resigned to the belief that there was nowhere for me in the world. Better to have fear where I could see it then lurking in the unknown. I was overwhelmed and lost.

***

Five memories stand out from those very, early days. We went to his friend's party; he was busy drinking beer and talking to mates around the barbeque. I didn't know anyone there. Someone started talking to me, and this person happened to be male. We were just chatting. I tried to socialise. It's nice to be able to just chat when you're at a party, rather than stand all alone in the crowd. The music was on, I was young and my partner was busy socialising.

This pleasant man asked me for a dance. I love music and dancing. It felt good, just having a dance, nothing more. We danced but not close and not touching. It helped pass the night when the Wolf was doing his own thing. When we got home, I was blasted for inappropriate behaviour. I told myself he was jealous because he loved me. How could I get upset at someone who wanted me so much, when no one else had shown any feelings about wanting me? I convinced myself that his jealousy was 'love'.

One day as we left to go out on a date, he lifted the suit jacket open and showed me the holster with a gun inside. Later in our home, he left his guns, rifles and shotguns under the bed and in the wardrobe. He left the bullets lying around on his desk. He showed me a photo of him standing like Rambo, legs apart with guns strapped all over him.

One night I was in the bathroom with my daughter and his son. My daughter was about to hop into the bath. We both froze as we heard his car drive up the driveway. She stood beside the bath, her urine running to the floor. She was fully toilet trained. Fear was palpable in both of us. If only I was who I am now, I would have grabbed her and run to the neighbours to get away, before anything more could happen.

I can remember one of his brothers coming over. On more than one occasion the two of them would fight, goodness knows what about —

full on, scary, physical, on the ground rolling around and fighting. I would run out of the room, scared and shut down. I could hear them in the next room. This wild and unpredictable violence scared me and left me feeling I shouldn't do anything to upset him, as I didn't want to be on the other end of that aggression.

Everything just froze me even deeper. Every piece added another layer to me, withdrawing deeper into myself and not rocking the boat.

This was our 'honeymoon stage'. Within weeks after meeting him we had begun living together. He was unrelenting in his questions and demands – including verbally and emotionally pushing and pushing for me to become pregnant. He had a son from a previous marriage. Wouldn't it be nice to have a complete family, a his, hers and ours with all the children close in age? Rationally or was it ideally, it made sense; but again the feeling of reality did not match this sequential logic. Like Little Red Riding Hood, I was disconnected from seeing and knowing what was in the corners.

He constantly interrogated me, and would hound me with impossible dilemmas; I was meant to give the 'right' answer to him. He would keep at me, pushing for an answer when I didn't want to answer his mad, irrational questions. But it was so ingrained in my system to respond to what the other person wants. It was obvious what he wanted. He wanted me to put him and his son before me and my daughter. He would question me for what seemed hours, that if I were on a boat with my daughter and his son, whom would I save first? I was torn. I was so conditioned to please and not get anyone angry, I was scared – I knew now of his unpredictable anger and violent outbursts. How did I know that the next outburst wouldn't be at me?

I didn't have money or visible family support or any friends to talk to. I was just so used to being alone, bullied and in survival mode. I did know how to look after my daughter and give her the love I never had. I ignored my own concerns out of habit. I did know how to try to make the best of a bad situation. I didn't know how to protect my daughter and me from the environment we were in. I didn't know how to move. My behaviours were frozen, locked away.

The madness. He wanted to look after me. He wanted to look after my daughter more than her own father did. He wanted a family. Children were important to him. I wasn't used to seeing a man who really wanted to have a family and spend time playing with the children. From living with the abnormal, I imagined this must be what normal was.

But there were all these things that kept creeping in. Getting mad at me because the man at the milk bar was friendly towards me; complaining about the neighbour and how he wanted to put something explosive in her letterbox because he didn't like what she'd said to him. He would boast about his past, those kinds of activities that highlighted his strength: his black belt in karate, his previous career that required physical strength.

On occasions we would go to my father's house for dinner, every time we came home he would tell me off for something offensive I had apparently said to my father, which I could not for the life of me recall saying. I would doubt myself and it would tie me up in knots. Had I really said the wrong thing? I would regularly ring my father late at night after our visits to check. He always said the same thing: 'No, you didn't say anything wrong.' I would hang up, but still feel something was wrong.

Every day was about control and punishment. Unpredictable and explosive. One day I came back from a rare visit to the hairdressers and he exploded because my hair was one inch, maybe two inches shorter than he had ordered. The rage vomited out of him, throwing and smashing objects. For about a year after, there was a plastered, unpainted part of the wall where he smashed it and had to repair the damage.

I never knew what would set him off. How could I have thought that my hair being cut a bit shorter than he ordered would lead him to explode? Nothing made sense. I couldn't predict anything or keep myself, or the children, safe. When he was in that mood I never knew if in the next moment he would turn and it would be me, not the wall.

Another time he got angry because apparently the dinner wasn't warm enough. He punched the fridge and took the hot frying pan in his hand. Later that night, recovering from the shock of his explosion, my baby daughter – my toddler – came to me and spoke about that big knife in his hand, when he was angry standing over me. In the speed of the explosion, I didn't even remember seeing the knife in his hand when he was in my face.

He would criticise me and tell me off for what I said, thought or believed, tearing my spiritual beliefs apart. He would tell me that he was in the perfect industry to kill someone and hide the body. Later having police friends, he got D24 tapes and would listen over and over and over, hundreds of times, to cases such as one where a girl was murdered by her father when he didn't want to return her on a contact visit. Not much incentive for a mother to leave and believe she could keep her children safe.

Chapter 2: In the Wolf's Belly

I can remember him playing with the children. At first, I was so impressed that he wanted to get down and play with the children. But things changed so fast. He'd take his glasses off to have a 'play fight' with his son and of course my daughter would want to be included in this play. But the 'play' accelerated every single time to the point of him sweating profusely, as he would roll around on the ground with them both. While he was grunting and rolling around the ground, gripping the children and taking them with him, I would be moving the coffee tables and things out of the way, because he was so fast and rough. I was in damage control. They always would end up crying, bruised and hurt.

One year, his son received some Teenage Mutant Ninja Turtles plastic green handcuffs for his birthday. These handcuffs got included in the 'play fight' type of 'games'. But they kept breaking. He came home from work one day all excited; he'd found some better handcuffs that wouldn't break. I looked at what he was holding in his hands and was shocked. They were made from stainless steel. He would put them on the children and laugh as they struggled with the handcuffs; they tightened on their tiny wrists as they wriggled.

Every night I would talk to him about the way he interacted with the children. I tried to explain. I would ask him to look at their faces: 'Can't you see they're scared and they're getting hurt? What you're doing, can't you see this is too much?'

Other times he would speak how much the children meant to him, yet he could not see the fear in their eyes and their meek and helpless body posture. I realise now that he didn't hear what I said during my nightly appeals. At that point in my life, I couldn't understand or integrate the possibility of someone hearing the truth and not recognising or stopping and going, 'Oh my god, this has gotten out of control.' I had this unrealistic expectation that if I kept telling him about what was really wrong, he would come to his senses and stop. But he never did.

He wouldn't silence me when I was trying to make him realise his brutality. He would let me talk, on and on, but nothing would change. Because he didn't stop me or argue with me, I thought he was listening to me and I hoped we would get somewhere. But each day, nothing changed. Sorry, things did change – they got worse.

The Wolf loved to take over and control and be King. Back then, in my early twenties, I was susceptible to being taken over, as this was a similar experience from childhood. I was not equipped and too scared to be in charge of my own life. He would control the way I looked, how long my hair needed to be, how I styled my hair, the particular way *he* needed it to be slicked back. He changed my makeup, giving me white foundation to wear to be like the women in the 'Simply Irresistible' video clip. He chose what clothes and shoes I wore. He controlled whom I had the opportunity to speak to, and where and who I socialised with, limiting my contact with family. He even changed my name, introducing me to his family as Tammy. Some of them never realised until later that it was not my name.

All I wanted was to be able to stay home and look after my children. He would provide for us – and for that, it seemed he thought he could do what he wanted. He ruled.

Sometimes he would admit that he was scared he had given his son brain damage from hitting him over the head. He used to say he was scared the neighbours would hear noises and would call the police and report him. So he knew what he was doing was wrong. But he didn't stop.

He worked closely with the police. Many of his friends were police and were over at our house all the time. He warned me not to call the police any time, as it would ruin his career. Again, he knew what he did was wrong. But he didn't stop.

When you're physically hurt, you feel it hurts; you know it's wrong. It's clear and it's reinforced in society. It's a criminal offence. But when someone denies what they say or do and denies what you say, feel and need – every day, year in, year out – and there's no one to dispute this reality, you begin to mistrust your perceptions. It plays with your mind. It's maddening. When no one is around to reflect how you've changed or how there is a look of fear in your child's eyes, then it starts to become 'normal' and inside this war-zone you believe this must be life. Shell-shocked, you go through the motions and don't question it, like everyone else.

Emotional, verbal and psychological mind games and punishments are slippery, elusive and evasive. There is no bruise or mark from the layers of emotional abuse. This abuse is not concrete, like a broken bone is. This abuse is not factual, like a slap. This abuse can be twisted to be perceived as just words and perceptions, and everyone has a different reality, don't we? But the Wolf's picture of reality didn't include mine and led me to doubt that my reality was important. A bruise is non-negotiable but we can turn ourselves inside out with meanings and words. Especially when no one outside questions or disagrees with the 'reality'.

When all those words and looks and actions manipulate, deny, control and reduce your life to something very small, your sense of self gets lost. Some part of the psyche hides away the essence of self, so it also doesn't get killed off from all the unrelenting attack. Left to be a shell.

It is easy from the other side to see that those words and actions are abusive. But when you are in the Wolf's belly and those daily words, looks and actions deny the reality of your subjective experience, your foundation is eroded. The trust in your perception is shattered; you don't trust your picture of reality to help find a way out of the Wolf's belly.

So you disconnect, going into survival mode. Some part of the self goes underground and is hidden away so he can't kill every part of you. In the distant dreamy hope that at some point, the Woodcutter will come.

Emotional and psychological abuse is the most dangerous and impactful wound, because it is often unseen – there is no evidence of the crazy-making torture and little validation in society of these criminal acts.

Often there is no Woodcutter to cut through and stop the torture. Even if someone sees some things that are going on, you get laughed at and told, 'I'm just making a joke. You haven't got a sense of humour … don't be so sensitive.' Or, 'I didn't mean it that way … if you loved me you'd understand …'

On a visit, my sister told me that he shouldn't speak to me that way, but that was it. There was no more conversation. In her mind, she thought she had spoken up for me and tried to reach me. Those words didn't help me because I couldn't stop him from speaking to me that way. She was speaking about him, not about me. He was unstoppable. I needed her to reach out to me, asking, 'You don't look happy, how can I help you?' This conversation did not take place. She too did not know what else to do. She did the best she could.

I was in a constant vigilant mode. Attack could come from any irrational and unpredictable direction, and at that stage could take the form of up to nine of the fourteen types of abuse. It got to the point that he would just look at me and I would involuntarily flinch. He would ask in puzzlement, 'Why did you just flinch?' I would not even realise it was happening until he asked me. Just a look or the tone of his voice would trigger fear in my system.

He forced sexual acts on me. I had already learnt he would not listen to my assertions to protect the children. I would try to object for me but he wouldn't hear my quiet no. I remember lying on the bed thinking he doesn't listen to my *no* – maybe if I show my vulnerability … if I lie still, distressed and pained emotionally, it will register. But nothing. He raped me. He put me in sexual positions, took photos of me and then showed them to some of his friends. After I'd given birth to our child, of course he wanted sex very soon after. And with me not knowing how to say no, he got it. Having sex made me feel as if I was desirable. It gave me some sense of power, though in reality, in the act of sex I had no power.

It was as if there was a survival-based part of me under the false impression that being able to go over the threshold of what was okay showed I was strong. He wanted sex two or three times a day. Going along with sex felt like, 'Yes, I can handle this. I can walk up to the lion and look in his mouth. I can stick my head in and count his teeth.'

This is counterintuitive. When the healthy response is to run away from the lion, the counterphobic response goes towards that which is anxiety-provoking. This is seen as an attempt to cope with inner anxiety and face the fear but ends up keeping you in a hyper-aroused state of stress. The ongoing stress depletes and wears you down more and more.

The stress pattern developed from my early family life did not include the activation of escape via the fight/flight response. I was habituated in the freeze response, the fear, threat, aggression and power of the Wolf maintaining my freeze response. The combination of my fear at 'home' and my fear of the world left me with no way out. No money and being isolated, helped maintain my counterintuitive response pattern of 'strength and endurance' with no solution in sight.

I could never escape. I had to endure. I needed to find some way of feeling strong. Enduring made me feel strong in some crazy kind of way. It's a false sense of strength to be able to tolerate and endure even more cruelty, as this kind of strength backlashes.

I constantly had urinary tract infections (UTI). I'd never previously had them in my life. It puzzled me. I had to go to the doctor again and again with another UTI. It was so painful and uncomfortable. I discovered later that UTIs are common when sex is rough. I've never had them since.

He would urinate on me. 'Golden showers,' he called them. For me it was insulting to be urinated on. I felt like an object with him standing over me. No matter what I objected to, my response was ignored as if I didn't exist.

No matter whether I was able to object or not, my face and body would not have shown pleasure, but he was in a world of his own. His fantasy where he was King and I was his subordinate slave.

He attacked my reality every day, telling me what I felt, what I thought and what I said was not real. Day in, day out. After a while, I just shut down. There was no point disagreeing with him because he always had to win. He was unrelenting and persistent. He would gloat, supposedly quoting from the Bible that as a woman it was my duty to be 'subordinate'.

I had more important things going on, to give my children a 'normal' life inside the madness. So I would cope with, manage or escape, while trying to shield the children – there was no space to have a clear head and reflect. When you're isolated and you're never believed, there is no space to question what you're actually living with. There's too much shock and overwhelm to really take in what is actually happening. When a threat or explosion was over I was immediately immersed in play with my children, school duties and play dates, cooking and keeping house.

He would buy me fancy clothes. Some people commented, 'How lucky you have. How generous he is.' But I was not allowed to choose my own clothes – not the style, not the colour and not what I actually needed. He kept buying me eveningwear. How he wanted me to be, not what I needed. I was a stay at home mum. I wore holes in my jeans during the day while he laid out evening clothes for me to wear when he would take me out.

I used to have to record a TV show every day for him while he was at work, *The Bold and the Beautiful*. He modelled himself on the father of this empire. He would tell me that was the way to be as a man. Though I don't think he actually was like that character. There was a distortion, a grandiose quality of wanting that kind of empire and power. It was all about the women being beautiful objects for the men's pleasure and the men being all-powerful.

He wanted me to cut his nails, do those personal care things that any adult does for themselves; he wanted me to fuss over him in every way possible and ask him constantly if he was enjoying his meal. He wanted me to do everything for him as well as pander to him as if he was a baby. When I didn't I was told off, repeatedly.

He'd watch music videos over and over and want me to live out his fantasies so that how I looked matched some of the music videos. He wanted to idolise me and could not believe that I did those bodily functions like going to the toilet, farting or burping.

Something in me wanted to be adored due to the feeling of being unloved my whole life. But there was no healthy love and healthy adoring; nor was there a healthy perspective. I was left to be idolised. But the deep cost of idolisation with a Wolf is that at some point you will be punished, as you cannot be more powerful than him. So there was a brief moment of being adored or idolised – and then stripped naked and punished.

He would take all of us to fancy restaurants, regularly buy expensive champagne, and occasionally treat me to a concert. Again, people commented, 'What a great guy, aren't you lucky.' But every moment was so stressful. He was living out his dream, enacting what he thought was a good life, but it was just a facade. The children and I were paralysed with fear, puppets to his commands. His presentation never matched his actions. The Wolf had two faces. One face to the world, that was so helpful and confident – and yet when the door closed, he was cruel, harsh, scary and cold.

Every time we would go to the restaurant, the children and I would spend half the time making a beeline to the bathroom. It was so unbearable to be in his angry but controlled (and controlling) presence that our nervous tension just needed to go to the toilet and get breathing space away from him. We genuinely needed to go to the bathroom ten or more times in the space of a couple of hours. Every time the three children and me would go together. No one would want to be left with the Wolf.

He not only controlled the way I looked, he also controlled the children's appearances, clothes and hair. He'd change their hairstyles, which would mean they would have to sit for extraordinarily long periods of time at such a young age, uncomfortable and hurting from the hair crimper and the heat. When you're just little, it's too much. They would protest, but it was to deaf ears.

He sexualised the girls through his behaviours towards them, including styling their hair. Treating them like objects and dolls. He would kiss my youngest daughter, holding her like you would a lover, not your baby. Like you see in the movies with the head moving from side to side, holding her – a closed mouth kiss, but still, it was wrong.

I couldn't stop him and I didn't have the safety to leave. I felt undeserving of support and grateful and obliged, because the Wolf was willing to provide for my daughter and me. I didn't want to have her put in childcare when she was so young. I'd had a very lonely, scary childhood. I wanted to be there for my child every day and it felt at that time that the only way I could do that was being swallowed up and in the Wolf's belly. Living with the Wolf allowed me to be with my daughter and not be terrified of being alone in the world. In my fearful state it felt more tolerable to be in the same house with the Wolf and know where he was, than be out in the world and live in constant terror of lurking Wolves.

I tried to focus on looking after my daughter, being a good step-mum and looking after our new little baby. I was trying to make sure that the children were okay, and unconsciously trying to make sure that my fear for being alone was kept away. I was constantly walking on eggshells, placing hope in the unrealistic fantasy that if I just say and do those pleasing things, he'll be happy. After all, if I was doing the things that he wanted, there wouldn't be any more eruptions, would there? I had the misbelief that if I did the 'right' things, he'd do the right things and be reasonable, too.

After an explosion, he would come and just stand in the doorway and say, 'You know, if we went to court and you had to swear on the Bible, you could not say that I punched you.' That's true, he never punched me. He dragged me, pulled me, pushed me so that I'd be pressed up against the wall. But more often than not, the physical explosions were around me.

What was daily was the physical explosion of words and the threats. It was the control, and it was the conquest of my identity and my social circle, not having access to any money or any of my own choices. It was the sexual abuse and the sexualising and objectifying of me. It was the madness of him acting as if everything was right when it wasn't, twisting things so that the reality that I experienced did not exist. It was only his reality. The emotional and psychological abuse was the biggest torment that kept me trapped in this prison – but back then I didn't even realise it was abuse. Emotional and psychological rigid rules that did not include my reality were the 'norm'.

One day, when the Wolf was resting, his son came up to me with those stainless steel handcuffs and silently handed them to me. I got it. He wanted me to make them disappear. I never had known where they were kept. I only saw them come out when the Wolf was 'playing' with the children. We walked very quietly while I was thinking, *where could I hide these?* My young step-son watched me hide them and we never said another word about those handcuffs.

Keep reading and you will learn how I came to realise what I was living in was abuse. In Part 2, each chapter will help explain how it can be possible to not know that you are living in abuse.

You know the experience, if you step into a hot bath when your body temperature hasn't acclimatised to it – perhaps it's a cold winter day – the water feels scalding and you don't step in. It's too hot. But if you put your toes in at the very tip, letting them adjust and then slowly inch down, more and more, then what was scalding becomes comfortable to be in.

So too when you're bombarded with all different types of abuses, walking on eggshells, trying to make sure he doesn't get mad. You're isolated and you're trying to take care of your children and give them a normal life: feeding them, taking them to school, participating in school programs, taking them to their friend's house, going shopping, cleaning … when you're being strong for your children and trying to give your children a normal life, as well as managing the constant fall-outs, there's not much space left in the day to reflect on or question your life.

When you are so busy trying to keep your children in a cocoon, to keep what is unbearable away from them, you too can get caught in a cocoon of how you want life to be, in order to protect the reality from breaking through and shattering all of you.

I wanted my children to be protected from the abuse, to not show the reality in my eyes, voice and behaviours. So I blindly and unconsciously acted as if it was not happening. I could not bear to see reality. The Wolf was also in denial of reality, acting as if we were a happy family and as if his distorted fantasy about whom we both were was true. For different reasons, we were all denying reality. That way, if I deny reality and can't mirror the reality back to the Wolf, I am not at risk of challenging him – and if the children don't mirror reality back at me, I am not at risk of failing them. They needed me to not fall apart and on some level they would have known that I couldn't cope to know, so as children they modelled what was shown. But the sad thing is that we all knew it – in the cells of our being we knew it. It changed our behaviours and choices – we just couldn't speak about it in the way that was needed.

Abuse is illogical – it is a mad space, it is never understandable. When you are inside the Wolf's belly, you keep accommodating those subtle things that at first were excused as 'just an outburst of jealousy' – a bit more control, a bit more punishment, until you're totally shrouded and suffocated in all the layers of abuse and control and fear.

This was daily life inside the Wolf's belly. When you're in survival mode, it's really hard to see the big picture; you only see the gut lining from the inside – not a great perspective. You're just focusing on the moment by moment details, to get by.

***

I have described what it is like inside the belly of the Wolf. Daily life. Nearly six years of my life. My children's early developmental years. Their foundation. We needed a Woodcutter that could hear the noise of fear. We needed a Woodcutter to come in and act.

I think of family, friends, police, the legal system and other parts of our social system being like the potential Woodcutters, who could hear and intervene. But if they remain silent and don't interject, the continuation of abuse continues unopposed. If there is silence or a shoo of a fly instead of the fullness of cutting the Wolf open to get Little Red Riding Hood and her grandmother out, women and children remain swallowed up in the Wolf's belly. We need Woodcutters who have the courage and skill to notice the quiet sounds and can bear being with the blood and the guts; who can bear being with the mess.

In the Little Red Cap version of the story, Little Red Riding Hood and the grandmother both have the opportunity and capacity to fill the Wolf with heavy stones. They are witnessed and supported by the Woodcutter to give back to the Wolf the weight of his own actions. When he gets up, he can't stand with the weight of what is inside him. The shame, blame and weight of his actions need to stand with him, not Little Red Riding Hood or the grandmother. The Wolf has an opportunity when he can bear the weight of what he has done to repair and change. Any death in a fairy tale does not necessarily mean a literal death, but there is the necessity of the death of the Wolf within the masculine psyche that is harnessed to control the feminine. That needs to die.

We need to know more about the Woodcutter in our society and the development of the Woodcutter Within.

The lack of adequate response by our social system is a bit like an absent Woodcutter or the laissez faire parent. Remember, the Wolf stays away when the Woodcutter is nearby. When the boundaries and consequences are in place there is less space for the Wolf to prowl.

When parenting, if you provide a small consequence to a child, it doesn't necessarily interrupt their attention or energy. Often children incorporate the small consequence, like brushing away a fly that is annoying them, and they keep going. However, if you give a consequence that interrupts their process, then they really stop and pay attention – they need the consequence to affect them for any possibility of change to their behaviour. So too, the Wolf needs society to be bigger than him and give him a large enough consequence that is not like a small fly. A consequence that contains and affects him. If we're not affected, we're not changed.

When Little Red Riding Hood is in the Wolf's belly, she needs someone outside the belly to act to create safety and support. There is very little opportunity to act inside his belly. It is only when society creates these opportunities and acceptance that Little Red Riding Hood can see, feel and hear, that she has some hope of taking some action too.

Reflect now, after hearing about life in the belly of the Wolf, to think about those people in your life who leave you questioning your reality. Is there a Dr Jekyll and Mr Hyde duality in their behaviours behind closed doors? Do their words match their actions? Is there a Wolf in a Suit? Or a Wolf in sheep's clothing? Do you excuse it because you believe 'he is not abusive and doesn't hit you'? Write your responses to these questions in your notepad. Is your reality compartmentalised, with different people knowing only part of the truth? How do you determine who can know what, and who or what is being protected? At what cost?

Is there space and support to be different? To disagree? To have different needs? To have your friends? Your time? Your interests? The food you like? The clothes you like? The music you like to listen to? Your own money? Your future plans?

Are you allowed to say no? After all, who has the right to bestow or take away your birthright to say no? No one.

Is this the kind of relationship you would want your daughter (whether you have a daughter or not) to have? Your best friend? Your sister? Is this the life you dreamed of for you? Or are there too many secrets or excuses?

All these questions can be valuable to ask yourself – or if you're a therapist, family member or friend, to explore in your own life and your relationships. Before you gently and respectfully explore these issues with any client or friend you have concerns about, it is important to know your own landscape, your own skeletons, your own blinkers. Ask yourself the questions that may not have been asked. Asking these questions is relevant when the answers impact you, your life, choices and relationships. If you can't see the shadows in your story you will want to avoid or minimise other people's shadows or cut them off from speaking of them. Can you live inside the belly of your existence or are you swallowed by someone, either currently in your life or perhaps from the past that is still impacting on a part of or whole areas of you and your life?

Chapter 3:
The Woodcutter Within

The Woodcutter in the story of Little Red Cap becomes suspicious. He acts on his instincts. He is connected to nature. He doesn't just ignore signals or sounds that seem odd. He doesn't think it is none of his business. He stays open. He becomes involved. He has the strength of character to follow his instincts and ethics, rather than being structured or defined by someone or something outside of him. The Woodcutter represents the healthy, masculine attribute which is connected to nature (and the nature of the feminine); the ability to cut through what is necessary. A fierce ruthlessness that has a positive intention to break through what is destructive to release the good.

The Woodcutter is that energy and approach that can cut through trickery and the veils of illusion. We all need, regardless of being a woman or a man, an internal figure who can be like this Woodcutter. One who listens, feels and senses what does not feel right and can take action based on those inner sensations, without second-guessing or doubting. Without the need to be convinced. Just willing to go with the quiet and find out. Having the courage to contain doubts or fear and still take action. The Woodcutter finds out more information and does whatever is necessary, not allowing uncertainty, assumptions or future, fear-based perceptions to block the necessary action.

The Woodcutter Within does three things: (1) interrupts the destructive power path by (2) cutting through and creating an opening, which allows (3) a release. The Woodcutter Within has the capacity to tolerate the uncomfortable, to bear the blood and guts spilling out – to take risks, even the possibility of being wrong. This is all for the purpose and intention to allow a return of life energy.

My release from being inside the Wolf's belly came in increments. There was no Woodcutter around me who was consistent to follow through to get me out. So it took moments of external Woodcutters paving a way for me to build my own Woodcutter and internalise the beginnings of skills and capacities.

The Woodcutter Within always needs external Woodcutters to help bring about what is needed. After all, as humans we are social creatures. I couldn't do it on my own. We learn and introject through social modelling. It took a while, but bit by bit, different events and experiences meshed together to create my stages of awakening, eventually ripping me out from within the belly of the Wolf.

As the years inside the Wolf's belly went on, the underground, unmetabolised memories of pain pushing inside my unconscious, accumulated and stirred restlessly. My pain and fear, and my daughter's pain and fear, were leaking in and around my whole psyche; we felt trapped, while being tossed through the different faces of abuse, again and again. Seeing the violence through their faces was so disturbing – instead of seeing their faces with the innocence, spontaneity, joy and lightness of being that should have been there in their childhood. All this pain grew and grew thicker and bigger and heavier – and my reality gradually became more and more uncomfortable and indisputable.

All of these layers swirled around in my system, knocking me about. My children were getting bigger. They were going out more in the world. This meant I had some space to connect to me and more permission to go out in the world – for their sake. Slowly snippets of opportunities and experiences with Woodcutters in the world could reach in and open the internal door, which was holding my pain. It started a slow ripple effect of realising what was so wrong about my life and what was missing – connecting me to other experiences. My reality began surfacing.

Here are some of the experiences that started to knock against me as I lay squashed and trapped in the Wolf's belly. These experiences helped to get me and the girls out. See if you can notice the three themes that flow throughout the stream of my experiences.

I fell pregnant only a few weeks after our daughter was born. (Sex was one of his ways of control and having sex soon after giving birth seemed to be his way of remaining number one). Falling pregnant whilst breastfeeding was something I didn't expect and alarm bells went off inside me. If I had a second child with this man, I would never, ever be able to leave. I was surprised to have this spontaneous thought float up of its own accord. After my initial collapse into helplessness, I had not consciously let myself recognise I wanted to get away, or have any plan to escape.

If I got pregnant again, how would I ever be able to leave? I would then have three children to look after as well as his child. It felt as if I would be lost in looking after all the children, with no energy or space to escape. The thought of having to protect two children that he would lay claim over and a right to see, seemed as if it would establish a greater power and rights to preside over his 'kingdom'.

I spoke to him about the pregnancy and made out I was not coping. 'That

Chapter 3: The Woodcutter Within

it was too soon ... too hard for me to have two children so close together in age'. I pleaded that I needed to have a termination, something that never in my life I would have imagined I would ever, ever consider or do. How could I choose to end the life of my own flesh and blood?

I had a termination. For the life of my two children and me. So we could at some point get out. I still mourn for this little one. My baby's life was sacrificed so that my two children and I could have the possibility to escape. It is hard to believe that this was my life. That this would forever be part of my life story. For eternity. I don't like the word 'termination' or 'abortion'. They are so clinical and final for such an emotional, conflicting and tumultuous experience that is far-reaching. The whole experience was awful. I was numb.

Time passed and in my never-ending attempt to be the one to help make things better and end the pain, I asked to speak to his medical practitioner. I knew the Wolf would only tell part of the story about what was going on with his health. I wanted to tell someone in authority what life was really like at home. I thought, *he can't get better when this is not addressed*. I wanted his medical practitioner to know the uncensored story and the stress we were all under. I was desperate for help from someone.

For some reason, a stranger seemed easier to talk to than family. Professionals in health care had in my perspective a clear mandate to help, whereas my family map was everyone for themselves. I went in and told him what was going on. I said it the way it really was. Nothing censored but no poor me, just concern. I felt safe as he was a practitioner and the Wolf was not in the room. I felt being a doctor he was an authority and I naively thought that just as doctors have to prescribe the correct medicine for an illness, they would also take action when something is wrong; after all, isn't that what they do? His patient was sick in many ways and he needed to know the full extent of his sickness.

He did nothing. Actually, later he did something, but that will come out in 'The Snarling Wolf'.

I was good at making the best of a hard situation and I continued to manage. I looked forward to the simplest of things. Every week I looked forward to driving from the suburb I lived in, back to my suburb from my other life before him. This was my weekly outing to go grocery shopping. I went to my old health food shop, and across the road were the greengrocers: two brothers and their mother who were so friendly and cheerful. This is where I had shopped for years.

Community and relationship. The greengrocers would always give my girls a piece of fruit and welcome them warmly. The health food shop man engaged so beautifully with the children, involving them in our shopping experience and encouraging them to climb up to the counter and help him. They would punch in some of the shopping items on the cash register and he'd give them a sugarless lollipop. He was friendly, calm, inclusive and gentle. Not pushy or controlling. We used to have 'normal' conversations about our common interest in health.

These simple shopping visits were my one weekly pleasure. I was out in the world where things felt normal. The other pleasure was, of course, when the Wolf was at work and I could play freely with the children or go help out at their school.

Doing our weekly shopping was such a contrast to what happened at home. An essential part of the gradual awakening was brought about by this contrast. It was a reminder of the madness against the normality. It was a reminder of there being some men out in the world who are gentle and considerate and appropriate with children. This personal connection was different to being a no one at a global supermarket. These welcoming men kept the door open, just a crack from a total encapsulation and isolation in the belly of the Wolf.

I occupied myself trying to be the best mother and partner. I've always been interested in health and thanks to the health food shop owner's encouragement, I asked the Wolf if I could go to some macrobiotic cooking classes, which I loved the idea of. Cooking healthy food really made a difference to my awakening. I had always cooked healthy food, but this was another level. It felt okay for me to ask the Wolf to go to this class as it would benefit the whole family. I could never have asked for something just for me.

The contact from shopping led to the cooking classes. If I had been so isolated that I was not allowed out to even do the regular grocery shopping, I would have been even more alienated and unlikely to take any steps out in the world. Each step led to another. The health food guy led to the cooking female teacher and her husband, who were both shiatsu practitioners. Over the years, they each helped in significant and different ways. A community of care was being built.

Every week in the class, I started to feel like a person, not an object. My desire to contribute and connect was stirring. At home, putting more time

Chapter 3: The Woodcutter Within

and mindful care and attunement into what my family and I ate started to create an interruption and space in my embedded survival pattern. I was starting to treat myself as a person, not an object in the way significant others in my life, including my partner and my parents, had treated me. I felt nourished and calmer.

Eating in this macrobiotic way changed my mood and my energy. The macrobiotic approach is not just about what you eat, but the energy you cook, the method you cook and how you cut your food and more. There is an attunement with nature and rhythms. Something lifted within me. I felt clear in my mind. I started exercising and meditating in the lounge room in the early hours before the children woke up. I was feeling clearer and stronger.

My energy was moving out of the stress and survival response to the everyday response. I was awakening.

One day, I read what was on the noticeboard while in the doctor's waiting room. I loved to read. I didn't like spaces of nothing. I had a habit from childhood to fill the silence and the gaps — to not leave space for my own feelings and thoughts to bubble up, as that would reveal the pain and the situation that I felt trapped, unskilled and helpless in. Reading was a good way of filling those spaces and taking me away from me.

At these times, it didn't really matter much what I would read. I was just doing what you do when you're in survival mode: keep busy, keep focusing on something; don't leave space to realise what you're actually living in.

On the noticeboard was a square sheet of paper and there was a list on it, with boxes after each statement. Each line was a description in the form of a question. In my head the answer was yes to each question. Yes, I experienced that. Yep, that one too. Yep, yep, yep, yep … and then I got to the bottom of that flyer and it was saying that I was in an abusive relationship. I was blown away. Could this be true? All of these questions were statements describing an abusive relationship.

I didn't really comprehend what 'abuse' was. I didn't really have a sense of the difference between healthy and unhealthy — but here it was, straight in front of me, and it was indisputable.

It was a shock to connect the label 'abuse' with the way he spoke to me and the way he treated me. I had not made that connection. I had never really heard that term or heard any conversations about abuse. Abuse had never been contextualised in what it looks like in daily life.

I had led a pretty sheltered life: no TV, not many people in our life other than grandparents and first cousins. No conversations in our house other than what our parents told us to do or to believe. I didn't have school friends and it seemed to me that even though my sisters had friends, not many people were over at our place. All I remember is that our house was pretty quiet, scary and isolated, not very connected to the world.

We were inside a very small world. Ours was not the kind of house where people dropped by. There was no laughter or lightness in our house. I remember being scared of my dad as a child and people from school telling me my dad was scary. Someone told me many years later that after visiting our home one day, they had asked their mother to never leave them alone at our place again. My dad was too scary. I had grown up accepting this as 'normal'. Here I was again accepting what was normal, when now I discover this pattern of power, control, threats, withholding, neglect and denial was abuse. This was why I had not felt safe. It was not me.

I didn't know what to do with this piece of information from the noticeboard. It was overwhelming, so it got put away somewhere in my system. Instead, I returned my focus on the daily task of surviving, taking care of the children and keeping the peace so (I hoped) there would not be another rupture or explosion.

I went home but I could do nothing with this information. It was just another piece in the awakening. There was no step at the end of this powerful piece of paper of what I should do, now that I knew this. Or if there was the next step in small print, I didn't see it. The shock was too much or the next step was too big to bridge to.

Bit by bit, all these pieces started to slowly link up. Like the time I heard him in the next room talking softly to his son while I was in the other room, nursing where I'd just been hurt by him. Sure it was in a 'game' but he still had no care or remorse for hurting me. I could hear him saying reassuringly to his son, 'I love you, I won't hurt you.' Something shattered in me. Another phase of awakening. *Oh my god, he doesn't love me, because he is saying he doesn't hurt people that he loves.* At that point I didn't make the connection, *well, he hurts the children, too.* But I got what was important. *He doesn't love me.* The bond of commitment was breaking.

The more I awakened, the more my fear palpably increased. Towards the end, I would wait a long time after he had gone to bed before I would feel safe to go to bed. I would stay up, keeping busy, waiting until he was in a deep sleep. I didn't want to go to bed and feel and hear and smell him. I didn't want him reaching over to me and wanting something from me. I was so terrified of him reaching for me, I would sleep with all my clothes on, lying as stiff as a board and as far to the edge of my side of the bed as I could reach, without falling out until the early hours of the morning. Then I would wake up early, before him, and begin my morning routine.

Another opening to being able to leave was through a very tragic event. While I was engaged to him, my younger sister was hit by a car and killed. I was devastated. She was my baby sister. The one I had shared a room with growing up. The sister who had stayed with me in the bathroom with my terrors. The sister I would seek refuge with in the school ground and sometimes play after school with her and her best friend. She was the one I was closest to in the world.

The Wolf suggested since I was grieving and she was going to be part of the bridal party that we postpone the wedding. I was in such a state of grief and chronic stress that I could not think clearly or plan. I agreed. I would not have thought of this tragedy as an opportunity to create some space before the even tighter binding to him in marriage, but he gave that to me through her death. My template was to endure, not to make adjustments or take space for me. I had some temporary space from further entrapment.

One year later I was gone. If we had married in that time it would have made the separation so much trickier. I think the legal and financial complications of marriage would have made my mental and emotional mindset so much harder for me to leave.

There came a time when he was taken into hospital. I was alone with the children for a period of time. What space … what a sigh of relief. This was a significant light bulb moment. I will never, ever forget this one night when I was serving our dinner. It was such a contrast. The lightness, the pleasure, the ease in me and in my children's faces and behaviours. *Ahh, so this is what life is meant to be like. I like this.* I was reminded of what is possible and healthy. My mind was felt so different and so clear for the first time in years. I was out of the survival mode now that he was temporarily not a threat or controlling my daily life.

I would visit him daily when he was in hospital. I didn't say anything. He was recovering. When it was time for him to return home and I was driving him back home from the hospital, I told him, 'I'm taking my life back.'

He said, 'Well go, I'll train another sixteen year old.' He blamed me, trying to make me feel guilt and responsibility. He said if I left he'd commit suicide. He blamed the problems of the relationship on him being unwell and said, 'Just wait until I get better and everything will be good.' But I knew that it was nothing to do with him being unwell. The problems had been there since day one.

The Wolf suggested we go to couple's counselling. I couldn't say no. Saying no was never an option. He always had to win. I didn't see that saying no would make anything easier, given that whenever he wanted something, he would hound and interrogate me until I would collapse. He chose a counsellor from the hospital and I agreed to attend.

We went to see this woman and in the safety of the room with her, somehow I started speaking about how it really was. I don't know where I got the bravery from – maybe because he was not fully himself and still under the effect of a lot of medication. He was still weak from his hospital stay. I felt some courage in speaking out. I spoke uncensored, maybe not saying everything, but enough.

Towards the end of the first session – with me describing what daily life was like and him responding to each of her questions, 'Yes, but it's no big deal, really' – she asked him to leave the room, making some excuse for him to leave.

He went to the car. I can't remember the details she gave him, it was something to do with getting the child seat ready in the car for our daughter who was with us. When he left the room she turned to me and said, 'Get out. Get out as quick as you can, do not take anything. It's not going to get better. It's only going to get worse. Just get out, now.'

I am forever grateful to this Woodcutter Woman who had the courage to speak out and acknowledge the depth of what was going on. I went home not saying anything to him.

I started planning by talking to Centrelink and looking for housing.

The accumulation of my gradual awakening, his decline in health and the counsellor's warning enabled me to gather the dislocated pieces together and see the bigger picture. My sister's death also brought on the immense preciousness of life and the fine line between life, death and regret. Bringing all these pieces together made my reality too uncomfortable to ignore. What I was living with was no longer avoidable and there was a momentum waiting to be acted on – by me this time. I began to sort out the belongings while he was out or asleep, in secret, but I made sure I was fair. I was always fair.

In dividing the belongings and going through my process of leaving in that final week, I happened to answer the phone when the Wolf's best friend, a police officer, rang. I told him vaguely what was going on. I didn't say much but I clearly hinted at the abuse. He basically said to me, 'I'm not surprised you're going. I could see the way he treated you was not good.'

I remember laughing incredulously inside, in shock or surprise. My internal dialogue: 'Wow! Really? You didn't see anything that was going on. You saw him on his best behaviour and you can get why I'm leaving? Wow …' I didn't make my response obvious – after all, this was his best friend. I couldn't trust him. I had not told the Wolf I was leaving so I didn't want to cause suspicion on the phone. I was also used to holding in my responses, protecting and not offending or challenging.

I wished his best friend had spoken up and challenged the Wolf while we were together. Who knows? Maybe he did but I never saw any result or change from it.

Yet I doubt he would have challenged his friend about the 'minor' things he had seen. He never spoke out in front of me at those 'minor' times when he witnessed how I was being treated. Those times that he was now saying were not okay. His silence sent a message that how the Wolf behaved was acceptable. If he did not speak out at the 'minor' incidents how would he be able to enquire about, know to or challenge his friend, the Wolf about major incidents. If his best friend was not able to speak up or create change, I doubt the Wolf would listen and respect anyone else's opinion. Silence is powerful and sends the wrong message when you don't communicate anything different to your surroundings. The unspoken sent message was that how he treated me was acceptable by other males. The mateship of not showing up another male. Any secret objections that remain unspoken contribute to the continuation of abuse, sending the message that it's acceptable and not worthy of being acted on.

I began to tell my family. It felt a very formal process. My memory is that none of them displayed much visible concern, comforting hugs or practical steps to help. I was left with a sense of them hearing my words – 'I'm going to leave'. I walked out of their homes, with me feeling alone and without a circle of support around me.

My family does not know how to be with a family member's feelings and experiences. There is so much pain and brokenness, it is as if everyone is too full. Almost as if showing feelings might open their own Pandora's box and our whole family could be destroyed by all the pain. Their words are often blame and a defending of themselves instead of being with someone's reality and the grief of how it is. I too was still caught inside this web of closed feelings; I would report what I was doing and not show my feelings.

The exception was one sister, who told me in private that when she used to leave after visiting us, she would cry in the car when going home. Something had seemed seriously wrong. She didn't like the way he was. Yet, like everyone else, this sister had not spoken to me or gone to the family with concern so together everyone could create an intervention to either ask me about it, or help me and the children get out when something seemed so very wrong. Instead my family was silent. Passive. It left me feeling what was happening was normal, no big deal and deep down that no one cared; that I was forgotten and unimportant.

The children and I, the ones who were helpless and trapped left, were left to take action. No one came singly or as a group, to stop what needed to be stopped. There were no Woodcutters in this family.

I organised financial support through Centrelink. I then found a place to rent. A first floor apartment. I would not feel safe in a unit or house or on the ground floor. I needed as many walls and doors separating me from him and his revenge. He always punished people when he didn't get his way and when he didn't like their response. He particularly didn't like women who were strong or had their own opinion. He always spoke about these women with disgust and dislike.

I planned our departure when he was out. During the two weeks before, I had gone through the whole house, taking back what I'd brought in before meeting him, my fridge, washing machine and some crockery and linen. My mother helped me. I asked my sister and father to meet me when the removalist arrived. They would stay and keep a lookout while the removalist took my things to our new home. While this was going on, I went to the local courthouse to apply for an interim intervention order.

Even at that point, I felt guilty for leaving him when he was not fully well, but I knew that staying would not help him get better. I knew that his family would rally around and he would be taken care of. The guilt that I had for leaving led me to contact one of his brothers and tell him the day I was going, so that he would be prepared to support his brother when he came home to find us gone. Even when I was escaping, I was looking after him and feeling guilty. I knew I had no need for guilt as he had been abusive from the first day I met him, and I was taking the children so they could feel safe. I would not be leaving if he were not abusive. This was a consequence to his behaviour that was his to carry, not mine to bear. But I still felt guilt.

I came to use these removalists a few times as we moved from place to place. They were wonderful and gave me a free couch left behind from another home as we had virtually nothing. I had ended up leaving a lot, as I did not want take memories with me in the furniture. The concern in the removalist's eyes and his openness in talking to me about what was going on was balm for my tired soul. These kinds of experiences helped me feel the world was not so harsh and unwelcoming.

But the kindness and generosity tended to come from outside my family. When I asked my family they would do tasks, like stay with my belongings while the removalist was there or mind the children when I was at court. There was little emotional or physical comfort. No one asked if I felt safe at night or what it was like to hand the children over. There were no regular dinners over, checking in on me or asking me how I was going as a single mum. It wasn't that we didn't talk but it was more a 'retelling' rather than emotional and practical pacing where I was at.

I realise now that one of the major reasons that I was able to leave was that he was unwell. He was incapacitated and sleeping a lot; he was not full of his usual strength and energy. Being on medication left him drowsy and not very aware of what was going on. I truly believe that I would not have been able to escape if he had remained well.

I mentioned there were three themes throughout these awakening experiences. The first theme was people. From information written by caring people as well as people connecting to me. Through the sign in the medical clinic, the couple counsellor speaking out, the men at the greengrocer's and health food store, the macrobiotic and shiatsu teachers each reminding me of what is possible, including the children looking free when the Wolf was in hospital. Different people making a difference to my existence in the world. Mirroring back about me and my reality, as well as their joy, warmth or concern. Responses reaching out and taking what was happening seriously, through care for me and being kind.

Bridging the cracks was very much dependent on other people. I couldn't do it on my own.

Space was also created through people, but this time created through the absence of people: space away from his energy when I went out shopping, space from wedding him through the death of my sister, and space from the Wolf when he was sick. Space is the second, significant theme.

I truly believe it was this combination of people connecting and space opening up by people that led to me being able to take risks and step out. When other people were taking some positive action towards me in my life, I was receiving the cellular message that I was seen, I exist and I deserve care and space.

The third theme which helped create an opening for my awakening was through people again – but this layer was health. The macrobiotic cooking, exercise and meditation created an interruption to the foggy, survival-based brain, and I began to see more clearly what was going on, develop emotional, mental and physical muscle, as well as access the strength of spirit to think clearly and begin to piece things together. I was more in my body. My energy was less scattered and more centred and in flow.

***

Consider people/connections, space and health in your life.

How do you ensure you get some regular contact that involves a nourishing connection with other people? Whatever regular means for you. Even if it's only a few minutes in a week, just as when I would go for my weekly shopping expedition. How can you keep the thread open to remind you of what is healthy? Where can you feel some relaxation and comfort in being with yourself as I did through cooking, meditating and exercise?

Who can help you connect to the world, even in simple ways? I am in deep gratitude to the greengrocer and the health food shop man. They were my thread to normalcy. I ask you, who can you talk to who can help you feel a part of humanity? You may not find yourself talking about the abuse, you may just begin with a smile and gratitude for an interaction. Bigger conversations can come later.

Who can you connect to, to help keep you safe? To help you know you exist and are important? It may be the woman who makes eye contact with you at the cash register and seems genuinely happy to see you, your hairdresser or your Doctor. These tiny steps may not seem like much, but they are stepping stones that allow you, at some point, to leave the abuse and take protective action for you or your children.

Wherever you are in your life, for whatever reason you're reading this book – whether it's to help yourself or someone else – asking, 'Who can you speak to, to help keep you safe or help you through an overwhelming challenge?' is a really important question.

So take some time in your notebook to consider and reflect what we have gone over. How do you take care of yourself and your wellbeing? How do you make space for you? That was one of the elements that saved me: making the space to be with myself and being in the moment in caring ways, validating I am alive and I exist. Me taking care of myself on a deeper level, through food, exercise and meditation, allowed my mind and my strength of spirit to be able to see and take in more, building my emotional muscle while strengthening my body. And from there, I was able to take action.

***

A client came to me one day: a woman troubled by her relationship. She spoke of feeling concerned about what was going on, but it was almost as if she couldn't say directly that she wanted to leave the relationship. I spoke of how it sounded like she was in a controlling and abusive relationship. It was confronting to name what was unspoken in her. We needed to take some time to explore her guilt, self-blame and sense of betrayal – however, when these fears were addressed there was a calm that her reality was real and important. She had needed me to name the elephant in the room, to pace her awareness and to respond to the internal fears and judgements.

Once I had created a space in which it was okay to speak about what was unspeakable, the details of what she was living with came pouring out.

We created a plan on how to leave, because she was so caught up in the binds of walking on eggshells and the belief that she needed to say more to him than he needed to know, or what was good for her safety. She was in overwhelm and caught in the Little Red Riding Hood Effect: not wanting to upset him and not knowing how to stay safe and leave.

She left the session with a concrete and specific plan. We had also identified a friend she would call on to have a role in keeping her safe and help her follow her plan to completion. She had not known how to do this without telling her partner everything and putting herself at risk of getting trapped or punished again.

Creating that safety plan can be a really important step, especially with the help of a professional. In many circumstances this safety plan may need to be set in place before you take the steps to leave. In other instances, there will not be time for a plan.

If needed, the plan can breakdown the fear and overwhelm. A plan helps come to terms with the reality of the seriousness of the situation. A plan anchors the floating, unnamed crazy-making abuses to reality. All the fears can be taken care of and addressed. This can make what feels unimaginable, possible. Bit by bit. It's easier when you have a safety net of what needs to happen when, and knowing that you are not going through the steps alone – that you have someone helping watch out for you.

Each person's timing and urgency is going to be different. Starting to collect important papers – bank account details, names and account numbers of loans, rental agreements and any contracts – is important so that you can remove yourself from any future STDs (sexually transmitted debts) that are not yours to carry. As is collecting copies of keys, some money, scanning photos, locating anything that is really significant and leaving them with a trusted person outside of your house.

I didn't tell the Wolf the truth of when I was going to leave. I didn't tell him the truth about needing a termination. Sometimes a little bit of information or none is necessary. The Woodcutter comes in to cut through what is necessary and not give away what is not to be given away. The Woodcutter does not hand over the axe for someone to use against him. He keeps certain information and tools to himself. He doesn't give the Wolf a warning.

Follow the Woodcutter, use the scissors, not the gun. The action of scissors is quiet, focused, mindful and connected; it can cut through. We can only put a certain thickness of material between the scissor blades. Scissors cannot take on too much at once. Being loud is not necessarily successful. Simple works, just like David and Goliath. The skill of scissors is something anyone can handle. You can use your fingers in contact with the scissors to adjust control. You also have control over both hands to manage the material with the scissors to adjust control. Far more control and flexible responsiveness than the complicated skill of using a gun. Scissors can be used immediately, guns need training. Don't use tools that are bigger than you – it will backfire or be used against you. Guns are loud and messy and the connection between you and the gun is unsteadier. With the gun in the air, the gun can be out a few centimetres and not reach the target. You do not have a steady anchor between you, the gun and the target, leading to disconnection. When facing danger, you need scissors not guns. Quiet and steady – and as good a guarantee as possible that you can cut through.

Let him bear the weight (stones) of his actions. Get yourself out of his belly and back into the world. Find the Woodcutter Within and find some Woodcutters to be in your life. Find someone who can help you remove the stones and weight of his actions from your shoulders and heart.

Chapter 4: The Snarling Wolf

Wolves snarl, yet they are known to be very social animals. Perhaps a bit like the charming and terrible face of Dr Jekyll and Mr Hyde. But let's get to the bottom line: wolves are predators who live in a pack, run by an alpha male that rules. You don't want to get on the wrong side of the alpha wolf. The pack is complex and there is a hierarchy based on dominance and submission. Very different from the social structure inside a herd of elephants.

I was scared of the snarl of this Wolf. The act of leaving meant I was no longer 'being subordinate' – one of his favourite phrases. I was not playing by his rules of domination and submission. I didn't know what he would do next but I knew that punishment and revenge would predictably come when he was not 'in control'.

I didn't know how, where or when. But I knew it was inevitable.

The walking on eggshells continued and my fear increased because there was no longer this arrangement of domination and submission. I was in new territory and terrified. It is far easier to keep track of the Wolf when you live together. At least you think you can keep track of him, when you live together. But not living together, I had no idea when he would appear or what revenge he would take. After all, having explosions over my hair being cut shorter than he liked was nothing compared to me leaving.

When we were together, the violence towards me and the girls predictably heightened after his son went back to his ex-wife's home. His son suffered from his abuse too but I don't think he was ever there for the biggest explosions. As the years went by I could see a pattern of increased violence when the Wolf couldn't control life, such as when returning his son who he didn't want to separate from, my haircuts or having a full on fight with our three-year-old daughter because he did not want her to take her toy bag out of the car. I can still remember her upset and holding on tight to her bag – and him, raised voice, towering over her, wrestling with and hurting her clenched, little hand. This was not a typical picture of a parent wanting a child to leave a toy in the car. This was bullying and abusive.

Some secrets, memories and vows, which had left me chilled to the bone and frozen to the possibility of leaving, stirred as I packed and left. I had images and sounds ringing in my ears of him sitting in his fake leather armchair, listening to D24 tapes over and over and over again. Police tapes secretly handed over for his listening pleasure. It disturbed me to hear them in the middle of our home – it disturbed me even further that the children may be playing in or walk by the lounge room and hear the horrors unfolding in the recording. 'Shots fired, shots fired …'

I left, even though I was scared he would kill me. He'd said that he was in the perfect industry to kill and bury me. I left, even after hearing about his pact with his brother. They had bonded over their recent shared depression. They agreed that if they decided to commit suicide, that they would kill each other's partners or ex-partners first. I think they thought they were pretty clever, that they could get away with murder without consequence. No one can put them in jail if they've already killed themselves. The mentality of 'I can get away with anything.'

These threats were pretty real as his brother had already made one attempt of suicide and in the final stages of leaving the Wolf had spoken of suicide many times. He also did not follow his doctor's instructions about what foods were not to be combined with his medication, which had risk of death. He was flaunting with danger and he would not listen to anyone. No one could stop him – and worse still, no one wanted to stop him.

So with all these vows and threats reverberating in the cells of my being, I was terrified and very alone, apart from my two little girls. Even though I had an interim intervention order from the day I left, I was terrified, because he didn't need to be near me for a bullet to reach me.

I left with no money – the only thing I was thinking of when I left was the safety of my children and me. I had no income or savings. I even left the tiny bit of my sister's inheritance to me in the shared bank account, which in the panic of survival and protecting my girls, I forgot about until years later. Money wasn't my priority but a part of me feels angry that even that little bit from my sister didn't come back to me.

Soon after leaving I had to find a family lawyer to protect me and the girls. I did not want to willingly hand over our daughter for contact visits when I had seen him being so brutal in the relationship, with no remorse other than the fear that he would give his son brain damage. But never any remorse towards me or the girls. Even though he had that fear towards his son's health, he never (to my knowledge) made any attempt to get help for his abusive behaviours.

What scared me the most about his abuse and violence was that he never admitted his wrongs to me. He always denied he had done anything wrong. The scariest aspect of the abuse was that he didn't have a conscience. If he was never sorry, how could he recognise what he did and prevent more abuse happening? I lived in constant fear.

I was later to discover the meaning of a psychopath. He ticked all these boxes, except that he did not have an inability to plan for his future. He built his own profitable business.

- Lack of empathy and shallow emotions
- Uncaring; cold-hearted
- Lack of shame, guilt, embarrassment and fear
- Irresponsible, externalising blame onto others
- Admissions of guilt when forced in a corner but with no shame or remorse – and behaviours don't change
- Superficial charm and smooth with words
- Insincere; constantly lies
- Inflating and distorting stories for the benefit of self
- Overconfidence
- Inflated and grandiose sense of self, the 'Ruler of the Empire'
- Narrowing of attention that does not allow all the situational information into awareness
- Lack of flexible responsiveness to a situation
- Impulsive
- Selfishness
- Incapacity for love, egocentric
- Parasitic lifestyle, wanting to be looked after
- Inability to plan for the future
- Low tolerance of frustration
- Irritability, aggression, repeated fights and violent acts (Hirstein 2013a)

The unrestrained psychopathic tendencies in the Wolf meant I had to return to the Magistrate's Court shortly after I applied for the interim intervention order. He was contesting the need for the order. Here I was in trauma, trying to help my daughters heal from their fear and trauma, and I was being forced into the court because of his psychopathic denial. It was one unrelenting trauma after another, all based on his denial. Due to the way our system is, I was forced to be exposed to him and his actions again when all I wanted to do was protect my girls and me.

So I had to go through the court process when I just wanted to find a new school for my daughter. I had wanted her to remain in the beautiful little local school, surrounded by her friends and her wonderfully warm and caring teachers. Her school had been a haven for us. But his punishing ways had continued. When I left he took my car from me. Even though he had given me the car one Christmas to be my own car, I discovered after I left it was in his name. He had his lawyers write me a letter to return the car.

I remember when I got this car as a gift. It really only came about because my wealthy, ex-sister-in-law's father had complained to the Wolf that he should not let me drive me and the children around in such an old bomb of a car. The car he had originally bought me. So he bought me a better quality car. A very expensive car. The contrast in cars was dramatic. Not because we needed one that expensive but because he had been shown up and he needed to prove a point. Instead of giving me a safer car he bought one to make him look good in the powerful older man's eyes. Then he took the car away when it no longer served his purposes to impress. Revenge was more important than keeping the children in a safe car. I was car-less and with no money to buy a car.

I could no longer take my daughter to school. We tried, but it was too far to get to school by public transport from our new home. She was struggling to last longer days together on public transport to and from her school. I hadn't wanted to rent a home in the same suburb as him so I'd moved closer to my family and the area where I had grown up. Only twenty minutes away but back to somewhere familiar and not surrounded by the suburb of bad memories. I would not want to bump into him at the local shops.

My children were upset, tired and shaken by the changes to home and school and the fear of his wrath. There was no getting back to or creating a normal life. We were in survival mode.

I still remember the day he contested my intervention order. His lawyer interrogated me. It was an excruciating day. I was representing myself. I could not afford a lawyer and did not know how to access legal aid at this early stage of just being a few weeks out from inside the Wolf's belly. I was lost in the system.

That day at the stand, after swearing on the Bible and facing the magistrate,

I had to work so very hard to prove that I genuinely needed an intervention order. It was my word against his. He had a lawyer and was all dressed up in a suit. I felt desperate that I couldn't leave the court without this piece of paper, the only hope I had of protection out in the world. So as I stood in fear, I spoke of some of my most personal, intimate, brutal experiences. I did not want to miss my chance of being protected so I said the worst. It was brutal for me to stand and tell the public my deepest secrets. To tell strangers, and anyone who wanted to walk into the room, my most personal and vulnerable secrets.

Time passed so very slowly. I remember feeling wrung out and taken advantage of as I left the courthouse with my hard-won piece of paper. It was not a win. It was a life necessity.

One of the most uncomfortable parts of this day was that this was the one and only time my father came to court with me. I can't remember if he asked to come or if I asked him to come. It was good to have someone there, but for my father to hear these most private aspects of my life was unbearable. He never, ever said a word about it, then or later. He never came to another day of court through the long seven years. I felt overcome that he had heard my most intimate details. We both walked out of the local courtroom in silence. The sun outside was warm but I felt no warmth that day. There was no privacy or honour in this process.

It took me about six attempts to find a lawyer to help me protect my children. The first lawyer was just interested in me being a client and giving him money. Despite knowing the circumstances, he didn't enquire about my financial situation or help guide me to get legal aid. At that initial point I had no understanding of the legal system. After I left the Wolf I sold my belongings and the little bit of jewellery I had to pay legal fees – I did not know I was entitled to legal aid.

My sister appealed to my grandparents to help pay for some fees. I felt guilty that in their older years, they would spend money on my legal fees. They had worked so hard to establish themselves after a very, very tough early life in Europe in World War II. I felt so unsupported and not guided by this lawyer that I left to find a lawyer who would help me with my situation. The awful thing was this lawyer actually knew my grandparents and did not do the right thing by them or by me. He should have helped me navigate the system, whether he knew them or not. Knowing people doesn't always help.

One lawyer asked me to write down everything that had happened and keep a daily diary of what the children were saying and doing – as well as what happened with the Wolf from now on. It was hard work to write down everything and keep track of everything. You naturally want to ignore and minimise what is painful but through the need to protect all of us, I had to pay close attention to all the painful words and actions and then write them down before I could block them out.

This really screws up being in the moment. This keeps you focused on needing to pay attention to the terrible. A good lead-in to depression, with the ongoing anxiety, fear and focus on the negative ...

Later when I found my true lawyer, I felt angry that the first lawyer did not provide the service I deserved and instead expected my grandparents to pay for the personal and legal injustice of power and my right to protect my children. My grandparents didn't pay for long. I stopped asking them for money. I couldn't bear to take money from them.

The second lawyer actually said to me, 'Children are resilient,' and was virtually telling me that it's not that bad, that they would get over it. How can a lawyer, someone standing for justice, protection and truth, say that a child should tolerate daily fear, abuse and be forced into the experience of being taken over? How can a lawyer turn a blind eye and not protect a vulnerable adult or child, when they are not protected from their basic human right to being able to say no to someone or feel safe in their own home?

How could I trust this man to protect my children or myself? I couldn't. This was my children's life and their innocence; they had a right to be protected and safe and he was telling me that they're resilient. Sure, my children could live through this if they didn't get killed, but what parent would agree to that being the standard of care and life? What parent would want their child to have a childhood of fear and suffering and betrayal? So I left this lawyer and went searching again.

Each lawyer would have this kind of response or not follow up on breaches, not taking the situation seriously, so I would go searching for a lawyer that could really represent us.

I was scared the court system would misunderstand all the changes as the Wolf was already twisting my actions since leaving, describing me as someone who wanted to send the children to numerous counsellors. The

Wolf wanted to show the world his concern of the impact from all these changes on the children. Of course, he was oblivious to the impact he had put on them, abusing them and me, and that his abuse was what was driving all the therapy. He was oblivious to how he continued to have an impact on the children by taking the car from me, as they were torn away from their familiar network of support and school. He was oblivious to the impact on his own son or my daughters by not letting me see my stepson, who I had brought up. He would not let my girls see his son unless they were all with him. His control … and there was more. Breach after breach.

I just needed to find the right legal support for my girls and me. They were showing emotional, physical and social effects from all the years of abuse. I was scared and worried.

I became a regular in the Family Court building and in my lawyer's office. I was going into the city two or more times a month, sometimes weekly, year in, year out, to protect both my children. Constantly in and out of Family Court, in and out of another affidavit, always with more letters for my lawyer to send to his lawyer, because he would breach the interim contact orders or intervention orders, time and time again. The courts never, ever gave out any consequences for any breaches.

The court process was not skilled to understand that he was now instigating legal abuse, which can lead to legal abuse syndrome (LAS, a form of PTSD identified by Dr. K. Heffer). The court was not skilled to understand what it is like to be in the court system with a history of and context for abuse that we were still inside of. The court system would not take into account what the children would spontaneously say to me, unprompted. My eldest daughter would say she hated him and never wanted to see him. My youngest daughter would say she was scared he would kill her.

Court mindset suggested that I would influence the girls. Which was a laugh, as it was the Wolf who influenced them through bribes, punishment and unrelenting interrogation. The court logic appeared to be that if the children lived more with me, then I was more powerful in influencing what the children would say. The reality was, their fear would override anything and their survival system would shut them down. As far as I know, they never spoke to anyone other than me about the full detail of what really went on. I held the truth for the three of us. No one was validating or supporting our truth. I was alone.

I didn't want my children to have to carry the burden of proof. They were children. They shouldn't have been asked to be bigger than anyone else and explain what was going on, when adults – the Wolf and his family – could not even tell the truth. Why was the pressure put on my children to tell when the adults were keeping secrets? The Wolf was let off the hook for not speaking, yet the children were not let off the hook for being unable to speak.

I would never bad mouth the Wolf or speak ill of him in front of them. I actually didn't even behind their back. I just told my lawyer what he did, the same as if anyone had asked me. I just spoke about his actions. In concrete and specific descriptions. I didn't need to badmouth him. His actions spoke for themselves.

If the girls were with me when someone asked why I left, I would just say I had been in an abusive relationship. I gave it a name but never any detail. It was important to me that I not pretend. I did not want to keep the abuse a secret. I wanted to model to my children not to keep secrets that shouldn't be secrets. At the same time I did not want to expose them to more detail than they had the capacity to bear and process for their age, especially given the context of their relationship to him.

My girls were four and eight years old – only tiny. They had enough to cope with in getting through each day. I thought I would hold the stories they told me until they were big enough to bear their memories, remember and ask questions. Only then they could ask, if they wanted to ask me about our past.

I could understand that for my younger daughter it would be particularly tricky, as this was about her father – the person who was meant to protect and love her. Such a double bind for a child. It was easier for my daughter who was not his biological child. She had space to hate him. She didn't feel an obligation to love him, as he was not her father.

It actually stunned me as the years went by how much they both silently buried the past. I could see it was developmentally healthy for them to focus on rebuilding themselves and their social lives. This was not the time to be turning inwards and to the past; they needed to be able to shine and grow into their future.

I hoped the court system could recognise their developmental needs and not place a burden on them that was too big for their little shoulders and voices. I am glad my girls prioritised their health and development rather

Chapter 4: The Snarling Wolf

than get trapped in the story of abuse, but it made my battle to protect them so much harder.

I would not let my girls be exposed to the court machinations and appointments unless the court required their involvement. I was in a bind because as time progressed the court wanted my children to talk to court-appointed people, but my children didn't know or trust these strangers ... so why would they share their fears with them? Even when my daughter was seeing a counsellor, who she liked and shared a lot with about what was going on, she still only said some of the worst things to me.

They were scared, little children. They told their mummy their secrets, not strangers. Aren't we taught not to speak to strangers? What a double bind to put to children. After all, would you feel safe to speak up about a Wolf if you were helpless, dependent, still very little and your mother and the world were still asking you to go to the Wolf? Would you feel safe to say what you wanted when you saw the Wolf getting his own way and trampling over everyone else, with no one stopping him?

I wonder if my girls were thinking, *what he does must be okay if Mum still sends me there and the courts don't stop him* ...

How do we expect children to feel safe enough to speak up if they have no choice but to go on contact visits? How do we expect children to feel safe enough to speak up if there is no consequence for all the types of abuse or for the breaches in court orders?

Finally I found a decent lawyer. It took years.

It was hard to *try* to live a *normal* life *and* keep a record of the pain, but I would do whatever was necessary to protect my girls.

My first intervention order ended after a year, as they do. The Wolf assaulted me when he dropped the children off from a contact visit. They would immediately run straight inside to their room and in a flash, when they were out of sight, he would get mad at me and assault me. So in control ... when no one was watching. No witnesses to see his terrible face. No one to dispel the myth of how good he was. Changing faces. He could switch so suddenly. There was no warning. The smiling assassin.

Sometimes the girls would hear something but they learnt to stay away. One time I called out for them to call 000. I didn't want my girls to be involved in what was too much for them to see but in that moment I had no option. Funny when I first remember this, I doubt myself that it really happened. I wonder if I imagined it, but I know I did call out. I was scared and I wanted some way of stopping him going at me.

You see, when you have been in abuse and no one has witnessed it, and the Wolf is in denial and still continuing the torment, you are in a nightmare. No one sees the hell you are going through. When no one validates what is going on, you start to doubt what is real, it becomes crazy making. Even now when I tell you these truths, my doubting self has me double-checking. The doubting self exists because our environment does not validate reality. If my memory is uncertain then I ask myself, 'Did I think that?' or, 'Did it really happen?' and I then go down a path of sorting the fear from the memory. It is so hard to reclaim my memory when the natural desire is to disconnect from horror.

But I don't need to exaggerate or lie. The truth was bad enough.

These doubts and checks that come up as I write my memories are a soft echo of a stronger response when I went through all the years of court. The shock is so large that it is hard to believe what happened. So I can understand when the public doesn't believe it could really happen. I can understand that the public finds it hard to believe the charming Wolf has another face. I find it hard to believe this is what happened to me. But I know my fear is there for a reason. *Fear does not grow on trees – it is planted.*

The intervention order had seemed to be working, even if the court contact orders were being breached. I had hoped that the absence of violence for the duration of the intervention order was a sign he had learnt that he couldn't hurt me anymore. I had hoped that if I was constantly going to Family Court, reporting on his breaches and what was happening for the children, then he would know that I am not staying silent. I had hoped that at least I wouldn't need to go back to the Magistrate's Court for intervention orders. During this time, I was still repeatedly going back to the Family Court for breaches of contact and to advocate for conditions of protection for both girls in any ongoing and future contact – but none of these actions were about violence towards me.

So when he breached the first intervention order by assaulting me, I went back to court. The court granted me a second intervention order. Again the year became absent of assaults or threats directly at me, though again he was breaching the orders in the context of still harming the children emotionally and physically, (emotional control, verbal interrogation and bullying; including, tying my daughter to a rope on school holiday contact whilst on holidays camping) and not returning them when he was meant to.

I thought or hoped that with the second intervention order in place, he would really learn that I would go to court every time he broke the order. That I would no longer be silent, just as I was no longer silent through the Family Court. Every time he broke any part of the order, I was back in my lawyer's office. The second year of an intervention order meant that again he wasn't physically threatening towards me. Again, I hoped he had finally learnt he couldn't control, threaten, harm or punish me. One more year passed and I let the second order lapse; I was tired of court and all this consuming my life. I didn't want to go back to court. I had hoped he knew his behaviour was unacceptable after a second order. But again, he assaulted me after dropping off the girls. Always when no one else was watching.

I went back to court to get my third intervention order. I was so tired. I was a robot going through the motions – 'this is what I am meant to do'. My judge offered me a lifetime intervention order. My judge. Funny how I write it that way. *My* ... The only court person who was affected and responded appropriately to me. He was the only one in the decision-making process of the legal system who actually made a decision for me that was valid and protective.

I felt deep relief and gratitude for the first time. Even now as I type this, my whole body opens up and a deep breath runs through me, the exhale of relief and relaxation. Someone in the courtroom was actually treating me with the concern that was warranted.

But the Family Court still didn't trust what the children said to me as being worth listening to and acting upon. It was perceived that maybe they were saying what I wanted them to say, or more accurately, what the court perceived I wanted them to say. Are they telling me I would put my child through all those years of hell for my own desire for revenge? I cannot understand this punishment of the many for the evil of the few.

My mother instinct was always wanting to say, 'No, you can't have them.' Not wanting to be home at pick-up contact time. Not wanting to hand them over. Wanting to say, 'No matter what, I'm not going to pass them over to you.' Feeling like every week I was betraying my girls, because they were telling me they were scared and they didn't want to go, yet I was the one opening the door to him and sending them into his arms.

All because I'd been advised by my lawyers that if I don't send them, I'm in breach and I could be put in jail. I did not want to take that risk. So I was forced to betray my children. I was forced to be part of the abusive system. I was forced to betray their trust, their security, their love, their safety.

I remember one time my youngest daughter had a vaginal infection, possibly due to the prolonged bedwetting she lived with. Bedwetting is understood to happen in families where there is a controlling parent. My daughter had been toilet trained and only began bedwetting when contact began, after we had left the Wolf. She was a highly stressed little girl.

I recall handing her over on one contact visit with the cream prescribed for the infection; the label on the cream, as well as my own explanation, informed him that the cream needed to be put externally on her. When she returned after that weekend he advised me with a smile that he had put the cream internally. I was shocked and revolted. Despite telling my lawyer, who took the appropriate action in the system, nothing changed and there was no consequence. It was as if this intrusion was of no consequence and that nothing wrong had happened.

In my eyes, this is sexual abuse. This is the type of behaviour that happened over and over again; they were inappropriate behaviours, constant reminders that he was the one in control of their bodies, as previously with mine. Slippery behaviours that may not look like typical sexual or physical abuse, but abuse all the same. He was more in control then the police or any judge – nothing stopped him.

I used to dread anniversaries, Christmas, Easter, Father's Day, Mother's Day and birthdays. I came to know about the full moon – these, I discovered, were predictable times, when he would not return the children. There would be some petty reason that he would find an objection and he would keep them overnight. I would contact the police to say that he hadn't returned the children. They would just shrug their shoulders and say there's no order, because at that time we were still going through Family Court, so there was only signed conditions. Court-signed conditions, but apparently not enough.

I would just have to wait for him to return them. It was always a long and painful night when the children were not returned. I was so very alone. I felt for them, so little and so alone with the big, loud, strong, scary Wolf. I didn't know when he would choose to return them, or if they would return. I would wonder what they were feeling and thinking and how I had let them down in not being able to bring them home and protect them.

I couldn't bear to think of what was going on for them, not wanting to be there with him. The pain in not being able to contact or speak to my girls and get them out was excruciating. I would lie in bed, praying and hoping that he would return them the next day. It was hard to fall asleep. Those nights were long.

There were many lonely and scary nights when the children were with him on contact visits or on longer stretches during the school holidays or summer holidays, and I would not be able to sleep. During those dark nights, I felt the ache of not being able to protect my little girls.

It was excruciatingly painful day in, day out to live with this knowing – to bear the knowledge that I was contributing to the continuing abuse, even while I was finally strong enough to act. Year in, year out. I couldn't explain this to my girls either, as that would be asking them to understand my predicament and not remain with their reality.

It was bad enough that I felt guilty that this was their childhood and I had contributed to robbing their innocence. That I had contributed to my children having to grow up too fast and not being able to protect them. That I had contributed to the limited capacity my children had to play, be spontaneous and develop their whole self through the safety of playing.

I would struggle to go to sleep. When my girls were with the Wolf I would listen to a tape of positive affirmations, or some gentle chanting. Something gentle on repeat all through the night, to try to help me switch off and get some sleep. I would pray my old tapes and tape recorder could handle this beating over and over.

I would have to wait for Monday to yet again ring my lawyer and tell her how he had broken the order, again – naturally breaches would happen after business hours, when I could not access my lawyers. Again my lawyers would write another letter.

All this fear and control meant there was no opportunity for me to consider working or trying to earn some money. I was exhausted from all the legal appointments. My time was swallowed up by helping my girls emotionally and mentally get through each day. They both had different behaviours and ways of coping. The two extremes: one withdrawn, not wanting to be here, and feeling suicidal at eight years old; and the other aggressive and defiant. It was hard for both of them to immerse themselves in the social innocence of their peers.

I was constantly in court, writing new affidavits, taking notes for my lawyers, going to conference meetings, taking the children and myself to our different appointments for health issues and for counselling. It took up a lot of space and energy. I did not have the space or energy to hold down a job. I was already working, but this work was still about being in survival mode. Meanwhile, the Wolf continued his unrelenting, punishing and vengeful behaviour.

I had hoped contact between his son and my eldest daughter could continue in my presence as he had initially agreed when I left. The children naturally had become close, both being young and living together as a family. I guess it was unrealistic of me to hope it could continue, given his punishing nature. I just had not imagined that anyone would involve children. After he took me to court for contact rights to see our daughter he stopped any promise of contact between his son, my eldest daughter and me.

Because I was holding firm through the court of my concern for our daughter's safety, he retaliated and not only stopped this contact to see his son, but he also applied to the court to see my eldest daughter. He began saying she saw him like a father and he saw her like his daughter. Despite my eldest daughter seeing her own father for regular usual contact conditions. The revenge continued. This was part of his predictable, punishing vengeful behaviour in response to me speaking up and trying to protect the children and myself.

After years of court proceedings and getting nowhere because neither of us would change our story, I was advised that the children needed to have their own legal representation. A separate representative was provided for the children. Picture this: the Wolf had a lawyer, I had a lawyer, and the children had a lawyer. It was complicated. I was then told the court wanted the father of my eldest daughter to become involved. It was not enough for him to write an affidavit to prove that my daughter had a father and did not want to see the Wolf. The court wanted him involved.

Despite all of this representation – and a record of a children's counsellors witnessing my daughter say she did not want to see the Wolf – the courts still, for a very, very, long period of time, kept the involuntary contact between my eldest daughter and the Wolf.

In one of the series of meetings in the court, the Wolf's medical practitioner put in a report advocating that the Wolf was suitable and safe for the children to be left in his care on contact visits. It shocked me that a medical professional could write that in a report, despite what I had disclosed to him in my meeting with him shortly before I had left the Wolf. He was protecting his client and putting three young children at risk.

My daily life revolved around me trying to contain and soothe my children's moods and behaviours and create a normal life. Trying to create a safe, normal, warm environment while still isolated, and with this pain and shock intruding on all of us. I had no time to make friends or socialise. I was so busy with court and helping my daughters with their own challenges and struggles. I just wanted my girls to have friends and play.

I don't know how I got through each day, holding each of our challenges and struggles and not having anyone to talk to. I was still very isolated and doing it tough. I was used to enduring.

Enduring not having a good lawyer for years, enduring breaches, scared children, no money, no car, difficulty getting to appointments or taking the children to school. This 'lifestyle' made it difficult to help my children socialise and play with friends after school. Everything was harder. Nothing was easy.

But there was one positive thing about not having a car and walking everywhere. I truly believe that all that walking helped prevent me from becoming severely depressed. Being out in the world, feeling the fresh air and the sun, and moving was good for all of us. I would be occupied trying to keep my girls happy and interested in the world so they would manage walking long distances. We would talk to the people passing by and we got to experience a friendly world. Often I would have one girl in a stroller and one on my back. These were pockets of normal life and warmth. I loved our walking, though it was tiring as their little legs struggled walking that far. Everything took longer.

I was constantly with my children's pain and fears and it was excruciating that I couldn't take the steps to protect them. Every day was agony. No one was listening. They were severely affected, both emotionally and physically. My eldest daughter shut down. She was so upset that she was being forced to see the Wolf, who was not her father, and was unable to have contact with which she considered her brother.

She was scared. She didn't want to see the Wolf. But I guess she saw that neither I nor her father, nor the court, could stop him. She saw him as the biggest power, which I imagine made her feel even more terrified and helpless.

After all, he applied to court to see her and the court said yes – despite her wish, my wish, and her father's wish for this not to happen. She was forced to go. Wednesday was her day to go. She began speaking of hating Wednesdays. Every Wednesday. They were no longer just a day in the week. They were hateful days.

She would tell me after she came back from a contact visit to not speak to her, because he had questioned her over and over and she could not bear the thought to be spoken to. She spoke of wanting to climb onto the top of her bunk and jump out the window. We lived in a flat on the first floor. My little girl. A little girl shouldn't have those kinds of feelings.

She would tell me – but not the counsellors, because they were strangers – the things that he would say and that she didn't want to go. But the court system didn't believe my voice for her. The court in their legal world, not in the real world, thinking that it was hearsay if I said it or that I made it up. I would not be able to think up the madness he would do – it was unthinkable yet true.

The courts continued to close their eyes and ears to what was happening, despite me passing on to the court everything my girls were telling me. I was still writing all the words they said and all the behaviours from each day in my diary. Days, months, years of writing. I still have this diary locked far away in a secret place … with the handcuffs.

My little eight-year-old princess became so quiet and tired. She began falling asleep at school. She had never done this before we left. She had always been quiet, but not like this and not falling asleep at school. She had been so bright and surrounded by friends in her first school. She used to love school and had been so social. She had shut down. I put it down to what she was living through. I felt no option but to take her out of the new school as she was not coping. She could not participate in school, away from her friends, and start again.

She was affected by so much. Much more than I could even realise. Years later she told me that it was even difficult to sit on leather couches, because they reminded her of the couch we used to have with him at home. Another time as she got older, she spoke of finding it hard to show spontaneity and pleasure.

My youngest daughter, my little one, had a dilemma that my older daughter didn't have. My older daughter, even though it was excruciating and severely impactful on her growing self, had room to hate him and not like what was going on. She didn't have the conflict that my younger daughter had – that this Wolf was her father – so my eldest daughter could tell me how she hated him and I could encourage her to release the anger safely. She would whack a pillow against the wall, declaring her hatred, releasing her hate.

But my younger daughter did not have that space to hate him. She had absorbed the pressure and expectation that she had to love him, as he was her flesh and blood. He repeated over and over that he loved her – and would demand she reply how much she loved him. She had to love him to the moon and back. She learnt by rote what he needed her to say. She learnt to block her feelings of hate or aversion going to him, but it had to go somewhere.

A child should never be forced emotionally, psychologically or verbally to say they love someone. It should be a voluntary act that comes out of the feeling of love.

I can remember when we were living with the Wolf, he would ask her for a hug or a kiss; she would say her kisses had 'gone to the park'. I used to silently admire her creative way of trying to say no to her father, without a direct confrontation. But he would never listen and respect that kind of communication. He crushed all their messages: verbal and non-verbal.

This Wolf was her father. It was almost as if when we left, and the heightened punishing behaviours began and along with being forced to go on contact visits, that she made a choice. She decided to not be like me and suffer in helplessness and pain. She found a place for the hate and aversion to go. *If there are only two ways – either the way Mum is, or the way Dad is – I'll be like Dad.* I had this huge shock shortly after I left the Wolf. There was this aggressive behaviour coming out of her that was far bigger than her size. I thought I had left the abuse and here I was, still living with abuse. This time I couldn't leave.

It can be hard to imagine or to describe to someone that someone as young as four or five years old can be so unrelentingly defiant, scary, aggressive and out of control.

She would bully her sister, her cousins and the schoolchildren. Even her primary school teacher – a tall, big boned woman – told me one time how she felt intimidated by my little girl. I can remember one time later when she was in high school one night, when she was being aggressive – I felt so threatened and scared by her I wanted to call the police. It was painful to feel the need to call the police on my own child. I didn't, but that night was tough to contain her.

The fierceness, hate and aggression in her words and actions were very intense, but this aggression hid the deep fear that over time she would share: that he would kill her. The tough misbehaviour also contrasted with the regressive bedwetting and babyish behaviour that continued for years longer than is typical. Behind the fierceness lay the fear and the little girl.

I tried everything in my parenting power to reach my little girl and contain the aggression.

I was constantly holding boundaries, providing consistency, providing support through taking her to counselling, and at home supporting her to express her feelings and anger in healthy ways, using conversation, stories, drawing, even puppets. Of course I was enforcing natural consequences and not punishing or shaming her. Nothing seemed to shift her behaviour, but I kept trying and doing what felt right in how to teach her how to be with these difficult feelings. Sometimes it got so bad I had to shut myself in another room with my other daughter as she was so unrelenting in her taunting and I could not stop her. I remember holding the door shut against her trying to come in. The most awful feeling to be barricading yourself from your own child. Leaving her angry and upset alone on the other side of the door, banging, yelling and struggling to get in.

I tried in so many ways to support her in shifting from the misbehaviour, aggression and defiance that was incredibly pervasive in our daily life, and which put an incredible pressure on me, her and my other daughter. Her aggression structured my day, as did the Wolf's ongoing abuse and control. When she wasn't aggressive, she was regressing and behaving younger than her age, like a little baby or toddler. Her play consisted of control over other children, aggression and sexualised behaviours, all of which reminded me of the Wolf's interactions with the girls.

Then she would flip, cling to me and tell me she wanted to marry me. She would try to kiss me the way her father had kissed her or want to be held like a baby.

My eldest daughter wanted to leave home … my primary school daughter wanted to leave home. This was too early. It broke my heart that I couldn't provide a home where we could all be safe and connect and have fun together. It was too difficult for my eldest daughter to live with the constant aggression and defiant behaviour from her sister. There was no solution that could make this better, not even the Wolf disappearing now. The imprint on all of us was playing out, especially on my youngest.

It was very difficult for the girls to live in the same bedroom together in our little unit. A small house meant that the bullying was like a pressure cooker, thick in all the corners of the home. I would move from home to home, trying to rent something that had a bit more space so the intensity and energy of what was happening in our house from the bullying was not so much in everyone's face. Also, so my eldest daughter could have her own space at home and hopefully have a break in her corner of home. At times my eldest daughter would disappear. I used to be scared she had gone walking the streets but eventually I would find her up on the roof – getting some space.

I will never forget the day I returned from court and I could finally tell my eldest daughter she no longer had to have forced contact with the Wolf. What a relief after so long. She looked in shock. That night she had her first seizure. It was one of the most terrifying experiences of my life. Alone with her convulsing, eyes rolled back, saliva falling out of her mouth. I remember silently promising her that I would always look after her no matter what happened. I had no clue what was happening, or if she would be able to recover and not be brain damaged.

I rang 000 and they helped me through the convulsions. Afterwards they guided me to prop her up wrapped in a blanket, warning me she would be very tired. We waited for the ambulance. I rang her father.

The next night around bedtime, we were both scared that it might happen again. Sure enough, the same thing happened. It was terrifying but this time I knew what was happening. I rang 000 again. We went in by ambulance. We saw medical specialists and they wanted her put on anticonvulsants, giving me a list of things to be careful of, such as disco lights and how to turn the taps on and off in the shower in case there were more seizures.

I didn't want to put her on medication. I felt like it was too synchronistic, happening the night she found out she no longer had to see the Wolf. I trusted that her body was discharging a huge amount of fear, shock and emotional pain and just needed some support to heal. I contacted my traditional Chinese medicine (TCM) practitioner; he suggested I change what she was eating and gave her specific TCM treatments of shiatsu, including moxibustion. This was the husband of the macrobiotic cooking teacher. He has been a major support through our lives. There were no more seizures. To this day, twenty years later.

Towards the end of the court process, I can remember the counselling centre where my youngest daughter had been going for quite a while, saying she would only improve when she was no longer obligated to see him. They held serious concern for her wellbeing.

I had to pull her out of school for her regular appointments. I hated doing that and making her different from her peers but this was the only time I could get to the clinic.

In all the seven or so years of court, there was only one consequence for him breaking the orders. At the time it was a big consequence. It appeared my ongoing detailed affidavits gave the court concern and at one point they decided to stop his contact for one year. I remember sitting in court and hearing the decision to suspend contact for one year. I did not feel like I had won. It was painful. I wanted to protect my daughter but I did not want to separate a father from a daughter. I didn't want this to be the reality for my daughter.

If only he was not abusive. If only he was not in denial of his behaviours and attitudes and willing to change. Everything could have been different.

In this sixth year of court, when she was not forced to see him, her behaviour changed dramatically. The aggression stopped. Spontaneity and play came out for the first time. Everyone noticed the changes. Previously it had been very difficult for her to play freely and without aggression. In this year of space she bloomed and blossomed. Her natural gentleness and innocence came out again. Her primary school teacher noticed the changes. People were commenting to me. The bedwetting ceased. She became calmer and easier to be with, and she began talking of her own accord again about the fear of him killing her.

Towards the end of the one year of no contact, the court ordered an assessment. We were all called in separately: me, both my girls and the Wolf. I requested to the psychologist who was assessing us that the Wolf not have contact with the girls before they have their assessment with him – so that there could be no inappropriate influence on the Wolf's part. He assured me that would not happen. I thought this was the best opportunity for her to speak of her reality without any force or threat coming from the Wolf, given he had no opportunity to pressure her over the past year.

It was hard for me. There was a lot resting on this meeting. I was scared of what she would say. I wanted to make sure she said what was true for her, but I kept silent. I knew it was not appropriate for me to say anything. I just encouraged her to say what she felt and needed.

I trusted the child psychologist – after all, he was appointed to address the serious concerns about children. The children were playing in the waiting room while I was alone in my assessment session. I did not have anyone with me. I was not good at asking for help and I was imprinted with the reality of having to do things on my own, so there was no one to watch out for my girls while I had my assessment. They were old enough to play in the waiting room. This was a safe area, or so I thought. The Wolf was not around, or so I thought.

I had no assertiveness at this stage to ask for one of my girls to go first, so that I could stay with my other daughter in the waiting room and keep an eye on things, and for me to go last. I did not know when the Wolf's appointment was and did not think it my place to check if it was immediately following ours – I just assumed his appointment would naturally be on another day. The counsellor had said he would make sure they did not have contact prior the assessment. I trusted him.

When I came out of my assessment, the Wolf was in the waiting room with the girls. He was promising them lots of presents. My heart sank. I felt betrayed and concerned about what this would mean to my daughter.

What my daughter said in that assessment session appeared to be very different to what she had been saying earlier that day or that week or the rest of that previous year. She had been saying she was scared of him killing her – but her story was suddenly very different. She was about ten and hearing about all the Christmas presents that had been stored up, waiting for her, from the Wolf and all his family. This was too seductive for her. She wanted presents, fun and playing, or for survival's sake she was going along with how he wanted her to be; either way, I was devastated at the change in story but I didn't show it.

Towards the very end of those tough seven years of legal involvement, I received a letter to say legal aid was going to stop. I had received all the money that was allocated for me. This was just before the final trial.

I rang legal aid and pleaded with them to continue funding my case, for the sake of my children's safety. Thank goodness they did recognise this and continued to fund my application until the closure of my case.

Now when I think of legal aid wanting to end my funding, I think how wrong it is that I was the one put in the position of possibly being unable to continue protecting my children. I was not willingly choosing to have this legal bill or be in the system. I was only in the system because no one was holding the Wolf accountable. I did not want to be in the system for so many years. That was the court's process, not mine. I would have been happy for a one day or one week process, not seven years.

The only reason my legal bill was huge was because of society's ignorance and denial about abuse, and their lack of restraint and consequence on a revengeful, abusive Wolf – yet I was the one made out to look like I was a drain on society.

I remember my lawyer saying that she didn't think she'd ever put my file away. It was the longest file she had, stretching from one wall to the other with all of the folders and papers relating to all the years.

After seven years of going to court and legal interventions, we went to the final hearing. I had been advised by my lawyers to accept a roundtable decision rather than go the four-day trial we had been planning for. His doctor, the child psychologist reports on all of us (who both failed in their integrity of their role) and other male professionals were backing him. He had a respected role in the community. I had gathered affidavits from numerous witnesses and family members – females and primarily non professionals. The risks of trial, given there was no clear evidence as it was my word against his, became too risky. My lawyer was concerned. Everything had happened behind closed doors, which made a trial risky.

So we agreed on a roundtable conference to create the final order. All day, in and out of rooms, lawyers talking with lawyers and coming back to fill me in, back and forth. Exhausting. My daughter's fate in the hands of strangers. In the end, he received what any healthy parent receives. No restriction on fortnightly contact, midweek contact and half of every holiday. About seven agonising years of court to get to this.

What could I do? Nothing. I had tried my best, as had my lawyer in a limited system. Then to top it off, my lawyer told me the other lawyers had said that if everything I had reported in my affidavits was true, then the outcome should have really been very different. That was such an insult to hear after all my honesty, my hard effort over seven years of trying to protect my children and writing everything down in the huge diary that had grown through all the painstaking, daily conversations and behaviours from our life with and after the Wolf. Their words and experiences were never honoured, listened or responded to – falling on deaf ears. There was too much that was unresolved. All the years of doing the right thing that the system asked of me. For nothing. Honesty doesn't work in the justice system.

I still don't have words, so many years later, to share my utter desolation and anger at a system that can only arrive at this pitiful kind of result. Every day had been a challenge to make ends meet, from when I left the Wolf, during all the court years and after them too. Unfortunately, from talking to women as I write this book, I know this kind of result is not a rarity and atrocities are still happening in 2016, in Melbourne, Australia and all over the world.

***

This chapter holds a lot of painful experiences. I share these experiences not to tell on anyone, or to blame or tell stories, but to speak the story of our life and the consequences of actions *and* inactions. I am naming the missing pieces people don't see when they go about their day and it appears as if everything is okay now. After all, we are out now and the children are going to school and playing with friends … but there is far more to work through and it takes years to recover.

I am naming the truth – the reality of what it's like, in some instances for a mother and children – in trying to break free and be safe from family violence, and the prolonged traumatic effect when society does not know how to respond or has an inadequate response.

I want people to understand the gaps and the long term costs – emotionally, physically and financially – of how our system is and how our society functions. Ask any woman who has gone through abuse and she will more than likely say it takes a lifetime to recover. She may appear over it on the outside, but the scars inside are deep and take a long time to heal, if they ever do. Unfortunately, some women don't find those skilled people who can help them heal.

As well as the internal scars, there are the social, spiritual and financial scars that have long-lasting effects. It is very difficult to work full time, attend court, attend therapy and look after yourself and your children – and move forward.

Later I returned to study to build a new life. There is time and money spent in rebuilding a life. It is a slow process with little support. Money has been a struggle for me. Then there is the priority of being there for your children with the additional bumps that come along the way, due to the past. There is often a choice of developing a good income or being there for the family. I made the choice of being there for my family and help them get through the bumps.

I want you to understand the amount of everyday moments that are robbed when trying to recover from and live with all the complexities thrown at families working to rebuild their lives. I want you to get how little space there is to get on with life, sit back at the cafe with friends, do those normal fun things and reconnect to people, when you are still not free – even though you look free. I want people to get and not forget how people still need support to recover, for a long time after. This is what I am saying.

Despite all this pain, there is one important thing I want you to take from this chapter of my life that was told to me by a counsellor many years ago. Remember that you only need one constant, loving person in your life who wants the best for you, to get through life's traumas. One person to love, see and accept you.

For the better part of my childhood, the loving constant was the characters in the books I read. I could escape my life and being in my body and live in their world. Later, it was my counsellor. At another point it was my doctor. In another way, my grandmother as well, though she couldn't see what was going on in my life – it would bring up too much for her about our family if she really saw how things were. But I knew she loved me. She was warm and she hugged me. She told me she loved me and showed me. I knew she wanted good things for me. She wanted me to be happy and nurtured my creative spirit. She also wanted me to be famous – maybe that will come true!

That one positive constant doesn't have to be the same person all the way through, but for a period of time, especially during childhood, it is optimal for there to be a loving constancy from someone. See if you can find a person. Sometimes there is no one and we find a constancy in fantasy or spirituality.

Find your rock. Your rudder that you can hold on to, even when times are rough. Being betrayed by people and those who are meant to care for you is devastating and can have a severe impact on you and your spiritual beliefs.

For me, when I was going through those years of court, I clung to my belief in Jesus. I was not a religious person. I was not even Christian, but in primary school and high school there were positive associations to Jesus and caring for children. The hymns, which sang of beauty and order. Children are also bombarded with two symbols that offer presents on the two major Christian holidays. As a scared and deprived child I longed for fun and gifts. Gifts acknowledge you are valuable and you exist. The surprise of seeing the Easter bunny through the class window when we were at recess activated an eagerness to go find some Easter eggs. Santa coming to school offered a picture of something good that was beyond the scary environment I grew up in. I associated these symbols offering gifts and excitement with Christianity.

Along the way someone had given me a picture of Jesus, with his arms outstretched to the children and sheep gathered around. There was something about the image: the positive, softness and warmth of the masculine protective of innocent children. It gave me hope that there was positive masculine energy and people in the world who wanted to protect the innocent. I kept this image in my room to comfort me. I still have it.

Many years ago, I had also been given a small inspirational book of passages from the Bible. When I was alone during the court years I would get this book out, often daily, and open it up to a page, trusting I was being guided to read that passage. These readings gave me comfort and hope for the future – of a different world and the protection of the good and innocent. The verses enabled me to hold the belief that there was a positive something, greater than humans that wanted the best for everyone. Rather than hold onto fear, I held onto Jesus, clinging with hope. In those years I was alone, praying was my experience of the positive masculine because I had not found comfort in men, either in the legal system or in more personal connections. Praying was my comfort when there was no personal comfort.

***

Through these rough years, I taught my children a number of strategies to help them. I think those strategies were good for me too, so I want to share a few of them as they might be helpful for you, or for someone you know personally or professionally.

I taught my children the difference between secrets and surprises. Children don't need to keep secrets. Children need adults to know what is going on so they can be protected. No one should ask a child to keep a secret. Surprises are only for a short period of time and then they always get shared and talked about. There is nothing any child *has* to bear and withhold.

I taught my children about good feelings and bad feelings. *yes* and *no* feelings. We went through *yes* and *no* feelings on all different levels, sensing them in their body, feelings, words, thoughts and examples in normal life from their interactions with people. I wanted them to be able to identify and differentiate their *yes* and *no* feelings and have choices on how to act on it and not be frozen, like we were in the Wolf's belly.

It was really important to me that, when they noticed *no* feelings, they could speak to me about it during those years of forced contact. I also wanted to make sure if they didn't or couldn't speak to me, that they would have other options. So I would draw their hand on a piece of paper and inside each of the fingers we would write down the name of a trusted adult that they could go to, whether it was a schoolteacher or someone in the family or someone else they could trust and talk to. I would encourage them through the court years to keep talking until whatever it is they needed to talk about was listened to – and to never, ever give up.

I helped them name and express their unthinkable thoughts and unbearable feelings in constructive and creative ways. I was their witness to what no one wanted to see or acknowledge.

All this applies to big people too.

Chapter 5:
Changing Paths

How do you recognise if you are on the path into the dark woods or the path to where you truly want to go? How do you find out which 'rules' to follow and which to drop? Do you discover and choose what path you are on or do you fall onto a path? What lets you know whether to trust and continue on just the way you always have or the way everyone around you does things, or not? How do you discover which path you need to be on?

How do you find out what you need so you don't get tricked or swallowed up by a life or a person that isn't right for you?

Who do you know, or do you know how to find that person who can help you become aware, change or become curious about your path?

Do you stop, reflect and question or does life define your path for you?

So many questions and layers to attend to when you are in the process of changing paths! This chapter of my life feels messy, with a lot of loose ends to tie up in the transition to begin a new path and leave the old path behind. I was awakening and needed to make order out of the disorder.

You may feel muddled at times going through this part of my journey. Welcome to my field of experience! Not all things are smooth and neat. Being in the right place sometimes means standing in the mess to sort it out.

Now it's time to take Little Red Riding Hood away from the 'good girl' path of powerlessness. We leave the path of 'niceties' and following rules without question – we leave the path of not having alternatives, and we leave the path of not protecting ourselves from the Wolf. I was no longer staying on the path of doing the 'dutiful' thing; I was no longer taking care of the Wolf without regard for my wellbeing. I was no longer in the court system.

This is a time of confusion. Changing paths requires questioning and becoming uncertain, as this allows new information to come in. We can feel vulnerable and uncomfortable as we become exposed to new feelings and thoughts, all necessary to help broaden our perspective.

We're changing direction – allowing emotions to inform and direct us, to be expressive and responsive to our own needs and environment, staying in tune with our instinct to discern. Remaining inside our own process, taking on our own path – our truth.

Changing the path and direction for my girls and me meant I needed to go over what had happened, so I could understand and never get caught like this again. This chapter is about 'sorting the beans' – a task often set in fairy tales. Sorting out what I had missed and what I needed to develop in moving forward to prevent this happening again. This chapter of my life was dependent on sorting out the seeing, knowing, sensing, feeling and thinking in my reality, which I had been disconnected from. After all, if I can't connect to it in my short-term memory, how can I move it to be filed away in long-term memory? I wanted to be free in the present, not persecuted by my past. I wanted to be clear, free and released into the spaciousness and possibilities of my present reality.

Overwhelming experiences inevitably hold big material. I needed to grow big enough (build emotional muscle) to contain this big material. *You can't release what you can't contain.* When the material to be integrated is big, this is a process. It takes time. Healing and change is not an overnight development. Done in the 'right' (skilled and mindful) way, suffering can become meaningful, rather than just suffering over and over again.

I needed to be able to pause in the discomfort and examine what I had fallen into. I needed to examine what it was that had not enabled me to access my instinctual, protective, intelligent self. I needed to identify what I had lost and how I could grow the skills necessary for my development.

I had reached the bottom of hell and there was only one way to go – up. I felt as if I had unfortunately needed this horrific experience of abuse to wake me up, otherwise I think I would have continued to drift around disconnected and lost. I had needed something to wake me.

I had fallen through the cracks. No one had seen me fall – or maybe someone saw me fall, but no one made a sustained effort to connect with me, get to know me, follow up and have a relationship with me. To establish my new path I needed to go back to my template where my neural pathways had been interrupted in their development and imprint of survival and identity patterns.

From a young age we absorb so much from our environment. 'Nature' is strong but 'nurture' is very, very powerful too. We are social creatures, introjecting from other either positive attributes and experience of ourselves or a negative view of ourselves, depending on our experience. We take in the verbal and non-verbal expectations and projections from others into ourselves. Naturally there is often going to be some combination of both, depending on the atmosphere in our environment and relationships.

The gaze of delight and love for a child enable a child to positively introject an experience of herself through that shared external response. This defines an experience of being lovable and safe. Eyes of frustration, hate, or rage regardless of whether intentionally directed at the child – if they are in the adults eyes, the young child introjects these projections as reality and so shapes their sense of self in the world.

I had internalised and being defined by a denial of my existence. I had grown up not even recognising my own thoughts, feelings and needs. I was so intent on pleasing people to be able to exist. My default map said I couldn't have a thought that was different or in opposition to another person. It was too threatening for me to risk being rejected, shamed and punished for challenging another person's view. The cost and consequences were shattering and alienating.

In our optimal development, we need at least one person to see and accept us, so that we can feel and know that we are seen and valued. That we can exist and are welcomed. We need those early years of receiving an adoring gaze and feeling that we are the centre of the universe. This experience of being adored supports, protects and cocoons us. We develop the capacity to negotiate future mis-attunements and disappointments, which inevitably occur over the unfolding of life.

What happens when we don't have this? We know the impact on the developing sense of self. So when you can, find someone, such as a skilled therapist. Friends and family are wonderful however these relationships need to be inclusive of and respect both people in the relationship whereas the gift of therapy is it is all about you. Here you have the potential to receive the gaze of acceptance and maybe love that can open up the space to heal alongside practical skilled work. With a therapist, there is no guilt to unpack your uncensored self and this process of taking up the space and not holding back for another is vital for healing and establishing your new path.

We are social beings and rely on significant people around us to mirror who we are. No matter what we experience growing up, the look in their eyes, the tone of their voice and their actions are what we internalise about who we are. In those early years, our brain is not fully developed. We are in a hypnagogic state, absorbing everything without the capacity to filter or discern. We absorb what is in our conscious and unconscious field. We don't have the rational developed mind to sort out the intricacies of what is going on – what is about us and what is not about us. We don't have a sophisticated filter to distinguish or block – that comes later as the brain develops. We are raw, open and affected. We experience, absorb and introject. No filter.

The unconscious is always present and we are open to the ocean of information of whatever is present. This information is inclusive of what our parents are conscious of and what is in their unconscious that is disowned but palpable in the field. I know this professionally through client stories and personally from the Ancestor Syndrome – in carrying World War II trauma of my mother's that were enacted in some of my extreme childhood fears and in my paintings as an adult. There are psychotherapy studies, therapies and books on trans-generational and ancestral trauma.

When we are young, we don't have the sophisticated brain capacity and ego development to differentiate between someone else's face, feelings and attitudes and our own. We need 'other' to be the 'good object' for us to survive. In our simple, young way, anything 'bad' coming from our environment or 'other people's stuff' that is not taken care of by other becomes internalised as 'our bad' for the sake of our survival. To love and hate the one person is a sophisticated and challenging process. We don't have the brain structure in place when we are young to negotiate the emotional complexities of loving and hating the one person; especially when this person is someone we are dependent on for our life.

Our simple mind is black and white, this *or* that. This is good, that is bad. We love this and hate that. If our parent is coming from their worst face and not able to own their 'bad', the child's simple, young mind is left with the incomplete interpretation we must be bad for this bad experience to occur.

The necessity of survival combined with our simple brain development of our early years, we are led to idealise our parents. This idealisation is because we can't integrate their limited self in the context of the intensity of our unregulated feelings and needs. We conclude we are 'bad' or at fault if we see and feel their displeasure. This tips the balance in 'others' favour to help us feel some security (real or false) that we will survive, because they are 'good'. Here we meet the template of the fundamental core wound of 'not good enough', 'bad', 'unworthy' or 'flawed' and the denial to look at the gaps in mother, father and society.

Anger and disapproval do not connect us. They separate us. *Our optimal survival depends on those significant people connecting to us even when anger is present*; we need them to be good rather than bad for us to survive. Only later in our development can we negotiate good and bad being in one person. To be able to bear and integrate the conflicting information about the one person is a sophisticated process.

We are destined to fall into the Little Red Riding Hood Effect to some degree when we are helpless or powerless as a child, (as all parents have their limitations) and be 'good', so our parent is not displeased and the 'security' of our survival is ensured. It just depends how much the parent is able to own their limits and relate to their own 'bad', so the child does not wear the 'bad'. As a child, we are focused on pleasing others to help ensure we are looked after – especially if we are a girl, as this is socially reinforced. As a girl, we are not led away from this ground of being pleasing, as this is seen as attractive. Yet a boy is encouraged to not please others and 'be a man', so he is not a 'girl'. We will talk much more about this in Part 2.

I needed to become 'response-able' for me. I needed to 'see me' and re-parent myself. I needed to move out of my stress-freeze response, self-reliant and 'pleaser' mode to free up my ability to be responsible for me and to me. That meant reaching out for support, rather than trying to work everything out on my own.

It is an uncomfortable thing when you can reach out to support others and not do this for yourself, especially when you are an adult. In experiencing the wrong, you automatically know what is right and give it to others. Yet the neural pathways about having this in your own life occupy a different branch in the brain to the branch towards 'other.' The branch about your own self has been interrupted. I was totally blank in having permission to be. The branch for 'other' was modelled, encouraged and educated on how to continue to grow and extend.

The early gaps in those interrupted pathways had filled with inaccurate meanings about me and the world, based on the behaviours and effect of those around me. There was no safety, permission, or modelling steps of behaviours, skills and beliefs to cross those gaps. I had no way to transfer the skills, security and assuredness from the branch of other people's birthright to feel, have and do to this also being my birthright. I could not incorporate this for me on my own or through logic. Logic was not available on the young interrupted, neural pathways where the survival/threat was embedded.

It may seem very logical to just transfer knowledge across neural pathways, but our brain is motivated by emotion. Our emotions, not logic fire up and create new neural pathways.

Our emotions are inextricably linked to our physiological being – these two areas are neglected in our modern attitude of 'I think, therefore I am'. This gap creates a loss of soul and flow in our culture. We are caught in the rush of thinking, doing and having. Our feelings, body, being and unconscious are ravaged and or neglected.

When you are in the emotion of the moment, your brain will go on what was safe and possible in the past. Deep down, I consciously knew what I wanted but I kept looping. It was as if there was a screen between me and the right to be me. I couldn't do it on my own.

When you can't be in the emotion of the moment and your instinct is locked away, you are vulnerable to be shaped by the dominating force of your environment and the corresponding, deep, repetitious sculpturing out on your neural pathways.

I had not been able to see what was going on, so clearly there were blind spots within me. This is why *work with the unconscious is such an important and missing part of the conversation about abuse*. I needed someone to be able to see my blind spots and give my unconscious and my body guidance and permission to connect to my inner sensings – to my reality and instinct. I needed steps and safety so I could follow through and meet my needs. So that I could become 'response-able' towards me.

I needed someone who would create the space for my path without overlaying what or how they thought my path should look like. This process was integral to reclaiming and restoring my sense of self, safety and possibility on my unique path (in my life and pathways in my brain) – and begin to create a safer world for my girls.

How do you recognise who can help you? It is tricky. I needed a professional. I had such a small circle of people in my life. No one was modelling what

I needed. I didn't know how to get out of this inner landscape of not seeing and helplessness. I was still vulnerable to get caught. I needed to find someone outside of my own landscape, which was all that I knew; who could help me travel and connect to people not in this chaotic and traumatic land.

It was a bit like I grew up knowing the Frankston train line, but I didn't know the Sandringham line. So I kept getting off at stations on the Frankston line in the hope of getting to Sandringham, but ending up at the same destination, never recognising any linking stations, which could take me out of the Frankston line and on to other lines and other futures.

A stranger was a more comfortable idea then for me to reveal my story to people I knew. I had an imprint in my default map not to reveal myself to people in my life. A counsellor was not part of this map. There was a branch in association with 'counsellors', which allowed some of me to come out, which would not come out through the state-dependent pattern in my life with personal connections. In some way I had absorbed from society that counsellors are an exception. Here was an opening. People in my life triggered me and reinforced my state-dependent memory about the way I had learnt to stay safe in the world – disconnected and alone on my train line. It was unthinkable to speak out in my world. It was not even that I would have felt shame or judgement or not want their bias. It was just not possible. I was too disconnected.

So I went to see a counsellor. It was uncomfortable but far more preferable to the discomfort of abuse. There was a comfort in the uncomfortable (with the right, skilled therapist) to begin to be seen. There is potential for some positive out of this discomfort.

It took about six counsellors, over a few years, to find someone who could help me beyond what I already knew. The counsellors were all well-meaning and caring but it was hard to find someone who could help me negotiate what was overwhelming and out of my conscious awareness or control. I needed someone to go beyond the insights I already could work out. I needed someone who I felt 'got' me, had a warmth and care and didn't just offer me rational insight therapy.

Neither rational insight therapy nor cognitive behavioural therapy is helpful for trauma. Of course, I would have wanted to act from those rational beliefs, if I had the space to. You can think something but not *know* or be convinced of it. You can want to stop smoking and *know* it is bad for your health, but your impulses and feelings are what direct your choices and behaviours. Thinking the rational beliefs didn't help me believe, feel or know them. Someone telling me how I should think didn't help either. It just made me feel stupid and a failure. Repeating the rational beliefs was not a convincer for 'that in me' which had unconscious blocks, preventing me to dare believe those rational beliefs.

Thinking about those rational beliefs did not dissolve the conflict inside me. The conflict was linked with feelings, experiences and survival. In the moments of life, those old, or rather young (undeveloped) inner conflicts would override my conscious desires and longing for the rational beliefs to be true and unopposed. Old because they have been there a long time and young because they were the involuntary young self's default map. I was stuck.

I could use willpower or positive thinking to convince myself for a time and if the circumstances of the conflict was not too strong – but that was only temporarily tricking myself. I still wasn't convinced and would loop back to the default map.

I could know it in my head but I needed every cell of my body to know and be convinced of what was the truth. I wanted to know I could hold permission for my feelings, reality and needs to be my guide of what was healthy and good for me. I needed my truth to follow, believe and trust my intuition and instinct. This meant I had to uncover the unconscious conflicts and how they were blocking me from being all on the one page.

I became curious. Why didn't I feel or know those rational, cognitive beliefs? After all, they made sense. What was getting in the way? I needed therapy to help me unravel this.

After trying a few therapists I found one I liked. I would go every week and in the beginning, just tell my story. This was important as I had never told my story before. I had never even listened to my own story. I had been too busy surviving and keeping silent. History had taught me that attention on me was never a good thing. So telling my story brought me to the place of being able to have attention on me. Telling my story brought me back into my body and my feelings. It is an interesting phenomenon to hear yourself speak and not be focused on the other person.

Every week I would tell more of my story and the ongoing fear and stress of the court proceedings, as well as about my darling children's pain and trauma-based behaviours. Every week I would tell my story and tears would pour down my face. It felt as if I cried through every session. But something felt good about it. I felt lighter.

My recollection of the room is that it was quite dark. I don't think it could have been, but certainly the space I filled was dark. It was comforting that she was with me in this darkness. For the first time I was not alone. She didn't try to fix it or make me feel better. She sat with me while I told my story and let the terrible take up the big space, as it had in my life; but this time I was not alone. The healing had begun.

***

I remember as a girl, I longed to grow up. Growing up meant no pimples and no bullying. Grownups had friends and clear skin. Growing up felt like I would be free and everything would be okay. I guess I had the fantasy that being grown up meant I would know everything; that school and learning was done, ticked off, complete. I had no concept of what was necessary to transition across. It just felt there was magic in becoming an adult and BOOM, I would be there. But it isn't that way …

It can be uncomfortable to be an adult and feel the needy or inadequate young self. The young inadequate self can feel so wrong and out of place inside the body of an adult. We also *often expect as an adult, that we should just know, before we can know.* That when we are adults we just know, and that it is childish to experiment or take risks; to become curious and not know. Our environment often does not allow or encourage us to reach out and continue growing and learning. Our environment goads us to be the same, fitted to a pre-determined image of how we should become.

I had a dilemma, I felt like an orphan child, not an adult. I needed to play and connect to lost parts of my innocent child self to find my confident, adult self. Play brings about spaciousness for something new to arise and to be more than who we are. Play enables us to trust in self, enjoy spontaneity, being care-free (losing control), being in the moment, being with the unknown, uncertainty, experimenting, accessing the creative self, curiosity and being taken over (by life-energy, pleasure and flow). Play is a mistake free zone. We need play to suspend our rational thinking and allow the unknown to come in.

When we know 'true play' it is far harder to be misled by 'degraded play', which the Wolf uses to seduce and trick. Our nose can sniff it out. We can say no, to what doesn't feel right when we know how true play feels.

Shame and judgement make it hard to play and unthinkable to expose gaps or feel okay to learn from another. Even when we have not experienced full abuse, don't we all recall being at school and not wanting to put up our hand to answer a question, in case we get it wrong and were laughed at? Where did we learn this inhibition? Think about where and how you learnt this, from the eyes of the child in you.

So here we were, not in the Wolf's belly anymore, but we still didn't fit in with 'normal' life – or at least, I felt like we didn't fit in. When I was standing beside other adults I felt like a child. For sure, in real life I am not tall, but I felt so *little*, so young. I wanted to feel my adult self, irrespective of my physical size, but I still felt like a child with no power.

Yet I was an adult with two children depending on me. I had an 'appropriate' serious adult facade. I don't know how much my anxiety affected my girls when I was putting on my 'adult' face and managing my conflicts of feeling little. I didn't know how to have fun, be silly, play and trust myself in the wide world. Play builds confidence and the emotional muscle to be in your own flow and be different. Play is about difference and connection.

In different ways it was difficult for my girls to fit in and be carefree like the innocent children they deserved to be. Their innocence had been robbed and they were both battling, in different ways, to be free and open up to others. Their trust and mine was impacted. Who could we trust? Society, including the Wolf, had reinforced that the charming ways of the Wolf were to be trusted over all. The message was to ignore and deny our own instinctual and spontaneous selves.

Navigating trust in other begins with trusting your own feelings and instinct. We all needed to develop trust, confidence and lightness. These qualities all help repair the isolation and build closeness. They are qualities that attract friends unlike shame, guilt and fear.

I wanted to help my girls establish the missing link to switch into relax and play rather than be in hypervigilant, freeze, flight or fight mode. I wanted to help enable them to be their whole self. I didn't realise at the time I needed this too.

I wanted my girls to be able to play – especially as play is a creative, safe space, which allows growth and experimentation. Play enables us to come into ourselves and our self-expression. Play is a necessary state in the process of learning and healthy risk-taking. Play helps us be in our body and locate ourselves in the world. Play is a safe avenue to express different parts of ourselves. We can play out rage and hopefully not get into trouble. We can play out the clown, the powerful one or the one who wants attention. We can play and discover more without immediately incorporating it into our identity. Play allows us to explore and experiment without being locked into a fixed identity.

It is hard to play when you are in survival mode. Survival mode means you have to disconnect from your play state. Survival mode means you are disconnected from and ignoring your deep, creative, instinctual self.

One of the ingredients necessary to immerse in true, explorative play is safety. To be able to switch off the internal, vigilant guard. You can't be both guarded and surrender to play; they don't go together. Otherwise, play becomes 'regressive', controlling and repetitive. It is not true play when a child has to keep the guard switched on. Regressive play does not show the relaxed, creative, imaginative, connecting and healing elements of true play.

This is what happened with my younger daughter. She did not have the skills to play. Instead her play mostly consisted of regressive, aggressive or repetitive activities, whereas my other daughter had been safe in the first four years of her life. She had greater safety and access to playing and the imagination.

To immerse in play and the imagination we need the space and permission to be able to say no. Imagine if you were playing a game with someone and you couldn't say no if you needed to. Not very inviting, is it? If we can't say no, we don't have the safety to say yes and immerse ourselves in something. Saying no allows us to surrender and experience being taken over in a positive way.

The ability to say no allows us to feel safe to surrender even further into the experience of play and be taken over by the experience of play, 'yes' and being creative. The ability to say no enables us to develop the emotional muscle to be in the moment and not have to remain in control. Saying no enables a trust and repair to be built to enable being in the unknown and discover that good can come out of the unknown.

When we have experienced the abusive side of being taken over, we learn to stay in control to protect ourselves. We are not comfortable being taken over, even in a positive way. It is too risky. After all, *bad events interrupt good moments*. Our internal self-protector will never again want us to be taken over. 'Taken over' becomes associated with 'bad', 'smothered', 'squashed', 'engulfed' and 'suffocated'. So the internal protector does a really good job of sensing any element of losing control and keeping us away from those experiences of being taken over – *even the positive ones*, to be super cautious. Growth is limited without support.

Moving out of isolation from the abuse and into closeness is tricky when these obstacles about play, 'no' and 'yes' are present. Abuse impacts our capacity to trust. When we can't trust our reality, ourselves and our sensings, it is difficult to know who to trust. Trusting another and entering intimacy, looking into someone's eyes or fully immersing into enjoyment or pleasure, is part of the unknown – and danger is associated with the unknown. Eyes can often signal danger to the survival centre (amygdalla) when we have experienced the worst of another. We may skirt more superficially, appearing to be with the experience but standing at the edges of it and not really look into another's eyes.

The thoroughness of our internal protector is a bit like what happens if a dog scares us. We don't tend to be scared of just that dog, or even that species of dogs, but we become afraid of all dogs. The internal protector is very thorough to cover all possibilities and prevent another experience of the unbearable. This is an example too of when we consciously know we don't need to be scared of all dogs, but there is an involuntary response overriding those rational cognitive awareness's. As I said, our internal protector is strong, and thorough.

Whether healing through therapy or play, when we have our *no*, we automatically know we can enter deeper into the *yes*. When we have access to our *no* on call, this allows us safety, fluidity and flexibility while exploring and experimenting. If being taken over has been a controlled and cruel experience, our system will remain on rigid, on alert and stay in control. We need a therapist who can model and enable us to have our 'no', even when it is challenging her/him.

We also know there can be positive experiences of being taken over that builds relaxation and a positive sense of self, such as a mother gently yet firmly holding her child when the child is distressed and in a tantrum, or the momentum of experience at your favourite music performance, or while watching a captivating movie. Meditation and hypnosis/trance are other avenues of surrendering and being taken over by the positive.

Children need someone bigger than them to hold and contain their unregulated emotions. Children need someone bigger than those big emotions flooding them. My children were on alert. I could see it in their faces, their worried eyes, their seriousness, their quietness, their stiff little bodies. I could see they were on alert by the absence of spontaneity, the limited childhood laughter and imaginative play. I had not been able to keep them safe, even though we had now left the Wolf. This was shocking to me.

The difference, now that I was out of survival mode, was that I could become more aware of how shocking it was. But I was still coming out of my frozen state, so I could only bear so much; particularly because now I had the added momentum and urgency to want and need to take further action. I was flooded with more consciousness about theirs and my pain. I could feel more out of my frozen self. Back then, my action had been frozen, unsafe and unsupported to take up. I was still not fully free to feel and know my pain and my thoughts but there was a melting happening. I was in another phase of transition in the survival/repair mode and trying to identify what we needed. At the same time, my focus was on my children. It was hard to heal and do life.

I had naively thought everything would be okay at home now. I guess our mind protects us from the hard road ahead. But how could everything be okay when I still could not keep them safe because the law was upholding the Wolf's 'right' as a father. I thought the damage was done, but *the constant contact until they were old enough to have their own choice was reinforcing their early life 'training'*. We were not out of the woods yet. I needed to help my girls recover. I needed assistance to help my girls recover. This was tricky, as the fear had been so strong for all of us. There was a strong reinforcement to keep holding in, hiding and coping, each in our own ways.

I needed to connect to libidinal, positive life energy; and not live life through the fear and trauma my childhood had imprinted. I wanted this for my girls too, so we could surround ourselves with people whom felt good to be around. So we could feel safe to bring out our positive sense of self that had gotten buried in an effort to protect it from further abuse. It is difficult to have confidence, closeness and intimacy if we can't play and be open. We needed our positive, life energy so we could laugh, play and be openly vulnerable in a positive way as well as being a necessary ingredient in protection from wolves. We needed to have access to healthy play to be able to sniff out the play of the predator.

When you are Little Red Riding Hood and the Wolf has charmed and tricked you with flowers, gifts, nice words and invitations, you can unconsciously become suspicious of play and beautiful things; they unfortunately got associated with trauma and danger.

I needed help on how to have a sense of play and belonging on this new path for my girls and me. I needed to be able to laugh and take risks to develop my sense of self, and I needed a positive circle of support. I needed people and a space where I could tentatively trust my inner creative self and also have a sense of being grown up. I needed to have the courage to be vulnerable in healthy ways. I needed to be able to listen to my creative, positive self.

My girls began to get some version of this through school but I needed this for me and also so I could offer my girls a bridge to these necessary life skills outside of school. Play and a sense of belonging are integral to claiming positive life skills and gifts. With these, I thought we could reintegrate into society – even if life now wasn't how I had planned.

It's so hard when you feel helpless, restricted and not in control because of laws and processes that are bigger than you. When you want to fit in with society around you but feel so different. I needed help to feel powerful and whole and belong, even if my life was not like everyone else's. I couldn't pretend I was the same; it would have denied my reality and I couldn't do the denial thing anymore. I needed a therapist to help me learn how to play.

My children could play at school but they too couldn't pretend that their life was like everyone else's. We were exhausted from years of fear and hiding our reality. Our differences needed to be seen and loved compassionately. We needed skills beyond what I could do. We needed counselling.

I was very mindful about my children's mental, emotional and physical health concerns, and was careful of what I was doing and where I was taking them. In affidavits, the Wolf had been scathing in attacks about me taking them to therapy. Over the seven years of court this led me to worry the judges would criticise me for taking my children into different counselling centres with different practitioners.

Getting out of the Wolf's belly, I was forced by the way of the system to bring different practitioners and counsellors to my girls. Not because I wanted another counsellor for my children, but because of the way the system worked. The counsellors referred other specialists and the system would require different people for different concerns and reports. I was in the system, and the level of chaos and awareness in the system is reflective of the trauma and chaos in our culture and society around abuse and family. But this was the only system available to me, when you don't have the money to go to private therapy.

Going through all those years in court and taking my children to different specialists, I didn't see it as putting my children through institutions, though the lawyers for the Wolf tried to use that against me. I was forced to be in this broken system. The professionals involved were doing the best they could to help my children, when they too were helpless and caught in a system that was broken.

The system colluded to not allow me to be powerful and act in the ways that were best and necessary for my children in protecting them. Here was systemic abuse, which continued the powerlessness and prolonged the healing and recovery. All because the system was not able to be with the whole story and does not have the skills or awareness to believe what is presented when only relying on witnessed 'proof' or supposed socialised credibility, such as being a Justice of the Peace.

The bottom line for me was that my every decision was made to help my children overcome what they were struggling with, and what was outside of their power. There was still a lot beyond my power, as the law continued to not allow me to follow my instinct and protect my children through their entire childhood.

My children needed to know that what they were going through was real and important, and worthy enough of attention and time. I wanted to teach my children not to give up. I wanted my children to receive the bridging support to cross through what they were going through in the most constructive way possible. I couldn't do anything about the fact that their innocence was robbed and they had had to grow up faster, but I could be there for them and find the environment to facilitate healing. It was a hard, slow and at times disappointing process (with many practitioners having no trauma skills).

My own therapy process was tough too. Therapy confronted me with the guilt and shame of what my children had been exposed to. The Wolf had been a significant part of the shaping of their identity, life and childhood and how despite my best effort, I had not been able to protect them. The self-blame and responsibility I was carrying felt unbearable to bring out and expose. It was a slow, bit-at-a-time process to release what was mine and what was not mine to bear.

The mother in me wanted to take responsibility for all of his abusive behaviour on my children. It was as if I was under the illusion that if I was fully responsible and it was 'my fault', then maybe I could have the illusion of control too. It would feel much better to be angry with myself and have a sense that I could change things, than this unbearable helplessness, isolation and emotional pain at not having the skills and resources to take a different path. Pointing the finger at me implied that if it was my fault I could have done something about it. So my guilt was there in this illusionary attempt to act as if I could have stopped it all and they could have had a normal childhood. My guilt, shame, over-responsibility and imagined choice of control were a defence against my helplessness and the ensuing emotional pain, heartache and loss.

I had to be really careful to make sure that the past limited aspects of me, which hadn't been able to protect me from him and exposed us to horrific traumas, didn't rob them or me of being functional now. I couldn't whip myself over the back and punish and tear myself to strips about how I *should have* been and what I *should have* known. The reality was I was limited back then. I couldn't change the past, but I could influence our future. If I had ripped myself to shreds with guilt and blame, I would have been useless in helping my girls or me move forward. They needed me to get out and not be sacrificed for them to live. They needed me with them.

An important part of getting out of the woods and changing the path for me was being able to know that I did the best I could. To know in my deepest self that I never, ever wanted my children to be exposed to anything other than a safe and loving childhood. Every day I was trying my best to protect my children.

I was not responsible for someone else's brutality and crossing boundaries. I was not responsible for the limitations imposed on me by my upbringing. Yes, back then I'd had limited skills in protecting our boundaries; but like any person with limited skills, I was not responsible for someone else's wrongs.

***

Life was not only a struggle emotionally, untangling from the past, but also financially. Court costs were ongoing throughout the revenge tactics and legal games. I wasn't able to work due to the high needs of my children and the demands of going through such a long, involved court process. The financial abuse of family violence can continue for many years after. There's little capacity to build a superannuation or build a career. Rebuilding a life leaves little space for a new relationship and a potential second income for support.

Both of my daughters' fathers were self-employed. Self-employed people can tell lots of stories and hide their income. One of the fathers did not pay child support for many years and the other would pay but I was penalised with my limited income spent on healing and protection. I would travel by public transport to court and to take all of us to our counselling sessions at different times of the week, along with other medical and miscellaneous appointments all tied to the effect of the abuse. This was very time consuming. Going across a couple of suburbs on public transport is a lot longer when a car is so much faster. Fewer hours to have that 'normal life' or earn an income.

The Wolf's inability to stop being abusive meant that I spent years in court and in counselling, trying to establish safety, stability and a positive sense of self for my children. This impacted my capacity to work and to have a normal week or a social life. Recovering from abuse was our world and life, which meant healing was much slower and time-consuming.

Changing the path led me to become quite involved in the counselling agency where I'd been a client. Their care, knowledge about relationship abuse and professionalism assisted me on so many levels. This place felt like my home. I remember walking in the front entrance and seeing the rocking horse, which the girls would run to and have a ride. A moment of joy and being carefree. That horse helped all three of us so much. This centre was a constant for us, always there. It was where I felt safe and where I could grow. It was the place where I knew they wanted me to be seen. They celebrated me. I felt comfort and strength to grow.

There came a time when my counsellor told me I had completed my private session therapy and suggested I begin the group work program. I came to love the group. This was where I began as the nervous, silent one who couldn't get a word in, but became able to speak up amongst all the other voices jostling to be heard. It was like children at the table. They became my family and I learnt to push forward and be heard.

I learnt to develop beyond my biological family; to jump in *and* not feel bad for taking up space. You get something from group therapy that is not possible in individual therapy. So too you get something in individual therapy that is not possible in group therapy. With skilled therapists, each has many precious healing gifts.

There were a few things that stunned me when journeying in these groups as a client. How many women who were professional and competent workers. Another surprising fact was how many women were nurses. The women in these groups really demonstrated there wasn't a stereotype of what kind of women are in abusive relationships. These were not all women with drug addictions or low socioeconomic status; these were women that you'd walk past in the street, some quite wealthy. These were caring, competent, intelligent women. Sure, there were some women that fit the stereotype but they were the minority.

I loved the group work program so much I kept repeating the courses. After repeating the program a few times, I was told that I had reached the limit of what the groups could offer me. I was basically kicked out of the nest in the most loving way possible. I was told I couldn't repeat the two group programs anymore. I had graduated! It was painful to know I couldn't remain in this safe, nurturing group, but it was bittersweet, as they were showing me that they believed in me. They believed I was ready to take the next step.

I could rejoin the world. But I couldn't leave this place. I needed another transitional step. For me this next step led to becoming a volunteer at this agency and training to become a Family Support Worker. I loved what they had given me. I wanted to be part of giving back. I couldn't leave yet. I wanted to see women who felt unseen, a bit like me, and help them rejoin the world, like they had gifted me. I had such fond memories of this place looking after me and my girls that I wanted to be connected forever. I became a life member.

Volunteering enabled me to put to test the idea that was forming inside me. Was it the right idea for me, as someone who had left school at sixteen years old, to take the big step and go to university to study to be a counsellor?

Let me remind you of a bit of my work backstory. Before my children I had worked my way from being office junior to accounts receivable, to accounts payable and bookkeeping. I had loved it. In each job I held, my role advanced to more responsibilities; but when I left to have my first child I knew when I returned to the workforce, I wanted a job where I participated more with people than with numbers. I felt safe to be around people now. I had not known what career it would be and trusted I would figure it out along the way. Here was my answer.

So after doing the agency volunteer training and becoming a volunteer, I found out that *yes*, this was what I wanted to do. It was a step in experimenting and stepping out of my comfort zone.

I was scared to go to university given I had left school at sixteen and had never had a pleasant experience at school. I found out I could do a short self-paced course to make sure I was of the standard to complete university studies. Another small step in the right direction. Having a bridging step was helpful, and necessary to give me the confidence to step into the unknown.

I began studying part time while the girls were at school. They were my priority. I could still be the one to take them to school and be with them to support them socially, emotionally and mentally when they came home from school. I would be there to greet them and talk to them about their day, or take them to a friend's place after school. I couldn't leave them in after school care. I needed to see them and maybe assuage my guilt that I was there for them now, when I hadn't been there protecting them adequately beforehand. I wanted them to feel secure and have a regular rhythm, a daily constancy. I would drop them off at school and go to class.

I loved every minute of study. Every subject was fascinating. I loved the teachers and felt inspired and supported by them. University became the next safe place I could practice speaking out. I made friends for the first time in my life. I was not alone. I belonged. I became stronger. I worked so intently on each assignment, wanting to do my best.

I was so excited to finish my university degree. Bachelor of Human Services (Human Behaviour)! I felt I was integrating into the normal world. I had completed something that other people did – something normal. I was blown away that at the end of my degree I was invited to become a member of the Golden Key National Honour Society for my consistent high marks.

I was fortunate enough to get a job shortly after I finished my degree. I was excited as my first position as counsellor was at the counselling agency where I'd been a client!

I began work with individual clients. I was also involved in running the groups I had previously been a client in. I contributed to changing the group program to further enhance what I personally and professionally understood these women needed in their journey away from abuse.

I loved working with these women. They were brave, clever and inspiring. I would tell each group of women about my life before being employed as a counsellor. When the women knew that I also had lived the life that they lived, they would ask me to write a book so people could understand why we get caught and why it's difficult to leave. I promised I would.

Being employed at this counselling agency and working with these women was one of the most constructive things I've ever done in my life. This work enabled me to deepen my confidence and my authority in what I knew. The child/adult inside was growing up, bit by bit.

I loved working with all my clients, but something wasn't feeling right. In working with a wide variety of people, I was exposed to many different life experiences and traumas. I knew I needed more skills and resources than what I was equipped with from my university degree.

Working and being out in the world meant that at times, things would come up for me personally. This counselling agency had the appropriate policy that once you're working there, whether as a volunteer or financially employed, you were no longer able to access the counselling services there – but they encouraged me to seek support from outside the agency.

Again I went looking for the next therapist to help me transition through my development on my path. This therapist was trained as a Soul Centred Psychotherapist. This is where I finally came to discover how deep change could take place beyond insight, beyond what I could understand rationally. This is where the richness of therapy could hold me easefully and with quicker and sustainable results.

My therapy with previous counsellors had achieved some important groundwork in naming my story and being validated. The group work had also helped establish my ego-centred sense of self, so that now in meeting this psychotherapist I had enough of a sense of self to enter deep work to release unconscious blocks.

Finally, deep cellular changes could dissolve the involuntary behaviours and limiting patterns that had shaped me. I was able to recognise more about my past and how it had shaped me. The personal and skilled presence of my therapist was a healing bridge between the gaps in my system, at a time when I did not have the emotional repertoire to fill me. Her genuine feelings and skills towards me helped me to do the same for myself.

After a while, I returned to study. I began studying this mode of therapy, Soul-Centred Psychotherapy and Counselling, in the private psychotherapy training at the Kairos Centre. This four-year course worked with the whole psyche, incorporating studies from current Western sciences of the brain, the body and trauma, including child development and developmental trauma and more. This course worked within a Jungian approach of working with the unconscious and also energy work drawing from Eastern traditions. The teachers, Kaalii and Andrew, took theories and developed them further, drawing on energy psychology (including meridian therapy) and Eye Movement Desensitisation Reprocessing (EMDR) as well as advances in hypnosis.

I remember watching my teacher's engaged and genuine responses as they taught the class and thinking, *oh, is that what it is to be human.* My early life had been so disconnected from the personal that I had no modelling to socialise. The combination of the mad and impersonal daily life, along with abuse and neglect, had impacted me more than I realised.

The experiential and exploratory work of the course was deep and life-changing. In therapy (compulsory in this course) I could attend to my own processing and this gave me space to engage with clients with a fullness I'd never had before. I just needed to be a few step ahead of my clients!

I could be part of a supportive transformation of my client's trauma and painful places. I felt satisfied in having greater resources and responses to do something beyond developing insight about what was happening. The skills in this course filled me with substance and enabled me to attend to my girls in a more solid and nourishing way.

Sometime later I left this wonderful workplace to work for myself. This counselling agency continues to do incredible work for their local community.

I wanted to keep helping people for as long as they wanted to see me, and not have the conditions and restrictions that government or community funded organisations are limited to through their funding conditions. Many of my clients had been involuntary, with a lot of trauma – including generational trauma. Often there was a deep mistrust from feeling betrayed and being exposed to many practitioners, of different abilities, over the years. Often it was hard for the clients to develop trust and repair when organisational rules did not allow long-term work with individual clients.

I wanted to work with people who could have free will on their choices about therapy and not continue a theme of powerlessness where they can't choose who they see or for how long. For my own self-care, I also wanted to be able to choose how many people I saw in a day, with more space in between sessions and less meetings!

***

Leaving the Wolf woke me up to what I had lived in; it felt like I had reached the absolute bottom of hell. In realising what I had just come out of, I was left with the sense that it had taken landing at that very dark, deep bottom of a hole in that dark place to truly wake up.

As my life and therapy process continued to unfold I made some important promises to myself that arose of their own accord, out of my instinctual self, from the free-flow of this new, safer place.

I'd had to be asleep – or as the psychotherapist in me would now name, 'dissociated' – through my childhood to survive. However, being asleep or dissociated made me vulnerable. Becoming a mother woke me up to a point, but it showed how asleep and how far down the black hole I was, still unable to respond to the need to leave the Wolf to keep my children safe back then.

As my children grew, I grew as a mother, which helped to wake me more fully to the abuse. I don't think I could have woken up and spoken out in the couple counselling session, if it were not for my children. I did not have enough value or love for myself to warrant speaking out for me, but I could speak for my children. I was worried about them. Seeking help for my children helped wake me.

'No more secrets' was the first promise. This didn't mean that I would go tell everyone everything about me, but just that I don't have to keep secrets anymore; just because it might not be what someone else wants to hear, if what I needed to say was important for my wellbeing or for a vulnerable other.

This promise to myself of no secrets meant that when I met new people and they asked a little bit about me, I would say, 'I'm a single mum, I left an abusive relationship.' I didn't need to say names; I didn't need to say details. I didn't need to expose my children to awful stories. I believed that the children had a right to have their childhood and not be swallowed up in the past. I held the belief that if I named the abuse clearly, the children would know at any time they could come to me and ask me questions, in their own time. I wanted them to be in control of what to ask, when and how much they wanted to know.

Naming and not keeping the secret about what I had come out of was enough. The amount of times I was responded to with, 'Yes, that's happened to me, too,' blew me away. I started to see that I really wasn't alone and abuse is far more prevalent than most people are aware of. If I had kept this secret, I would still feel alone and different – when I was now discovering that I wasn't different.

Approximately one in three women report abuse. I believe the number of women being abused is higher than that. Many women have said to me that they never contacted the police or told anyone. Also, some women do not define they have lived with abuse. They call it other names – 'controlling' and 'jealous' – though further details of their relationship indicate abuse. This means that we all know women and families who are living with abuse or have lived with abuse but have not reported it or entered the system to be counted.

They say it takes seven times for a woman to leave an abusive relationship. I left once but later in a series of relationships I found myself with controlling or narcissist men. What fires together is wired together (the one to love is the threatening and denying one). It took some time to find the type of therapy to untangle this madness from the imprint of love.

This is why I wrote this book: to tell the story that some women are not comfortable to know or tell. To help protect women who cannot yet know their reality. To help women who are confused about and still been shaped in limiting ways by their relationship (or past).

I want women who are living in toxic relationships, but who may or may not recognise they are living with abuse, to be in a community who recognises the abuse. I want women in abusive relationships to have women in their lives who know what to say and what not to say to a woman, or anyone in an abusive environment. I want a ripple effect.

Every woman in a toxic or abusive relationship knows at least one other woman in her life, and if every other woman has a clarity about and differentiation of what is abuse – and clarity of communication on how to explore these sensitive topics – we will create a ripple effect among women and an environment that supports more effective communication. Society can change without us waiting for some men, policies or institutions to catch up.

So my promise to myself was this new lifeline of truth and integrity: No more secrets. Not those kinds of secrets that protect other people at the cost of my children, or me never again. I don't have to hide who I am or what I need.

I came to a place of believing that it is okay to rock the boat when you have a positive, necessary and constructive intention. Even if the other person doesn't like it. By necessary and constructive intention, I mean to act when something is stopping a natural and healthy right, reality or need of a person. Response-able.

We need a society that is 'response-able' for individuals to be able to be responsible.

I came out of my personal experience believing that if I'm seeing something and it's absolutely wrong, I'm not going to be silent. I knew what it was like to be on the other end of silence and be trapped and helpless. I don't want anyone to go through the isolation, emotional pain and helplessness when they have someone in their life who could make a difference. Remember, my sister who only told me after I'd left that she had been worried about the children and me? I want to educate women like my sister to respond differently. I only discovered when writing this book that my two sisters would talk together of their concern but didn't find a way to talk to me. I want this to end.

I do not want to be part of bystander society silence and the inevitable entrapment. I do not want to be part of the social tendency to stay silent, 'obey authority' and not listen to my conscience.

Milgram was also concerned about this social tendency and in 1963 undertook a social psychological experiment about authority and obedience. The subject was given control of a dial that delivered 'electric shocks' to another participant – who, unknown to the subject, was a hired actor. Obedience to the 'authority' in the lab coat led the unsuspecting subject to the perception that when they were increasing the dial, each time there was an error in the other participant's answer to a question, that there was a higher electric shock administered. Across eighteen separate trials, 65% of the participants continued to the highest shock level: 450 volts. All the participants continued to 300 volts despite hearing the 'actor' screaming and despite discomfort about following the instructions. They were reassured there was no harm yet continued to administer perceived electric shocks.

Milgram found authority figures in family, school and workplace shape our tendency to override personal concerns in an effort to remain obedient to authority.

***

No matter what theory or range of influences, I had developed such poor emotional muscle in our family. Neither parent had a warm, flexibly responsive emotional muscle. It was not okay to rock the boat. Both parents had very fixed views and were not willing to be wrong and own their own vulnerability. We had learnt so well not to disturb other people's emotional state. So my sisters, possibly without thinking, spoke to each other but not me. Such a disconnection from instinct and feelings/actions of love. Perhaps they did not want to upset me or rock our relationship, so they didn't speak to me.

Back then I was trapped. I wish I had known then my sisters saw something and cared. I wish my sisters had named what I could not name. Maybe I could have spoken up. Maybe we could have come up with a plan together.

I want to educate about the brain body trauma response and how knowing this can influence greater communication skills for women and children who are trapped and for the women and men in their lives.

This pain and abandonment led me to develop the courage to speak up on my new path; even if it meant rocking the boat or risking a relationship. I did not want to be part of that dysfunctional family pattern. I see the need for safety of someone who is being abused as being something bigger than the relationship and I am prepared to take the risk and speak up.

There is a risk and a cost when speaking up. With skill there is an optimal way of speaking up and no need to take on guilt about the outcome. Each person has their free will. But there are many choices and opportunities along the way. I don't just speak up and wipe my hands of someone I love. I keep trying in different ways.

I don't regret speaking up, even when I have gotten burnt. Though some pain lingered for a time when betrayal was involved. At least I can go to bed at night with a clear conscience, proud of speaking up for those who are impacted by injustice or limited skills. Through time and getting burnt, I have now learnt to evaluate a person's level of helplessness or willingness to receive and leave people to their own choices. I do not need to become the archetypal hero (there is too great a cost), but I will speak up if someone is unable due to safety concerns, such as in an abusive relationship.

Even if my sister had said something to me back then and I couldn't have heard it, it would have been sitting somewhere in my system to knock about a bit with everything else. Imagine if many people had seeded their concerns about me? Who knows how it might have helped to stir me to awaken sooner? To know that even if I didn't agree, she was engaging with and cared for me. Who knows what could have changed if my sisters and family had spoken up? Their silence left me in a void. To me their silence meant I didn't matter. Love is a verb, an action. An absence of action communicates something, whether we like it or not.

I don't want to repeat this cycle. I want to be the one who speaks up, even if the other person objects to what I say. I want to extend my hand and heart in love and (whether you agree with or like what I'm saying) say, 'I'm here for you and I am not going away. I won't ridicule, shame, punish or reject you, or fall to pieces, no matter what your response is. My love for you is bigger than all that.'

This doesn't mean we force someone to make changes in their life. But we leave the door open to the possibility that they can receive your intention to match or meet them. That you can, as one of my nieces says, 'be the wall'. Solid, not falling to pieces. Able to receive and let things bounce and move. But importantly, you are not crumbling if they do not accept your reality (e.g. that their relationship is abusive). That wall that silently communicates that whatever is coming back at you is not going to break the connection and love, because you are solid like a wall.

This emotional muscle is also an important protection from Wolves. I remember one partner later who had an affair. When I named that I believed this was happening, he denied it. I initially let his emotional charge be bigger than my quiet knowing. It is so important to let your stance not be scattered just because someone else has a strong response. It is important to know small can be true. Loud does not equate truth. Developing emotional muscle helps keep you embodied, strong, resilient and connected.

I was exercising at the time and lifting heavy weights. When I would lift each weight I would spontaneously say to myself that I wanted to be as strong emotionally as my muscles were, so his (or anyone's) protest would not be louder than my quiet knowing. This came true and his denial no longer kept me in limbo. One night I sensed he was betraying me and I went there. I went to prove it to myself and give my outer self the proof of my inner knowing. That night, I went from facing them both, straight to dancing. I felt joy, empowered and free. From then on, I always trusted my quiet, inner self no matter how loud someone would deny or protest.

How can you build an embodied protection of feelings and beliefs within and around you, so that someone else's reactions does not determine your conviction, even if your voice is quiet and theirs is loud? After all, loud does not equal right.

This process of quiet conviction has not been an easy road. I felt very alone and severed from my family for many years. There have been a number of serious betrayals and backlashes at me. No one spoke up through a series of injustices, which unfolded within the family. I had to bring up certain injustices - more than once - as they were not acknowledged in the family. I could not arrive at family gatherings and act as if nothing was happening though they all were. I received many objections, rationalisations, excuses and rejection.

My mother punished, rejected and betrayed me and my children on a number of occasions and my sisters colluded with her. This led to permanent damage in our family. They didn't rock the boat and along with their partners, were harsh in silencing me.

On a significant birthday of my youngest daughter, with the Wolf and his family present along with my family, my two sisters were mingling and chatting with the Wolf's family. They went up to the Wolf's brother and chatted for a while. The one who was in the agreement to kill me in the suicide pact. My eldest daughter came up to me, disturbed and upset and asked me what were they doing. I was silently furious. Here they were sending the message again to the Wolf and his family that nothing bad happened. A few days later, I spent hours trying to explain the pain and betrayal to one sister. She was absorbed in her defence and her spiritual perspective of 'forgiveness', despite my personal request to support her niece(s) or myself. I gave up in talking to my other sister as I knew she was even more heavily into this spiritual perspective, handed down from our mother, which required a type of spirituality which denied the personal and relating. I was too exhausted and emotionally beaten by the blindness in my 'family'. There are a number of these experiences, where my sisters betray and fight for others but not for my children or me.

No matter what, I am proud for speaking up when something wrong was happening. I developed a deep inner strength and trust in myself and my ability to overcome huge obstacles and continue growing. Through my pain, I learnt I did not need my family to behave a particular way for me to feel acceptable and in my truth. My family's gaps helped set me free.

These challenges pushed me out into the world to find my tribe. A circle of women and men I could trust and be supported by. My world opened and my 'family and community' grew in different ways. I can go my own path and I also have safety and support to return to my 'community' for nourishment and continual growth.

I have described feeling so alone through this time, and of my family not able to be there in the way that I needed. I also need to acknowledge that there were times of support, like my sister offering to look after my girls while I typed my past on her computer. I asked two sisters to mind my girls when they were too little to go to school and I had to see my lawyers so regularly. But then I would pick up the girls and go home and for me it was like we were on another planet, forgotten by all the family. They were struggling with the behaviour of my youngest daughter towards their children. Nothing was easy. They didn't know how to bridge beyond their struggles.

Our family would talk to each other. Don't get me wrong. But this talking for me was more like reporting the news. Going through the motions of updating the family, but there was no emotional interaction of love to me, or how it was for me and how I was feeling. Maybe they were in shock too and didn't know what to say or do but I see this as an ongoing state in our family. How can we educate families and community to communicate heartfully from the fullness of what is happening. Otherwise, the silence and walking on eggshells continues on both sides of the circle.

How sad that society and family does not know how to be with the stuff of life. What can we do in our immediate circles to change this, rather than protest and defend the occasions when we were there in an attempt to push away or deny what was missing? Defending leads to denying the reality of the gap. It takes courage and emotional muscle to be with our own gaps.

When I left the Wolf he contacted my father and would visit him when he had the children on contact visits. When I found out, I asked my father why he had the Wolf over. He said so he could see the children. Yet I brought the children over to visit him. For me it was a betrayal and sending a message to the Wolf that what had happened did not exist as my father was acting just like the Wolf and towards the Wolf, sending the message as if nothing bad had happened.

I would be invited over to dinner to my father's. It was nice to be included with a family meal, especially when my sisters were invited too. It was nice to all be together. But there was no space made to talk to me, asking me how I really was. No one did. Communication was very formal and superficial in our house. Oh, except my Nana.

Over the years, Nana had come up to me and asked, over and over, 'Are you really happy?' I didn't have the heart to tell her what I couldn't speak of and she didn't have the skill to help me through this. I also knew she had been through so much pain in her life. Maybe on some level, I didn't want to be a burden on her. Life is such a complicated mess, whether we acknowledge the unconscious existence or deny it. Life is not so simple, ordered or rational. There are many layers going on. Maybe in some way the child in me who absorbed those early years knew of her pain, my mother's pain, knew of her unconscious and how big her story was in living through World War II in Poland with my mother. How could what I am going through be a big deal compared to surviving the Holocaust? This is a challenge for any child of a parent who has lived through trauma – that your life is nothing compared to what they went through and you should be grateful. This is not necessarily spoken but absorbed when the parent does not empathise and support the child's experience.

Sometimes I stayed overnight at my father's house when it was near a birthday or some legal challenge as I would be scared to stay alone with the girls, in case the Wolf did something unpredictable. I am grateful for these times but I wish I had had someone to hold and comfort me, and help create a space where the pain and anger could be shared.

Sometimes my father said and did things that were so wrong and I didn't know what to do with it. I would freeze. I can remember lying in my old bedroom one night when I stayed overnight, next door to his room. My step-mother was in hospital. I lay there howling and howling. I had regressed to being a little girl, triggered and scared by the control, threat and intimidation of what he had said to my little girl. I was too scared to get away. She was in his bed. I just cried and cried, loud and tormented. Hoping he would come and I would see the good face of my father. No one came.

Nothing was said the next morning.

My second promise to myself: I vow that I will never again let anyone structure my life to not feel safe to show myself. I vow that I won't let fear govern my choices. I vow that in my own home, I can express and show myself and be safe. That doesn't mean that fear never structures my decisions or choices. I am human, but I can recognise fear much quicker and I can always recover from the effect of it. New information always emerges when fear is activated, so I thank the gift the fear brings me. This information helps me protect myself from the gaps.

When I left the relationship and made that vow of never letting anyone structure my life; I began to think, 'Well, in my home I'm going to put up this little picture I was given, on my bedroom wall.' It was that small card of Jesus with his hands out to a young boy and girl surrounded by sheep. To me this image was a symbol of love and protecting the innocent. This image was part of what filled a gap in my system. It was a symbol of the positive masculine, being gentle and looking after the child. This picture comforted me through the terror of being alone while protecting my children and gave me the strength to keep on alone in a tough situation through all the years of court. I didn't want to hide what was important to me. I wanted it out in my home so it could comfort me as I walked past. I am free. I wanted to be free and safe to show myself and be respected.

Years ago, I had also been given a small book with passages from the Bible – through the court years, this helped keep me going. I would come home from court or a legal appointment and in a quiet moment, I would open a page and read the comfort and hope. I kept this book out so it was in easy reach when I needed comfort. I didn't want to hide it.

I knew my father, who was Jewish, would come to visit me at some point. He did not visit often as it was his expectation I visit him. I didn't want to have to run and hide this one picture or one little book. I feared if he saw them he would be displeased. I was scared. I didn't want to have to hide something that was positive, especially not in my own home. So I went to my father to tell him how I prayed to Jesus. How Jesus had been comforting me through these years.

Back then I was still so scared of my father's disapproval, given his ways when I was a child. Maybe I believed I needed to confess, so I could get his approval and not live with anticipatory fear. Maybe I wanted to be the one in control and face the fear before he found out and it was out of my control. I felt I'd never had his approval or blessing. He had so often looked disappointed, stern, angry or critical. There were too many memories reinforcing this. Just like when he wrote to me about living with my first partner, as he was not Jewish. He could not be happy as I was not living 'his' way, yet he wrote that family was what was most important. He was not walking the talk. He could not be happy that I was happy. His way of caring was through criticising, perhaps driven by worry and anxiety. How can we as a culture address the uncomfortable instead of alienate those we care for?

I was still so isolated and had such little support that I did not have the emotional resilience to bear his displeasure. I was still tentative in showing the world who I was, and I was caught needing someone to accept me so I could feel acceptable. We are, after all, social creatures and need to belong.

I could not bear the anticipation of waiting for him to come and show his displeasure. Growing up, I had absorbed so many negative messages from his words, actions and looks of displeasure. I needed to confront him rather than let it happen out of the blue. I could not bear the waiting. I wanted to be in control of the bad thing happening. I knew he would not like to see this in my home, given I had grown up in a Jewish household.

I told him how Jesus had been there for me when I felt alone. He disowned me and told me I was no longer his daughter.

I walked out of his house that day in shock. This freeze and shock was such a familiar state of survival. I was dissociated from my feelings. 'Just keep on going' was my mantra. I could not even contemplate the possibility of having outrage or grief about his rejection of my healthy action – of gaining comfort from praying to a picture when I was alone, especially when I did not have the circle of support I needed.

I didn't want my children to have another layer of a broken family. I arranged to drop off my children regularly so they could still see their grandparents, even though I was no longer a daughter. I was not allowed in their house. It was painful dropping them off at the gate.

One year later my father wrote me a letter apologising for his wrongful action. I honour his capacity to own his mistake and we began a careful and slow repair process. This has been the healing with my father: that despite his limitations through life, he is doing his best and through our tussles he is there for me now, unconditionally and without judgement. This 'without judgement' came about through a series of confrontations of me holding him to boundaries and reflecting to him when what he was saying and doing was inappropriate or heartless. From this a new ground developed and he relates very differently and compassionately to me now.

Getting out of the woods, being on my new path and holding intentions like not keeping secrets and being true to myself, led to events that still brought their own grief and pain. Being true did not stop rejection, judgement, grief and pain coming in. But I would not change what I said to my father, because just as I walk into his house and respect the symbols that sponsor and support him, I am equally important to have the symbols around me in my home that support me. It is irrelevant as to what label or description those symbols have when they offer support. I was willing to take a stand for myself, in the way I needed my parents take a stand for me growing up. If it did not happen back then, I was at risk of not doing it for myself now, unless I did something different at these choice points. I could do it for me now.

This new path meant I was challenged to come to terms with my grief and my anger towards the Wolf's family. I never spoke to them after I left. I had imagined they would have known something of the truth, given that the Wolf and I went to court for so many years. I imagined they must have read some affidavits of my account of what had happened. I imagine the Wolf must have feigned hurt about the 'lies' I had written. I couldn't believe that with them knowing my nature and knowing their son(s), that they would really think any of it was an exaggeration or a lie.

Everything I said in every single affidavit was one hundred per cent accurate. So I could not believe when the process in court continued and there appeared to be no pressure from his side of the family to stop what he was doing for the sake of the children. Control and revenge continued over the years of their childhood. Not one member of his family visibly took action to protect the children who were being dragged through the court system. They could have easily put pressure on him by challenging him.

I believe they could have had a role in preventing or limiting the legal persecution to protect the children's right for safety. They had never seen me being revengeful or inappropriate, so maybe they needed to consider that there was truth to my affidavits or contact me to hear my truth. After all, two of the brothers actually knew the truth about the Wolf's violence, yet there appeared to be no pressure on him. They stayed silent and preferred to bury their heads in the sand and sacrifice the children.

In his family as in mine, the social silence was palpable to me. I would guess that what happened in my family was a version of what happened in the Wolf's family: silence, denial and not rocking the boat or affecting the one who is 'difficult' or 'different'. We recognise and accept social silence. Silence can be taken as support if there is no visible objection. Families and even movies and advertising can have a large destructive influence, yet we continue to not take up the constructive elements to being an influence for positive means.

Words cannot describe my opinion of his family for supporting him, for protecting him rather than protecting these children. Protecting his reputation, rather than protecting the lives and development of these children. As adults, let us think hard about what and who we protect – are we content to live with those consequences? Are we living our values? What kind of society do we want for our children and grandchildren? Feeling uncomfortable can result in positive action. Avoiding discomfort can be dangerous.

Everyone in society has a part to play. If people are silent, abuse continues. It is people who abuse and people who make up society. The silence and abuse in society affects and shapes what happens to people. Abuse is not something separate to society – unfortunately it is woven into the very threads of society.

I was also angry at the legal system because I thought it was meant to be there for justice and for protection. The justice system, I discovered, isn't about doing what is just. The justice system gets so involved in black and white rationality. You've got to be able to show proof that an experience is true and this is difficult in abuse behind closed doors. Real truths become reduced to being invalid. Of course, facts and proof are important but if decisions and outcomes are only dependent on 'witnessed proof', then some context, such as what goes on behind closed doors, falls through the gaps. This means some of the most vulnerable members of society fall through the gaps.

This kind of mentality also means that the experience of emotional and psychological abuse gets discounted. Your experience and needs are invalidated because there is no external proof when you live with emotional or psychological abuse.

I remember in the early days coming back from a day at court and one of the counsellors at the counselling agency saying to me that I was now being abused by the legal system.

It's taken me many years to process the anger I have held towards the Wolf's family, my own family and the legal system. I am truly grateful for therapy and the process of writing this book. There is something healing in writing a book because a book can reach community when our pain and truth originally couldn't. The public becomes involved, which is so vital in the process of healing. I trust the risks I have shared in being human can be received to understand the consequences of actions and non actions. So my raw pain and everyone's limited actions described in this book can create a bridge of change for all other women and children going through abuse.

We currently have a fragile connection to the presence, capability and value that is possible in the circle of community – witnessing, mirroring and supporting. Just as writing this book has opened up so much in me, it has also opened up so many connections to people. This book has given me the last key to complete healing: transforming my 'righteous anger' into peace and finding a new place inside my memories and in society. I think that's the final 'why' this book had to be written, because that anger of betrayal and emotional pain needed to be turned into something constructive.

I see so many women and men who are angry and have good reason to be, or who are righteously defending their position. Righteous anger divides, competes and polarises. Righteous anger builds bitterness, resentment, alienation and keeps some level of helplessness. I want righteous anger to dissolve into anger that protects life. That is the purpose of anger. To protect our life-giving energy. Anger has been derailed and been given a bad rap.

I want my anger, emotional pain, helplessness and other people's anger and helplessness to unite and create policies that bring our community to witness and support. I want a society and humanity that uses the left and the right brain to make the best decisions, created from both the information of logic and the information within the truth of feelings and the body. Responses which can incorporate how stress and trauma influence and shape who we are, for the abused and the Wolves. So we don't rely on cognitive recognition as the saviour or the solution – because right now it is failing all of us. The whole of society is affected. We are not separate.

Our thinking, feeling and decision-making can inform through five ways:

- The left brain thinking over its own brain dump
- The right brain revealing its creative outpouring and it's depth beyond word
- The left brain thinking about the right brain's feeling and bodily information
- The right brain feeling about the left brain's thoughts
- Finally, what they bring together as a whole, which is more than the sum of the parts.

This way, each part can inform and talk to the other – just how we need to as participants in society. A whole and varied combination of ways of gathering information.

***

As I continued on this new path, I had to continue facing my anger and my grief over my children's lost childhood. This also led me to be with my own grief, despair and anger about my own childhood and the deep losses of my innocence that could never be recovered. Cycling through both again and again over the years at different times. Each time a new layer became integrated. A bit at a time, as the depth to comprehend the immensity of each loss is beyond conception to integrate all in one go.

This anger at both family and society turning what felt like a blind eye touched a deep wound of abandonment in me. The pain brought the wounded child in me to the surface to have her childhood experience validated and made real as being as big as it truly felt. Validation of my anger and my reality allowed what was unacknowledged to become more fully present. The repetition of the family betrayals and the denial reinforced the truth of the family pattern. As a result, there was less censoring of my memories; and so painful memories shifted and comforting memories surfaced.

Being with my anger brought me healing, in more ways that I could have imagined. Allowing the anger to flow with recognition of my past and how it had shaped me, surprisingly did not stop me from growing and developing, freeing myself from the hooks and bonds of the past. My anger could protect me. I was also now in an environment where those past influences could change through deep therapeutic processes. Healing brought a deep compassion for my younger self – which in its own time spread to a compassion for others in my story.

Despite grieving and anger processing taking its own time, my capacity to bear the growing awareness of the magnitude of this loss has allowed me to become wiser, softer and more courageous over the years. That my heart may increase to hold all that I grow into has been a blessing. Thank goodness my sense of my self has not been held back with the pain. Thank goodness to the solid structure built through my psychotherapy journey. So this processing has been just as it could be in the ebb and flow of life, imperfect and opening, engaging with the limits and magic of life.

I knew I couldn't change my past, but I had to come to terms with the emotional pain. No matter what good I bring into my life now, I could not change my childhood and my children's childhood. This new path built a deep and solid foundation to accept and move on. It's a funny thing, aging – I did not want to disown my past as it had shaped me to be a person I am proud to be and brought me two children who are my gold. Denying my past would be a trauma, as it would deny my reality, yet I needed to find a way to live with it and not torture myself or be tortured by it.

***

This path was bringing me back to *me*. Changing paths was about coming back to the real world. About having the courage to face the Wolf and see him for what he is: a charming trickster.

'The Real World' is about cutting the Wolf's belly open, to bring out what is trapped and pulsing with life within it. It is about seeing past the skin and facade of the Wolf that is not actually powerful, but cowardly. 'The Real World' looks into the environment that feeds the Wolf and questions the placement (and displacement) of power.

'The Real World' is all about how to leave the old skin and insecurities behind. How to begin to trust again – both in yourself and others. Trust can begin when what is real and true is acknowledged and the myths and fairy tales are put to bed.

The journey through my anger and my grief, though painful betrayal and many losses along the way, helped me to find the edges of myself and the little lost girl within who was still influencing my choices and the amount of power I could access.

Journeying with my own children through their pain enabled me to develop the emotional muscle to see and feel and know what the little girl in me had needed, had lived without and had lost. I could know, through my love for my children, what they needed and what was lost. I could then find the love that had been lost to me, in me.

This new path really showed me that positive thinking and willpower aren't enough. We all need different things, but we all need the same things too. This new path highlighted how important it is to be able to take action and seek out help to discover what has been missing for me, and for you.

I had to gather my missing parts. They came in all different shapes, symbols and forms. I found a poem I wrote when I was very young of being a wispy, little lost cloud separated from my mother. When I was a little girl I drifted about lost like that wispy little cloud. No one helping me locate myself in the chaotic, messy bigness of my surroundings. No one was mirroring back to me what was really going on. I had no roots to plant into fertile soil. My feelings and realities were floating about in this vast, ethereal sky. I grew older but this little lost cloud girl was still stuck and unable to move on, as she had never been found. Until I began my therapy process. We need to recognise the impact of neglect and abuse in childhood. We don't just get over things just because we become adult.

Entering my new path had elements similar to a simple daily activity that we all do each day. We all pick up something and take it from one room to the next, whether it's a cup of tea, a book or a phone. This function of being able to take something from one room to the next happens because we have a picture and a name for what we are looking for, and therefore we can find that match and identify it. Only then can we take it from one room to the next.

If we don't have that picture and name of what it actually is, the elements can't connect and the task can't be completed. So too when changing paths;

the naming and the symbols, and all else that makes something what it is, needs to be identified to be able to move it from our current self-experience into long term memory – so that we can truly, cleanly and completely move on.

Something can't go from one room to another if a part of it is left behind. It needs the whole kit and caboodle to be able to change places. So too, life events that are overwhelming and have been too uncomfortable and chaotic to be processed, stay in limbo in our system until the whole of it can move. This means when there is a part that is unbearable or unthinkable, the memory and the coping mechanisms are stuck on repeat, constantly getting triggered.

When these memories are in limbo, floating around in our conscious self, they cannot be made whole and find their final long term resting place. This means that when we are in similar situations, or there is some partial resonance in the present to those fragmented past events, we are limited to those old life-coping strategies involuntarily getting activated and shaping our choices and actions. This is what trauma theory looks like in everyday reality.

To be able to make the healing links so the past can move into long-term memory, certain skills and capacities are necessary to process what we couldn't integrate originally, but are essential to integrate to be complete. So now there was a different kind of fear in getting out of the Woods and out from Little Red Riding Hood's cape. The pieces that needed connecting were uncomfortable to be with but there was also the fear of stepping out of my comfortable, familiar zone. Thank goodness for therapeutic tools I could use at any moment, which helped soothe me and be with the unfamiliar in creative, comforting and fulfilling ways.

***

This process of moving out onto this new path was about my vows and promises to myself. It was about me being with unbearable anger, grief and loss. It was about helping me and my daughters integrate back into life and build our future. It was about me studying and becoming employed.

It was also about people starting to ask me, 'So when are you going to start dating?' I would say I was not interested. Maybe never!

After about two years of therapy, I thought maybe I'd look into this dating scene …

I went to one of those singles dinners. It was a large room of people. We were all seated, alternating male-female. I was talking to the two men on either side of me. I was not interested in either man and thankfully one became busy socialising elsewhere. But the other man remained and me in my Little Red Riding Hood shadows, felt obligated to stay and talk with him. That if I walked away he would feel rejected. I had such a painful history of early rejection, that my default position did not like me in any way rejecting another. So the whole night I politely stayed by his side.

I went home regretting my limited self and feeling miserable that the excitement of the night had been sabotaged. I made a promise to go back and have a plan on how to get away from any man that I didn't feel interest in. This is what I kept doing, along each step on my path; I kept building the new next step when I hit a bump, which revealed what skills were missing.

The next time I returned, I had my lines ready to use to get away and mingle more. I mingled and met someone of interest. We began dating.

This was my first relationship after the Wolf. We had a common interest in psychology. One day he gave me a small Myers Briggs tool (not the full process) for me to complete. I am not sure why he gave it to me. If you don't know the Myers Briggs test, it is a series of personal questions, which creates a profile of your personality style, all based on choosing your preferences.

It wasn't meant to take long to complete. It was just a small, simple multiple choice asking which option I prefer more. It took me hours to complete. I was shocked that I couldn't comfortably and clearly say what I preferred. I was so attuned to and habituated to what the world wanted from me. My identity was still more fragmented that I had realised.

This new path was uncomfortable, but in a different and healthier way then the discomfort and pain of living with abuse. This new path meant that I was going out, meeting people and trying new things, which exposed me to deeper understandings about my strengths and the places in me that needed some rebuilding. Most of the time this healing process happened via people. It is far easier for our wounds and limits to remain hidden when we stay at home and without much social contact.

The wounds that we receive over a lifetime tend to happen via another person. It helps for the healing to also be with people. After all, isn't the success in our life, family, relationships and business a lot about how well we can be ourselves with others?

So I offer this book as a beginning, a middle or an end in your path. I also offer me to be there for you, beyond this book, via a range of healing processes in working with me through my other books and workshops – and through my talks, webinars, online courses, retreats, or individual sessions to support you in your healing journey. Because in this part of the journey, finding yourself and stepping out of the comfort zone can, in some ways, be even more challenging than living with the abuse. Avoiding our self can be easier than facing our self – our past, present or future.

There can be a painful comfort in handing over the power to someone else; in not making a choice. No matter how bad it was, I had a perception of knowing what to expect and I had a sense of my enduring spirit soldiering on. Whether my perception was accurate or not. *I felt secure in being unsafe.* Paradoxical and illogical, for sure – but my original safe place via my parents, was not safe. So I had a map of safety not being safe and this being normal.

I'd had a sense, maybe false, that I could endure the old life with the Wolf – even though it would have been a very small, painful life with great costs to me. After all, he kept me isolated and controlled. Beyond his unpredictable mood and actions, there was not much uncertainty. It was a life of certainty despite the chaos and abuse. I was certain to not have power, be controlled, remain uncertain and not be in the world or have choices.

Now my life was filled with uncertainty and the full spectrum of feelings, choices and possibilities. Such a contrast.

One day, during this time of rebuilding my path, I could hear the girls playing while I was cooking dinner. I was chopping vegetables and even though at the time we were still in the court process, I could feel this joy flowing through me. There was such relief that no matter what was going on around me, I could feel joy and contentment and that I truly had achieved what I wanted. That no matter what, his cruelty and fear-dominating ways were not going to structure my inner world and my life.

I really was free now. He wasn't ruling my life, my feelings or my environment, even if I was still inside a court process. He was not structuring me. My emotional muscle was stronger. I was free!

***

During those early years on my new path, I had no other life other than my girls, my study, therapy and my work, with all this structured around their school and bedtime hours so I could be there for them. I only saw my new boyfriend on the fortnight the girls were away with their dad's until it was really clear we were going to remain in a relationship.

I was building my strength in so many ways. Taking risks by trying new things. Starting university despite leaving school at sixteen years old. Speaking up in class in university, speaking at a university rally with a microphone to people, speaking up at my workplace as an authority for my clients, becoming involved in the children's school, building my strength in dating and in my relationship.

I can remember when my eldest daughter was in Year 11. We were having a heated conversation. I am not sure what the details were about now, but what came up was her pain about being different from the other families, and the family violence that she had been exposed to.

We reached a point of back and forth. I felt such emotional pain as we couldn't connect with each other. She was in a painful place and for some reason I couldn't reach her, but I didn't stop talking. It didn't matter what was coming out of her mouth or my mouth, what mattered was that both of us were talking. That was a huge *aha* moment for me.

I realised, that in the end, love is not necessarily about saying the right thing at the right time; this is not a perfect world. None of us are perfect. Perfection is not the reality of being human, but it's about being able to keep desiring and being motivated to re-attune, reconnect and be available. The fact that both her and I kept standing there talking, even if whatever we were both saying was gobbledegook, we kept the channels open by staying and waiting for that reconnection to happen. And at one point, something just sparked. We held each other in a deep hug.

Somehow we got from being on different roads back into connection. Electricity was running all through me. *This is what love is: staying with it, through the tough moments until the reconnection.* Sometimes we can't do more than we're doing, but as long as we just keep *staying*, the reconnection will come back.

I really felt the importance of attunement, and also mis-attunement.

Connection and disconnection. Mis-attunement happens, but just keep staying there. Don't get tricked by the mis-attunements when there is a healthy original connection. Keep showing up for when re-attunement can come in. Otherwise, how can re-attunement happen if you leave the conversation? Friends, family members, counsellors and other members of society – this is for you too! Don't give up if there are mis-attunements! Keep staying with your emotional muscle, present and available for the re-attunement to take place.

Attunement is being present to what is happening; being aware and responsive to the verbal and non-verbal, emotional, physical elements of the person you are communicating or present with. It is also about being empathic, accepting, inviting, permissive and open to more information. Mis-attunement is when there is closing down, ignoring, invalidating and not being with the unspoken content.

Use these stories about relationships and family as an opportunity to reflect on your communication skills and where your tendency to tune out or defend is triggered. What are you or the other person needing at those moments? Sometimes we don't attune to uncomfortable content and it becomes the elephant in the room, which can leave the connection in a mis-attunement to yourself or the other, and needing to be addressed..

I can remember one part of a conversation with my daughter, to do with the past and how much it was impacting her at this time of her transition in Year 11; it was robbing her because she hadn't had that whole family unit of support, like her friends or the advantages and benefits that go with it.

Something in me came out without thinking. It came from a 'tough' or 'fierce' mother, but not a 'cruel' or 'disconnected' mother; it was as if I drew the line for her to say that these terrible things have happened, it was shocking and you lost out on lots of fronts, but that's not all of who you are. Enough. Don't let it eat you up. Don't let it define you right now. Don't let it narrow your world down. Don't let it rob you of now.

So in this new path I was building emotional muscle, which increased my capacity to engage in all my relationships, my social zone and expand every frontier of my life.

***

This is my offering for you, wherever you are in the process of changing your path or helping someone change their path. Be willing to name, validate and acknowledge all the creative, generative qualities of you, them and the world. Then be flexibly responsive to be willing to put aside those generative qualities for a time if that would get in the way of you being with your whole reality and the calling to be inside your truth.

Use your anger that you have towards the world or towards certain people to motivate and fuel the life you want. Educate relevant people on what you need or like. Do it for you, not for them. If you say, 'I am tired of being the one to educate someone,' (with that someone who has already shown they are capable of inclusiveness, acceptance, reflection and growth), *remember you are doing it for you*, not for them. Don't let your past experience of people who could not be educated get in the way of creating healthy relationships now. Reclaim who you are and your right to be seen and accepted.

This new path's focus and energy, of changing my life path, came about from using my anger in constructive ways. My anger helped me to separate, cut through and name the abuses and the wrongs and get away. My anger led me to fight and not give up when the first few lawyers and counsellors didn't know what to do to help me. My anger led me to find someone experienced to help me resolve the trauma, the overwhelm and the shock. My anger helped me unlock and restore my true self. My anger led me to say, 'You can't continue to control and ruin my life, either in the world or in my head'.

Your anger can help you unlock your (or your friend or client's) true self, being able to relax and trust – and learning to say no. The no which allows you to say yes, when it is safe to. Accessing *no* allows you to feel safe to enter even more deeply into *yes*, so you can enter into deeper layers of *yes*. Greater feelings of pleasure, joy and intimacy. Entering into deeper layers of *yes*, when we have held tightly to our no, can almost be as if we went through life in black and white and are now experiencing the world in colours so bright and pure that it can feel too much to contain.

Teenage years are a time when children are exposed to a greater 'yes' to life. When my children were teenagers I realised: how can they fully and freely transition out into the world with joy, lightness and confidence if they've got a mother inhabiting a very small world and not being fulfilled? Not that I didn't feel fulfilled. I was content being safe at home, with my girls being my world. But my girls needed to go out into the world and I needed to show them the world is a good and interesting place to be in.

The *no* and anger on my path allowed me to take healthy risks, to begin to play in the world and have my world open up. At first, it was a real challenge for me to step outside of the safe structures of mothering, study or work and open the door to building a social life. This was something that had never been accessible to me due to my family environment, being bullied at school and the abuse. I realised that I needed to go out and find my fun, so that when my children go out and have their fun, they can do that freely and not be held back worrying about me. This is part of the job on the new path: find your fun! I have had some incredible adventures and memories, which helped me become safe in the world and filled me with joy and a growing confidence. It is wonderful to have positive memories available to keep washing over you and fill you with pleasure, safety and capability rather than painful flashbacks.

So in changing the path, remember these three key things.

- Find your anger and grief and use it constructively.
- Find someone to help you. Someone to help you take healthy risks, while being able to say no and yes.
- Find a symbol, a visual/verbal reminder, which speaks to you. Something to support you in staying on track on your path. I have an elephant in my room, because as a child I learnt to not speak about the elephant in the room. It became so automatic when noticing something for it to become automatically buried. Find your elephant!

The elephant in the room is to remind me to use that information – to speak from it, act from it, feel from it. The elephant in my room reminds me to incorporate what I'm noticing with my eyes, ears and senses. The elephant can help remind you to make your own connections. Go get yourself an elephant or some symbol that resonates for you, to help you to cross those boundaries to name the unnamable.

If you want further support in how to talk to someone you love about concerns over their toxic or abusive relationship, or on how to talk to yourself and begin to change your mindset about what is really going on, read either of my books: *Urgent and Unspoken,* my short, free ebook; or my book: *From Unspoken to Spoken Conversations about the Wolf: Helping your Friend Recognise her Abusive Relationship.*

From Unspoken to Spoken is the expanded and in-depth version of the ebook.

This book is a conversation guide on what questions to ask yourself and the person you are concerned about. This book provides practical stages of communication, such as what to say and what not to say. People out of love, concern or nervousness tend to jump into having the final conversation before they have the essential series of preparatory conversations, and their friend often then doesn't want to talk about it again as the conversation has failed. Or people don't know what to say, so they don't say anything. This book sets out all the steps and questions and complements the educational information in Part 2 of *The Wolf in a Suit.*.

Chapter 6:
Where are Mother and Father?

Where were the mother and father in Little Red Riding Hood? For most of the story, Little Red Riding Hood is alone, or with the Wolf, without anyone there for support or guidance. She is in an environment that is bigger than her and her capabilities. Even as adults we can feel unskilled and overwhelmed in our environment, beyond what parents could teach or offer. How can we change this, for children, adults and for ourselves?

The absence of support from the parents to Little Red Riding Hood speaks of the child not receiving help in navigating those aspects of life; when she is faced with something bigger than her out in the world. Sometimes, unfortunately, we face this in our own home. Where can we go to learn how to respond, in ways, which are effective and protective? Who teaches us the skills required, which involve being able to recognise, understand and negotiate deception, trickery and ulterior motives? Where do we turn when we meet those people in life who aren't fair or reasonable?

If we are not learning about this at home, who teaches this out in the world? Often when it is not available in the family, we move out into the world with this lack of knowledge and seem to end up in a group also reflecting the lack of the knowledge and not know how to find what we need. *Society is a reflection of our families, and families are a reflection of our society.* So out into the world we stumble along, habituated to not seeking or not responding even when we feel or see a lack. We adapt so well that we put up with what we can't change, and continue this even when circumstances change and we have more options.

How many ways do we minimise or tell each other or ourselves to not seek, question or follow the uncomfortable and the unknown. 'You can't complain, look what happened to so-and-so, just get on with things, stop being selfish and demanding. No one else is complaining so there must be something wrong with you, this didn't happen to my sister so something must be wrong with me, don't show you don't know what to do you'll be laughed at or ridiculed …'

In Little Red Riding Hood, we only hear the mother saying the 'do-good things'. Mother is not inviting Little Red Riding Hood to consider and take into account Little Red Riding Hood's own needs or experience as part of the big picture. Is this a remnant of 'children should be seen and not heard'? Are only adult needs valued? How well do we attend to the whole of the child, and not just the outer needs?

As mentioned before, we don't hear Little Red Riding Hood's mother teach her how to navigate the tricksters and Wolves of the world. The focus is on taking care of another (her grandmother). The focus is on taking care of someone older than her. Is this the task for a young and dependent child? This is not a young woman being asked to visit her grandmother. This is a child. Does this suggest that children are sometimes asked to take care of their parents or other adults' needs? When I refer to 'taking care of', I am talking about in emotional as well as practical ways.

If we want to tell a teaching story on how to be considerate and helpful, can't we tell the story differently?

I think there is something inappropriate in this. Too often parents have a lack of being with the uncomfortable and do not know how to take a child through their experience, as they themselves do not know how to do this for themselves.

We have a society with an epidemic and inability in being with the uncomfortable and transposes some emotions as being negative, instead of recognising that feelings come out of experiences and environments. Feelings are not bad, they are messages about our experience. We have a society that is highly sophisticated, yet ill at ease on the instinctual and feeling level. A large part of our society still perceives passionate, emotional expression as 'hysterical', 'ranting', 'over the top', 'mad' or 'weak'. Our society still has difficulty differentiating between trauma, hysteria and healthy, emotional expression. When family and the reflections in society are still ill at ease with uncomfortable experiences, and intensity of feelings, we are left with narrow choices to respond either as an individual or in a collective response. Yet after the fact, or when it's too late, we express regret, outrage or disappointment.

Often, we do not have an adequate response until we have reached a major upset or catastrophe. We have a range of possible alternatives: put off, minimise, create deletions or disconnections in our thoughts (or words, feelings or actions), become depressed, fill with despair, hopelessness or become isolated.

We live in a society where the pattern of control and denial is prevalent to different degrees across many social structures: family, school, work, socialising and the legal and political systems. In this pattern there is a direct or indirect demand for one person to ignore or cover the gap for another, rather than own one's own limitations and gaps.

There is an expectation for children to accommodate an adult's limitations. We have a society where adults have perhaps buried or chosen to not own their limitations. Perhaps because they carried the burden of their own parents' gaps and are too depleted with the demands of our social structure to take time out and do their own sorting, owning and healing – and so the wound is passed on.

We have created a society where the ability to feel safe to respond is limited by shame, control and fear of rejection; and where many people have become disconnected from even knowing or showing the free flow of what their response is.

If we are truly honest, this pattern of abuse is present in many relationships. I think we prefer to identify abuse as belonging with the families we see on the news and separate our situation from theirs; yet abusive tendencies are common, but ignored. We are inside the fairy tale of the Emperor's New Clothes, where together we pretend what is happening is different to how it really is. We muddle along, and through our blindness we leave the message that what is not okay is normal.

Children know when something is not okay but when the environment acts as if it is normal or nothing wrong is happening they often adapt to their social surroundings. We have normalised the wounds of abandonment and neglect and the impact on our individual psyche and on our society. We are all covering gaps for each other, while we nurse our own wounds, minimising what we missed. But for whose sake? At what cost? Passing the gaps down? For the adult's needs, comfort or pleasure?

How can we change this for the child's sake, for our future generations, for ourselves? In our own circle of family and friends now?

Sending Little Red Riding Hood off with the basket of food does not send a message about valuing the innocent and vulnerable or with skills to take care of yourself. But you say, *children like copying adults and taking on responsibility*. There is a difference between healthy and unhealthy taking on. Where is the mindful adult ensuring that the child is not out of their depth? So they take on some responsibility with joy and pride, and guided through appropriate stages.

Where is the needed guide in this life stage out in the world, out in the woods? In one version of the story, the Woodcutter is around and temporarily prevents the Wolf from coming near her – but because there is no teaching or transferring skill for prevention and to take care of herself, she is vulnerable and taken when the Woodcutter is not around. The Woodcutter then comes in when it is too late and trauma has happened. Is this revealing a gap in our parenting and social structure? We are there, but not there to teach and transfer what we have gaps about?

The father is absent. Why? We don't hear about a father in this story. A father can be at home but still be absent. The absence is not necessarily literal, but symbolic. A passive or abusive father is still absent despite being present.

A father has a necessary role in supporting the young feminine in going out in the world. The father has the opportunity to teach those skills which are aligned with masculine attributes: to negotiate being out in the world – including developing the inner eyes to see those aspects which are aggressive, deceptive and cruel, and be given permission to prioritise and protect your reality and needs. Where is the father modelling, teaching and encouraging her to cut through the tricks and charms used out there to take advantage of the feminine attributes of feelings, tenderness and receptiveness? Where is the father honouring the feminine so she can internalise the knowledge she is worthy of protection and her needs being attended to?

This, by the way, is relevant for fathers teaching and instilling girls *and* boys to be with both their feminine and masculine attributes – after all, we all contain both. The masculine within needs to protect and honour the feminine within, irrespective of whether we are female or male.

***

The modern world and some people in the world take, take, take and just want what suits them. How are the mother and absent father supporting Little Red Riding Hood to not get swallowed up by these people, organisations and energies? Where is the modelling of healthy boundaries and providing a safe place for self-care and self-soothing being incorporated? Is his absence reflecting that he does not oppose or does not care what the mother is doing and how his daughter is shaped?

Both the mother and father are absent each in their own way and not available for the necessary development of Little Red Riding Hood. They teach Little Red Riding Hood a one-sidedness about how to be in the world. There is a focus on being nice, serving others and fitting in to group needs without objection. There is an unspoken consequence when serving others. This is filling the gaps of others' gaps and carrying their responsibilities, such as Little Red Riding Hood taking on some of the parent's duties. Why wasn't the mother going that long distance to look after her own mother? Why was a little girl doing that, through the dark and dangerous woods?

This story illustrates gaps in our social structure for the child, or the one like a child who is not skilled or resourced left alone and without resources. The story of Little Red Riding Hood also tells the story of a sick grandmother who is taken advantage of in her own vulnerability. Does this story also highlight those vulnerable adults who are ill-equipped to face Wolves, perhaps evident in elder abuse, who need a healthy society to look after the vulnerable, whether young or old?

Let's look at the inappropriateness of some expectations placed on Little Red Riding Hood and on females in life. As I said, her father didn't teach her how to negotiate the world. He didn't step in and prevent inappropriate consequences from taking place. Where was the power and capacity of the father to help Little Red Riding Hood wise up and assert herself? To be street-smart and not get tricked? Where was the permission and celebration to defy and follow one's truth and instincts, even if others are displeased?

In both versions of Little Red Riding Hood, the Wolf knows to keep away when the Woodcutter is nearby. Little Red Riding Hood is only vulnerable when the parents or the Woodcutter are not around. Innocence becomes naivety without protection.

Little Red Riding Hood's needs were not taken seriously and she was not equipped with Woodcutter skills. There was no transition to walk beside the Woodcutter so he could educate, teach, model and guide her to step into her power. The Woodcutter, an aspect of the masculine, could teach her to cut through deception and charmers, and utilise the skills and instinct required to negotiate whatever she would come across.

It was significantly wrong to send her out into the world to be exposed to all types, with no resources at all and no one to witness what she could not observe from her limited, developmental age of naivety. We all have limited areas of development, which inhibit our ability to question and have choices. How do our parents and society provide us with 'good enough' skills in the safety of our home before we are thrown out into the world? We often learn, from home and reinforced in school, to fit in and not disturb group and adult needs. Often we have to fit into a structure that is not necessarily equipped to respond to our own timing and needs.

What happens to our development when our parents have their own limitations and self-absorption? Where and how does community and society step in to educate and support, with the intention to prevent a continuation of lack and greater tragedies? How do we support future generations to be more than their previous generation? This is evolvement.

Little Red Riding Hood wasn't given the permission, skills and capacity to listen to her own instinct. When Little Red Riding Hood knocked on the door and was asked to come in, what she heard was meant to be grandmother's voice. But she *knew* the voice didn't sound like her grandmother. She knew. Her instinct said, *something's not right*. Yet, she didn't listen to her internal voice. She listened to the external voice. She listened to the voice that was trying to persuade her to not listen to her instincts, and instead please others. She listened to the external voice that was using persuasion and reassurance for their own needs and benefit.

What is it that we need, to enable that quiet inner voice to become stronger and louder than what is outside us? 'Louder', in the sense of us hearing and connecting to our voice more clearly and directly than someone else's loud voice. Quiet is not necessarily less 'right' than the outer loud voice. Bigger is not necessarily more 'true' than the soft, inner voice. There is no equation that says whatever is louder is more right. Attending to the soft, inner voice and supporting it to have its strength, into becoming a strong inner voice, is not the same as someone else's loud outer voice coming at you – because your inner voice is connected to your truth and reality.

Don't we want our children to have this trust in and strength of spirit? If we all listen to and value our truth, wouldn't relationships be either clearer and more functional, or circumnavigated out at warning signs ?

What skills do our parents need to give us and encourage us to have? What capacities do our parents need to develop to bear being wrong and acknowledge and model when they are wrong and how to self-soothe when wrong (rather than the child be the one to soothe them better for being wrong)?

What resources do our parents need to develop to allow us to object, whether we are right or wrong, and not lead to shame or rejection? To guide us to discover what we need to learn and develop when we are wrong. What skills do our parents need to develop to allow us the right to be where we are in that moment, just as they are in their imperfect self as an adult?

Of course, this doesn't mean that they don't teach us what we need to learn, but the teaching can be complementary to allowing our objection – so one is not exclusive to another. Even if the child's objections will at times be wrong, allowing us to listen to those instinctual stirrings can bring about guided learnings to discern and strengthen what to listen to – and what not to listen to.

Things are not necessarily how they seem. How do parents teach children to trust what we know, see and feel when parents themselves often deny the reality for their own purpose or out of overwhelm or confusion? This is, after all, a human dilemma and survival strategy: to keep away from discomfort. But this reaction is not necessarily in our best interests. After all, we would not start a new job, learn a sport, instrument or language if we persisted with keeping away from discomfort.

When Little Red Riding Hood was saying, 'What big ears you have,' 'What big teeth you have,' she was putting her concerns out there, but she wasn't doing it in the way that was protective of her. She was seeking a reality check from something that she was mistrustful of.

There's something flawed there: that the place where she goes to check information is the very place where there is something not quite right. It would have been better for her to say to herself, when she's knocking at the door, 'Hold on, this doesn't sound or feel right. I need to return home, because this does not sound like the person that I know to be my grandmother. Even if I am wrong, it is better to not take the risk. My mother will want me to, above all, look after myself, if I am scared or uncertain. It won't be catastrophic if I make a mistake, but entering could be catastrophic.'

Leaving when she hesitated at the door would have been a better option instead of walking into the place that holds risk. So many women I speak with have shared this knowledge, now that they have escaped the Wolf: they knew early of warning signs where they had felt caution and concern but overrode it in entering a relationship with a Wolf.

The childhood experience of not following the 'invisible' quiet truth becomes serious when we are an adult in our relationships, career or in the legal system and have learnt to ignore the soft and the quiet which does not immediately or necessarily prove itself in visible ways, yet is still true.

I always tell my clients it is far easier to address things when they are little, at the first step. Don't turn yourself inside out as to whether or not that was right or wrong; just keep listening and acting from the little/soft. If you are wrong, the likelihood is that the situation can be returned to and this time with a deeper clarity and sense of trust or safety, because it is okay to listen to yourself and follow through even without 'visible' proof. Turning yourself inside out is often a sign something is not okay. There is a conflict in your system and there needs to be space to identify what the conflict is about.

Is the conflict about needing to move away from something that you are getting warning signs about, or is the conflict about wanting to move towards something, which leaves us feeling vulnerable?

What are the signs and signals that help us identify the different types of conflict? Or do we feel conflict and react because we are missing a particular skill or resource to be with the discomfort and 'sort the beans' of what is going on. When we jump into things reactively and do not develop the links and information that is between the conflict and what we are seeing, sensing, feeling, hearing and our thoughts and meanings we inevitably get caught.

You can prevent many events by saying 'no' when something doesn't feel right. *I will not open the door to more contact. I will not send mixed signals.* Why do we wait for the subtle sign to become bigger and create problems? This could have been Little Red Riding Hood – it could have been me, when I left home with unresolved fear and anxiety on that night at the party.

How many times as parents do we force our children via social niceties to betray their soul, their body, their feelings with someone they would not feel compelled to voluntarily and spontaneously touch or connect to intimately? Why do we minimise the experience in the moment? Why don't we teach our children a third alternative to the 'yes' or the 'uncomfortable no' overloaded with rejection or shame about 'making' someone (an example of blame and over-responsibility imposed on someone else) else feel uncomfortable?

The third alternative is 'no' given with support, pride and ease to tune in and disallow. How much permission do we give our children to be able to follow their mood and their experience of the energy of the other person or themselves on the day to respond reflexively, instead of in a fixed and compulsive way? Let children guide the kind of closeness they feel good about. Isn't that what we want for them as adults? Isn't this proactive towards building healthy relationships? Why can't children show what they like and don't like and we respect it?

How comfortable can a child or teenager (female or male) or even adult be in saying, 'No, I don't like the way that person is talking to me,' and just leave or name a boundary? Why do we endure, stay silent and tolerate? Who does this serve?

Make life simpler for yourself; life is complicated enough with things we can't control. Control what you can and be around people where communication is respected, clear, open and direct. Where questions can be named, responded to and valued. You don't have to be constantly on guard, sorting through madness over what their words or actions mean. Who wants to be exposed to someone else's attitudes and actions that don't feel good, create confusion and leave you unclear, doubting and having to deal with questions and conflicts that arise from their 'hard work behaviour'? The hard work of sorting through the mind games and madness of, *were you too sensitive*, *did you say something wrong*, and so on. How often do we jump out of our own skin and listen to those 'social', 'other' or 'family' voices, which want us to be the way that pleases others?

Instead, surround yourself with people whom you feel relaxed around and feel comfortable with. Surround yourself with those who want you to listen to your soft inner voice, those little stirrings and want you to act on them. Those people who don't want things to get drawn out until it is a big, intense drama. Don't wait for 'it' to get bigger and snowball into something bigger.

We can get caught in the mindset of 'now it is big, it should not be ignored' or 'okay, this is serious, I need to act on it now.' *The essence of concern is the same, whether it is big or little – it is founded on what is not okay.* The only difference is how much the snowball has accumulated over time.

Being able to respond early on is far easier. There is less snowball accumulation. It is often not as large or intense as there are fewer events, memories and effects to deplete energy, beliefs and behaviours. When you respond early, the consequence of what you do generally isn't going to be as huge, and so it's going to be less stressful, less complicated.

With parents who are present we can develop a Woodcutter Within, a solid sense of self which can trust our own reality: our own feelings, thoughts and experience. When our reality is received, incorporated and responded to with respect and regard, we can grow up confident, secure and solid in our own experience, needs and expression. When we have not had this optimal upbringing, find and learn from people who model those skills we are lacking. If you don't feel confident to be among these people you are at risk of being caught. Who can you find and trust to help you bridge to the circle of people you want around you?

Take yourself off the hook that you've got to keep over-extending yourself to other people and situations. Listen and trust yourself. These are the kinds of messages that Little Red Riding Hood needed to have received from her mother and father – and this is the kind of message that I needed to receive verbally and non-verbally from my parents.

Where were my mother and father before the snowball that my life accumulated to? I have mentioned a bit about my childhood and I think it is important to take some time to explain a bit more so you have a greater understanding. Why? So you can start to develop questions about your own life and important people around you. To support you to start to ask the relevant questions and ask for what you or another person needs as well as to repair what has been neglected and managed.

It's really important for me to say that my parents did the best they could. This is not meant to be a tearing down of all of who they are. I am holding what was good and that can stay intact. This is what I say with clients. Let us put the good to one side, so it is not tarnished by what unfolds. The good does not take away from the necessity to be with what your parents were unconscious to or limited by. *So you can move beyond your parents' unconsciousness.*

We are not skilled in our society of being with both the good *and* the bad. It is almost as if when we name the bad we fear it means we are betraying the good, instead of coming to terms with the reality that both exist. We fill with guilt and want to include their good to justify. This is an indicator we have jumped out of our reality and skin, into the reality and skin of our parents – and their defence and justification. In this leap out of ourselves, we have inevitably denied the full extent of how it was for us. In this abandonment of our experience we leave our experience incomplete. This incompletion means we have difficulty to integrate and move on, as we are no longer with ourselves.

When a child is with their experience they will have a strong response. As adults we may find the intensity of a child's strong response in the moment to be amusing and out of context; but for the child, that is all there is in the moment and the fullness of their affect is true and valid.

As we grow up we might think we have developed sophisticated responses and don't have intense feelings, but I beg to differ. I think we still have the depth of feelings and it is not that they don't exist, but we need to engage with them differently so our outward expression is the regulated response but we allow the depth of the feelings of being human to have their own space, truth and expression. Otherwise we are at risk of extreme feelings, moods, addictions, impulses and obsessions gripping us.

Admit it – we are deep, feeling creatures. Even if our thoughts can be very sophisticated, we still have a depth of soul aching to be known, whether through depression or obsession, poetry, music, art, drugs or something else. Our language illustrates the depth of our soul; we are stabbed in the back, torn apart and broken into pieces, ravaged with despair in a black hole.

I am not going to name the good things, just as I can't name all the details from my family as this book would go on forever otherwise. The bad needs to stand alone and not be minimised by the good. This book is a revealing of what was not named – the elephant in the room, in family and society, the consequence and an unpacking of the impact. What we don't acknowledge has power. What we don't acknowledge is still there – we bump into it again and again. When we can't respond to the elephant in the room and don't acknowledge its existence, abuse continues.

***

People often think, speak and act in deletions. Our choices and behaviours reflect those deletions. We need to say things as they really are. After all, isn't that what being an adult is about? Adults who can be with the whole truth of what is going on; with the power, skills and choices to bear the big picture and respond.

This is quite different to the situation of a child, who is dependent and still unregulated in all their feelings and thoughts. They are limited by their own developmental capabilities as well as limited by their own parents' capacity to be with the big picture; and therefore by how much of the big picture is available to them.

By deletions I mean not being with the complete, specific, clear statement of what is going on. For example, 'She rejected me' could more accurately (and without the deletion) be, 'I feel rejected when she was tired and went to bed.' We can then see we have joined two separate experiences and compacted them as one creating a cause and blame that is not accurate. Then we can become curious about our sensitivity to rejection when someone is unavailable or taking care of their own needs.

Trauma, stress or overwhelm leads us to compact, reduce, generalise, nominalise, minimise and delete information about concerns. Listen to those concerns and untangle the things we have linked through experience that are not necessarily true. Trust yourself. For example, 'He is angry at me' could more accurately (and without the deletion) be, 'He is angry because he doesn't like that I am not prioritising his needs over my needs'.

Let your concerns guide you to find the right person to support you and build your emotional muscle so you can respond in an optimal way rather than in the 'coping' survival response. This is one of the deep layers of how I got caught: staying with the deletions and not taking in the true and bigger picture. Non-verbally and verbally I was encouraged and rewarded to listen to my parents' concerns, interests and reality through their 'absolute beliefs' and turn down the dial to my own reality and needs. There was the non-verbal message to take their deletions as the 'truth', which left the child me with an experience of neglect and abandonment, and where a child experiences some consistent form of rejection and possible threat to collude and maintain the deletion's perspective.

I was a good student at school. I was quiet, studious and conscientious. I knew how to work hard. 'Conscientious' was often what was written in my school reports. I was doing my tasks efficiently and carefully. There were deletions in the behaviours and attitudes to being vigilant to please others at school just as I did at home. Make sure your conscientiousness is motivated not only for an 'other' but also for desires, experiences and interests of the 'self.'

The conscientious child in me was so eager to please because she was so hungry to be seen and loved. The child within any adult who is suffering from relationship abuse in reflection can often see a connection between a gap in the way they were parented and their relationship story. It is really important to acknowledge when the child in you, did not receive what you developmentally needed from your parents. Many children don't. Not all, but too many.

If I speak from the perspective and understanding of my parents, I betray my child self's reality. I repeat the wound of having to grow up fast inside other peoples' realities and not being able to take on the reality and the needs of my own experience. If I don't speak up about the child's experience, I am continuing to protect my parents and not the helpless child who lived through this. The child who was imprinted by these failures and whose reality fell through the cracks – and was left vulnerable to be caught by a Wolf due to an invisible sense of self. The wound gets carried on and onto our children ... unless we speak up and face our gaps as families and communities.

If there are not enough voices speaking this truth of needs not being met, the needs get muffled. These needs are then made to be wrong, bad, demanding and shameful. We bury them and fill ourselves with self-hate and disgust for our intrinsic, developmental needs. We need to make it acceptable to say what is really going on behind closed doors in families, for the sake of our desire for a healthy community.

So I am proud to be part of a movement to name the unspoken and share real stories about families. I do not believe that in meeting women in all ranges of professions I am having some freak experience of meeting all the women who have been in abusive relationships, and that somewhere else in the world this is not happening. I believe abuse and neglect is not the rarity, but runs through the fabric of many relationships and generations, just as trauma does.

Both my parents came with a whole lot of trauma from war experiences, from needing to leave their home country learning the English language and integrating into a new culture. They had their own grief, losses, challenges and difficulties to belong and thrive in the world and in a new country. They both found their own ways of withdrawing or coping in the world. Both of them in different ways, yet each acting as if we as a family lived a normal life.

As an adult I can understand more layers of their experience. As a child I didn't know about those layers and could only perceive and make sense of them in my limited way, which influenced how I could be in the world. As a child I couldn't do this sophisticated perceiving and I believed the way they were was a reflection of me. That I was unlovable and too much. I believe every parent has a responsibility to be with the parts of their lives that do not sit comfortably with them, for the sake of their children and their grandchildren.

As a child I could not make meaning of the layers of my parents, that they could not as adults, even make meaning about. We act as if children are not exposed to what is going on, as if just because they don't have sophisticated language that they are immune from the impact of their environment. I was still impacted by their relationship, their past, as well as those aspects, which lay in their unconscious, unrelated and disowned. Those memories, feelings, thoughts and experiences they could not integrate or metabolise were floating around, whether they could relate to them or not. My child self absorbed this.

We know the first six years as children we are in a hypnagogic state, where we can't filter and we just absorb. A child that young is not able to distinguish the conscious from the unconscious. All is present. Much is absorbed.

When a parent does not own and integrate their experience, the unconscious, uncomfortable, unbearable material is untethered, alienated from its context. The material is not anchored to who it belongs to. The child is like a sponge and the disowned, disconnected experience of the parent is present to the child, just as the conscious experience of the parent is present to the child. The context or meaning may be lost to the child but the imprint of the unbearable and uncomfortable still comes through and the child absorbs the imprint. When this material is unrelated to, this imprint is impersonal and becomes scary. It can intensify and take on a bigger projection.

I could not know the context, but what I did know was the feeling of the looks they would give me, the tone of voice, the actions they would take. I couldn't differentiate what was related to me and what was not. As a child you take it to be about you. I grew up with certain perceptions about me, about them and about the level of safety I could have with them. Unfortunately over time, these were never reclaimed, repaired or addressed.

I grew up in a strict environment. We didn't really have a social life other than visiting grandparents and one set of cousins. I wasn't allowed to speak English to my father; he wanted us to speak in the language that he had grown up with, so that we could be bilingual, but the problem was that our mother did not speak this language. It's very hard to learn a language, speak, connect and share about your day when you're little and your dad is away with work. When because of your age you go to bed early and you're not allowed to speak in the language that you know. It is very hard to build a relationship when you can't talk.

This lack of conversation meant that I also couldn't speak with my paternal grandparents, as I was not allowed to speak in English with them. They followed my father's instructions and would not speak to me if I did not use their language. This rigid rule meant that through my whole childhood I had extremely limited connections with my grandparents and aunt and uncle, despite seeing them weekly. I felt imprisoned by the language barrier and the strict rules. I can understand that the ability to speak bilingually is fantastic. It is just that the way we were expected to learn was harsh and demanding, not a connecting, special experience. There was not enough play and lightness in our family.

As a child, conversations with my father were serious, difficult and limited. I experienced his face, tone and words as frowning and disapproving. Communication was just that – communication, not spontaneous and only a response to his instructions.

I recall only two conversations through my childhood, both very brief: one where my father was enquiring about my secondary school choices and the other when he was connecting to me: he bought me a book he thought I would like to read. I grew used to being alone and not understood. I grew up not expecting people to want to get to know me. After all, no one put effort into me, so I mustn't be worth it. I grew up feeling unimportant. Those every day conversations are so important.

It is hard as an adult for me to sit with two contrasting experiences of my father and so I don't know how I could integrate this as a child. It is a difficult concept to be with the polarities of being hungry for and wanting comfort from the 'ideal father', so wanting to sit in your father's arms in the car at night going home from our grandparents or sitting with him to watch our favourite movies at his parents place. Did I want to sit with him because I truly liked him - this is so unspeakable and unthinkable to say - or because I liked the movie, didn't want to offend him and because my cousins and sisters weren't including me in their games. I didn't feel safe or comfortable with him, yet these pictures of childhood pressured me to add positive information to the picture, in stark contrast with his stern rules and self-absorption which left me feeling an aversion to this dark and distant figure.

As a child I felt invisible. I fell through the cracks. There were language and communication barriers with both parents. My mother was in so much trauma from her war-torn childhood that she struggled to be a mother, let alone to manage the home and be fully in her marriage. Even if she was there, she was not present. She was a shell. She would spend hours meditating and being with her spiritual beliefs, which I imagine held, supported and guided her and also very much influenced her communication with me. We were lucky our Nana was over so often to help out and bring cooked food.

I remember being left alone as a baby. I remember me standing, crying, holding the bars inside my cot, and her walking past my open door, left alone as if I didn't exist.

When she would talk to me, her words were not about connecting to me or how my day was. Her words were not about communication, but about explaining spiritual laws. To me now it was her way of controlling her environment, making meaning and distancing herself from what she didn't know what to do with. Her words were about how God needed me to be (how she needed me to be). Quiet. Obedient. Reflecting her as being good and whole.

I can remember one day being seated at the table with her. I was busy talking to her. I stopped abruptly halfway when I saw her start meditating. She praised me when she came out of her meditation. I was 'doing the right thing'.

Her meditation would interrupt many moments. She was not in tune with her social or relational surroundings. She could not find another way to self-soothe that would give her the opportunity to connect with me in a personal and warm way.

I learnt that I was not a relevant part of the picture. I was hungry for attention. When she did praise me it was like food nourishing my soul. This praise led me to do more of how she wanted me to be. This meant me being silent and helping her in any way she wanted. I was starving for love, and the attention and praise for being quiet was better than nothing. After all, if she felt better, then I could feel better.

I became creative in finding a way to connect with her in an attempt to 'wake' her from her dissociated spirited states. I was starving for connection. I had to find a way to be rewarded with a smile, eye contact or some sense of pleasure, love and connection between us. So I would say, 'Guess what?' 'What?' she would ask. 'I love you,' I would whisper.

My mother had an all-pervasive commentary about living your life the way God wants you to, that God sees all. God would not want me to be angry or feel hate, and if I did, 'He was watching all the time' – I would be punished and return again and again to Earth. I just wanted her approval, so I wanted to 'pass the class' and do the right thing by not being angry. Therefore my anger and protest had to go underground. I had to be pleasing and happy. I wasn't allowed to be angry. Anger was bad.

Growing up, it seemed that my father was the only one in our family who was allowed to be angry. He was the loudest and the most frightening. When you have both parents who don't want you to be angry, your level of confidence and sense of self are limited because you can't be an authority on your own feelings and boundaries.

As a child I knew of my mother's fragility before any cognitive awareness. But that knowing can't protect or immunise a child from the pain and impact of an absent mother or disembodied words and actions, disconnected from relating.

Later, when I asked my father as an adult about our childhood, he said, 'What could I do? I was at work.' If only he had been able to acknowledge rather than blame or defend, maybe the pain could have been held and grieved. If only he had been able to check in with me when he came home from work and have a 'real' conversation, maybe things would have been different. Later I came to realise my father was quite anxious, worried a lot and was sad about significant parts of his life. His way of managing seemed to be to criticise in an attempt to have some control.

As an adult I can understand he had his own history and challenges, as we all do. I can see now his criticism was his way to protect me. I want to name these failings to the child and the consequential challenges because I think as a society, we need to look at our own anxiety – our own grief, helplessness, anger and trauma – and not deceive ourselves that we can manage it or imagine that no one else is noticing or affected. We are not hermits. People in our life will be affected. It is inevitable. There is not enough support for those impacted in the many contexts in life, abuse, trauma, war and refugee and immigration displacement, alcohol and mental illness. The ripple effect continues.

When we deny reality, the process is blocked and the natural process of development and change is interrupted. We need a society that provides a way of being with the unbearable and not being shamed for it. We need a society where people around us don't pretend that everything is okay. We need a society where there is support for those who are vulnerable.

For many years I struggled to come to terms with my childhood. We are meaning-making creatures and I was trying to make meaning about my life. It was hard to make sense of the conflicting messages. I needed to know what was going on so I could be clear about what was real and how I could trust my reality. I needed to know what my thoughts, feelings and reality were so I could be mobilised into action, rather than remaining lost, frozen and desperately seeking 'love' from the wrong places.

I struggled with the knowledge that not everyone who has such life challenges imposes such cold, harsh judgments and actions on their children, to the point of disowning their flesh and blood. Both my parents have disowned me, though my father did re-attune and repair for the mis-attunement. My mother never wanted to repair, despite my numerous attempts. My father, in hindsight, realised his enforcement of no English was not the best decision. It is such a shame he remained inflexible and could not acknowledge his error earlier. What a profound modelling, healing and closeness that would have brought us.

I am naming these events because being caught in an abusive relationship often is not an isolated event – it is a series of events. The way I was related to by both parents was part of the shaping that kept me vulnerable and open to being abused. I was conditioned to be the way others wanted me to be, and to not show anything that could affect them – or I would be rejected, shamed or punished. It was almost as if 'love' was imprinted as danger, fear and instability, and not being able to get away and this was what my system responded to as normal.

Silence, denial, power and control are so dangerous. As an adult, when I would speak up to members of my family there was a backlash. I felt I was left to carry the burden of the family because no one wanted to share my reality. I became the scapegoat, the black sheep bearing the gaps in the family. So I was rejected and left to carry the unnamable so the rest of the tribe could, in some sense, keep on as 'normal', survive. 'That is where there is something wrong – over there in that person, not in the family.' In the survival pattern, there can be relief that it is not you who is being targeted, which can lead you to not speak up for the scapegoat …

Growing up, both my parents were quite spiritual, though in very different ways. They both valued obeying God, being 'good' and not being angry – which sounds nice, yet this was a black and white prescription shaped to benefit what they needed from their environment to cope, rather than a pure expression of faith. I have nothing against the values of leading a life of love and respect for religion. As an adult, I live a spiritually rich life. But my experience growing up was that religion and the idea of god was used to dominate and oppress.

The god that I grew up with from both parents was the punishing god from the Old Testament. It was a god about black or white, right or wrong, 'don't displease'. It wasn't a forgiving god, nor an understanding or compassionate god. There was no accepting god – 'that was okay', 'it's not catastrophic'. It wasn't that kind of god. I grew up with messages of not being allowed to say or do. I was not allowed to object. I was not allowed to say no to either my father or my mother. I was not allowed to have my own power.

Again, I am naming this to illustrate the impact and consequences of what parents expose children to. I am sure my parents did not intend or want to send these messages, but children do not necessarily receive messages in the way parents intend when they have a limited, developing sense of self. Children are powerless, dependent for survival, and have not finished developing on all levels to be able to understand the nuances and intricacies of communication and complexes.

As parents, we need to hold our child in our awareness when we speak to them, mindful of their visible cues in response to our behaviours and check in on their understanding of our communication and relationship. We need to reflect on what message we are communicating in our words, tone and behaviours. We need a fine attunement to how they will turn themselves inside out to say and do what they think we want from them to keep us emotionally stable.

A child's capacity to receive the true message is compromised not only by their developmental capacity but also by the unresolved emotional pain that is visible in the parent's eyes, tone and behaviours. When a parent's unresolved or unconscious emotional pain is not integrated, and instead leaks out from those stressed internal places; this chaos stains the child. When the parent does not attune and repair, the child is left alone to manage this mess. The child believes it is theirs and it is too much for a child to metabolise and integrate.

My mother, with all her war trauma and other conditions, couldn't cope with being in the marriage, with having four young children and with battling her inner demons. I learnt on a very deep level that for my mother to cope with four children, she had to collapse the four of us into one to manage (she later explained this to me). Growing up we couldn't have separate identities in her experience, and we couldn't have separate needs. It was as if when something happened to one, then that was it; the rest of us didn't need it, or as if by osmosis we must have all received it. If one thought something, it must be the way all four of us thought. There was a denial of instinct and differences. I grew up without a sense of self. Her war trauma weighed heavily on me.

When I was very young I would have nightmares and wake kicking and screaming. I was terrified of being attacked; I saw evil male faces laughing at me from the toilet and bedroom windows and coming out from the showerhead. I was terrified of this evil male face that was always there in my most private times and places. I felt intruded upon and terrified.

I would come out of the shower and my whole body would feel like there was something lurking under my skin. I could feel an inner scream but I knew to be quiet, so I would scream inside. I would itch all over my body. The minute I would rub one area, the itch was in another location. This was indescribably excruciating. I felt hysterical but I could not show it. It would torture me for what seemed forever. Every day, but only after my shower. I would plead for my younger sister to come into the bathroom with me as I never wanted to be alone. I was terrified. (This was never explained through shower products as I tried numerous organic and natural ones as an adult. It did end after my deep therapy process and then the occasional occurrence ended after I painted my shower scene for the Dax Collection exhibition of children of the children from the Holocaust.)

Walking to school, I would constantly look behind me for the predator that I was expecting to be there. At home, when I was alone, I was looking behind doors, cupboards and dark spaces for the lurking predator. I saw it in shadows and behind doors. I was always checking. I was never at rest except when I was in my room with the door shut (except that Dad would keep re-opening my door), reading my Enid Blyton stories and other books.

I was bullied all through school, from kindergarten until I left high school at sixteen. I didn't have friends. I was so quiet and withdrawn. I guess I was an easy target to be picked on, to be scapegoated. I was quiet, I wore glasses, I was dressed in hand-me-down clothes and my hair was cut like a boy's (mum was the hairdresser). I felt awkward; I didn't fit in and didn't know how to talk to people.

My mother would talk about spirits, about Jesus and UFOs and about who she 'really' was. She'd say that you can walk through walls if you want to. There were lots of things she said that really scared me and were too much for me to hear as a little girl. She was scared of the world and she passed that fear on to me.

One day the cousins rang to ask if I wanted to go see a movie with them. I was excited. I didn't have much recollection of them reaching out to me before. I was usually left out. Mum spoke to me about the movie being scary and the risk of someone jabbing a needle into me at Flinders Street Station. I didn't go. Maybe she was right that I would have been scared by the movie: Jaws. It is just a shame that there was no suggestion to help organise another occasion with my cousins with a more suitable movie and bridge to my limited social self.

I had no one to talk to or to play with, to be a carefree child with other than my sisters, but as we had learnt to act as though what we had lived in was normal, it impacted on the way we could play and interact together.

We were really good at playing mummies and daddies or schools, but these were games with structure and rules and being a grown up or quiet at 'school'. Our environment didn't allow us to play beyond those structured games. Play where we could be the innocent child: spontaneous, noisy, messy, adventurous, mischievous, wild, loud, intense and immersed in a magical, imaginary world.

I do have beautiful memories of childhood games with my younger sister, who I shared a bedroom with. Playing hopscotch and jumping sticks outside with my sister. I remember taking it in turns with all my sisters to stand on the mattress at the end of the bed, and my eldest sister grabbing my legs and falling backwards onto the mattress – they were rare moments of squealing with delight. I remember playing busily with Barbie dolls and paper dolls, making them clothes, and a game with cherry trees. I remember making treasure maps with my younger sister. We'd scrunch up our hand drawn map and burn the edges. We would take each other on a treasure hunt to find some toy wrapped up we no longer wanted which became our treasure 'gift'. That was fun. I remember Dad teaching me how to play Backgammon and battleships, which I loved. I remember Mum teaching me cross-stitch, which I absolutely adored and found soothing.

I remember writing stories and poems and listening to my other sister's stories and poems. That was good. But all my poems were sad poems. I can remember my Nana saying, 'Write a happy poem.' I couldn't. Everything was bleak in my poems. Every poem was dark and despairing. When I tried to write one happy poem for her, it came out so sappy and didn't have the heart or depth of my other poems.

I have lots of memories on my own: trying to find a tree I could climb in our front or backyard, with not much luck. Longing to be in nature, loving throwing the ball against the wall over and over again, playing catch on my own. Hammering nails on a piece of wood and enjoying the connection between the hammer, nail and wood. I loved collecting stones and putting coloured tissue paper in different jars, watching the colour come out into the water. I enjoyed being in the sun and moving.

I remember playing with my doll, tucking her in my blue and white pram, feeling an enormous and deep love for her, so full and strong. Her name was Lucy and would shake her head no, as she didn't like spinach!

My maternal grandmother often fed us, showed love to us and encouraged us to write. Through my Nana I felt there was someone who wanted me to be happy and liked to do things that would make me smile and feel good: give me a chocolate milk drink, a teddy bear biscuit and a hug, dressing up like a little kid and being silly, taking us to the movies and asking about my poems. She was the only adult who tried to connect to me in my world as a child, rather than me having to go into the adult world to connect to my parents or any other adult. To me she seemed the one constant when I was little who was interested in my existence.

It felt to me that my parents only wanted to know if I was doing well at school or doing my jobs that needed to be done at home. They didn't ask how *I* was.

There was a family joke that I wouldn't eat; my father would come home from work and go on a hunt to find where I had hidden my food. He would eat my soggy honey sandwich when he found it. I would stand there silent. I couldn't eat at school. I don't recall either parent ever saying, 'I'm worried that you're not eating,' or, 'How come you don't eat your food at school?'

My parents' pain was too much for them – they didn't have room to move beyond that and see me. I grew up without friends, without a sense of self and without the skills to be able to interact with people, feel relaxed and experience support. I felt invisible and so unlovable. When you feel unloved, you feel ugly and unwanted. I did not feel the experience and support of, 'I want you in my life,' or interest in me.

I remember as a child occasionally putting my arm in a sling. I never injured my arm. I just felt wounded. I would silently walk around the house with my sling.

They did not show interest or curiosity to get to know me or show concern, such as why I didn't have friends or that I never invited anyone over. I remember feeling sad when I was a young adult to realise that my parents actually did not know me. They didn't know what I liked, if I had friends or anything about me other than I liked reading and I was a fast reader.

I had two very brief relationships as a teenager before I left home. These milestone events are important to share, because each story weaves its own messages and insights about what was unnamable. The new reveals the old. The good reveals the bad.

Adolescence began and in getting older, my sexuality: my libidinal life energy opened me up. I spoke up, wanting to join my older sister in the scouting group she was going to. It was hard work to get permission. My sister didn't want me to join. But finally, out from the famine of no friends I found a group I began to connect with.

Sexual energy offered me energy and courage, and opened me to the opportunity to meet someone who wanted me and was interested in me. I look back now and see how young I was in my first love interest. It felt so wonderful and so exciting to have someone interested in me, and who I was interested in. It was so special and I enjoyed our closeness. The connection was quite innocent and there was no pressure or urgency.

One day, as it happens, he went away with his family over the summer holidays. He was away for what felt a very long time. While he was away I 'hooked up' with another guy in our scouting friendship circle. Still from such a naive place. I was content to just sit on this other guy's lap; maybe there was a kiss but I don't remember one! Nothing more. My boyfriend came back and found out, and that was the end of our relationship. I never protested, of course. I had done wrong.

Now I can understand what actually happened on a deeper layer. When he left me for the holidays, the younger me felt abandoned and back alone in the world, in the desert of non-existence – of not being seen and cared for

– and it was unbearable. I needed the comfort and the contact of someone to feel some sense of love and safety. I couldn't bear to return to aloneness.

Sexuality was a way I could be loved. Funny how you learn that, even when we didn't have a TV. I was hungry for love and when there is not much around you find creative ways to get love, closeness and touch.

My second relationship was a bit less innocent. He was a little bit older than me and from my 'clinically good' life he was what I might call a 'bad boy'. Not really and truly a bad boy, just doing those things older teenage boys might do. Well-behaved in the appropriate circumstances but cheeky and adventurous when out with the boys. He was full of life and good-looking – I just loved being with him. He wasn't very skilled in or probably interested at that younger age, about the benefits of good communication in a relationship; he was more about having fun with the boys. When he broke up with me I was devastated and heartbroken. I fell sick and I missed exams at school. I had fantasised about a fairy tale life with him. I wrote a poem about my love for him and felt I would love him forever. I was heartbroken.

I returned to school feeling even more alone and lonely, struggling with the pressure looming ahead of what subjects to choose for the following year. I was getting older and questions were present in school paperwork to choose next year's subjects and how this would determine my future. The counsellor at the private school was no help. Neither of my parents were available to guide me or make the time to help talk me through what next. I felt even more lost and alone; there were no options. I didn't know where to turn. Everything felt hard work with no pleasure in sight. All I craved was love and company.

Thank goodness it was now the end of that school year. Summertime, at the beach. I met this young man on a hot summer's day. We connected without even really speaking. It was as if we just knew each other and were meant to be with each other. He just wanted to be with me and I just wanted to be with him. I had found someone I could bond with. For the first time in my life, I was truly not alone in the world. From the day we met, we spent every day together until about the last month before the relationship ended.

I remember when we first moved in together, just over one week later I stood at the front door to greet him when he drove home after work for our first night living together. I was naked under my nightgown. I was sixteen. I couldn't speak, flirt or play but I could share my body.

I would think thoughts and I wouldn't share them. I was probably so used to no one being interested or connecting to me, so when the thoughts of connection came they just floated away. It was as if just thinking was a completion and all of the communication that was required. The next step of sharing my thoughts was non-existent and unnecessary. I was so used to being in a world of my own that I didn't know how to connect.

Each story adds more layers to understanding how the vulnerabilities were built and how someone can get caught in family violence. Being in a family where there wasn't social interaction, growing up through school and family without social interactions, not being able to be expressive or be angry, and because of not feeling loved and seen, I was not equipped on how to interact with or protect myself from others.

When you have two parents with their own traumas and dislocation from their own country and war, and unable to connect with me, I was not equipped socially to be in the world. So I fell into my first relationship with an innocence and eagerness.

I had parents who couldn't connect with each other and couldn't connect with me. I grew up not being able to connect to myself or to adequately understand, for example, when I missed my first boyfriend. I didn't have the space to have the response, 'Okay, that's understandable and these are ways you can take care of yourself when you're missing someone.' I didn't have those self-care skills and capacities, so I just fell from one situation to another.

Later in life when I saw my psychotherapy teachers interacting, my spontaneous wonder made sense: *oh, is that what it is like to be in relationship.* I had been alienated as a child, having two parents that were neither personal nor relational. Two parents who both struggled in different ways to be in the world and built structures to hold and manage their anxieties and insecurities. So it was not surprising that I ended up in my first long term relationship with a man who I later discovered didn't like the world very much and wanted to stay hidden away – and then next a man who pretended the world was the dangerous thing he could protect me from and hide me from the world, instead of the reality that he was the danger.

I had received a reinforcing message from childhood and the two long-term relationships that the world is not a friendly place and men are not responsible, safe or appropriate. That they can't be trusted and women are there to accommodate the man. It is not about the woman's reality – she stays hidden.

***

Let's move forward to when I left the Wolf. I say Wolf because I don't like to say 'the abusive relationship', because to me the term 'abusive relationship' distorts things. Saying 'abusive relationship' is not placing the abuse where it belongs. It belongs to him, not to the relationship. Yes, the relationship was tainted by abuse, but I was not contributing to or creating an abusive relationship.

I also say 'Wolf' because one, I don't want to say his name (for my safety) and two, I don't want to say 'abusive man' and talk about him as being nothing but abusive. Irrespective of me not wanting to be in a relationship with him, he is more than the abusive part of him, though it seemed to me that he made a choice to let that part of him rule his life and future.

Yes, I had been ripe for capture. There were complications that had developed around love, aversion, misuse of love (and pseudo–love), anger and power. The difference between a child's experience of love and pseudo-love: when something has been interpreted or named as love that has not been sorted through. The misuse of love became messy and confusing, especially with me being a young adult hungry for love. I was naive with not knowing how to extricate myself from pseudo-love and not being able to differentiate the difference. We explore love much more deeply in 'Bluebeard's Seduction'.

We are building a list on what a child needs to be healthy, have a healthy sense of self and have healthy relationships. Play. Being seen. Talking and checking in. Attunement and re-attunement. Encouragement to be yourself and different. Checking what you need to grow and helping make that happen. Encouragement to enjoy your body and its strength and capabilities. A parent who is willing to reflect and work on their own shadow.

Shadow is an interesting thing: my father has difficulty being with my perspectives when they challenge his, the conversation gets shut down or abruptly changed to a topic of his choice; yet he has run a very, successful men's group for nearly thirty years. My mother taught art classes to children in a home for disadvantaged children but couldn't play with us. It can be very valuable to look at your strengths and shadows. Or ask someone you love or trust, their perspective of your shadow as it can be difficult to see it for yourself. I am lucky I have my daughters to remind me of my shadow!

The child needs a non-shaming other. An allowing other that can give us permission to experiment and take risks. A permissive other that opens the space to be big enough for both of us to be big and powerful, no matter our age. An other that allows us to be able to identify what's good and what's not good, and how to take steps about that. Otherwise we have constant levels of inner conflict and are left walking on eggshells.

We can feel and know what's not okay, but when we don't have the permission to bridge to our reality, make the connections or have the space to reveal to other what is okay and what is not okay, we can be caught in limbo. Being in limbo can mean we are vulnerable to remaining walking on eggshells, which can lead to crazy situations like relationship violence.

When we are inside relationship violence, and the circle of people in our life around us are not reaching out and recognising some version of what's going on, there is starvation through the whole system, not just in the relationship with the Wolf.

When we don't grow up with a rich environment of people who are nourishing and nurturing us on how to be with all the aspects of being human, both pleasant and unpleasant, we become vulnerable to being lost in a desert and starving. There is no pool to drink from to revive the self. Our society and many families have gone so far into 'I' that we have lost the 'we' and the desire to contribute for our heart's pleasure to the benefit of our community and the emotional muscle to be with the uncomfortable.

The child needs to know there is nothing wrong with having feelings or thoughts that are upset or angry. It's part of life; part of how we're affected on this journey of being alive. However, when we have parents who don't have the capacity to support us in being with these feelings and thoughts, then we can fall through the cracks. We need parents that let us know uncomfortable feelings and thoughts are just information. If parents can't be with their own painful or uncomfortable process of the informing thoughts and feelings, the family system is blocked. Parents may involuntarily blame, project, punish or deny to avoid seeing or feeling their own discomfort.

Children need to know that whatever we experience, it is our system giving us information about something that's going on for us. How you experience what you experience is neither right nor wrong. It just is, either pleasant or unpleasant at different times and here to tell you something.

When parents are not able to provide a mindful curiosity about what's going on, there is no guide to teach us to enquire and learn about what we can do about it. When all this is not happening, life becomes tricky and complications happen. Complications like relationship violence and bullying, or having to go through Family Court. Children's lives are then not being lived the way we would want children's lives to be. There is a ripple effect.

Start to reflect on your parent's best and worst faces. Start to reflect on your own best and worst face. Acknowledge these, so in your future you don't have to trip over them in any kind of way. For example, if I don't acknowledge that there's a coffee table in the room I could trip over it and our parents are more important than a coffee table, that's for sure! We need to be able to identify what is real and true to be able to develop better ways of moving around the world, instead of crashing into things and getting hurt.

We need to identify, when we're about to cross a road, if there's a car coming or not. Is that car driving appropriately or do you have to take extra precautions? You can't rely on someone else to do the right thing. You don't assume. You are guided by internal and external stimuli to stay safe. Just as Little Red Riding Hood needed to connect to her internal guide, as she went through the woods and at her grandmother's house. So too in becoming an adult, we need to reflect on our assumptions and what we have absorbed as our internal reference point in how we relate to others and ourselves rather than continue to be shaped by these unexamined external reference points that have been swallowed whole.

Start to reflect on the people in your life, their best face and worst face as well as your own. Not just how people want you to perceive them or how you want to be perceived. Become curious of your internal and external stimuli – and what you focus on, value or ignore.

In this chapter of reflections about the mother and father, start to question if there was something missing for you growing up. What do all children need from their mother and father; what skills and capacities were missing? Consider from the perspective of what all children need, as well as from what you personally felt was missing, as often we can 'understand' and minimise what wasn't provided for ourselves and deny what we needed but can more easily offer others those missing pieces. Create a list of what children need. Send me a copy! I would love to know what you believe is vital.

How can you restore those parts of you now? How can you assist your clients to guide them to getting the support they need? How can you help them to re-parent themselves? Who can you learn from to keep developing in your own journey? As you develop that in yourself, you can also be part of the ripple effect passing that on to others, personally or professionally, in your world.

How can you take care of your needs and not just those of others? I have seen the effect of that in me and with other women in family violence. We're so good at taking care of other people's needs and sometimes not so skilled in our own needs.

I've also seen the effect of taking care of your own needs, to the cost of vulnerable others and the impact of that – as I experienced from my parents when I was a child.

Both types of neglect, for the self or with others, are impactful. Recognise how those imbalances might be in your life so that you don't deny them and become lost in them. So you don't lose the connection to yourself or others.

***

Women need to take back their power and surround themselves with those who celebrate them to be real and true, powerful and emotional. Men need to examine and question their beliefs and attitudes towards female girls and women as well as how they are with their own feelings of vulnerability so they can be powerful and emotional. What does it mean to be a real man at this point in history? Of course, there are men who also need to take back their power and be real and true *and* be with their vulnerable self. Everything I say is relevant to all people. Women also need to reflect on their beliefs and attitudes about being a female and what a real man is.

***

We went back to my early life to unpack the different layers of being shaped to illustrate what gets built on what. After all, that is how systems and development in our world work, whether it is the bricks of a building or the bones of a skeleton or the babbling sounds of a baby to speaking to writing to reading. Life is a cycle of progressions. Your process of development will be different from mine, but I hope in my raw honesty it supports you to strip back your layers.

All babies and children are initially helpless, physiologically and emotionally unregulated, dependent, needy, developmentally raw and without the sophisticated refinements and resources which develop over time.

Human infants are amongst the most dependent and vulnerable of all species. When a child is left in a state of lacking support for too long, or too soon in their development, before they have the relevant capacities, the child becomes traumatised. When the parent does not repair from the rupture that left a child feeling unsafe, unloved or in fear, the trauma becomes embedded.

No trauma can be compared to another person's trauma. Trauma results from any experience that leaves a person in overwhelm, and unable to integrate the experience. Events are traumatic, but let's be clear: the trauma lies in the body, it is no longer the event. The trauma is what we are left with and reliving in our body and mind.

I have been speaking from the perspective of me as a child: the child's reality, the child's limited capacity to take things on and how it shaped me. In Part 2, 'The Real World', I will talk more about how as adults, we can bridge between the adult that we are now and the child that has been left with the incomplete capacities that are involuntarily impacting our choices and capacities.

As a child our neural pathways are being laid down, and despite the benefits of plasticity that is possible in adult life to change our neural pathways, the early patterning is significant and structures our relationships, sense of self and life choices. This needs to be recognised to be able to put the appropriate response in place, in the context of changing neural pathways. Our core identity and options were set under stress. The map for what is acceptable, and what is not, was built. This is the platform we work from when we begin dating.

When you receive a series of repetitive messages, verbal and non-verbal, throughout the life cycle through ages and stages – which hold a common theme of not listening to your reality – then a focus on another's perspective, and being rewarded with love or attention for that, overrides your true instinctual self.

This survival response often buries the true self to protect it from anticipated betrayal or further damage. The true self goes underground, and the survival or 'pleasing' response is reinforced, which then maintains certain dynamics that inhibit trust and free-flowing behavioural responses. This survival way becomes reinforced by our living context and so embedded in thoughts, feelings and choices; that it becomes so second nature it is perceived as being the identity and reality.

This survival perception of reality and identity is further reinforced by the ongoing distortions and biases of parents who are not providing what a child needs, and so reinforcing as the child develops that their perception is not a valid part of the picture.

When communication, reflections, concerns and questions are presented from the mother and father in a healthy way towards the child, they provide for a child. They allow the child to absorb a positive reality. A parent's curious, non-judgemental interest in the child's experience allows the child to take that reality in for themselves in their own kind of way when growing up.

If we have parents able to do this permissive kind of enquiry – this ability to differentiate our experience from theirs, and their experience from ours, with the kind of questioning that reflects and expresses our own concerns and creates boundaries – then we have the capacity to relinquish control of holding in and can be expressive and responsive. But if we don't experience this full repertoire via our parents, then it's very hard to have this internalised and do that for ourselves when we go out into the world.

Aren't these all the very skills Little Red Riding Hood needed to support her navigating the Wolf?

This is what was very difficult in my development as a child. The way I was learning about me and being in the world was influencing the way my brain was forming, and the way I could relate to others and the world.

My parents were silent, and years later each preferred to blame the other parent for the 'mistakes' or consequences. Each of my parents at some point brought up their guilt or their error, but in a way that it became more about them feeling bad and fragile then the impact on me. This can often leave the child/adult reassuring them that they did the best they could, so the apology is lost in becoming the caretaker to prevent the parent falling to pieces, rather than there being a receptiveness to the reality and the impact of their actions. The cycle can change when parents can stand, bear their own worst face and not have to excuse or defend. When the parent can be with the other's reality without trying to 'save face'. When the parent can see and say, 'I am sorry I was not there for you in the way you needed me'.

I am not suggesting that adult children need to go back to their parents or require them to receive validation on the reality of their childhood. Once we are adults, it is our own responsibility to resolve what has become our own. Otherwise our healing process can be as if we are a child again, dependent on our parents accepting our reality in order to heal.

So to clarify, I am naming what was needed for the child in an optimal family context, in the desire that parents reading this can make changes earlier on in their parenting to own their shadow and build emotional muscle. This is so they can bear their child expressing objection and reflecting a parent's worst face, and it being received in the safety of home and repair and development can take place sooner while the child is still at home.

This *parental healthy ownership provides a modelling of an emotional container for children to own their worst face and engage and relate to their worst face, as they see and experience their parents doing* – and so the ability to engage mindfully with our own experience and responses is developed and grown, not stunted and limited. Relationship abuse can be stopped. Otherwise, we continue a cycle of protecting the adults in the generation above and not protecting the children, even into adulthood. Let us be adults and protect the children and generation below and those to come.

Can you see that when we can own our worst face, we protect and prevent our children carrying someone else's worst face and being caught in violence being passed down?

I am writing this for the greater good of all – for our society to see the impact of what we bury in our unconscious and ignore in our desire or effort to uphold the belief that parents do the best they can. The adult in me can acknowledge they did the best they could. The vulnerable child and vulnerable young adult in me needs society to acknowledge and address the gaps.

We need to move beyond the personal defence and look at the real and bigger picture – and what needs to change when we acknowledge the real picture. Otherwise we are at risk of continuing an idealised view of mothers, fathers and childhood, and the fairy tales remain. Those kinds of fairy tales that hold the truth in their gruesome elements, all because we can't bear to be with the bigger truth.

Let's bear the gruesome 'full catastrophe of life'. Let's be with the joy and the suffering, so we can help future generations live through the dark and light. When we can embody our pain and suffering, we are free to embody our joy and power. When one is dampened, the other is too, in fear of the outcome from any release.

Let us now leave Little Red Riding Hood behind and explore the many layers of unspoken secrets and knowledge inside the real world, with the help of fairy tales and other surprises. Let's connect and reclaim the power of the feminine.

Part 2:
The Real World

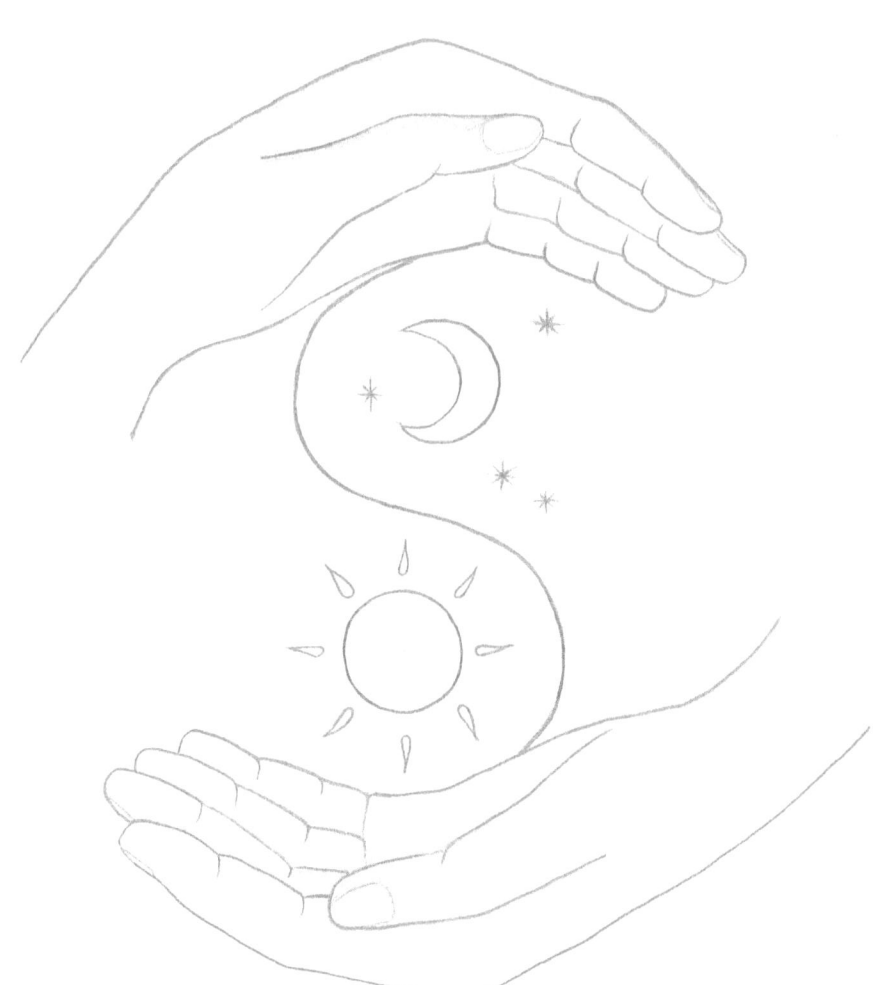

Chapter 7: Rumpelstiltskin

Rumpelstiltskin

A poor miller wants to be seen as important in the King's eyes. He lies that his beautiful and clever daughter can spin straw into gold. The King takes the girl and says he will cut off her head if she doesn't spin the room full of straw into gold by morning. She feels despair, when all of a sudden a little man appears. He says he will spin the straw into gold if in exchange, she gives him her necklace.

On the second night, the King gives her a bigger room of straw to spin into gold. The little man appears again and fulfils the task in exchange for her ring.

The third night, the King wants her to spin an even larger room of straw into gold. If she spins the straw into gold the King will marry her, otherwise he will kill her if she can't fulfil the task. The little man returns. She has nothing to exchange, so she promises to give him her firstborn.

The King marries her. The little man appears to take her firstborn. She offers him all the wealth from her marriage but he doesn't want it. He says if she can guess his name within three days he will go away. She spends two days guessing. She starts to panic and sends her messenger out to see if he can find out the little man's name.

The messenger searches for the little man and overhears him singing a tune about his name. The little man returns the third night. She initially pretends not to know his name. Finally she tells his true name, Rumpelstiltskin. The agreement is broken. Rumpelstiltskin leaves angry and defeated.

Adapted from Children's and Household Tales *(Grimm 1812)*

The only way the girl in the story of Rumpelstiltskin becomes free is by being able to say his name. This is equivalent to naming what is going on. Once she knows his name, he has no power over her. When we can't name what abuse is, or that abuse is a common occurrence in families, then we have a problem.

When I ask people what abuse is, they often start listing the types of abuse and do not understand what defines abuse. When you are not clear on the definition of abuse, it can be easy to not see abuse *as* abuse. You miss recognising what abuse is when you are only looking for the specific types of abuse you or society recognise. This is why many women do not realise they are living with abuse until after they have left the relationship.

Understanding the specific definition of abuse allows you the clarity to become aware of any type of abuse. If you just learn the types of abuse and not the context and definitions which make them all abusive, then you are still ill-equipped to identify other types of abuse and can easily be caught again by the charm and trickster of a Wolf. Just as with any concept, when you understand the theory, then you know the markers – so you don't have to try and remember all of the numerous forms within the fourteen different types of abuse.

Abuse is hidden behind closed doors, inside of family homes. Abuse has many different faces, behaviours and effects. When abuse is not hidden, we name it as criminal behaviour.

Abuse in the home is tricky, because reality gets twisted, manipulated, distorted and minimised. These tricks of reality are often highly slippery because society does not mirror back the errors in all forms of relationship violence. Abusive behaviours are intertwined and blended with the otherwise everyday actions of living. We make the error in thinking the relationship is normal when we do normal things together: eat and sleep, do housework, work, have children, make a cup of tea, talk and try to help, support and grow. We generously attribute 'normal' to the Wolf when it may be more likely that the 'normal' is in the fabric of the background rather than in their behaviours. We generously share 'normal' with the Wolf rather than see the crazy madness of their expectations and behaviours.

It becomes hard to separate the abuse (and respond to the abuse) from what is reasonable – to identify where the reasonable exists or where 'play acting' is going on. Like a 'con man' or a salesman, he tries to hide his shadow and instead own the reasonable and take that away from you. Abuse crosses boundaries and throws you inside confusion and blurred lines. There has to be a blend of both elements, the reasonable and the abuse; because you are in the picture too. When you are also flooded with stress chemicals and he is hurling blame and guilt at you, it is hard to see, and not safe to own that the reasonable only lives with you. Especially when society says he is such a nice guy or that it takes two to tango.

The Wolf will say something that's really wrong, but shroud it inside all these other things that you automatically know are good and right. So you get this automatic internal 'yes' from the series of the good and right things. That thing that is not quite right gets lost in the confusion and shock, and because we don't know what to do with it and no one has modelled an alternative. So we do this silly equation with our beliefs about love, boundaries and relationships that leaves us ignoring that which is wrong.

When there are all these other things that we have interpreted as sending a 'good' message, then the inconsistency leaves us uncertain. It is more comfortable to be with certainty even when we don't know how to be with the thing that is not okay, so we disconnect from the uncertainty and move towards the 'charming' and 'pleasing' elements.

Whatever is bigger is going to override the 'instinctual smell' that something is off. It may be his 'charming' behaviours. It may be our overriding limiting beliefs that belittle our needs and perspective, and bestow greater power on another person's reality. Or it may be, as it was for me, my extreme terror of being alone that overrode the 'off smell'. Whatever is most urgent in your current situation will override the 'instinctual smell'.

The combination of not attending to our 'instinctual smell' and the fact that abuse tends to start small creates a complex dynamic. The beginning is an inconsistency sandwiched between the charming, fun, impressive and 'nice' patterns. The appealing part of this sandwich can appear perfect, ideal and so tasty; but there is a gradual, sneaky and slippery piece of judgement, jealousy or another kind of outburst that is uncomfortable to face and is not going away.

Even with the Wolf, though I didn't want to make a connection, I admired his blue eyes, which could make contact and his ability to talk. I admired his confidence and ease in social circles. He had an air of not only wanting to take care of things but that he could. This was all so different from my previous relationship. Liking those qualities, combined with the unease of his unrelenting stalking seduction early on, meant I didn't know what to do about that inconsistency. I didn't know how to 'pay attention' to the instinctual smell. Now when I reflect, I wonder why there was *an implicit expectation that if I like certain behaviours or features, that I would have to like the person.* I don't. I can like this and not that and it does not need to lead to only one conclusion. The implicit expectation that if I 'like this then I have to like that' is the logical masculine attribution style whereas the feminine style is I 'like this and not that' and not have to follow through to the limited equation.

Despite the fact that I wasn't sending him signals to spend time with me, I was left with a triangle of conflicts. So I dropped the hot potato that I had no clue how to be with and focused on the 'good' and what was more certain and comfortable, not able to close the door to this form of 'good'.

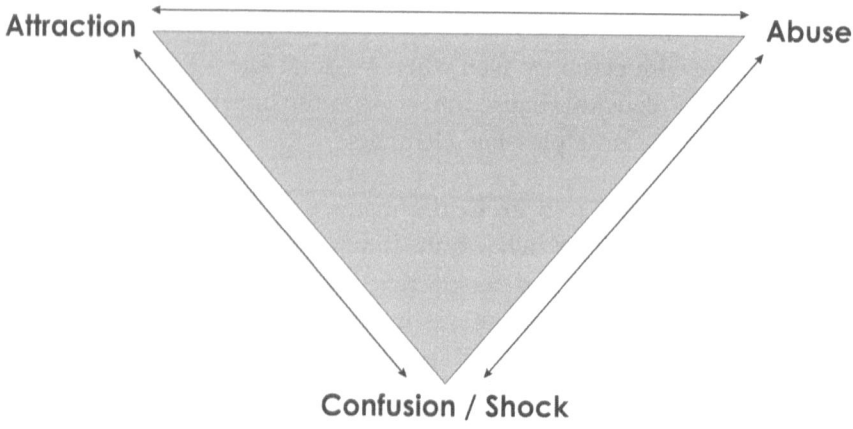

I created this abuse love triangle based on the conflict of opposites that don't gel together. This is what I believe abuse is founded on. I would love to know if this reflects your experience. Please email me and if you have a different triangle of conflicts, please send your version.

A distortion of reality, deception, and lies that just doesn't make sense. The shock and inability to integrate that, which does not make sense, creates cracks. We fall into these cracks because we don't have a map with a validated, modelled response. We are immobilised from our 'instinctual smell' response and move towards madness.

We see the cost of the unprepared Little Red Riding Hood, who has not been taught how to discern and question, or how to hold true to her own reality and her senses. The unsuspecting 'child' within waits in innocence or the 'woman' who has been taught to wait and 'follow' the man when the Wolf first approaches. The role of the feminine in being 'adult' and leading with her instinct has been messed with, instead allowing him to guide her into his structured nightmare.

The shock, confusion and outrage becomes immobilising when it is hard to believe that he 'said that' or 'did that' or 'expected that of you'. These behaviours are so far from what we have been taught in how to be 'nice' and 'kind' that we minimise, excuse and disconnect from what is hard to believe. Until we end up discovering that the sneaky bites of abuse have gradually grown and a pile has built up. Often, it then becomes the other way around: now the charming, pleasant part is the small piece sandwiched around the unpredictable and aggressive control and abuse. We have been worn out. Our reality is no longer of substance.

We need to define abuse that occurs in the home, because our society does not yet see this abuse for what it is, the same as abuse in other settings. Power over another through a disowned and over-inflated, distorted reality. Now, let's get really specific.

Domestic violence is *a pattern of denial, control and punishing behaviour within an intimate relationship, from one person to another, through the use of force.* In family violence, you may or may not be married, living together, separated or dating. It can happen in heterosexual or same sex relationships. Abuse, domestic violence, family violence, gender violence, interpersonal violence, relationship abuse ... whatever you want to call it, there's a particular behaviour of control and force (whether actual or threatened) from one person towards another, or towards property or animals, that causes that person whom it is directed at or witnessing to be under threat of psychological or physical harm or deprivation. When that threat or act is directed towards you, there is a fear of your personal wellbeing or safety.

Another way of describing abuse in a relationship, is when one person repeatedly denies and overrides the rights, reality and needs of another person, punishing and shaming them to extinguish their right to have their own response in their own surroundings.

Humans are made to adjust to our surroundings. Adaptability – it helps us survive. It also helps us accommodate 'the terrible'. Think of the people who have survived war trauma and torture camps. The human spirit is incredible in being able to adapt.

This adaptability makes it hard to identify abuse in the home for a number of reason, (1) because it's hidden and done in secret, (2) because being hidden and not spoken about leads most people to not even realise when they are first experiencing abuse, and (3) we don't notice it because we are a reflection of our society and have lost our 'instinctual smell' and clarity about what the specific definition of abuse is.

As our society finds it hard to recognise relationship violence, we don't have access to an external mirror that reflects what is unacceptable in relationships. There is still confusion and an aversion to confronting abuse in relationship – therefore, (4) there's often shame and shock and fear which make it hard to put the truth about our relationship out there. (5) We are under a collective fantasy that love is meant to be the fairy tale and turn ourselves inside out waiting for it or getting seduced by the illusion of the fairy tale. (6) So many women take on a level of care taking that is not theirs to carry, and feel they are to blame or something is wrong with them. When all of this is going on, (7) it's very hard to identify and therefore make the changes because the abuse impacts our identity, choices and our experience of being in the world.

The bottom line is, abuse is tricky, because with abuse comes all these unpleasant responses: guilt, fear, shame, shock, confusion, secrecy and expectations. This complicates things even further. These unpleasant responses slow us down, overload and overwhelm us. Overwhelm is the biggest obstacle for any progress, whether to do with abuse and relationships, doing our taxes or even spring-cleaning our home.

As a society, we are not very good at dealing with overwhelm and seeking help for what feels unbearable. Overwhelm in the context of trauma means we disconnect and so we adapt from a place of dis-integration.

I grew up in a hothouse of overwhelm. It was my daily diet. In my childhood, no adult identified or owned their behaviours as 'this is healthy', 'this is unhealthy', 'this is appropriate', or 'this is abusive', 'this is broken and needs repairing'. It was all merged and blended and smoothed over so as not to upset the adults.

As a child, when these factors aren't identified, separated and differentiated, it becomes tricky later in life to do this for yourself, as the blinkers have become so familiar that you don't even realise that you wear them. You have learnt a tendency to adapt, accommodate and make excuses for lots of things. Sometimes adaptation is not a good thing.

Now that we have identified what abuse is let's look at how many different types of abuse there are. When we can place pictures of what the pattern of control, denial and power over looks like in different contexts, we can clearly identify and affirm the reality of what has happened. Remember though, only when you recognise the key elements, which define abuse can you have the freedom and skill to identify the different types of abuse. It is only then you can talk about what's happened for you or someone who is trapped. Only when you know what you (or your client/friend/family member) are facing can you access choices, or regain a sense of self and reclaim personal existence and reality – to get closure and the growth to move on.

A flower can only thrive in soil that has nutrients in it. When a plant receives the required fertilisation, sun and rain, it grows and blossoms. We too have our requirements to thrive. The soil is our family and society. When the soil is deficient and the soil of our relationship becomes filled with different toxic behaviours, we wilt.

Too many times people outside the relationship think they know enough about abuse or someone's relationship and behave as if the problem should already be solved, but they don't have the whole picture. Take the time to really understand the definition of abuse so you can recognise its slippery forms and grasp more layers.

Too many times people outside the relationship, in their emotional haste, think they know enough and blurt out statements of action or care; but still do not have the comprehension on how to navigate what is unknown still to them. We may think we have it, but there are elements that slip through the gaps because of our blinkers and the lack of good earth, societal fertilisation – and so the response is piecemeal. It has holes in it. The lack of good societal fertilisation means we still have our own blinkers and we go back to the abuse or keep staying.

People outside the experience of abuse can't get what is fully going on when it is piecemeal, so society has difficulty being motivated to make changes. People judge and say silly things like, 'Why doesn't she leave,' or, 'But he's such a nice, fun guy,' when they don't know what is really goes on. They don't know how they, as a part of society, are contributing to maintaining denial of abusive patterns.

Let's look at the terms 'violence' and 'abuse'. People typically identify family violence as only physical or sexual and when speaking about the other types they tend to stop using the word violence or abuse. Violence is generally only considered abuse if it is in the literal, physical violent form and emotional and the other seemingly less direct or concrete forms are not defined as violent. Abuse and violence are often in social conversation considered different, as if violence is the 'physical' and 'worse' act and 'abuse' the lesser acts and not physical.

In my mind, abuse involves different types of violence. Violence is the intensity, the rupture, the intrusion on your physical, emotional and energetic boundary. Violence is naming the experience of abuse on our system. Violence is an expression of the energy within the abusive act that is anti-life, anti-connection and anti-flow. Abuse is a verb; it is the action, it is all the types of violence. Violence is a noun. It is naming what each of the types of abuse has the potential to do. Abuse is the forms of violence. So a reminder from my perspective: even when the abuse is not directly physical, each of the forms of violence is abusive and each abuse is violent.

Abuse can take many forms and all forms are impactful, not just physical abuses.

Did you know there are fourteen types of family violence? Often there is not one single type of abuse happening, but instead a weaving of a few types that mould into an abusive character with particular attitudes.

Let's get more detail about the fourteen different types of abuse, so you can be clear on what abuse is and what it isn't.

Physical abuse: actual or threatened, direct or indirect. Includes destroying your physical belongings, clothes and home space; throwing objects, smashing things against the wall, hit, suffocate, slap, choke, punch, spit, pull or drag by your hair, murder, detained, take away your keys, restrained, being rough, risky driving, use weapon or have weapons lying around. Forcing a diet, substance abuse, medication or under-medication. Belittling and minimising your medical and health needs, preventing medical or other help. A sense of force such as standing over you, locking you in or out of the house, raising a hand and then stopping to laugh. Treating you as an object. It includes defining how you should look and act: makeup, clothes, how you speak, even your name.

Physical abuse structures how you live, treating you like a servant. Driving past your workplace or social location or home (either when you live together when he is meant to be at work or when live in separate homes). Taking and reading your mail. The abuser acts like the master of the castle, forcing you to do illegal activities – using looks, violent actions and gestures, or deprivation and taunting your vulnerable state. Invasion of privacy. Stalking via excessive messages on social media, phone calls, texts, emails, letters. Turning up unexpectedly at places you are known to frequent.

Sexual abuse: any forced sexual acts and imposing beliefs about sex, sexuality, and sensuality. Rape and unwanted sexual behaviours including bestiality, forced pornography, sex on their conditions, denying sex or rationing sex. It's about sexualising you and how you dress or present yourself, talking about your sexual history or life to others, showing intimate or nude photographs of you to others, affairs, expecting too much sex from you to the point of getting urinary tract infections, and rough sex that is not enjoyable for you. Forced contraception, denying choice of, taking away contraception or forced abortion. Risky behaviours. Forcing sex in front of children.

Psychological abuse: giving you 'double binds', mind games and mixed messages: It's okay and then it's not okay. E.g. it is okay for you to look after your appearance and be beautiful 'for him' but if you do it when going out with girlfriends, you are a slut. Showing concern and 'love' as if your depression, confusion, grief or rage is because you 'have something wrong with you, such as a mental illness', which undermines your character and reality instead of recognising that your responses are normal in the face of abuse. Using your past to manipulate the validity of your current responses. Giving you too little money for housekeeping and then getting angry for 'not managing the money well'.

Part of the mind game is denying the effect and constantly changing the conditions of what is okay. Gaslighting: changing something and denying it has changed: attitudes or beliefs, physical belongings. Hiding something and blaming you: making up a story about something. He wants to be the centre of your world and gets jealous of friends, family or children and creates unrealistic propositions or arguments to prove your love of him through answering his fantasy.

He makes all the decisions and makes up some illogical reason why you are not able to participate in decision-making. Includes the children in adult decisions and excludes you. Forcing the children to side with his reality and turning the children against you. Threat of suicide. Spreading rumours of mental illness or affairs. Dr Jekyll and Mr Hyde: charming and then the Wolf, or the Wolf and then the Sheep in Wolf's clothing: in need of saving. Psychological abuse can include emotional blackmail.

Emotional abuse: can include jealousy, possessiveness, denying and dismissing your needs, feelings and reality. The abuser minimises and trivialises your experience or concerns, ignoring and neglecting your needs and reality, and emotional blackmail; blaming you so you feel an over-responsibility, shame, self-blame and guilt. Situations are created to scare and torment you, with threats such as suicide, taking the children away or putting you in a psych unit. It's playing mind games, making you feel guilty and humiliating you. Stripping away your self-esteem and undermining your character. Humiliating you in private and in public. Criticising your body and appearance.

The abuser may involve the children, making you feel guilty about them, or using the children to relay messages or provide servitude for what he wants, whether it's forced hugs and kisses or to dress a particular way. This forced affection or clothing can be directed towards the children or to the adult partner. Silent treatment. Shifting sands, not being consistent with values and interactions.

Verbal abuse: name calling, insults, threats, shouts and whispers. Finding faults and always correcting you, patronising, being inconsiderate in public, sarcasm, lies, threats, constant interruptions and dominating conversation, criticism and put-downs. It's about shaming you, your beliefs, values, emotions or actions defined by the abuser's perception; you're taunted, teased, ridiculed and humiliated publicly and privately, twisted to be a 'joke' and criticised for being 'too sensitive'. It involves making light of the abuse, but also includes harassment, accusations, denial, shame, interrogating, insults and threats (towards you, the children, pets, belongings and of self-harm) to control your behaviour. Being a though police.

Social abuse: isolating you from family or friends and humiliating you in public. Threatening friends or family to back off or lying about your feelings or thoughts about them. Needing complete attention. Bad mouthing your family and friends or bad mouthing about you to your family and friends. Stopping you from getting or keeping a job, studying, going out or getting a license. Preventing and restricting your work and social interactions and opportunities; picking you up and dropping you off for work and social events.

The abuser limits or sabotages who you talk to and see, and controls how often and for how long. Controlling what you can do and how you present yourself. Standing over you while you're on the phone or monitoring your phone use, messages and social media accounts. Controlling what you watch, read and where you go. Limiting outside involvement. Jealous outbursts to control and justify actions, such as talking to the milk bar man leading to a jealous outburst. Accusation of affairs. Hiding or smashing your mobile phone.

Financial abuse: controlling the money and rationing how much money you can have or spend, often making you plead or ask for money, and preventing you from keeping or getting a job. The abuser is the only one to access the family account and keeps secret accounts and assets. Money is used to reward or punish. You're unable to spend money for yourself, and are interrogated for what you spend your money on, often giving you too little for the family or your needs. You're forced to hand over all your pay and perhaps to sign paperwork even when you don't know what it is about, tying you to debts and credit cards in which you are not party to the benefits. Restricts your capacity to work and earn. Sets conditions on your choices about work and earning money and what happens with the money. Gambling, drinking away or spending family money on his own interests to the point that family needs are not met or your right to spend on yourself is impacted.

Spiritual abuse: quoting from and using religion to reinforce subjugation and servitude, using their 'religious' beliefs to justify their behaviour, deny and prevent you from practicing your spiritual beliefs or from attending in your spiritual community. Denying you sharing your spiritual beliefs with your children. Controlling what you read, what you watch and where you go. Ridiculing your spiritual beliefs and practices. Demanding you take on their beliefs.

All of these eight types of abuse are to different degrees commonly identified within the context of relationship abuse. I believe with any type of partner abuse, psychological and emotional are involved, so there are always two or more types of abuse occurring. Here are more types.

Pet abuse: rough or brutal to or kill animals or pets, or use animals to scare you and show his 'power over' male dominance. There is a strong correlation backed by research between domestic violence and pet abuse.

It is also important to look at partner abuse from the context of children who are related to either adult. Relationship abuse now has a broader impact. It is important to bring in this bigger picture, as otherwise we are at risk of denying the impact on children and the residual of the next three types of violence. Many people in relationship violence have experienced relationship abuse via their parents as a child.

Many people still hold the false belief that a perpetrator can be abusive to a partner and still be a 'good' parent. This is illogical due to the emotional binds between the child and adult being abused. Any partner violence affects all children involved in the family unit – whether the abuse is direct or indirect, whether they live with the adult being abused or not. When an adult (who may be a parent) is abusive to an adult (who also may be a parent), then automatically the children are abused as their environment and relationship is not safe. The threat is never separate. Our bonds to our child and child survival is greater than our physical self - we have an energetic self that senses and feels beyond the boundary of our skin.

- **Child abuse:** involves one or more of the above abuses, either directly towards the child or in being a witness to another family member. Sexual abuse does not necessarily just mean penetration (this is the same as for an adult); it can be via fingers, hands or other objects. Sexual abuse can occur even if it does not hurt. It also includes forcing sexualised behaviours, forcing to dress or behave sexually, forcing affection when the child does not want to – all this has impact on a child's development and right over their own body and expressions. Kissing a child in a sexualised way. Relating to the child as if they are their lover and the partner is excluded from this intimacy.

Child abuse typically involves psychological, emotional, verbal and social abuse – as well as physical and sexual. Financial abuse could be utilised in the form of money or gifts. Child abuse can involve manipulating their behaviour and forcing the child to be a servant, such as to get their beer or to be a pseudo-partner. Not allowing the child to have contact with school friends or develop friendships. Forcing the child to events for the adult's advantage. Children witnessing, hearing or seeing the emotional or physical effects and after of abuse from one adult to another or a threat or action directed to a pet

- **Sibling abuse:** power and control being perpetrated from one sibling to another, often re-enacting the violence from the Wolf without parental intervention or acknowledgement of the reality or protection. Sibling abuse could be encouraged by the abusive parent. Sibling abuse can be physical, sexual, psychological, verbal, emotional, social – or possibly even financial, forcing another to hand over money or steal money for them. Spiritual abuse in copying the force of beliefs over another. Sibling abuse can happen and the parents are aware of it but don't know how to deal with it, so they minimise it or rely on the child that's being abused to just bear it – almost as roles are reversed and the adult is the child and not able to cope for the child to bear what they are often powerless to change.

- **Child to parent abuse:** when the child means to intimidate, threaten and control the non-abusive parent. This is a traumatic re-enactment of the abuse of the Wolf to the other adult. This is serious and has severe implications on a child's growing identity and social competencies, as well as friendship and relationship development. It also has serious impact on siblings and their capacity to feel safe, relaxed and take up their own needs and space. I do not focus on this area in this book, though I have experienced this both professionally and, to some degree, personally.
- **Legal abuse syndrome:** Often when a woman leaves, the Wolf will take her through years of court to continue the abusive control, threats and punishment. Court proceedings can be opposing her orders for personal safety and applying for reciprocal orders as retaliation, court proceedings to hide finances and not pay child support or separation settlement, taking custody so the child has limited or no contact with the non abusive parent, and many variations to complicate contact. Dr Karin Huffer identified this type of abuse and identifies it as a subset of PTSD with research backing up about the impact on physical, mental and emotional health.

The last abuse is not covered in this book, but important to still define in the full context of family violence.

- **Elder abuse:** using power and control over elderly and vulnerable parents. Taking advantage of their age or frailties to gain control over possessions, finances, their legal rights, or their daily life choices and spirituality – where they live, changing the will, influencing who has power of attorney. Sometimes this abuse can be seen in the context of an early life of being abused by the parent, but this is not necessarily always so. Elder abuse is a complex area to identify due to assumptions about the cognition and abilities of the ageing parent or the degeneration of the ageing parent. All the more reason to be more diligent because ageing adults, just like children, often have less power in their life. Elder abuse can happen within family violence, but also within the community. It is common for society to be blind to the forms of elder abuse.

A friend shared a distressing experience about her ageing father. He was in his nursing home and over three days had complained to the staff that he didn't feel well. The staff ignored his complaints until suddenly there became a need for an ambulance. Again the staff made an error of minimisation and sent him to a clinic, so the urgency and pain this elderly man was going through was increasing until it was recognised he needed to be in hospital. An infection developed due to the slow uptake of the staff, which led to increased frailty, possibly the cause of a fall, which occurred in that week adding to further complications and serious and risky repercussions – all because his reality was dismissed because he was 'old'.

Through all these types of abuse we see the Wolf elevating his position and wanting to be seen as the centre of power at home. We all want to feel special and important however it is clear in the different pictures revealed in the types of abuse that the line has been crossed. There is no internal checkpoint or review to readjust inside the Wolf. He is uncontained. It is all about his reality and distorted picture of how things should be.

In the story of Rumpelstiltskin, there is a passing mention of the father who wants to elevate his importance in the eyes of the King. When we look symbolically, how do father's not see their son and share the ground of the masculine with him. Each father is a King for the son. How many father's compete and do not let the son take over and go past him. The competition to be the centre and feel special is a major wound for many men. Often the son is verbally or non-verbally told to mirror and be the version his father is otherwise he is unacceptable.

The feminine within the man is often discouraged, told to toughen up and the man turns into a Wolf in his relationship, doing to his partner what happened to his softer side. Triggered when the woman's attention is with a close friend or birthed a baby, the Wolf will roar and lash out in not maintaining her centre.

In the story of Rumpelstiltskin, the father is willing to sacrifice and betray his daughter to gain this outward 'medal' of success. How awful is that, you say? That would never happen in your family or in your circle of friends …

My hard-working parents were doing their best to contribute to society but the difference between the ideal and reality in our family was shattering. The combination of what was passed down from parents, the environment and circumstances of the times, such as a focus on rebuilding after World

War II; there was limited possibility of a bestowal to take up our own space and power and a sacrifice was made of the young. Is this another version of the father in the story, who was over-focused on an ideal image of self or family and sacrificed his daughter?

When sacrifices for an ideal are seen as special and become established, they create a pre-occupation from the parent and a demand for the child to care-take the parent gets passed down. Anxiety builds. Feeling out of control and busy as an adult keeping it all together in that soldiering on way, the adult to child or adult to partner personal relationship is sold out for the longing to have the perfect picture and receive an entitlement of what feels long overdue.

Does this family pattern of ideal and sacrifice influence men to perpetuate the 'patriarchal power over' with an over-focus on image rather than personal connection, difference and respect? Does this kind of father influence women to move in circles with this mindset as being 'normal'? We don't shut the door to 'normal' connections.

Just as the father wanted to be connected to the King, don't we all want to be special, and belong in the tribe and the land of abundance? But at what cost? The King, like the father, has a narcissistic wound, and is self-centred. By making this agreement with the father it appears they are both obsessed with building their ideal image, as well as how the King threatens the daughter. In this mindset there is the 'boys club', looking out for each other's wounds and the attitude that 'they know best'. The feminine is sacrificed for this masculine wound.

This story highlights we need to go beyond our own nature, just as the 'girl' had to, to set herself free from the binds and expectations of others. We need to find the messengers within and those supporters out in the world who can bridge information from what we know to the bigger picture of what is going on. Otherwise, there is a risk that what gets sacrificed are the feminine qualities of creativity, difference and feelings.

Even when we think we know what we know, we need to be aware that there is a risk of blind spots. 'The Emperor's New Clothes' is a fine example. There is an art to being confident and open to learn more, instead of a defensive, arrogant or inflated confidence.

When no one names what is going on a collusion can develop and the monkey mind can enter a maze of confounding conflicts and tricks. We may sense something but by not externalising and putting a name to the whole picture through a real and specific context, we are left bound. Just as with the Wolf or in my childhood, when my father could not name what was not okay in our family and tried to be the King needlessly sacrificing the feminine, or when my sisters knew something smelled wrong with the Wolf but did not speak. When some aspects are unspoken or secret the next step is limited. There was no enquiry to take the behavioural and emotional cues from behaviours – and there were many clues. The whole system is out of healthy flow with instinct, communication and connection.

This approach of communication in response to something out of flow, of course, expands to extended family, workplaces and even schools. Conversations to vulnerable ones are happening but not necessarily in an optimal way. People and organisations are caught following rules and structures that do not allow flexibility and are bent on not rocking the boat for funding, employment or prescribed outcomes over individual people's wellbeing. This leaks into a cost on society's ability to flourish and maintain connections.

Bullying and power over others is still highly prevalent in families, workplaces, schools and online communities. We strive to support and create healthier families, and therefore communities, but we still don't have enough understanding and shared skills to create a momentum of generative communication and action flow into a healthy, supportive and healing community.

We acknowledge workplaces and schools are part of our community, but create limited opportunities for working together, developing skilled communication and maintaining being real. We have created such unrealistic expectations of our social system and therefore our people, despite the fact that these systems are made up of people. There is inflexibility and lack of responsiveness and skill to prioritise relationships and affect.

Whether at home, school or work, we compartmentalise what troubles us, feeling shame and inadequacy while not wanting to trouble others, instead of seeking our communities to help us through. There are too many stories where people have sought out help in work or school, but the response was far from skilled, appropriate or useful – and so we manage and move on, accumulating more stress and disappointment in our social networks.

Industrialisation and all that followed has interrupted natural community flow, support, rhythms and rituals. We have not caught up and found how we can develop *and* still maintain community connection and support. Instead we have received non-verbal or verbal messages in family, schools and workplaces on what is encouraged or known how to respond to – and what would get in the way.

When a family has not been able to respond, we as a society do not provide enough normalising opportunities to learn and heal. Instead we commonly provide stigmatising attitudes, structures and organisations that divide, reduce and diminish. The fact is, the school and the workplace is where we spend a lot of time. The more connected, inclusive and supportive these communities are, the more each individual and family unit can thrive and contribute and our society can flourish.

We have created an unnatural environment in how we learn, move, connect, socialise, eat and work that is removed from our natural, bio-mechanical, psychosocial rhythms and instead enforces a type of productivity that is removed from its wholeness. The perception is that productivity can only be achieved through the masculine styled environment – rather than the alternatives such as in the Steiner School system, where there is far greater inclusiveness about developmental teaching relevant to the whole person (mind, physical and emotional development). This means class-time is present to the world of the child and so it is not an interruption from learning for there to be a discussion about what is going on in the social or emotional circle of their life. We are so busy 'doing' we forget to teach and support 'being'.

We need to live closer to the truth that it takes a village to raise a child – where the burden is off two people, and the community or tribe are available in inclusive and constructive ways, rather than community being there in stigmatising and limiting ways.

If there had been an adult to see and enquire after me through my growing years, it would have made such a difference to what was real, true and possible. If there had been someone who could have named Rumpelstiltskin to me.

My family is not the only one where parents are burdened through trauma and stress and lose sight of the truth and importance of how the child experiences them and the world. Life is challenging when we live inside unnatural structures and social responses that are not inclusive of the whole experience.

You will find that in many fairy tales, just like Little Red Riding Hood and Rumpelstiltskin, the father is absent or passive. This theme highlights it is not only necessary to know the foreground message – to be able to name Rumpelstiltskin – but also to know the background story, the patriarchal transactions which influence, shape and set the story which each have a cost. We need to know what is necessary to name in our family circles and about significant people and environments – such as parents and leaders, who are not always responding to those with less power, or changing structures which have created injustice and toxic environments.

The setting in the story Rumpelstiltskin is where the miller is poor and his daughter is beautiful and clever. The miller set his daughter up to something that was beyond her. Sure as a parent we need to challenge our children out of their comfort zone but to do this while teaching the steps, not abandoning the child. He was risking her life for some fleeting recognition.

Clients, over many years, speak of childhood memories of parents ridiculing and shaming them for their innocence, for their talents, for their capacity to name and see the wound in the family. Many times a child is scapegoated. We may brush off incidents as 'just having a laugh' or 'they're just children' – however, from a psychological perspective this can be damaging. I doubt the father or mother would laugh at their friend or ridicule them in the same way. When a parent has had their own innocence robbed, an involuntary re-enactment may take place with their child. Does the father in Rumpelstiltskin give his daughter away, as a re-enactment of his feminine, gentle or soft side, which was not allowed ... that was given away. Maybe the father is absent or passive in many fairy tales because in a patriarchal society their true masculine essence is not fully here. Where is the connection to the earth, to his body for a constructive purpose? Where are the rituals to become a man and the circle of men to teach and mentor him?

The Wolf often uses envious attacks to steal their partner's goodness for themselves. Jealousy is where we want something someone else has, but we accept it is theirs, whereas envy is where we want something and we don't want the other person to have it. Sisters or friends can unconsciously do this too.

But enough for now. Let us focus on another important facet of this fairy tale. She only needs to know his name to be free; she does not require anything from him to become free. Isn't that wonderful? You are not dependent on the other person approving or agreeing with the truth to set you free. This is the ground of the adult.

Becoming free arises from the daughter's internal resources and the connections she creates outside of her. Rumpelstiltskin is not instrumental in her path to freedom, only the power of naming is. After all, we cannot protect ourselves from what we don't know. This is what Rumpelstiltskin is all about.

The story of Rumpelstiltskin reminds us to keep trying and go beyond what we know. She doesn't give up the first time she gets his name wrong or the first time she thinks she can't achieve what the King demands. Each wrong answer gets her closer to the right answer.

When we look at fairy tales, we often find there is a creature, messenger or something from nature that assists the main character in the story. We can take this to mean that we have to go beyond our own nature; go beyond our familiar territory and call on something new to discover those qualities, skills and strengths needed to explore and cross thresholds.

We need to connect to a bigger nature that is not known to us yet. Nature that has been disowned but is calling us back to be in our full, natural, instinctual self. Disowned and un-related to nature can appear odd when not integrated, like a little man. Unfamiliar and strange, because we don't have a relationship with it. This nature that requires us to travel beyond the territories and comfort zones that we already know, to rediscover what is ours, can at first appear wrong, dangerous and not to be trusted.

Rumpelstiltskin may even be a reminder that we will find the necessary information in unexpected places. So remain open and don't pre-judge who or where the information can come from. The only requirement is to ask, 'Am I putting myself out of my comfort zone to seek my full nature or to release myself from that which limiting me?'

The miller's daughter remains full of possibility and hope for a solution, even when she cannot know what this is. She asks for help from the messenger. She is not limited by what she does not yet know. Many times when I work with women and unpack their unconscious beliefs, we find a block in the form of fear of the unknown and a future of which they cannot know the answer to. This fear does not take 'healthy' risks. *We cannot know before we can know, yet, because we don't know we don't make a move.*

In Rumpelstiltskin she does not pre-judge or jump to an imagined conclusion when she does not know. She experiments to open the door to the next step. The future is where you will be given the new and 'right' information. Sometimes you can only know once you have got there and then are able to integrate the new information that has presented itself.

I want to help you to start identifying, in your own life and those around you, whether people are displaying some of these fourteen types of behaviours. Let's wake up. Waking can be confronting, but not confronting can be more painful. Confronting reality leads to greater potential of less stress and greater choices, freedom and peace and a closer community. Become curious so you can be open to new information.

Imagine if we all wake up, recognise where abuse is happening, name and respond. Our society boundaries of blindness and collusion will change and our society will be more functional and response-able. We need to get over the fear of seeing what is there and feeling precious about our illusion of society or family.

If we stay with the mindset that no one in our life circle is abusive or in an abusive situation, we won't open the window to see what is truly there. When you are open to identify abuse, only then can you be in a place to address the warning signs when something's not right, so that you can get assistance for you or for others.

Your time being alive is precious and worth protecting. The circle of people in your life is important. This may mean over time a change in choices, people and environment, but this change is a pathway to being surrounded by life-giving support and people. It is never too late.

Start noticing if you've experienced one or more of the different types of abuse, now or in your past. Sometimes our unconscious picks up on subtle signals before we have more information, and we discredit what the unconscious can know. The conscious mind likes to think it is top dog and knows everything first, yet we have an unconscious that can know what the conscious does not know. Sometimes our unconscious is picking up on information that is there, but we have our modern society- or family-learnt blinkers moulded on, which deny the wisdom and power of the unconscious.

Great ideas and inventions come from the unconscious. Start to give your unconscious some credit. It has a huge part to play in recognising, healing and moving on.

Sometimes, we might not be able to put a finger on exactly what's going on but feel something's not right. When we can identify the specific, core foundation of what abuse is, we can know details about the different types of abuse and have greater opportunity to put our finger on what is not right then we can be clear on boundaries. It becomes easier to be able to really put a finger on what's going on for our clients, friends or for ourselves to enable a progression and moving on, and ensure you have not left a part of you or vital information behind.

If we don't take the time to understand what abuse really is or the different types of abuse, then as a society we're going to continue to accept the unacceptable and those things that are not normal. Then we maintain everything is normal and ignore that elephant in the room, so we have to disconnect in some kind of way; we have to split off. Not such a great environment to be around – not feeling, nor seen, heard, supported and with people blaming and ignoring – acting as if 'not normal' is 'normal'. Instead imagine what creative opportunities could arise when people feel safer and connected.

It's really important that we take the time to really understand what abuse is and what the different types are, so that we can make the changes to incorporate that elephant in the room and all the information that elephant offers us, to be able to take the actions and change society. Otherwise, when we continue to misidentify what abuse is and how many different types of abuse there are, there's going to continue to be generations and thousands, if not millions of missed people impacted by abuse.

When we're only picking up about physical or sexual abuse and we're missing the others, we're limited and not able to help so many people who are caught in serious and damaging situations. When we identify what abuse really is and all the types of abuses, we can become proactive, hopefully before it escalates.

Emotional abuse is always the precursor to worse acts of abuse, so the better we get at identifying and closing the door to the Wolf the less damage he can do. He will be in a smaller space with consistent restrictions and boundaries in all relational and social structures.

More and more research is showing the connection between relationship violence and the stress and impact it imposes on our mental, emotional, physical and social health. The impact of abuse is significant on the whole person. This impact is especially significant for children exposed during their developmental growth phases. Abuse either directly or indirectly impacts neural pathway development, changing our attachment style and our perceptions of love, boundaries, anger and power – and whether or not the world is a safe place.

We will continue to see people's health, relationships and our society structure deteriorate in an ongoing crisis with family and relationship violence escalating, unless we can see the whole problem. Identifying what abuse really is and seeing all the different types of abuse is a necessary beginning so we can start to make changes and become more proactive to interrupt abusive patterns and nourish what needs to be nourished.

The elephant in the room continues when the perpetuation of accepting the unacceptable continues. When we stay silent about what happens in abuse, the abuse continues. Right now, abuse is normal – meaning it is so common that it has become a 'normal' part of the fabric of everyday society. But we are still so uncomfortable to bring the conversation of abuse into our personal life stories and chats. If we don't make it personal and instead hold it out as a topic from the newspaper and not how it is present in our life we are limited in our capacity to protect ourselves, sisters, daughters, friends and clients. Change of awareness, knowledge and actions needs to take place in society for individual realities about abuse to be contained within a tighter social boundary.

Imagine having conversations about the stress someone is under and how they are reacting and offering someone a place to talk or have time out. We will feel closer and more relaxed because we are not having to jump around the elephant. We can share, normalise and talk non-shamingly how many of us have lived on the continuum of abuse at some part of our life. This creates empathy and the capacity to face it, change and move on. It can become part of our personal and social history but not the face of our personal and social imprint when we face it. *Hidden it becomes fixed, faced it can be transformed.*

When the elephant is in the room, there are missed cases of abuse, a decrease in health, and relationships deteriorate – as well as the ongoing crisis and massive financial cost that perpetuates and weakens our entire social structure. Abuse is re-enacted in organisations: sports, schools, business, the police force, the legal system. In Australia police deal with domestic violence every two minutes yet they believe they are only called to 40-50% of domestic violence incidents. It has leaked everywhere, yet we pretend it is rare or doesn't exist.

***

While I've been taking you through the fourteen types of abuse and describing them in more detail, you may have found that at times you had some niggling or loud objections. Often we minimise our own experience to cope. Abuse is abuse. Even if what you experienced is not as 'severe' as another person's abuse, it does not mean that the impact is not severe. It has impacted your right to feel safe, feel, speak and do. Abuse is not comparable.

You may recall other people in these situations having objections like, 'It's my fault, I didn't stop it – I let it happen'. 'I can't talk about that as I'm part of the problem', 'I can't say what was really going on, because I'm to blame, too'. 'It takes two to tango.' Or, 'There is no point talking about it as I can't change anything, it was in the past.' My answer is that you are not at fault and you are not to blame; just because you had a limited capacity to protect your natural, healthy boundaries that is a completely different issue to him crossing boundaries into abuse.

When I say you are not at fault, it is also important to look at that false belief of the Wolf 'losing control'. Many people who have been abused will recognise that abuse happens in chosen situations where the Wolf does not feel a threat or risk of a repercussion. It does not happen in front of people the Wolf is concerned could create a problem for them.

The second point is that the Wolf, in the outbursts of 'losing control', will very rarely destroy their own belongings. I am talking about the choices available to the Wolf in his strategic ways of abuse, or to parents who neglect or abuse who both still hold an accountability that is not yours to carry. You can only do so much when you are caught inside the abuse and the many complex layers – that is not your fault.

Just as a child is not at fault for a parent's abusive or neglectful behaviours because they are dependent and not equipped to protect themselves, so too an adult who is in a state of trauma or unable to protect themselves is not at fault in being unable to protect themselves.

There are many adults who have been exposed to abusive parents and are not abusive. There are choices and there are avenues to get help. It is possible when you seek help to keep on going until you get the specific help you need (just as I had to through lawyers and counsellors) or to take yourself away from the woman/child(ren) at risk, so you do not continue to abuse.

It is possible for an awake society to sniff something is odd, notice and step in when either adult in the abusive relationship is unable to respond. It is not your fault. You are part of a system that is not fully skilled in being proactive, protective or responsive when there is a need.

Even if you did something you are not proud of, that does not mean someone else has a right to be abusive. Even if you are difficult, angry or disappointed, as we all are at times; the man inside the Wolf has the choice to walk away and get help for his abusive behaviours.

If you say to yourself, 'It's my fault because I let it happen,' then you are taking the responsibility for someone else's behaviour. This is one issue, yet both the responsibility and the event, has gotten inappropriately split amongst two people.

Whether you have the capacity to take responsibility and whether they can own their responsibility for their own behaviour are two separate responsibility issues. *It is irrelevant whether you have a capacity to hold boundaries or not; someone else's capacity about whether they overstep and be abusive is a completely separate issue* and a separate conversation to whether you can hold boundaries or not.

Re-read those two previous sentences. They are so important.

Abuse happens because one person does not respect boundaries. It is not dependent on your capacity to maintain a boundary when abuse is happening. The very nature of abuse is that it happens *because of overriding boundaries*. If you could stop it, abuse would not exist. It happens everywhere in the world; why would you think you can stop all of it? Abuse happens because there is a misuse of power. The fact you are unable to stop it is a consequence. We place such unrealistic expectations on ourselves and on others, especially when our society is still not backing up the full extent of intimate partner violence.

If you say there is no point talking about it because it was in the past ... I can't tell you how many women I speak with, whom have had their trust and life choices limited because of the past. So even while women say there is no point speaking about the past, it is still often influencing them, their identity and choices – so, in some way, it is not in the past, and what is unresolved is still alive and structuring the present.

My heart aches when I hear from caring and intelligent women who have felt their only option was to reduce their life capacity in some form, because they didn't know of the range of possibilities and support available or their fear was too great. I know of women who get flung involuntarily into the painful past when they walk past a man with a particular aftershave, tone of voice or look – or when driving past a location. Women who believe triggers are now an inevitable part of their life forevermore. They believe they need to forgive or be more loving or something else. *No*; these involuntary responses are indicators of unresolved memories. You *can* do something about them so that your system is free of intrusions. These triggers mean past memories have not been processed.

I will explain more about memories and coping styles specific to women and solutions, which involve these stress and trauma responses, so keep reading!

If someone says to you, or if you have an internal voice that says, 'It's your fault, you brought it on by nagging or being selfish' – or if that voice says 'he works hard', or 'you should feel guilty' because you stay at home and he provides financially for you – then you are caught in a limiting belief system. If you say to yourself, 'Each adult is meant to bring something in and I'm not doing my part, I can understand he gets upset and angry with me,' that lets him off the hook and there is a limiting belief in here.

As I mentioned before, you not being perfect does not give him the right to be abusive. It does not let someone off the hook from their abusive behaviour. The story that you say to yourself about the cause of the abuse and how you share responsibility are two entirely separate issues. Abuse is not acceptable, full stop.

I would say more often than not, if we sat down in a room together and talked about all the things you do for the family – your contribution, including your emotional contribution to the family and for the children – you could be bringing more to the family than what he's bringing in.

It is not even about contribution being measured to become 50% each, but that the contribution of each is appreciated and that the ratio is acceptable for both people. I want to emphasise that most people in relationships are contributing; we just do it in different ways and different capacities and this can vary through time and need.

Just as there are nine recognised types of intelligence, we all contribute based on different strengths and intelligences:

1. naturalist/nature
2. music
3. logical/reasoning/mathematical
4. emotional
5. interpersonal/people-smart
6. body/kinaesthetic
7. linguistic/word-smart
8. intra-psychic/self
9. picture-smart/spatial.[1]

Being an adult also means we can move out of the mindset we learnt as a child that says we have to be fair and equal at the same time and to the same amount. In healthy relationships there is fluid movement, responsiveness and flexibility rather than a static and rigid, fixed expectation. He may be supporting you financially now and you may support him at another time in life, or you're supporting him already in another way that is incredibly valuable through a variety of the different intelligences.

In this chapter I have defined what abuse is and the different types of abuse. We also need to clarify the difference between arguments, conflict, stress and abuse. My working interpretation of the difference between abuse and arguments in a relationship is that *abuse involves an environment and pattern* of denial, punishment, fear and control, which systematically denies one person's reality, feelings, needs and differences. Whereas, *arguments and conflict may involve someone denying another person's feelings or opinions in the moment, but you are not in fear of them or of consequences, and it is not embedded within a systematic process of control and denial.*

This can be confusing if you have some unresolved trauma in your past which inhibits your freedom of self and limits your responses, and may influence a misattribution of a look or tone of voice, action or words; however, when your partner is *not* abusive, there will not be a match between the misattributed words and actions and what actions and responses actually occurs. There won't be any 'proof' of abuse. This can be tricky

---

[1]. Based on the current model of psychologist Howard Gardner, original developer of the multiple intelligence theory, as of 2016.

with emotional and psychological abuse, so it can be very, important to speak with a skilled and neutral professional; so you do not dismiss your past trauma as excusing his abusive behaviour.

The 'walk and the talk' will either be congruent or incongruent. When it is incongruent it is either because he is not matching 'walk to the talk' due to his abusive behaviours (whether you have a history of trauma or not) or it is because the incongruence is from his own trauma that is perpetuating abuse and though you feel you have choices, are choosing to remain. Again this is important to sort through the beliefs and reality of your choices with a skilled and neutral professional, so your perception of choices and safety is accurate, as well as looking at the accumulative effect and risks of living with this abuse.

Often what happens in arguments and conflict is that there is a habitual response, which we can confuse with powerlessness from abuse. To discern the difference in these instances as to whether it is conflict or abuse, stop and consider whether you could do something different.

There may be strong displeasure or temporary punitive behaviour, but that it is *still possible to do something different.* In non-abusive relationships but with some conflict there are opportunities in the relationship that are not limiting, threatening or punishing on how you define your choices of behaviour. There are opportunities for both people to reorient to the conflict and change position.

In some instances there is unresolved abuse from a previous or childhood relationship that is influencing or colouring our view of our current choices and reality. It can feel tricky to define the difference here; each individual situation has its own details and truth, so it is important to keep the conversation going to sort out how you tell the difference between your responses and your partner's willingness for you to have greater responses, or a trauma pattern that inhibits you from taking up some choices. The response from your partner when you talk about what is going on and his capacity to allow your responses without shaming you, rejection or punishment will help sort out what is going on.

Remember to refer back to the definition of abuse and the types of abuse in the context of control, denial, punishment and threats, and reflect on interactions and daily life, habits and patterns in your relationship.

Of course, just because someone has a history of trauma does not mean that their trauma is 'to blame' and the partner is cleared of being abusive. Someone with past trauma can have trauma and still be abusive – these are two issues, which are not your responsibility.

It is important to not base your decisions about keeping safe on the fact that someone has trauma, but rather base your decisions on what actions are needed to keep you safe and that are not dependent on him. Likewise, the woman suffering from unresolved trauma does not give the Wolf a free ticket out from his own abusive behaviour nor take away his responsibility when the Wolf has his own past trauma.

Each situation is unique and it is important to recognise the whole of what is going on to understand what is necessary to protect and guide the people involved. Please refer to a skilled trauma and abuse specialist to help you navigate this territory. Please check your therapist has had in-depth training about trauma and abuse.

Remember to look out for how you can differentiate abuse from limiting beliefs, guilt and past experiences, which may deny the abuse. Even if you don't 'pull your weight' in the relationship, it doesn't mean abuse is an acceptable response. Abuse is never acceptable.

All this information may feel complex or confronting, but we have faced the elephant in the room. Working through abuse means being with the uncomfortable. We can't get out individually or as a society if we don't build our emotional muscle to be with the uncomfortable.

Memories may arise as your conscious mind questions and your unconscious works to make deeper connections and clarify what was okay and what was not okay. Different memories may arise, which require sorting out how to tell the difference between the two types of experiences, within abuse and conflict: what was okay and what was not okay.

We may recognise abuse that we have not identified before. Sometimes this is accurate and sometimes we still don't have all the pieces to feel fully clear and certain. Take your time and leave possibilities open rather than making a fast conclusion. Allow new information to sit with your questions. This can be uncomfortable for the conscious mind, which likes certainty but this also assists building emotional muscle and emotional intelligence as you continue to gather more pieces and layers through each of the chapters.

Human beings are meaning-making creatures; the way we understand things best is by making personal and meaningful connections, so it is natural to question the meanings you previously made. Just allow yourself to question – to wonder the unthinkable and not lock anything down until you have more information. Abuse is unthinkable so some information may have become stored as unthinkable and unbearable but which hold truth, reality and meaning.

This may be a time to contact a skilled somatic psychotherapist to help guide and support you through your questions.

It can be helpful to hold a position of curiosity. To hold the stance of being observer and witness as you continue reading to allow space for your system to gather the information and take what is relevant and resonates for you. Rather than you rushing the process, trying to figure everything out or get to a 'better place', you can allow your system to gather the pieces and make new connections. Trying to get to the 'better place' too soon can mean you skip gathering important pieces of information and so can't reach the natural and real conclusion.

Your task is just to stay open and ask questions, as well as to self-soothe and take care of yourself through the uncomfortable journey into the unthinkable.

As you go along, you will build an emotional muscle that allows you to feel and think, rather than deny or minimise. You will build emotional muscle from gradually gathering more pieces through each chapter. As we walk together, we can walk around 'family or partner abuse' and get to know more of what is really going on. It will get clearer as you place more meaning and context on these different parts of the elephant in the room.

As we move further into the detail of unpacking about abuse you may want to write down questions, memories and personal connections about abuse and the types of abuse that may have been triggered in your memories, from reading this chapter.

Please contact me with any questions or to share your experiences. We are on this journey together.

Chapter 8:
The Handless Maiden

The Handless Maiden

There lived a poor miller in hard times – all he had left was his milling shed and a beautiful apple tree behind it. One day a strange man came up to him in the forest and said, 'I can offer you riches if you give me what is behind your mill.'

The miller, thinking there was nothing important behind the mill, made the agreement. The strange man laughed and said he would return in three years for what belonged to him. When the miller returned home his wife came running to asking him what had happened, as their home was filling with riches even as they spoke.

The miller told his wife about the bargain. His wife began crying, telling him the strange man was the Devil – and what was behind the mill was the apple tree, but their daughter was there sweeping in the garden.

Three years passed and the Devil came to collect the daughter. She bathed, dressed in white and drew a circle around herself. The Devil was unable to get to her and he screamed out in fury that she was not to bathe and he would return.

Weeks passed and the daughter was covered in dirt and matted hair. When the Devil came close, she began crying and her tears dropped onto her arms and hands, revealing her white skin. The Devil again cried out in fury, that they were to chop off her hands and he would return. The father protested at the thought, but the Devil said everything would die including the miller, his wife and the fields if he did not submit.

The father apologised to his daughter and sharpened the axe. The daughter was submissive and agreed this was what he had to do. The father and daughter cried together as he chopped off her hands.

When the Devil returned she was crying and her stumps were clean from her tears. Again the Devil was thwarted by the forces of life and tears and not able to take her. He went away cursing never to return.

Her parents had aged but promised to take care of her in a castle of riches forever; however, she felt she needed to become a beggar girl and rely on the goodness of others. Leaving home, her stumps bandaged in gauze, she walked and walked until she found herself near a royal garden, full of fruit trees. Collapsing to the ground in hunger, she was unable to get to the fruit.

A white spirit appeared and helped her get across. As she walked through the garden, she sensed all the pears were numbered and accounted for, but one branch was bent so low and she was so hungry that she found her lips biting into the juicy pear. As the moonlight shone down on her muddy and handless form, the gardener saw her. He also saw the spirit so he left her alone. She went back into the woods to sleep.

The next day the King discovered a pear was missing. The gardener explained what had happened. The next night the King sat with his gardener and magician to watch for the Handless Maiden. When she came for another pear, the magician went over and asked her if she was of this world, and if she was human or spirit. When she said she was both, the King leapt up and spoke from his heart that he wanted to look after her and he would not abandon her.

The King made the Handless Maiden some silver hands to attach to her arms and they married.

When the King had to go to war, he asked his mother to care for his beloved wife and to send him a message if she gave birth to their child. When the Queen gave birth to a child, the mother sent a messenger to tell the King the good news.

Along the way, the messenger was tired and fell asleep. The Devil came across the messenger and switched the message to say that the child was born and was half dog.

The King was horrified to receive the message, but sent a message back to care for the Queen at this time. When the messenger was returning, he fell asleep again and the Devil changed the message to say, 'Kill the mother and child.'

The mother was upset to read the message and did not follow the instructions. So a series of messages went back and forth to check the intention. Each time the Devil would change the message, making it worse until the Devil was saying, 'Keep the tongue and eyes to prove the death of the Queen.' The Mother could not bear to do this to the kind Queen, and so killed a deer and sent the eyes and tongue of the deer instead. She then bade the mother to leave with the child and hide. The mother and Queen cried in parting.

The Queen found herself in the wildest forest she had ever seen. Walking through the forest she came across the same white spirit. This time the spirit led her to a poor inn. The innkeepers recognised who she was and invited her to stay. They stayed together for seven years. During this time, the Queen's hands began to grow back.

During this time, the King returned home and his mother cried, asking him why he asked her to bring the eyes and tongue of his wife. The King was horrified and cried in deep pain. When the mother saw this, she told him that they belonged to a deer and she had sent them off to the forest.

The King promised he would not eat or drink until he found them. He wandered the earth searching for them, becoming dirty and matted, yet some life force kept him alive. He stumbled across the inn and stayed the night. When he woke, there was a woman and child standing beside him. She told him she was his wife and explained how her hands had grown back. She brought her silver hands out of the cupboard to show him. The King rejoiced and they all returned home.

Adapted from Children's and Household Tales *(Grimm 1812)*

This is such a big story. Can you see a theme of the father (again) symbolically being blind to the awareness of his daughter and so sacrificing her for an easy life? The father was so consumed with his own desire of grandness that he did not think before making such a big contract about why this man would give him so much for apparently so little. Can you also see the theme of a submissive mother who is not aware of what is happening and not involved in a big decision to prevent the father from cutting off the daughter's hands?

The tears represent her feeling life. Her tears of grief help protect her. Her tears acknowledge truth and honour her life. This is something the Devil does not have: feelings. Your tears of grief can help protect you as they bring awareness, value and the cost of what has happened. Your tears help you heal. Our tears of grief as a society can help us become awake to actions needed to protect and prevent abuse.

Her hands represent her ability to feel and touch. This is her feminine essence of being. Out in the world, her feminine way of being, with feeling and sensing are not valued and are betrayed. Once betrayed, she does not want to live in the superficial richness that cost the maiden her hands and live with parents who betrayed her. She prefers to leave. She takes a leap of trust and follows her integrity. She does not choose to stay home out of any fear of change, helplessness or limitations. Instead she steps into the unknown. Once she begins and is outside her comfort zone, something from outside her world comes to help her.

The King sees her with his heart and sees beyond her dirty and dismembered state. He does not want her to suffer. This healing love helps her grow through the challenges of life that are evil. The King and his mother, refuse to betray her no matter what challenge appears, are such a contrast to her early life with her parents. Even when it seems things are bad, they trust what they know to be true. They listen to their instinct. Through them, through their love and trust of instinct and not betraying her, her own hands have the optimal environment and opportunity to grow back. Through finding a place in the world where she is honoured and loved; she can heal and grow into a woman with her hands fully available for her.

Hands sense and encompass the ability to give, receive and take. Being handless, she has lost touch, is helpless and unable to take care of herself – an introjection and reflection of how her parent's were with her. Her parents had lost touch and were impersonal. Through her journey, she develops and grows into being able to touch, help herself and grow. Now she can be reunited with those who love her.

'The Handless Maiden' is the woman's journey of a lifetime growing hands. 'We do not just go on to go on. Endurance means we are making something substantial.' This is where we need to make the differentiation between endurance to go on and on inside a survival state, and endurance and persistence through challenges, which have an opportunity for meaningful and creative transformation. 'The Handless Maiden' is the story of unrelenting endurance, which, when met with certain requirements, can then 'make sturdy, to make robust, to strengthen' (Estés 1992, p. 388).

In 'The Handless Maiden' we have a contrast between love, commitment and honour against control, selfishness at cost of the other and betrayal.

Just as in the previous two fairy tales – 'Little Red Riding Hood' and 'Rumpelstiltskin' – there is betrayal, neglect, selfishness and sacrifice. These tales highlight a dynamic that unfortunately does happen in families. The reality is that even though families are meant to be where we feel safe and can grow, often it is within families that we experience our biggest wounds and betrayals. Fairy tales are a gentle way of bringing truth to what can feel unspeakable.

When families are a safe place to grow, the family and society provide opportunity, encouragement and modelling for the girl to create her own destiny rather than dominance over her life path. Can her environment give her the space to put her hand on what she wants and create her own life, or is she forced to be the shape others want? Would putting her hand to her life calling be seen as too much, too powerful or unfitting?

This story tells the experience of the innocent feminine thrown into betrayal and abandonment, brutalised by those who use tricks and deceptions. Endurance is required – and through time and with some love, she develops intentions and purpose so the development and transformation from 'handless' to 'capable' can be complete. The transformation of endurance is only possible through love and mindful differentiation (the King and his mother).

The terrible was not her fault. Bad things happen to good people. Bad things happen in innocent moments, when we're not prepared and we don't think we have to defend or protect ourselves. It's childlike to imagine bad things only happen to bad people.

Patriarchy has a template to blame women, instead of attributing responsibility and accountability to the man and his misuse of power. So too, women in abusive relationships absorb this attribution style and often blame themselves for some cause and fault of the abuse. To be able to identify and name we need to recognise there are two layers of abuse, betrayal and deception; not taking an action, witholding, neglect (omission) and the act of (commission).

Just like 'The Handless Maiden', each woman living with abuse has at some point the potential to access the power within to endure and grow strong, staying open and positive and finding the way to not betray herself or leave the door open to others to continue to betray and harm her. But we are social creatures, we need support.

Our family, our culture, our society, and the spiritual or religious environment we grow up in each play a part in shaping us and infusing us with a template of being. We are not a clean slate when we meet someone. We have a range of conflicts, beliefs, strengths and vulnerabilities that are formed through time and influences, which direct how we are in the world and what our choices are.

Our family lives inside a society that is a blend of cultural, religious and historical influences. We are going to identify some of the subtle ways that our identity and choices are influenced by this blend, which we absorb without even realising. If we were transported to another time and another country, it would be far easier to recognise what our own society is infused with because we would be removed from it.

I invite you to begin to be curious about how your family, culture and religion have woven threads through your environment and created a particular lens of how you and your world 'should' be.

How and what our family values or allows, creates an influence. Are our feelings, separateness and sensitivities valued and protected, or are parts of ourselves rejected and cut off? Can we be different, challenging and opposing of our family or environment? Or are we sacrificed for the 'image' or the 'good' of the family? Are we denied having our instincts, which would allow us our hands in the world?

Remember when I spoke of the flower in the soil? Our family, and the culture and society, is our soil. Has there been enough nourishment in the soil or are we lacking some nutrient that leaves us deficient?

Family is an important area to explore, to understand those layers that are more indirect and maybe more pervasive than we realise in influencing who we are and what we accept – or don't accept.

Our conscious mind likes to convince us that we are separate and adult now; that our parents don't have the influence they had when we were young. Is this really true? How do you tell the difference between upholding a belief or attitude because you believe it or because your family asked it of you? How do you recognise if you are still following family patterns – and how do you discover your own way and have the courage to enter the wild forest? Or do you prefer to live in the comfort and richness of the parents' castle – staying in their mindset, appeasing their guilt or your own in seeking their approval, staying limited and handless under the glass ceiling of the family?

It is tricky, this thing of difference and separation, individuation or 'stay in the tribe' mind-set; after all, we humans are social creatures. We want to stay connected yet we also need separation to grow. We learn through modelling and socialisation. We need each other – we like to belong and find our tribe, those who are like us. There are millions of people on Facebook seeking likes and joining groups. There are thousands and thousands of Meetup groups. We are hungry to connect, even if we are not currently great at it. We are independent but very dependent on each other to grow, learn and love and even to be able to eat.

Whether we like it or not, we are dependent beings. I walk into my home and I trust that a whole system of people – other social creatures, strangers to me – have made the effort to go to work to make it possible that when I switch on the light, the electricity flows through. When I walk to the shops, I am relying on a system of human beings who grow and deliver the food, making it available for me to be able to buy it. Healthy adulthood is a fluidity between independence, dependence and interdependence.

We are dependent on so many levels to our tribe. If we don't recognise where our dependence lies, we are bound to it instead of having a choice and making adjustments. This is why understanding the individual through the lens of history, culture, society and family is an important element. We need to understand the soil of what we grew up in. We need to know what fertiliser has nourished us and what fertiliser has just been shit. This is one of the areas I unpack even more when I run workshops or explore specifically when I work personally with individuals.

There are many unique layers of influence that have come about through family, culture, society and religion. They often meld into each other. Let's first look at one of the early influences within the family: the development of our attachments styles (John Bowlby; Mary Ainsworth). Our attachment style is the emotional bond we develop from the direct relationship we initially experienced with our significant care-givers, usually our parents in our early-life interactions. The degree of security, warmth, consistency, containment and care that our parent/caregiver responds towards us and the environment we are in shapes which attachment style we develop. The other side of the secure, confident and trusting attachment style is insecurity, avoidance, dismissiveness, chaos or anxiety.

These attachment styles are dependent on trust and feeling secure. The feeling of security develops from having at least one sensitive, responsive and consistent parent who is available when needed. When the parent does mis-attune, the sensitive parent repairs and re-attunes to the child, building more security. The consistency and predictability of an available and soothing parent builds a secure attachment style. Less stability, insensitive responsiveness and unpredictability creates either 'anxious ambivalent', 'anxious avoidant' or unstable 'disorganised' attachment patterns.

It has been suggested that the map of trust and security, displayed in adult relationships, is built from this template of early attachment.

Within the family the different attachment styles are dependent on the interactions with the parent, so let's just briefly go through what they are and what parental behaviours influence different attachment styles, which in turn influence how we respond to others. It can be really valuable to know your attachment style, your weak spot and what it is that you need to develop to take care of that part of you.

Secure attachment is when the mother's responsiveness to her child's signals and needs is quick, sensitive and consistent, which leads to the child's general state of being as secure, explorative and happy. The child believes and trusts that their needs will be met. This child will show distress when the mother leaves, yet be able to regulate themselves, play and then show pleasure when mother returns. This is all because the mother is responsive, does not over-extend beyond the child's developmental needs and returns in an appropriate time.

However, when the mother's responsiveness to the child's signals and needs is distant, disengaged and takes too long for the developmental stage, then the child is not so explorative and more emotionally distant. Anxiety develops in response to this **avoidant attachment** style. The ambivalent attachment style occurs when the mother's responsiveness to her child's signals and needs are inconsistent, emotionally unavailable, unresponsive, ignore, reject, and are sometimes insensitive or neglectful. She may often rationalise her lack of emotional response, discourage an emotional response in her infant and encourage premature independence.

This creates an anxious and insecure child who is unsure their needs will be met. Underneath is an angry child, though the anger may need to be disowned due to lack of permission to have feelings and risk of rejection. This type of parenting creates a self-reliant personality who, under stress, has a preference to withdraw in an attempt not to distress the parent and so at least please the parent in appearing independent and similar to the parent, not displaying feelings.

Lastly, there's the **disorganised attachment**. The mother's responsiveness to her child's signals and needs is extremely erratic, unpredictable, frightening, passive or intrusive, which leads to the child's state of being as depressed, angry and non-responsive. The mother frightens the child, has unrealistic expectations of the child and does not communicate verbally and non-verbally their feelings in a clear and appropriate way, sending confusing messages about their own feelings and state of being. Intrinsically this child is often severely confused, with no strategy to have their needs met because the stress response wants to flee to safety (mother), but the parent is unsafe. These children often need to dissociate to cope because the parent has not provided a solution to the fright associated with the parent.

The parent may have a history of trauma, neglect or abuse. It is not necessarily about how bad that trauma was but the parent's capacity to feel it and make meaning and resolution from it. Otherwise, the trauma continues its effect through the relationship when the parent involuntarily becomes triggered through a low tolerance to a range of emotions, reacting and totally unaware of the impact on their child. This leaves a child with difficulty to make meaning of what happened, feeling unsafe and mistrustful of the world, resulting in difficulty socialising and self-soothing as well as trouble regulating their emotions.

There is so much to say about the multiple layers and connections within family which influence our relationships, sense of safety, choices, capabilities, as well as shaping, imprinting and embedding in how our brain, body form right down to our cells. Do you know science has found that we each carry cells that were our mother's? We have inherited in our DNA psychological and behavioural tendencies of our ancestors, and when we are in-utero the way we develop is influenced not only by our mother's (and father's) physical health, but also her mental health.[2] We are active in preparing for our own life after birth, absorbing the messages of her experience.

---

2. For more information on the topic of epigenetics see the works of neurobiologist Dr Michael Meaney and molecular biologist Dr Moshe Szyf.

This shaping of our own brain and mind-body system is so sensitive that if our mother's state change between in-utero to birth is different, it significantly affects our development; even if the change is for the better there is more negative impact than if the state remained consistent (Sandman et al 2011).

Cell migration even occurs from baby to mother to reside in many of her organs, including either the mother's brain, skin, kidneys and heart helping the mother heal from particular damage or illness years later (Dawe et al 2007). What an incredible survival system to seed healing for our care-giver's future and therefore enhancing the availability of the care-giver in the infant's life.

Do you know every cell carry's memory and molecules carry emotion (Pert 1997)? Can you begin to see how influential family is in shaping who we are? How important it is to be with and respond to the information and needs within the body and the unconscious.

The capacity or limitations of the primary care-giver to connect and open up to their own good feelings or process their own difficult feelings from the past opens or limits the capacity of the child's neural pathways, hormones, body structure and even health. Even the mother's heartbeat changes the way the child's brain develops.

A mother's emotions of pleasure or stress influence not just her physical health, changing the brain development and hormones of the foetus. Electrical signals from the mother's heart can be picked up on an EKG machine, which show them being transported through every muscle and every cell of the foetus and mother. A foetus heartbeat will often be in the same rhythm as the mother in 'entrainment' (Tassone n.d.). So too, as an adult our unique heartbeat rhythm will naturally synchronise with another when we are a certain distance apart.

One example of the close connection is the baby is dependent on which neurotransmitters are lit up in the mother. What she is experiencing when she is with us influences what neurotransmitters are lit up and activated. So if she is stressed and there's not enough serotonin getting activated, whether the stress is to do with us or not, as a child that influences the switches in our own system. A depressed or stressed mother has a huge influence on the default mood of the child.

Thank goodness with advanced mind-body psychotherapy we can now work with this template, and through neuroplasticity continue to develop the pathways and choices. However, the more we can attend mindfully and responsively to our child through their development, the less work there is to do later. This early patterning shows how our past influences us and how our cognitive self needs to be in a relationship with our feelings and our body. On another level it may even suggest our system is geared to match our parents', and the challenge in our choices is to go beyond the glass ceiling of what our parents feel or have in order to evolve. Perhaps it was once necessary to stay on the same wavelength for survival's sake …

Notice the original passivity in the Handless Maiden – a bit like her parents' passivity – and how with consistent and sensitive loving she becomes courageous, strong and flexibly responsive. Research shows evidence that consistent loving touch and love can dissolve and change the effects of trauma patterns (Sandman et al 2011).

***

Little Red Riding Hood demonstrates the passivity of her mother line and how this continues when she meets the Wolf. Just as I also continued the passivity from my early life, until I engaged in effective therapy.

In the case of the Handless Maiden, the passivity continued until she experienced the consistent love and touch from the King, mother-in-law, the innkeepers and her own child. These early attachment patterns can leave us vulnerable to get caught because we don't have our full, vital, responsive energy system available to us. The female in 'Rumpelstiltskin' didn't have as tough a time. I would say the precious items which belonged to her were symbolic that she had some value in herself that had been demonstrated to and bestowed on her; and this was reflected in less passive behaviour. She was not as deprived. The jewels are symbolic of owning some (internal) riches and resources.

Another layer of influence over the family is the attitudes around us that find their way into our family – those influences that have threads from our social, historical and cultural context. These contexts all influence and shape what we can express and connect to – and what is deemed unacceptable. This is something that we'll unpack now and in different ways in other chapters. I also expand this in private settings of my work beyond this book, as these areas are so personal and useful to explore in your own particular unique blend of family, social history and culture.

Another layer that crosses over the boundary of family, culture and society is the religious or spiritual atmosphere of what we've been infused in. Even if there isn't a specific religion present in your family of origin, the family is still influenced by the surrounding religious influences. The culture of the Western world is influenced by the Judeo-Christian laws and commandments, such as honouring your mother and father.

> Honour your father and your mother so that you may live long in the land your Lord your God is giving you.
>
> Exodus 20:12 (Bible, New International Version)

Honouring your parents has been associated with the same attitude to honouring God, irrespective of the personal experience within each home. A fixed, attitudinal, patriarchal, black and white perspective developed over time, as they were originally claimed as 'words' and 'utterances' and later reframed as the Commandments. This commandment, as it is now known, can get taken out of context through the particular values and instructions within society and interpreted in black and white ways in homes with neglect, trauma or abuse. When read as a commandment rather than an utterance, is taken so literally and without flexibility, and does not honour the reality of a child's experience growing up with their parent.

Don't we even feel as a child that our parents are gods? I know I did. It was as if they ruled the world. They were my world. They were like the gods and goddesses in myths who had arguments and threw my universe into disarray when they were displeased.

How do our parents collude with this commandment in their desire to be right and adored, and so keep us away from reflecting back to them to face their own humanity and frailties? If parents can display their humanity and not unconsciously or consciously ask the child to see them as gods, but instead allow the child to relate to them personally instead of as gods, then children may have a safe place to express and relate equally. Even if as parents they hold more power, the child's reality can begin to integrate the parent's shadow and humanity – and therefore there is space for the child's displeasure about the mis-attunement from the parent to go somewhere and know what they know.

When there is an integration of the best and worst face of mother and father, this can become a model for the child about being adult and not inadvertently lead us into relationships with 'false gods' or the Wolf in a suit. Our template of who to love can be real rather than idealistic. Plus we get the gift of seeing our parent's model and teach how to negotiate being with their best and worst faces. How resourceful, protective and preventative is this for future relationships?

As parents we tend to hide ourselves away and 'protect' our children from uncomfortable feelings, instead of sending the message that our feelings are not too much. Children are not traumatised when they experience us respond with capability to our uncomfortable emotions, even when they are big.

The Handless Maiden was the dutiful, submissive daughter who honoured her parents' wishes, even if it meant cutting off her hands. Her parents were willing to sacrifice her. Her parents did not concoct or attempt any plan for the whole family to escape to hide from the Devil to protect her from the deceptive contract, unlike the King and his mother.

I too followed what my parents valued: be quiet, be submissive, do as you're told, smile and show the world everything is okay even if your reality is not. I learnt that love is connected to fear, to not get angry and not to upset anyone.

My parents may not have intended these messages, but when you are very young, the immature brain cannot handle sophisticated sorting and it is left with the concrete reality of experiences and their impact. So I was left with a disorganised attachment pattern of love and fear. I remember the familiar experience and feeling of what felt a beautiful sensation of leaving my body and being on the ceiling. I was like Little Red Riding Hood, who had not developed the signals and skills to get away from the fear or from the Wolf. I was physically there but no one could recognise I was in trauma and dissociated. I had grown up immersed in fear and with no one to teach me how to come into my body and navigate the Wolves in the world.

Fear had been a 'normal' state for me growing up and I was not independent enough to fight or flee from this fear. When I met fear later in life, it did not register high enough that I needed to get away. My fight and flight response was damaged. The level of what I tolerated as 'normal' was out of whack, tolerating the intolerable.

I was acclimatised to being immobilised around fear, as I had repetitively experienced there was no escape. I could not get away, as a helpless and dependent child. As an adult this turned into feeling unable to get away from fear; I became switched off around fear and was susceptible to being caught. So it was almost as if I was destined to be with someone who used fear to control, as I had experienced no choices and inevitably been taken over and controlled through fear through my childhood.

In researching Judeo-Christian influence for *The Wolf in a Suit*, I came across some interesting information. In Rabbi Hayim Donin's book, *To Be A Jew*, he writes, 'A child is never to put a parent to shame or tell the other parent that one parent is doing the wrong thing as this can lead to one parent cursing another parent.' He writes that you do not interrupt or contradict, or even disturb the sleep of your parent. These kinds of laws limit or restrict a child when something wrong is happening. These kinds of laws protect parents, not helpless and dependent children. Even if your family did not follow these books or religion, was there a general expectation of this kind of attitude? Do you feel a sense of this around you in your society and culture?

It was interesting for me to find in my research how Jesus affirmed being obedient to God would overrule honouring your parents, especially if parents were disobeying god's laws. I am not religious and do not have objections about any particular religion, but I do have objections about anything in society, such as 'honour thy mother and thy father', which does not allow someone's reality to exist and be supported especially when they are vulnerable and dependent. Isn't it time we become clear about what and how we honour so we honour in a different way from denying one to elevate another? Otherwise, we are with the basis of abuse. In abuse, one person digs a hole for the other person to stand in, taking away their ground, and they use the dirt from that person's ground to build themselves a higher ground.

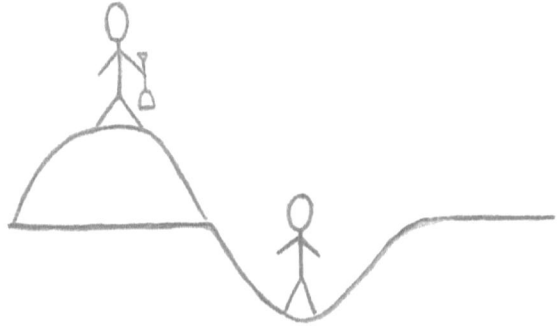

How many families are obedient to God overruling honouring your parents, above their own desire to be honoured; especially when their behaviour is not honourable? Jesus, whether you believe or not in following him, is speaking of an intrinsic belief that everyone has the right to be honoured. That there is no hierarchy of power, which bestows more honour on another. Each of us has a right to be loved, respected, kept safe and honoured.

It seems to me that Western society has such a strong 'honour thy father and thy mother' ideal that the general rules of correct behaviour have become lost in a focus to honour parents. This to me is a truth that doesn't seem to get understood or recognised in the many shades of reality within our own social, cultural and familial structures.

I see this in my therapy room. Many clients, initially talk about how good their upbringing was. I don't question this. I am not expecting everyone to have huge wounds from the past. However, at some point, our parents will fail us. Whether we can name their failings tells something about our family pattern and what we are carrying. They are human and for our child self, it will impact because we are dependent, limited and relying on our parents as our map develops with what we can feel and express. So no matter what your story, we need parents to provide us with the resources that allow our whole reality to be important rather than protect their face.

Isn't parents bearing their worst face and allowing room for our reality an important ongoing experience to enable the child to develop the skill to be confident, to trust ourselves and our reality, to develop emotional muscle, to build relationships, to share our perspective with others, to create the life we want, and to be resilient? This, when passed on, helps future generations bear their faults, own them and so intrinsically reduce violence.

The foundation of equality and honour for all members in the family, with parents having sophisticated power but not using that power to excuse their limitations, has the potential to create far healthier relationships and change the face of abuse. When a child grows up to feel and know that the laws of honouring include them too and not just the parents, and so feels safe to express, children can keep their raw power and affect and family violence would change in society. Healthy relationships and society is when we are able to affect and effect each other.

The reality now is that adults themselves, let alone children, have difficulty speaking up about their parents. It often takes time for an adult person to build the emotional muscle to speak up about their parents' failures. There is always such a desire to 'not betray my parents' and carry some of the responsibility. This carrying is an over-responsibility when the child is still unregulated and learning from the adults. The child can only learn as well as the environment around them allows. It is the teacher, not the student, who is responsible.

In time, without me steering client's awareness, they come to be able to name their reality. They can begin to see their experience through their own eyes, rather than seeing themselves through their parents' eyes. So their reality aligns with them, even when their parents were not behaving the way a parent needed to behave. When their child self can be seen, they no longer remain limited to protecting others, but instead can protect themselves. Life energy, confidence and safety are released.

Can you see how this immunises the self from depression and releases them from the child mode to be free as an adult in the moment, where there can be greater room for spontaneity, confidence, resiliency and more than one opinion and reality?

This is a respectful and appropriate orientation for the purpose and intention of moving on. Otherwise, there is a cost in always hiding and never acknowledging the impact parental gaps placed on you. How do I know there is a cost? When clients feel guilt, shame, 'bad', or that 'something is wrong with them', they feel alone in their child experience while naming certain things about what their parents said or did (either covertly or overtly), then I know that the guilt or shame is protecting the 'other' person and locking away part of the truth of their true, instinctual reality. Often there is a habit of over-responsibility or being pleasing to others which impacts on physical, mental and emotional health.

If client's struggle to do this with their parent, there often is somewhere else in their life where they are protecting another from the truth and feel powerless. Where they feel apprehensive they may affect or offend the 'other'. True intimacy is a two-way street of both affecting and being affected by each other.

How else do I know there is a cost? Because if the guilt or shame was not there, they may feel some anger, hate, grief, loss, abandonment, uncertainty, confusion, insecurity and so on – *and it would be okay to feel this.*

When we see our childhood through our parents' eyes, it can feel like opening Pandora's Box seeing through our own eyes, not knowing what will come out. There does not appear to be any gifts in there, only emotional pain.

The problem with having a closed Pandora's Box is that part of your reality stays out of the picture, and *all* the related feelings have value. Feelings are there for a reason. They inform and give value about our experience. Those feelings, when seen and valued, can release the past and develop the self in becoming protective, wise and discerning.

The guilt or shame may be a last resort to manage and stuff down those uncomfortable feelings, and a way of not offending or upsetting others when you don't know how to be with the discomfort. So you carry the discomfort. If an adult who is no longer dependent on their parent does not feel comfortable to be with those early life gaps with their parents, then that leaves me questioning what access they have to being with uncomfortable feelings and emotional muscle to protect themselves in life now. This 'managing' can become an in-built habit or pattern to not rock the boat and minimise reality – and can leave you vulnerable to dominant characters, bullies and Wolves in the world.

This 'managing' of the uncomfortable will also become an in-built pattern for the Wolf and inhibit developing emotional muscle to bear and own their actions and consequences.

Habits of managing are often connected to unresolved experiences that have ended up impacting our wellbeing and our choices. If we don't bring this topic up, the guilt or shame is always managing the stress, and so resolution is not successful. The guilt, shame and betrayal needs space to move through our system, rather than stay within a Pandora's box hidden somewhere in our system.

Our health, moods, choices, identity, strengths and vulnerabilities are all affected and shaped by this management and containment. Coming to understand and 'honour' your father and mother in the context of their limited capacity is not generally a clear and simple equation. We end up juggling because we don't know what to do with our uncomfortable pieces. There is a way through, without the childlike obedience to a law that sounds like a good instruction but does not allow a full experience within society.

In exploring the familial, societal, cultural, religious and historical patterns in the context of abuse, there is an important reality to consider. Humans are the biggest threat to other humans. We are more at risk of being harmed by another human than nature or an animal or a poisonous plant. This is why looking at our familial, societal, historical and religious patterns are important and fascinating! It does not need to be a dry and complex process. It can be informative and freeing.

Along the way, naturally there will be challenges. There are many double binds in partner violence. A double bind is when we receive two or more messages that conflict or oppose each other. 'I love you and I will harm you.' 'Honour your parents when your parents harm you.' 'Our life is normal (when it is not).' Our experience needs to be honoured and included to feel safe and secure, and prevent the costs from double binds.

We are a social creature who needs a tribe. We have a deep need to belong. We also have a deep fear of rejection, which goes back to tribal times. Historically, we are less likely to survive on our own. Being rejected by our tribe would often lead to death.

We have a double bind with both our need to belong and our need to separate from the shared reality to have our reality included. This can at times feel threatening to the cohesiveness of the tribe and the individual. We are geared to be sensitive to rejection, to prevent ostracising and risk of death. This puts a challenge on our system when as children we are not fully developed or resourced to ensure our own developmental needs. We are reliant on our parents' ability to honour our reality and own their limitations.

We need a society that can support the limitations of the adults without shame or punishment. Consequences need to be put in place to contain, educate and optimise potential for repair. Consequences need to provide choices, which also offer opportunity to show you can do it differently. Human survival and development is based on a social network of belonging that also provides a range of resources, non-shaming support and development.

Growth needs to come out of consequences, otherwise we are limited to the less optimal form of adaptability – which becomes 'managing the status quo' and not developing.

Recent research shows the same part of the brain that lights up for the experience of rejection, lights up when we experience physical pain. This is in contrast to the late 1800s and early 1900s when Dr Luther Emmett Holt and Dr John Watson, amongst others, began describing affection and touch of your child as primitive. In this period of history, natural instinct was seen as animal and not to be responded to. Patriarchal men had authority over motherhood. There was a significant drop in a baby's ability to thrive, with serious degeneration in mind and body – and even death. This changed when mothering was allowed to return to more natural mothering.

There have also been a number of research projects about Romania and Russia, where many orphans failed to thrive based on lack of care, connection and touch. One, the Bucharest Early Intervention Project (BEIP) was a twelve-year study of 136 abandoned orphans. A range of neuroscience tests, as well as MRIs and EEGs, were used to determine the impact on cognitive, social, language, emotional and physical development on institutionalised orphans, compared to those who were fostered out and those infants with their families. The institutionalised infants were the most damaged.

Love and connection is intrinsic to human life and development. We see the worst in the horrific lives of Genie and other 'feral' children. We need more than a roof over our heads. We need connection and touch.

Can you see how all these layers of family, society, religion, history and culture influence the complexity of abusive bonds? Some contact is better than the unbearableness of no one. In our DNA is the fear of not being wanted. 'If I leave, no one will want me – I can't survive if I don't belong.'

Let's look at what is woven through all these stories of society: patriarchy. The domination of one gender over another. The story of the Handless Maiden shows the expression of patriarchy with the father choosing for the family, blind to and disconnected from the feminine and placing an incredible ask on the feminine – the daughter. We see how the father's choices influence the daughter's life, identity and choices, changing the whole family unit. We see the King, showing another expression of masculine power. We see how the King's choices, aligned with the positive feminine in the mother, offer an alternative map of relating, choices and healing.

Gender power over the individual is not based on the personal attributes of any individual. Gender power is a blanket domination and authority of one person over another. Looking at the story of the Handless Maiden, we can see a representation of what happens in gender power. The father has a mindlessness and unconsciousness about what he is bargaining with and giving away. Patriarchy does away with valuing the gifts and differences of the feminine, as if they don't exist.

This patriarchal attitude is present in many cultures. There are a variety of patterns of domination in the context of genders. Focusing on patriarchy does not diminish the wrong of any domination over another, in all its forms. I am focusing here on patriarchy as the widespread and systematic use of patriarchal thinking and domination that has influenced and structured many societies and through time.

This patriarchal way of social organisation, no matter what our religion, is greatly influenced by a particular view of the masculine. The father is the powerful ruling figure within families, organisations, our law and politics. Patriarchy has a lot to do with perceiving and experiencing the feminine as being at fault, inferior or inadequate – and not valuing the feminine ways of learning, engaging, being and doing and not valuing instinct, the earth and nature.

Just to clarify, when I'm talking about masculinity or the masculine, I'm talking about patriarchal masculinity. There is the experience of the masculine from a very different, positive ground, which values the feminine and true equality. This positive masculine self can be with authority without domination. The positive masculine self can be with the thinking and the feeling self and with strength and vulnerability. The capacity to be with both the masculine and feminine as equal and powerful.

There is evidence that before patriarchy there were goddesses and polytheist religions, honouring multiple gods and goddesses. These inclusive religions existed before the masculine patriarchal god of Abraham. The gods and goddesses allowed many forms of the feminine as well as the masculine to coexist, honouring the strengths and the weaknesses of both. There was a place for everything. In the world of gods and goddesses there is more an attitude of being inclusive and being with 'this *and* that' rather than 'this *or* that'.

***

Humans are social creatures. We absorb stories of how to be, how to love and how to interact. All our influences – family, society, culture, religion, even history – all leave their traces on and through us. If we don't look at the bigger picture of what we are immersed or cooked in, we lose important details, to remain lying within our subconscious behaviours, thoughts and actions, yet all contributing to shape us. Therefore, we have less choice to change the ingredients and create new and better flavours.

We have a choice. Do we get tricked by the Wolf and the surroundings, as Little Red Riding Hood did? Or do we look beyond our current situation, trusting the emotional limbic brain, our body sensings and the unconscious to help reclaim our power and our instinctual inner eyes and ears? Do we keep our hands?

***

Neuroscience, psychoneuroimmunology and somatic psychotherapy recognise that our primary relationships shape our brain development; our neurotransmitters, our hormones, our attitudes, the way we stand, even our muscular positioning in the body. If we don't start to look at the detail of how we engage (including our attachment patterns) and find out what our habits are, rather than just automatically reacting from our habituated way, we will keep following Little Red Riding Hood down the path into the Wolf's belly, instead of following our own path and destiny. We will remain 'handless'.

***

The attitudes we absorb from our family and culture can be subtle and the rules may be unspoken, but nevertheless they *will* unfold in your family. The 'rules' may be verbal or non-verbal. We may not even be aware of them because they're so ever-present that we just take it for granted: that is the way our world works. We were born into it being this way. It is what it is and we adjust and accommodate, without question. The human capacity to survive is built on adaptability and tuning out the repetition.

Learning to drive is an example of 'absorbing and tuning out'. In the beginning we notice absolutely everything. There is so much information going on around us. Trees and houses flashing past when we drive down the street. All the instruments, mirrors and gears to keep track of in the car. Our heart pounding. The pedestrians, cyclists and traffic lights. Yet over time, we realise, 'Oh my god, I didn't even notice the traffic lights changed when I resumed driving. I'm just driving.' We just do it without noticing consciously all the details. We adapt and tune out every day.

Our system has built a map. We tune out from repetition. Our brain says 'I know this' and tunes out, lighting up the familiar pathway of response rather than create new pathways. Our brain is geared to go down the pathways that we have most recently and most frequently used, and what has worked; after all, it got us through. Often we are in a zone of a habituated response in which we move and choose from the unconscious. We grow into a family with so much information floating around and our young system absorbs it all, like a sponge, tuning out the repetition and shaped by what is expected, rewarded or punished.

***

This absorbing sponge begins early on. Up to the age of six we are in a hypnagogic state, below consciousness, with theta and delta brain waves. A trance state where a mix of the imagination, reality, perceptions and sensations of everything around us is downloaded into our neural pathways to create our beliefs. The words and statements our parents say become powerful hypnotic suggestions, as well as what is floating around disowned in the unconscious field of the family, influencing and shaping our map of who we are. We do not yet have the sophisticated skills to identify, separate and filter.

As we continue to live each day absorbing the field and the familiar, the tuning out happens; after all, it is useful to not have to pay attention to every single thing, to every little detail. But this tuning out also takes place in events where we have not had the most helpful resources, support or responses towards us. So we find ourselves doing things and not even realising better choices … sometimes until it's too late. Almost as if later, we come out of the spell. After all, we do know words are powerful and can be hypnotic.

As a child, especially in those early years when we have not developed full consciousness as we know it, we are hypnotised without even knowing or having a choice. Trance and hypnosis are shifts of consciousness where we are more absorbed in one aspect over the rest of the experience in the moment. You are in a trance state when you are at the movies and so absorbed with the movie that you feel as if you are in the movie and nothing else exists, including no awareness of the people beside you. We move from different states of consciousness or hypnotic trance states all throughout the day: regression (when we feel younger than we are or feel we are in a memory from the past), amnesia, future progression (race into the future) and more (Grinder and Bandler, Milton Erikson, Michael Yapko).

Our attitudes, influences and behaviours have been subtly infused by our surrounding experiences, shaping our choices, decisions and relationships to how we are in the world. We may not even be aware of the choices we have. This is why I am passionate about talking about all the layers. The more we can recognise the automated process we are in, the more opportunities we have of finding an exit.

Start to observe and witness the interactions you have with your family, friends and colleagues; begin to question how you are different in the different contexts. Why? What do you prefer in the differences of how you interact with the different groups of people? Which way works better for you? It may be a bit from both or something new. Becoming a curious witness to your habits and how your environment influences your mood, choices and expression can be very valuable. You can begin to see the unspoken rules of what's okay and what's influencing how you are in different contexts.

Is there permission and support within you or around you to question attitudes or expectations? Can you push on the family or societal culture and still have your reality included? Is there room for you to contribute, incorporating your new information to create constructive change? After all, nothing is static. Anytime we are in a situation that requires rigidity, there will be an inevitable eruption. Static is not flowing or growing energy. Something will need to be disrupted to create flow.

No matter how religious or non-religious you or your family are, attitudes and values can be shaped by the broader society. Start to become curious about what you have absorbed, so you can choose what you want to keep and what is not in your best interests. You can't change what you are not aware of.

With modern technology, we can't help but be so much more aware about the world around us. We seem to prefer to look at all the world then at our own immediate front yard. There are major crises within families all over the world, as well as between countries. There is a universal lack of honour. There is a lack of being with the vulnerable and the needy. Why do we as a society place this extraordinary expectation to honour our father and our mother, regardless of the reality of our relationships? This imposition and obligation acts as if there is no issue going on, when there are great struggles with power and inclusiveness on a global scale.

I am not implying that just because there are global problems in the world, not to forgive your family or culture. I am saying it is time to recognise that when pressures are imposed from the outside in, there will be long-term consequences. Recognise you are not just working to free yourself from your family or social binds, but there is an ancestral and historical link as well. So be kind to yourself. It is huge to step aside and do things differently. If it feels right for you, this is the time to recognise the unspoken pressures and choose what to push back against, to allow your feelings, needs and reality to be supported.

Find a tribe that values and supports you being with your reality and exploring what is right for you, without feeding you another external structure or 'rule' of how to be a good friend, partner or person.

Did you know 'fear-related social cues from individuals from one's own group/ethnicity have greater "power" then outside of our social group'? (Chiao et al 2008, cited by Perry 2009, p.247) There is a greater activation of the survival centre of the brain with someone in our group than with someone not in our group. There are such subtle pressures to conform to our tribe.

When I talk about the commandments and parents, I am not implying we demean and distance ourselves from our parents. (Though for some people it will be appropriate to create some distance, for a period of time or permanently.) There are many choices and opportunities for healing (that are not dependent on our parents acknowledging what our reality was as children) when we move out of black and white, 'blame' thinking.

Sometimes we don't challenge our mindset or our environment, refusing to step out of our comfort zone because we fear rejection and tribal abandonment. Our desire for change is circumnavigated via an assumption – by some static conclusion, some perceived answer, some end point often relating to the past and learnt coping patterns.

Often this 'answer' is from a patriarchal masculine way of thinking, reducing, rationalising and concluding; instead of a feminine viewpoint: which is fluid, dynamic, inclusive and ever-growing. How would it be to challenge our mindset or environment and not predict the outcome? What is possible may be different but better than you could imagine.

Instead, allow the feminine approach, where the outcome can develop and continue to grow through time, through relationship, through curiosity and gathering, through life experiences. Sometimes we project a limited conclusion based on what our conscious mind has already experienced or absorbed from our culture and past, instead of this dynamic, fluid path of possibilities which can incorporate the positive feminine and the positive masculine and take us beyond what we already know.

When we keep doing the same things we create the same outcome. We need to take a risk and create the new reality along the way, without even knowing what the next step will look like. Otherwise we keep recreating the past.

***

Can you see a theme? Here we are looking at those aspects of our life that influence us, which we have grown up with as a part of life – unquestioned, unrelated – that are still influencing our choices and perceptions. Not being aware of or understanding our assumptions, fears, beliefs and vulnerabilities in the context of rejection and not belonging can lead to ongoing managing, coping and not questioning. Even if you think there is nothing to question, I invite you to see if there is something that you are not aware of that can be revealed by the possibility of questioning.

Do you know '98% of what the brain does is outside of conscious awareness' (Gazzaniga 1998a)?

Early-life family, social and religious influences on our emotions shapes the way we think, the way our brains formed and our learnt patterns. These are all important facets to understand and become aware of in becoming free and accessing more from the unconscious material. Accessing more of the unconscious involves identifying involuntary emotional responses and beliefs. These areas are important to continue sorting and understanding in the context of abuse, or just in the context of being free to be ourselves in life and within our families.

The right brain can perceive things the left brain cannot. The left brain is for the managing and interpreting, as well as the ability to speak. Can you see when someone is upset and the right brain is activated, if the left brain and right brain are not talking to each other (disconnection happens under overwhelm and stress), then the left brain is forced to interpret without full perception and interpretations will be inaccurate.

We need skills and support to build emotional muscle so we can keep both hemispheres talking, even when highly aroused, so both brain halves keep connected and communicating. *When the right brain can perceive and the left brain speaks, without the left brain integrating the right brain information, there will be a confusing outcome with assumptions, jumps and gaps* (Gazzaniga 1998b). Think of what this means when we reflect on encouraging our boys to move and build and our girls to feel, we reinforce each relying on one side of the brain and not integrating or speaking from the whole picture.

Throughout patriarchal influence, boys are conditioned to be 'men' – to contain feelings so they don't appear out of control (pleasure, grief, vulnerability) and to feel and express aggression (to be strong and powerful); but not to express the multitude and depth of all feelings. Men are encouraged not to feel, express or communicate the multitude of feelings and vulnerabilities that are intrinsic in the human spectrum of experience.

Verbal and non-verbal messages are there in a man's family or cultural conditioning: to 'not be a girl'. It is so embedded that parents and others don't even realise the times they do it. Girls get touched and cuddled more, played with gently and boys are roughed and encouraged not to be weak, 'gay' or emotional. There is pride about being tough or strong, and there is shame and rejection about feeling scared or even cold.

Women in patriarchal societies and in many cultures and families are not encouraged to feel their healthy aggression or anger; if they are, they might be called a bitch or that they've got 'balls'. It's not 'feminine'. Woman and girls are not encouraged to be in their body and feel the strength and power of their body, to enjoy their body. Women and girls are encouraged to be kind, soft, understanding and gentle – not adventurous.

These attitudes and stereotypes shape the way we dress, think, move and our choices, influencing what's deemed as being pretty or attractive as a man or a woman, and so much more. There are real restrictions to being a male and female.

In this chapter we're talking a lot about how these different layers of our environment have influenced our experience and our capacity to have a flexible responsiveness to our experience. The outer (parents and society) creates and defines the inner (identity, choices, brain development) template. Choice in our brain either automatically go down those well-worn neural pathways (that society encourages), or having the freedom to choose the path that's most appropriate for ourselves at any given moment. This requires hard work and emotional muscle to create new neural pathways, enter the unknown and go beyond our tribe. A bit like pioneers on a new frontier.

To have freedom of choice, we need to recognise what we are immersed in. To be free within ourselves of those binds within our culture and family, we need to be able to look at the whole picture to truly see and understand what's happening – and to be able to have our appropriate response, to enable moving beyond familial and societal influences.

I want to share a little but powerful story. An old story from Jalalud-Din-Rumi (1207–1273 CE).

Six blind men live in a village. One day an elephant arrives in the village and the blind men want to go where the elephant is, because they've never seen one! Even though they can't see it, they want to go and have the experience of this unusual occurrence of the elephant in the village. They want to go and feel it.

One man touches the leg of the elephant and says, 'The elephant is like a pillar.'

The second man touches the tail and says, 'No, the elephant is like a rope.'

The third man touches the trunk and says, 'The elephant is like a thick branch of a tree.'

The fourth blind man says, 'No, the elephant is like a big hand fan,' as he touched the ear.

Another blind man was stroking the belly and says, 'Ahh, the elephant is a huge wall!'

The last blind man, feeling the tusk, says the elephant is like a solid pipe.

There was an argument about whose perception was right. A wise sage says, 'Each of you is correct and each of you is wrong. You only have a part and you need to put the whole together to get a picture of what the elephant is like.'

As we continue together on this journey and investigate all the different parts of the elephant – the individual, the family, society, culture, religion, history and beyond – you will build a greater understanding of how to be part of change. Change for anyone who lives with or lived with abuse, and also for anyone who wants to be free and confident to be themselves in their life. Everything I say is relevant for everyone. After all, we all want to love, belong and connect – and we all feel conflict, stress and uncertainty about the relationship between honouring oneself and honouring another.

I love Rumi. His poems and words are profound. I also love elephants. I have an elephant in my therapy room to help remind me to speak about the elephant in the room, either when I am working with someone or socialising. I don't need it as a reminder any more, but in the early days it was very helpful.

I was so used to the imprint from childhood: to not speak about what I would see, feel or hear. I had learnt to ignore the elephant in the room. I learnt that zoning out would protect me. Remember, that law of familiarity that tunes out what is repeated? I would dissociate from parts of my experience.

One of the things I love about this Sufi story is that despite the men being blind, they remain curious and open. They don't limit themselves to not being able to know more about their experience. They want to know more about what is going on. We need to recognise that we all carry some blindness and don't have the whole picture. We need to stop pretending we don't have our own blind spots. Leaving space or recognising we have a blind spot creates space and a place for new information to be able to come in.

In the story, the blind men need the wise man to help them bring each of the parts together. They can't do it on their own. Be like them: willing to take up the different parts of value from different people and places and from the dark spaces of the wise unconscious within you.

I hope you are loving this little exploration and research of the influences on family and society as much as I am. It seems we have compacted truths until they are reduced and have lost their truth and wholeness.

The parental obligations according to Ronald H Issacs' *The Jewish Book of Etiquette* are to teach, give boundaries, not favour or terrorise the child, teach the child according to their interests, and encourage mutual respect. That's very different to just 'honour thy father and thy mother'. Which is your experience of childhood? I know some fortunate adults received the better version as a child. I want more children to have this experience.

***

Despite this chapter being about family and society, you may have noticed a focus on the unconscious. We can't separate the conscious from the unconscious. It is within us and part of our ongoing development and engagement. A theme or thread running through all these areas that is endemic in patriarchal thinking is to value the power of the conscious mind, and deny the value of the unconscious.

> The causal role of conscious thought has been vastly overrated, and what we are in fact is not rational creatures, but rationalising creatures.
>   Robin Wright

Our environment influences the development of our beliefs and what is pushed into and stored within the unconscious. Patterns develop from the continual reinforcement of 'rules' and 'expectations' in our environment. Let's understand the word 'pattern', because we will keep seeing a pattern through the layers in each chapter. A pattern comes from the word 'patron', something serving as a model. What model do we want to create or change that becomes our pattern, or our children's pattern? Let our patterns be constructive, not destructive; inclusive, not exclusive.

Let's also begin with looking at the word 'gestalt'. The brain and senses do not just see or filter and process – they also interpret and fill the gaps. In psychology this is called 'closure' and 'gestalt'. It's the recognition that the brain will see something and add to create a conclusion, even if it is not the whole. Our brain will want to perceive some object as the whole, even if it is not. Our brain likes certainty and connections; it doesn't like the unknown or gaps.

THERE'S AN ELEPHANT

IN THE

THE ROOM

It's a bit like above, when we see those statements and the word 'the' might be in the statement two times, but our brain skips one. It continues to 'complete' things all the time, either by adding or taking away.

In psychology we talk about this in the terms of positive or negative hallucination. The positive when we're adding something into the picture, and negative when we don't see or hear something and we're taking something out of the experience. This is happening in our brain, adding and taking away to create something, that is not necessarily accurate every day.

A more real-time example is when you are at the supermarket and looking for a product. You are staring and staring at the shelves and it does not seem to be there. You ask a staff member, and they point it out to you. It is in different packaging so you don't see it. Your system created a negative hallucination because you could not find a match for the picture/imprint you were looking for.

An example of a positive hallucination is if you have an argument with someone and you honestly didn't say something, but they swear you did. They added something in that was not there. A partner can often have a positive hallucination (that doesn't feel very positive!), and feel as if you are being like their mother and nagging them … when you are just asking them to put their dirty washing away.

This filling-in phenomena is also in the physiology of vision, responsible for the completion of missing information across the physiological blind spot. We are geared to fill blind spots to survive. So we need to be proactive to be mindful what we find in our blind spot and how we fill them.

This chapter touches briefly on significant areas within and between the family, culture, religion, society and history. Each layer creating an environment that changes and directs what kind of wiring is fired off in the brain, as well as shaping the inter-relationship between the brain and our environment in a continual dance – influencing feelings, safety and what capacity we can have available in response to abuse or misappropriation of boundaries.

Our environment is affecting and developing our brain through birth and through the emotional experience of growing up. It is really important to connect all these social, familial and other powerful elements with the brain. If we, for example, look at the important role of the limbic brain, we can see nothing is separate. The limbic brain is the part of the brain to do with feelings, motivation and reactions. It's often called the emotional brain, and it's also very much to do with species preservation.

It is different to but not separate from the amygdala, which is in the reptilian brain. The amygdala is the part of the brain that wants us to pay attention. Reptiles do not have fear, they observe and have pure instinct reaction. They (and our amygdala) remain quietly vigilant and constantly on, scanning our environment. The amygdala is part of the limbic brain system but it is the limbic brain where fear or learned fear is activated in response to the message of needing to be aware (from the amygdala). As long as the amygdala and limbic brain are communicating with the sophisticated prefrontal cortex, there can be an accurate assessment of what is happening. But when there is disconnection between the three (which involuntarily happen when we are in overwhelm and stress) the amygdala message is taken by the limbic brain and the response can lead to hyper-vigilance, anxiety, panic and chaos. (Stephanie West Allen, JD in collaboration with

Jeffrey M Schwartz, MD from blog *Clearing up confusion: the amygdala is not the same as the reptile brain and it's probably not reserved for fear*).

Fear, sex and aggression become highly involved with the amygdala. The limbic brain responds particularly to emotional stimuli and therefore is setting our levels of arousal and motivation, as well as what behaviours to reinforce. It influences some types of memory and regulates our autonomic nervous system (connected to our organ function and so many systems within the body) and our endocrine (hormones, moods, sleep, tissue health, growth) functions. The autonomic functions involve the parasympathetic nervous system (relaxed response, rest, digest, breed) and the sympathetic nervous system (fight or flight response). We'll be talking about the secret in our stress response in 'The Red Shoes'.

So we can see we have a reinforcement – a pattern on a tribal, cultural, familial, religious and social level to belong as well, as on a cellular and brain function level, for belonging and survival. We can't escape the human experience, but we can relate and engage mindfully with it differently, when we include the whole self in the whole system.

***

Given that we're talking so much about history in this chapter, let's look at the history of a few words and the different understandings and interpretations that we might have about them. After all, this chapter is about identifying interpretations and perceptions.

Let's start with 'honour', as we have been talking about it a fair bit. When you look up honour in the dictionary, it is doing what's morally right. It's not a blanket 'honour someone' just because they are your partner or your parent. Honour is directly in context to behaviour and intrinsic laws of 'right' behaviour. It is not about value-based perceptions.

Now, let's look at 'responsibility', which comes from the word 'response'. It's about being present, *having the ability to respond*. Who has modelled and taught you effective skills and behaviours to inhabit your instinct and responses? Where do you have access to your ability to respond? Where don't you have your ability to respond? Where are there inhibitors to a natural response for a particular context, which will inevitably impact your capacity to be responsible?

We often twist and distort what our responsibility is, or we can take on someone else's response-ability when they don't. What limits your ability to respond? Is there a limiting belief that interrupts your natural response? Or is there a limiting feeling, such as aversive fear, confusion, guilt or anxiety that is interrupting your ability to respond freely in the context of a particular situation? Is there a limit on how acceptable your response is if others don't reflect the same view?

When you are in a tricky situation and you can't access your response or your response-ability for yourself, you can imagine how someone you admire would respond. This is a creative way of accessing the model you may have missed out on and can bridge to the neural pathways that have been interrupted.

The word 'discipline', if you look up its original etymology, comes from 'disciple'. The instruction given, teaching, learning, and knowledge; it's not about punishment or shame. It's about teaching. Teaching needs to involve modelling, consequences and choices to allow a person to grow.

I particularly love the origins of 'belonging'. The base 'be-long' comes from the Dutch word *gelang*, meaning 'at hand' or 'together with'. Not alienating or threatening, but an extended hand. There needs to be an extended hand to have the experience of belonging. Isn't this what's so important to increase women and children's safety in our community? That, as an individual, we have the ability to be at hand for someone else and when we need a hand we know there is one available? This means community needs to extend their hand, to be 'together with' rather than say 'this is not my business'.

The desire to belong and connect is so strong that though our hearts all have their own individual heart rhythm, it has been found that when we stand a certain distance from one another our hearts join and share the same rhythm (Pearsall 1999). We are primed to connect to our family, relationships, society. We just need to find ways to connect that do not negate our own truth and needs.

Another effective way to understand the different levels of how you're shaped within your own family system is looking at your family of origin. Drawing the generations helps to see the patterns. Go back three or more generations (i.e. your great-grandparents) and include miscarriages, diseases, terminations, deaths, half-siblings and step-children, family roles, careers, significant life events, religious and cultural influences of the time and individual characteristics.

Write down two or three descriptors for each person's character, and something that stands out about their life or their career. You can draw a key, like on a map, with different coloured patterns between the people who were close and squiggles or jagged lines between people who had conflict.

Once this is complete, it can be interesting to look for the themes down one and then the other side of your family. The history of your own family and their influence on you may reveal a theme of survival, or betrayal, or fear; a theme of strong women, alcoholics, sexual abuse or more. I found this a really interesting process to notice the family stories in the context of my story.

Fortunately there was the theme of endurance and survival in my family. For me this book is a lot about transforming endurance into empowerment.

How can someone caught in an abusive relationship have clear and clean skills and resources in the moment if some of these over-riding familial and social layers (as well as working to survive on such a deep level, Chapter '*The Red Shoes*') are going on? It's complex and tricky to go beyond the external and literal unfolding of each day when abuse is involved. There are so many layers, inhibitors, blocks and challenges that influence interactions on every single level. These pressures and expectations often confuse, distort and limit our choices.

The more you read, I'm hoping the more you understand how there are multiple triggers that involve our environment, as well as many layers within every element of our being – including the body, the limbic brain, the amygdala and our unconsciousness. There is so much more to explore! Don't be put off! The rewards are more than you can imagine in being free and comfortable in your own skin. You don't have to do all the conscious work for every single thread. With a skilled response, there will be a ripple effect between your unconscious and conscious self, through mind and body, clearing and healing. Though I would recommend you have a support team, including a skilled psychotherapist, along with if possible a friend(s) or family to help you through this journey.

When we look at these layers, we open up greater choices, which optimise the parasympathetic nervous system mode (rest, digest, feed and breed) rather than be in the sympathetic nervous system (fight and flight) where there is limited access to brain choices and significant impacts on our health. When we recognise what is happening in our brain body we can work with the messages and responses in our brain rather than fighting them. There is a simple body brain exercise to help the brain link out of the stress response and from there you can then process what is required (using the right mind body tools).

When we feel secure and relaxed in our body, then we have more reserves to handle stepping out of our comfort zone – but the first thing is making sure you are safe. It is very hard to process information if you are unsafe and still in the stress response. So don't pressure yourself. It is important to first off have the ability to switch out of the sympathetic nervous system and build up the parasympathetic nervous system, so you have fuel in the tank and space to tolerate some stress and still remain in your optimal arousal zone. So many people are trying to negotiate life from their sympathetic nervous limited brain/body function response or are constantly on the edge and tip over into the sympathetic nervous system when something happens. As a society if we want to have different conversations and create better actions and outcomes, we need to ensure we are all out of the stress response to be able to speak and process with the emotional muscle (which includes having resources to negotiate what we are confronting) to explore what we can do differently.

When we're in the stress response, our blood is going to specific parts of our brain and body. Different hormones are activated which determines what we focus on. The blood moves away from our frontal cortex, the front part of our brain that has more sophisticated thinking about our feelings. Our blood moves instead to the amygdala, that old part of the brain, and connections and processing cannot take place and it is just about activating learnt survival responses.

When we are in a stress response and our blood has moved away from our frontal cortex and into our amygdala, we can easily get a foggy head, be forgetful, get things back to front, feel muddled or mixed up, feel like we're wading through mud and have less energy. Our sleep and digestive functions are impacted as it is not time to rest or process but to stay vigilant to defend or escape. Circulation to our hands and feet are inhibited and can feel cold as our blood congregates around our organs. This is all involuntary, because the alarm system has been activated and we're in the emergency fight/flight mode. When we are in the constant environment of vigilance and alertness that an emotional or physically abusive situation demands, we are vulnerable to getting more depleted the longer we're living in this environment.

When there isn't a response in our environment that can help us switch off and we're constantly getting triggered, our system becomes exhausted and hypervigilant to risk. We are so trained to be on alert and focused on survival, and navigating the risks, that in our tired state we fall into going through the motions, with no room to reflect. We are in cleanup/lookout mode – there's no frontal cortex access to look at how we switch this off, because the brain's not thinking 'how' – it's in the mode of enduring or getting away from the immediate danger. Plus we don't have a society that has awareness and tools on how to resound to the brain body stress response. We are deserted and in chaos, no matter how many people are in our life or trying to help. We are not in reach or more accurately, they are out of reach and don't know how to reach us.

Looking at history, culture and patriarchy while holding awareness of the connection between stress and the body reminds me to tell you an unbelievable but true story from history. Hippocrates, the father of medicine, as well as the famous philosopher Plato, both believed that a woman's womb would 'wander' by itself in the body and create hysteria. Greek doctors were adamant that this troubling phenomenon created physical and mental problems for women, and this was why women were different to men. The Greek word for 'hysteria' actually is a derivative of the word 'womb'. Aristotle believed that a woman was 'deformed' and a 'mutilated male'.

Aretaeus of Cappadocia believed the womb was 'an animal within an animal' and could create sluggishness, vertigo, lack of strength, headaches, choking, loss of speech and sensibility – and even death. But apparently, the womb loved scents and doctors could calm the womb and lure it back to a correct position. So men decided that the way to control this 'wandering womb' was to keep the woman pregnant so the womb was not 'bored' and would stay in its rightful place. Doctors would prescribe a lot of sex. Isn't it understandable that women used to have panic attacks, exhaustion, headaches and other pains when they were treated this way? Other solutions included yelling at her and, for some reason, making her sneeze.

By the 1500s the belief of the wandering womb was no longer held but women were still held to believe that their womb made them irrational. By 1700 the cause shifted from physical ailments to psychological problems. By the 19th century remedies consisted of hypnosis, vibrating devices and strong jets of water directed into a woman's abdomen.

This part of patriarchal history tells us again that women, their feelings, instincts and their bodies were treated with disgust, made wrong for being different and trivialised. Perhaps also the tight corsets and being treated like a sexual object was how men tried to mould women to not be in their 'animal' nature, which created a significant impact on women's physical and psychological wellbeing. (King et al 1993; Tasca et al 2012).

***

We have cultural, societal and religious expectations where one person or group attitude is given greater value than another, yet we hold the value that it's important to think of others and not to be selfish. Combined together they are a dangerous, abusive cocktail. Relationships are not about one person or one attitude and are not so black and white. It doesn't have to be this *or* that; a relationship can be self-care *and* respect for others. These qualities don't have to be separate from each other. We don't have to throw the baby out with the bath water. There are many, good qualities in honouring, being responsible and not rejecting, considering others *and* considering self.

The problem is that the Wolf is not willing to be part of this and wants a one-sided arrangement. This is when one on one work with a skilled psychotherapist can assist you to find yourself, so past or current, strong or unconscious, societal and cultural beliefs don't inadvertently collude with the force coming from the Wolf. So you can find yourself inside choices that respect you inside the relationship. This can bring greater clarity about the health and flexibility of what is possible in your relationship.

We can be independent and dependent in healthy ways. We can be loving and maintain boundaries. We can be caring of ourselves and others, and not be overly responsible to completing another's unrealistic expectations. We can develop emotional muscle to bear disappointing others in order to maintain love and respect for our own sacred self.

Often there are layers as to how much we can access our healthy self beliefs such as 'thinking of others' and 'not being selfish', which tie in with spiritual beliefs and other facets of patterns and influences. This includes not wanting to be negative, suspicious, mistrustful, questioning or disagreeing. I ask you (or ask you to ask your client), do you want to be naive and get caught by the Wolf? These beliefs of not wanting to be negative, disagreeing or mistrustful are very black and white. There are shades that can allow trust, discernment, appropriate questioning and healthy risk-taking.

Do you want to develop greater emotional intelligence, so that you can be the one amongst the others who can see what really is there? Yes, it can be uncomfortable to not go with the crowd, but do you want to fit in with the crowd and betray yourself or your community, or be with the truth, like the child in the story 'The Emperor's New Clothes'? The child, the innocent who is not yet shut down and ingrained inside the tribal culture, is the one who can see that the Emperor is walking around naked. The crowd consists of people who follow and don't reflect on what is true (bystander effect), out of fear of being different, getting it wrong or rejection. You can become the child who is open and sees, no matter what your age or circumstance. Are you willing and comfortable to stand your ground to protect you, even if your community or society don't agree?

No one wants to be rejected – rejection is painful. But I ask you, are you willing to reject aspects of yourself, so that other people don't feel rejected? Would you ask that of your children or your closest friend?

In the history, culture and religion you have been immersed in, find what is nourishing, or not, find it elsewhere. Just find your rock and rudder. Find the intrinsic soulful values that can hold you and that are bigger than you or anything else. Sometimes I found this value in people's belief in me, music, creative arts, writing, nature, sometimes in prayer and sometimes in poetry.

During my challenging years, I found immense support in the form of a special poem. I would recall a particular verse when I needed to stand with courage and not betray myself in fear of being rejected. I want to share this very, very special poem with you. You may have heard it before.

The Invitation

It doesn't interest me
what you do for a living.
I want to know
what you ache for
and if you dare to dream
of meeting your heart's longing.

It doesn't interest me
how old you are.
I want to know
if you will risk

looking like a fool
for love
for your dream
for the adventure of being alive.

It doesn't interest me
what planets are
squaring your moon …
I want to know
if you have touched
the centre of your own sorrow
if you have been opened
by life's betrayals
or have become shrivelled and closed
from fear of further pain.

I want to know
if you can sit with pain
mine or your own
without moving to hide it
or fade it
or fix it.

I want to know
if you can be with joy
mine or your own
if you can dance with wildness
and let the ecstasy fill you
to the tips of your fingers and toes
without cautioning us
to be careful
to be realistic
to remember the limitations
of being human.

*It doesn't interest me
if the story you are telling me
is true.
I want to know if you can
disappoint another
to be true to yourself.
If you can bear
the accusation of betrayal
and not betray your own soul.
If you can be faithless
and therefore trustworthy.*

*I want to know if you can see Beauty
even when it is not pretty
every day.
And if you can source your own life
from its presence.*

*I want to know
if you can live with failure
yours and mine
and still stand at the edge of the lake
and shout to the silver of the full moon,
"Yes."*

*It doesn't interest me
to know where you live
or how much money you have.
I want to know if you can get up
after the night of grief and despair
weary and bruised to the bone
and do what needs to be done
to feed the children.*

It doesn't interest me

who you know
or how you came to be here.
I want to know if you will stand
in the centre of the fire
with me
and not shrink back.

It doesn't interest me
where or what or with whom
you have studied.
I want to know
what sustains you
from the inside
when all else falls away.

I want to know
if you can be alone
with yourself
and if you truly like
the company you keep
in the empty moments.

    Oriah @Mountain Dreaming

Thank you Oriah, for allowing me to share your profound poem.

I offer you Oriah's wise and soulful words to connect to. What part of these words resonate for you? I find her words are a mantra to live by. To be with the fullness of life's experiences and have the emotional muscle to stay with the truth rather than deny. I love her reminder to be mindful, that if we don't want others to betray us, how are we betraying our own soul? Don't use this question to beat yourself up or be cruel or harsh about your own limitations. But from this point moving forward, what steps can you take to not allow others to betray you? How can you make one change to not betray yourself? Even if it is in a small situation. Begin.

Write your own manifesto. It may help to first list the values, attitudes, beliefs, behaviours, habits, body sensations and postures that have grown out of your family, culture and religion – all of what you have absorbed.

Then write down a list of the attitudes, feelings, behaviours, etc., that you want to have beyond all of these influences that protect and honour your boundaries. Does anything need to be added to protect your values?

It's a bit like looking in a street directory. You've got to look on the map and locate where you are *and* where you want to get to. It's very hard to move anywhere if you only know the detail of where you presently are. It's also very hard to move towards what you want if you don't have concrete specific clarity and details of this new ground.

So be with these layers in specific ways, so that you can find your markers and direction and not be walking around lost. So that you have some sense of the basics of what you want or don't want. More can come when you have a clear and specific starting point.

When we look on a map and just know generally where we want to go, say we know a street in Melbourne, we're still not going to get there. We need specific, concrete detail – and so we need to unpack these details. What skills, strengths and structures do you need in order to find, develop and protect this new positive ground? What values and attitudes belong here? What will people notice about you when you walk through the door, fully embodying this ground? When our culture, history, religion and family have provided a structure that is not working for us, we need to find what can support our new map.

The more detail you put down, the more this ground can hold and you can find the gaps and what is needed to support you in ways that your culture or history hasn't offered you. This is so you are not waiting, longing, seeking approval or permission for a second longer. Start to claim your ground. Now.

Little steps, day by day. You can build and create what you want. Who can you seek out now to support you with taking these beginning steps? Because I hope you recognise by now that we can't do everything on our own.

Each chapter, we will open the door to a greater consciousness of what we know. Johari's Window, as you can see below, invites us to go beyond our limited picture of information and understand from four different orientations our experience of knowing.

'Knowing' does not reside fully in one orientation. In one window there is what I know about me and what another person also knows about me. In another window there is what I know about me and what another does not know about me. Then there is the window of what others know about me, that I don't know about me. Sometimes people have awareness about us, before we consciously do. Some people can see what we are unconscious about. In the final window, there is what both of us don't know about me. This is what is resting in the unconscious.

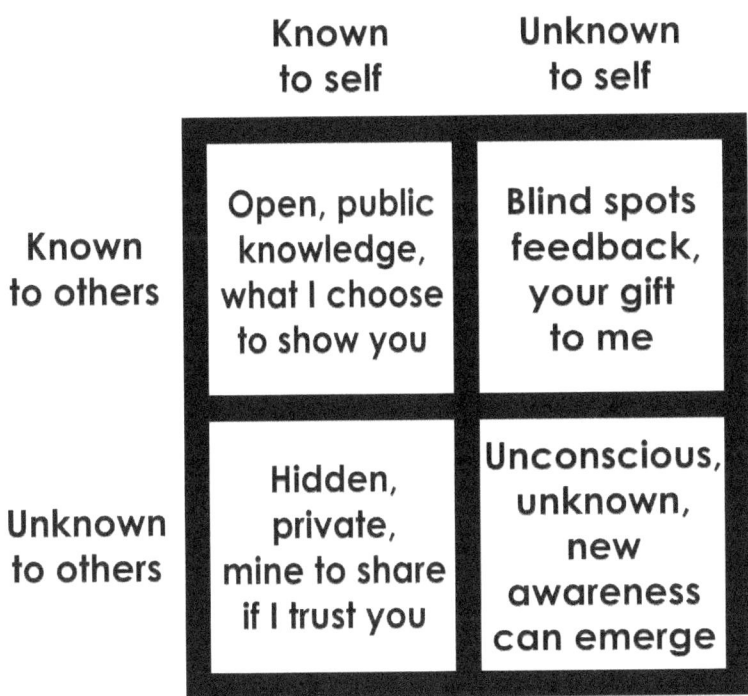

Johari's Window

When we stay inside our culture and society paradigm, we are limited on how much we can explore the wisdom in many of these quadrants. If we only rely on one of those quadrants, we're limited to the resources and awareness of just one perspective. Working with a skilled practitioner can help you connect and listen to your deep, creative and wise unconscious as well as take in more from others, so we can actually have access to and benefit from in varying degrees all four areas, including the unconscious.

Are you ready to take the next step?

The last thing for this chapter. Within the influence of our society, family, culture, history and religion is the creation of you. Remember, you can't move in the map to your desired destination, until you honestly locate where you are and where you want to get to. If you don't like yourself – if you reject your own feelings or thoughts – how can you find your destination and be with a circle of people who do? It is very hard to create change and set boundaries if you don't acknowledge how you feel or think. You don't have to like, agree or feel comfortable with all of yourself at this point, but you can want to include and allow what and who you are right now in the desire to get to who and what you want to be. So you can grow into you, without willpower or positive thinking forcing it into being (because neither approach lasts).

How can you start to love and accept yourself just the way you are for doing the best you can in this moment? You are a product of a long history. The act of naming your reality is the first act of love and acceptance.

Perhaps at some point you can honour and thank your history, but not necessarily right now. By thank, I mean feel pride for what you have come through and recognise how you are part of a long line of survivors through a culture of trauma and abuse. Through the combination of all that created and shaped you to be who you are, you would not have the depth of sensitivity, strength or courage if you had not lived through what you have. You may not recognise this yet; you will come to what you need to, in your own time.

Because despite everything, you got through to this point. You have choices and possibilities and are moving forward. You wouldn't be reading this book otherwise. I'm not saying, thank the abuser for hurting and wounding you. Thank that you got through and haven't given up. Thank that you managed to ask yourself questions and go beyond.

Chapter 9: Bluebeard's Seduction

Bluebeard's Seduction

Bluebeard was a big man, with a dark blue beard. He was a womaniser and once courted three sisters at the same time. They were scared of him, yet he liked the challenge. He courted them and dazzled them with abundance and a fun time. The two older sisters enjoyed the occasion but when they returned home, they were still suspicious of his intentions. The youngest sister started to convince herself of his good nature. She agreed to marry him.

After a while Bluebeard had to go away. He handed his wife a set of keys and told her that she could enjoy all the abundance of all the rooms in the house, except for the smallest key to one room. He encouraged her to invite her sisters over. When they came to visit they were curious and wanted to know what his instructions were.

The three sisters made a game of going through the hundreds of rooms to find which room matched the tiny key. They finally came to a small door; and without thinking they opened the door. They all screamed with what they saw by the small flame lighting up the darkness. There were skulls, blood and corpses lying in piles.

Quickly closing the door, the youngest saw there was blood on the key and wiped the key on her dress. Each of the sisters tried to wipe the blood off but the key kept bleeding. By the time they reached the kitchen her dress was stained with dark red blood. She tried to stop the key's bleeding using horsehair, ashes, heat, cobwebs – but nothing stopped the blood, so she hid the key in her wardrobe.

The next day Bluebeard returned and questioned her about everything she had done. When she said everything was fine, he asked for the keys back but noticed the smallest key was missing. She tried to say she must have lost it while out horse-riding. He got angry and grabbed her hair, throwing her to the ground and calling her names. He yelled out that she had been in the room and flung open her wardrobe to find the bleeding key staining all her beautiful clothes.

It was now her turn to enter this smallest room with all the dead wives' bones. She grabbed the doorframe and pleaded to have fifteen minutes to pray before her death. He agreed.

She ran to her room and asked her sisters to wait at the outer protective walls of the castle. She knelt down to pray, but instead she kept calling out if the sisters could see their brothers coming. Every minute seemed to go too fast with no sign of the brothers, until the sisters could see some dust in the distance.

Bluebeard began yelling for her to come for her beheading. Just as she called out to her sisters one last time, her sisters saw their brothers coming. Bluebeard came thudding over, the castle walls and floors crumbling with the weight of his rage. The brothers arrived just as he was entering her chambers. They cut him to pieces and she was free.

Adapted from Tales From Mother Goose *(Perrault 1697).*

Bluebeard likes to seduce. He pretends he is a lover but he is intent on tricking, charming and enticing someone who is unsuspecting or innocent. He is steadfast and focused on his own agenda. This agenda of tricking is presented in a seductive way, to confuse the person from any sense of alarm or caution. Bluebeard is clever at persuading and convincing through indirect ways. This trickster might present himself with something that appeals to you, not revealing his intention to kill you – not necessarily literally, but to kill your identity, your rights, your feelings, your reality. Though in truth, some women are physically killed by Bluebeard.

The story of Bluebeard takes us beyond the trapping of the Wolf inside the torture and control in the relationship that is presented as love.

Let's look at love, seduction, false love and some hooks. Getting tricked by the powerful man is not so simple. *A trick only becomes a trick because you can't see the deception.* So by naming the man as a trickster, there is already a disadvantage, because we are already aware of something that typically is not yet known.

To prevent being tricked, we need to look at where and how we form our love and our anger/assertion/power map. All the messages and skills that were missing from Little Red Riding Hood's basket set off into the woods. Again, we need to visit family and the unconscious. How do we learn to not get caught by these tricksters? After all, not everyone gets caught. Hopefully our home-life becomes the template and the safe place where we learn and explore how to navigate the world and our feelings via our parents.

Where in the story of Bluebeard were the parents to encourage the youngest daughter to not be tricked and remain listening to her original internal warnings? We may have sisters and the same parents but each child receives different messages, influenced by the different temperaments, different life events and different stages of the parent's lives when we each are growing up.

What is happening in the life of a family when one child is two and the other is four and another six, will be experienced very differently even though it is the same event but filtered through the children's different temperaments, different emotional, psychological and developmental capacities, let alone the mood and life events influencing the parent and their own capabilities at that time.

Where are the parents teaching her to allow her quiet, invisible, inner sensing to be bigger than Bluebeard's loud, visible seduction. The parents appear not to provide support, skills or encouragement for this daughter to sit with and hold firm through time, listen to her inner instinct and wisdom. The parents are not teaching how to build the emotional muscle so you do not respond out of fear or urgency in not finding the 'one'.

Maybe there was not a modelling of reflection, or questioning of what feels good and what doesn't feel good through the dating process. I would say this needs to be modelled way earlier than the dating years, taking the time to reflect and question how we feel and what our body tells us about our yes and no feelings. I would say there was not a solid emotional education or demonstration of love to model how to protect yourself. Maybe the parents were tired by the time the youngest daughter started dating and were more occupied in their own lives, leaving her to her own naivety.

The two sisters' suspicions in the story of Bluebeard can be literal sisters or symbolic of the instinctual whispers and wonderings in our own mind, which are so important to listen to. To me the brothers represent those masculine qualities we all need, just like the Woodcutter in Little Red Riding Hood; it's the ability to cut through and destroy what is bad, to protect what is good. This bad that needs destroying or stopping could be a bad attitude or behaviour that is not respectful or life-enhancing.

This skill of destroying the bad needs to be focused with a specific and flexible responsiveness to the concern – and not be indiscriminate and globalised in our concept of bad and good. The brothers also represent the capacity to act without question, to not hesitate. *To be able to stand on our own ground and not be swayed by the volume of someone else's protests.* As women we can be taught to be so attuned to other through patriarchy or through trauma that we get swayed too easily.

I know my parents did not give me a safe place to stay true to myself. Love was a confusing thing in my home. There was an unspoken expectation in the map of love that left me unsafe and uncomfortable. A double bind. The map of love became associated with fear, judgement, control, shame and rejection way before dating began. Tricky to have this template when you grow up and start dating. Start the basics early on!

Remember, I am talking from the child's experience. My parents may not have intended me to have that experience, but as a child we don't have the sophisticated processing that develops later in life. Experiences are either good or bad. If your parent is depressed, stressed or overwhelmed, and the look in their eyes or tone of voice does not tolerate your natural self to be expressed (whether it is related to the youth of your behaviour or not; the not coping or their emotional pain is still there when they look at you which you interpret as about you), then the child absorbs that they are not lovable or acceptable in their full self. The sense of not lovable or acceptable becomes a vulnerable hook and target and leads to being too accommodating of other when dating and in relationships.

You learn love comes with *conditions and limitations on being you* but not conditions about the other person. You learn that your parent is fragile. In some sense you become a caretaker and withhold aspects of yourself so you are not 'too much' for them. This translates to you fitting in to the emotional conditions set by the person you date and in relationships. You may be confident or excel professionally in other areas of your life, but there is a gap in your emotional love map. Something a Wolf will sniff out and find you a suitable target.

When the daily experience is of a parent (or parents) unable to resolve personal limitations and stresses, the entire household can become immersed in 'walking on eggshells', explosions or holding in.

I learnt to grow up fast and act as if everything was okay, because my parents were not coping. Love was caring for the 'wounded'. Love was caring for the child in them. Love was showing them the reflection they wanted to see, not what I saw – I had to carry that dark secret of what I saw and pretend it was not real.

This was the map of love I learnt. Love was not about being seen. Love was not about being free to be myself and being loved for that. I was loved for being the way they needed me to be. I was used to walking on eggshells being normal. What you tolerate you are at risk of taking into your adult relationships under the banner of normal and familiar. The boundary has been stretched.

In my young undeveloped state, I could not reveal the truth that they (my parents) were not enough. After all, I depended on them for my survival. I had to 'make them whole' so I could feel some sense of getting through each day.

If I'd truly had the capacity to consciously know what I know now about my parents, I do not think I could have gotten through each day. I would have been in so much more emotional pain, overwhelm, helplessness, grief and alienation. So I had to pretend so well to convince myself there was nothing behind the pretence. That way, I could manage and they would not see that I knew the truth. I couldn't reveal it in my eyes back to them. That way I was always reflecting they were fine and all was good back to them. Making what was not okay 'normal' became automatic and part of the template I was not aware was being created in my growing years.

There is often a 'family shared pretence' that everyone becomes convinced by and defends. When I tell my story now, I am devastated at what the child in me had to bear, acting as if nothing was broken. The imprint of love became me losing 'me' to keep my parents intact. A big task for a child to bear, but no one created the space or showed the constancy of presence and permission for me to be seen and come out.

We are all vulnerable to 'lose' parts of ourselves growing up, but hopefully there has been some good enough parenting which allows us, through adolescence and early adult years, to go out into the world, party, take risks, date, study, work and through these experiences, reclaim and reorganise a good enough sense of who we are. Throw out what didn't work from our family and keep what was of value.

My parents did not cheer me on to discover how to walk my path. They didn't seem interested in finding out what made me shine. Just as long as I was quiet, did my schoolwork and got the right marks, everything was good. They were absorbed in getting through each day. They didn't know about my day. They didn't know about what I liked or what scared me. They didn't ask.

I loved John Denver's 'Annie's Song'. I loved elephants. I loved Enid Blyton, Paddington Bear, 'The Muddle Headed Wombat' and the Adventure series by Willard Price. I loved trees and clouds. I treasured my poetry writings tucked away in my folder – that somehow vanished one day, even though I always kept it in a special place in my room.

The whole folder disappeared. One parent never knew about this loss and the other just made one comment, 'Maybe the cleaner threw it out' and walked off. There was no comfort or searching with me, or sharing the loss. What was most important to me, the expression of 'me' on paper, was lost and no one cared. I was left with the sense that I was not worth feelings or effort. These memories build a map of love or not feeling loved.

Back then, I was so busy surviving that I did not get the opportunity to discover or develop my interests and my sense of self, beyond my secret inner life. Reading was my passion and my coping strategy. I lived through the characters and through their joy and spiritedness, I could feel some joy. Yet, I couldn't make the best use of these characters and step more into my own character. I was used to revolving my life around others, being serious and not being the centre of my own world. There was no space or lightness to be me.

My parents didn't create a space where I could show my fear and be comforted. They couldn't just be with me. I internalised that, I wasn't acceptable for feeling or showing my fear. There was no curiosity about what made me so scared. I remember my father carrying me on his shoulders around his study in the dark and telling me, 'See, there is nothing there. You don't need to be afraid.' That was it, a moment in time, done. He thought that issue was resolved. Ticked off. But I was living with nightmares and terrors every day, my whole childhood, and there was no enquiry or curiosity to be with me inside my reality or follow up how I was going. There was no entering into the feelings together.

There was no pacing and helping me build the skills I needed. No conversations. No check-ins. Even if they didn't know what to do, not being alone would be enough. Children are easy to please. *Just be with me.* Acknowledge and help me express and soothe. There was no search for missing skills. There was no search for what in my environment was causing the fear and then changing what needed changing. I went into my adult life *not expecting I could create change to suit and support me.*

I learnt to always succumb to the person who appeared to have more power than me. The one who was louder, more controlling, bigger. Day in and day out, I had learnt to be quiet, passive and obedient. It starts to become habitual when there are little exceptions to this experience.

No wonder my favourite place was the library. Even now, when I walk into a library I feel comfort. It is quiet. It has something home didn't have: order, peace, space with no intrusion and wonderful stories. My tolerance for connection and intensity was fragile, which also left me vulnerable when dating. I did not know how to handle intensity or the chaos of feelings as an adult.

Everything at home that was encouraged was about being quiet and not about the embodied experience of spontaneous childlike play. Reading, drawing and writing were encouraged – all quiet activities. There was no area of my life where the noise of the child, the robustness of expression, could come out and play. Spontaneous play allows us to take up space and affect our surroundings. To be carefree and spontaneous. It builds confidence. These inhibitions have direct impact in our experience of dating and relationships. Dating and intimacy is about being playful. If we don't have a strong sense of being able to fully stand in our space, we are at risk.

I learnt to fit in, not stand out and definitely not be different. Being different felt too painful, as I already had too much experience of feeling alone and alienated, of feeling my parents were different in an unacceptable way and feeling different as a whole family. I desperately wanted to belong. The challenge to honour myself and show 'me' would mean being different and the risk of getting rejected, which could mean being on my own. I couldn't bear more of that.

The template of love and needing to be loved ripples out from childhood into adulthood, because we always need and want to feel loved and feel lovable. It is tricky when we don't feel lovable, we will turn ourselves inside out to be lovable for someone who will notice us.

Children need parents who celebrate the child having the energy to stay with their convictions, even if the parent 'loses face'; or when the child doesn't do what the parent thinks is best or when the child makes a mistake. Children need to experience parents engaging with their own best and worst feminine and masculine faces to be able to internalise and navigate love and false love and develop emotional muscle to the full spectrum in being human.

Become aware of the love messages you received growing up. Become aware of how you may get swayed, serenaded or tricked from being with the big picture in an effort to remain loved. Do you know your weak points? How can you discover what they are? What do Bluebeard's 'romantic' gestures feed in you? Is there a part of you that feels validated by Bluebeard, where he fills a void or silences a gap?

In looking at Bluebeard, we are looking at the adult experience of love and seduction. However, the map of love is an imprint from the experience of our first loves – our parents. The original imprint of love plays a significant part of how we experience love and whether we are labelling 'false' love as 'true' love, and how much we feel lovable and acceptable to receive love.

So there are two (of, I am sure, more!) fairy tales to consider in this dilemma of love and the relationship with the Wolf.

Some women may have had the experience of Little Red Riding Hood, where there may have been some family love but they weren't taught certain skills and not allowed to be with their full instinctual self.

For other women, they may have felt like the Ugly Duckling in their family – that who they were was not acceptable, despite possibly being loved or not. For some women, they experience a bit of both fairy tales growing up.

As we have already spent some time with Little Red Riding Hood and Bluebeard, we will now explore the love and abuse we are susceptible to in the experience of the child.

The Ugly Duckling

𝔐other Duck is sitting on the last egg, which has not broken open yet. She is proud of all her babies. This egg is bigger. An old duck says to leave it, as it's probably a turkey egg. The mother duck felt that since she had sat there for so long, she would wait a bit more.

Finally the egg cracked open and out came a large creature that didn't look like her other babies. Mother Duck thought maybe it was a turkey, but when they went to the water this baby swam well. The mother tried to see the beauty of this baby but she struggled.

Other creatures made fun of this baby and bullied it for being different. The mother tried her best, hoping that as her baby grew it would grow into itself, but when everyone else at the farm hissed, scratched and pecked him all the time this duckling was very gloomy. After a while Mother Duck became fed up and wished the duckling would just go.

The ugly duckling ran away. Exhausted, he collapsed by a marsh. Two geese came over and made fun of him. Suddenly gunshots fired and the two geese fell to the ground in pools of blood. The duckling hid and then flew on, wanting to get away from all the horror.

By nightfall, the duckling arrived at the poorest of houses where an old lady lived with her cat and hen. The cat caught mice and the hen laid eggs. The old lady hoped this creature would give her eggs or she could kill it for food.

The cat and hen picked on the duckling for not being able to offer anything. They didn't understand why the duckling wanted to be in the water. The duckling had to leave again. It was too painful to stay where he was made fun of for being different.

The weather was getting colder and colder by the time he arrived at a pond. He saw the most graceful birds flying above. When they saw him they called out. His heart leapt. He made a sound that he had never made before. He was also heartbroken as he felt a love he had never felt before – but he was alone now that they had gone. He felt the most alone he had ever felt.

He shuddered in the cold as the wind blew and ice, frost and snow came. He tried to move in the ice to keep warm but one day he became stuck. He felt he would die. Two mallards flew by and felt pity for what they saw: ugly and helpless. They flew off.

A farmer came by and freed the duckling from the ice. In the farmer's house, the children tried to grab the duckling, who flew in terror up to the ceiling, breaking pottery and escaping out the door. All winter the duckling flew from one pond to the next house, trying to stay alive.

Spring came and he stretched his wings. To his surprise they were much bigger and stronger. Flying above the pond he could see all the baby creatures coming out and some of the swans he had seen last autumn. His heart leapt again and he felt a calling to go over, but he was terrified they would laugh at him. They swam closer to him and he felt a fear they would kill him. He bowed his head, waiting to be killed, preferring to be killed by them rather than anyone else.

To his surprise he could see a reflection in the water of a beautiful swan. It was him! The other swans welcomed him. He belonged. He was home.

Adapted from the works of Hans Christian Andersen (1843)

The ugly duckling is born into a family where he doesn't fit in. Parents often have a view, partially unconscious, on how you should be to survive according to their world. Then there is a painful experience of trying to get you to fit into that shoebox. The Ugly Duckling does not look the way mother imagines. Sometimes, despite knowing rationally you are free to be your own person; it is not until you are in your thirties, forties or fifties that you can free yourself from the 'persona', 'relationship', 'lifestyle', 'attitude', 'habits', 'career' or whatever else your parents had decided was right for you. It can take a while to realise we don't have to please our parents and we can live our own life. Sometimes it is not until our parents die.

The mother tries but she can't sustain a position different to or beyond the farm view. She collapses and rejects her 'duckling' – emotional abandonment, until it appears that the duckling leaves rather than she had already left the duckling. The mother did not have the skills, support, resources or community to help her 'duckling' come into it's unique self.

> The ugly duckling goes from pillar to post trying to find a place to be at rest, while the instinct about exactly when to go may not be fully developed, the instinct to rove until one finds what one needs is well intact. Yet there is a kind of pathology – the ugly duckling Syndrome – one keeps knocking at the wrong door, even after one knows better. It is hard to imagine how a person is supposed to know which doors are the right doors if one has never known a right door to begin with. However, the wrong doors are those that cause you to feel outcast all over again.
> (Estés 1992, pp. 180–181)

Women, who do not feel a sense of belonging or who are not encouraged to be their own person in their full, powerful and feminine way, may go searching; meeting different men, going from one relationship to another, searching in other friendships, in hairstyles, fashion, in their career, or working out at the gym to find what is missing – not clear on what they are searching for, but knowing they need to search. A missing piece of themselves is calling them. A version of this also often happens with sensitive men not fitting the patriarchal, macho model their father expects of them.

In painful ways, anxiety or being with an abusive partner creates distance from a world they don't feel comfortable to be part of; either from their anxiety or toxic relationship sending the message that something is wrong with them – 'You are not acceptable' – instead of the message that something in their life is not acceptable.

Ugly ducklings may look different, feel different or are teased. Yet, we are all different. They are ridiculed and receive messages that they are not acceptable just the way they are. Ugly ducklings don't fit in. Why? Because a premature judgement is made that limits who the ugly duckling is.

Remember how we spoke about the habits of the brain, and how the brain likes to fill the gaps. Remember how we spoke about survival and the need to belong? Combine this with the imprint of love and the environment we grew up in as a child. Can you see how the pieces all fit together?

When we are young and still forming, there is still the unknown in us, still spaces to develop and spring forth and reveal our quirks, skills and personality; but we so quickly fill the unknown with certainties about who we/they are from the fixed messages determining what is acceptable and our destiny. A baby is born and we already try and place it looking like one parent, or what they will be when they grow up. Sure, there is a playful element to this, but it does hurry us out of the present moment where there is the unknown and fill a gap.

> A girl begins to believe that the negative images that her family and culture reflect back to her about herself are not only totally true, but also totally free of bias, opinions and personal preference. The girl begins to believe she is weak, ugly, unacceptable and that this will continue to be true no matter how hard she tries to reverse it. (Estés 1992, p. 171)

Here is a theme of non-acceptance, limitation and punishing consequences that keeps repeating in different ways in families – in how the brain processes, in our survival patterns, and in familial and cultural expectations that keep reinforcing the 'be less than who you are' (or you will be excluded and risk rejection and death of some sort). When family and society want us to fit in, there is an implicit expectation to not show our differences that challenge the family or social 'rules'.

The ugly duckling isn't being loved and accepted for who the ugly duckling is, even though the ugly duckling is actually a beautiful swan. But *if the parent does not know the experience of the swan, it does not recognise, appreciate or allow something that is different to what the parent is to develop and come into its own.*

When the ugly duckling is seen in the context of a swan's growth, it is apparent it is not ugly. The duckling has been labelled as ugly because there's a comparison. The duckling has been labelled as ugly because there is an interruption to the natural process and a hurried judgment made too early, before there has been a full evolution. The result is being made to feel wrong, and not being valued or admired for being unique or different.

We all have a deep need to find where we belong and where we're loved, accepted and admired. Everyone wants to feel valued and part of a group.

***

When we grow up in a family and important aspects of experience – love, anger, power and family – are misnamed and normalised, this can lead us down the wrong path.

The beliefs we developed from what we experienced about love can pull us into relationships and experiences that are not necessarily healthy. Beliefs about love, anger and power are tied to experiences and beliefs that develop within family patterns. Love and anger both influence our relationship choices and how much of a capacity we have to protect ourselves and discern what are true loving behaviours and attitudes. We look at anger and beliefs about power through Cinderella and the story of Lilith later on.

Beliefs and experiences about family, love and anger influence our role in the family and our connections within the family. All of these can be limiting or generative beliefs. Limiting beliefs become the hooks in relationships that make it difficult to extricate us from Wolves.

A hook is where there is some gap in our system – either a limiting belief, a lack of permission or lack of the skill to be a certain way. It leaves us vulnerable. A Wolf or Bluebeard sees this vulnerable gap and takes advantage by pulling us in, knowing we do not have the skill or strength to respond.

Let's explore some limiting beliefs about love. The first limiting belief that I'm going to say something about might be a challenge for you. *Unconditional love is a myth.*

Let me expand a bit more. I believe that every baby needs unconditional love. Full stop. A helpless infant cannot regulate their physical being, let alone their emotional and psychological being. A baby needs unconditional love as they learn how to regulate and process their experience. Adults are different and it is not needed, healthy or necessary to give unconditional love.

I guess I'd better define what I mean by unconditional love. Love is not constant. Our feelings for someone change all the time, dependent on a range of factors. Our feelings respond flexibly to a context of what is happening at the time within us and from a range of elements in our environment. To some degree our environment also needs to be flexible to us – it is not a one-way street. Except with a baby, we would hope that we don't show our upset towards an infant, no matter what is happening with the baby, as they are helpless. It is not their doing. The infant needs us to be there with a warm, consistent responsiveness to their needs.

With a young child, we are pacing ourselves to their capacity to feel and know. We hopefully still contain the majority of our unmediated responses and just share a tip of what is going on in a mediated way, depending on their age. We are holding them in unconditional love and it is the parents'/adults' responsibility to bear the extra 'stuff'.

As our children grow into teenagers, we gradually want to let in a bit more of how we are affected, while continuing to teach what we believe we need them to know. By this stage we want them to carry more, bit by bit so they build their emotional muscle to hold and feel and the capacity to mediate their own unmediated responses and also engage with how the other person is affected. So that the adult has modelled, allowing them to introject this healthy processing. In our relationships we need to incorporate how we are affected, so our children learn to healthily incorporate how others are affected in their relationships. By first being empathic to our children and then asking our growing children to consider their siblings, friends and us, we are helping them develop their empathic muscle, *towards themselves and to others,* which builds healthy relationships. We need a healthy self-to-self to be empathic to another and participate in a healthy relationship.

We want our children to not treat others as objects and not see the world from an entitled place. We want our children to feel love and empathy for others, *and* learn to regulate their unmediated self. This comes about by how we engage and model unconditional to conditional love. Don't we teach children and adolescents conditions on what is acceptable in loving relationships? So why do we think when dating that we should go back to square one, and offer unconditional love to another adult?

Bruce Perry is a psychiatrist and author specialising on the long-term effects of trauma in children. His book, *Born for Love: Empathy is Essential and Endangered*, is important reading. I believe empathy is the primary deficit in Wolves and Bluebeards. In our affect-aversive society, we are continuing to reinforce not being with the uncomfortable and losing our ability to bear witness, communicate and comfort. Violence occurs when someone does not have empathy.

A young boy wanted to play with a little four year old girl who hid behind the legs of her grandmother (me). The mother of the young boy asked the girl if she wanted to play with her son. The girl said no, strongly. The mother laughed and said, 'that's code for yes.' I imagine she didn't want her son to feel rejected so she twists the no. This is not empathic to the boy. This is teaching him to deny his hurt or disappointment. This is teaching him to not bear the fact that not everyone is going to like him or want him. The mother needed to be empathic to her son's vulnerable feelings of rejection and help him bear it, rather than set her son up to blame a female for his 'uncomfortable' feeling.

Daniel J Siegel is a leading neuropsychiatrist and author who specialises in trauma, thriving and the study of the brain from childhood, with its attachments through adolescence and adulthood. Daniel's work in parenting as well as being with the adult experience is profound, as is his work on the necessity of building a culture of empathy and compassion. He draws on interpersonal neurobiology, mindfulness, the right brain and cognition.

These two leading specialists, along with Brené Brown's seminal work on shame, have uncovered a lot of valuable research about the necessity of empathy as a skill that prevents violence. We need to be empathic to boys in all their range of feelings and instil this as part of being a strong man. We need empathy when a woman is angry and not shame her so she can find her depth of fire to hold her boundaries and her perspective, and not stifle her spirit from living the path that is only hers. We need to be able to differentiate about when and how to respond empathically to build healthy love and relationships.

Too many times I see boys *and* men being ridiculed for being human (hurt: physically and emotionally, vulnerable, tired or cold).

We need to not let our women be selfless vessels to provide unconditional love to men – for the sake of our boys and girls and preventing violence. We need mothers and fathers to teach boys to develop emotional skills and emotional muscle to be able to process and be with all their feelings, without requiring a partner to carry their emotional life – men often end up unconsciously asking their partner to carry the feelings in the relationship, and so they externalise their internal processes. This externalisation towards their female partner is a reflection of the re-enactment of what they do to their inner feminine self: punish and kill off the feeling life inside as being unacceptable and weak. This is not the partner's responsibility to carry or heal.

Likewise, the woman can unconsciously place their disowned and unconscious rage in the hands of their partner, where he carries all the anger and selfishness, and she says or does the 'right' thing. Where can her rage exist for her to engage with it and be informed by it in a creative and non-destructive way? How can she find and express her 'selfish' self for her own whole wellbeing?

The skill of being adult is when we can own both our full and shadow self, regulating the unmediated self and being in relationship to the other person. Two adults who are self-regulating themselves, taking care of their own emotional package and communicating what they need to, and what they need the other adult to know for understanding, boundaries and connection. Two adults who have skills to self soothe and take care of their emotional selves. This creates a healthy, intimate and powerful relationship. No one is being a caretaker for the other – instead, both are active caretakers of the third body - the relationship.

Is it making sense now, when I talk about unconditional love being a myth in adult relationships? An adult's obligation to another adult is not to give unconditional love. We are not a parent to another adult. When we parent each other, it backfires and we get the infantile rage that is not ours to bear or relate to. We are there to protect ourselves and our boundaries. We are there to provide unconditional love to ourselves and ask the other person, still with love, to respect our existence and experience. We are there to share life together, have fun together, build something together. Create, not destroy.

Let's be clear, the importance of setting boundaries and saying no is not about giving unconditional love to the other person. It is not about acting as if the other person is all amazing, when the reality is that sometimes there is something seriously wrong about their behaviour.

We don't do that with a child. *We wouldn't give a child unconditional love in the moment and act as if something was okay, when something is wrong* and they are old enough to own it in some capacity. Sometimes we blur unconditional love with the removal of facing our shadow, instead of holding the child with love *and* helping them see and metabolise their shadow and so grow in consciousness. We reflect back to the child, love *and* what is unacceptable. It is absolutely paramount to know that there is no need to do that for another adult. Sure you can do that with another adult, but there is no healthy reason to give unconditional love to another functioning adult when they will not own their shadow otherwise you can be caught in being their 'parent' or 'therapist' and the relationship is unequal and denying of your needs and existence.

The reality can't change if you tell yourself fairy tales. That will become even clearer in 'The Little Match Girl'. Telling the truth about your situation and your relationship to yourself and a kind witness - not to the person who is abusive, as that could place you at risk – (I recommend seeing a skilled counsellor or psychotherapist to help you navigate what to do) is crucial. The Ugly Duckling had to keep changing locations to find its tribe of acceptance and belong. The woman in Bluebeard had to wake up and find the person who could see the real story, her brothers, to respond to her reality and create change.

Exploring your identity in relation to love and breaking down the limiting beliefs about love and connection – discovering the unrealistic expectations, idealisations and myths that hook you in about love, relationships and anger – are all really important to enable you to reach your reality to be free. Free to be yourself in safety and full expression to protect and express yourself. To have your reality of being and desires able to affect and interact with others and your environment. Free to grow, experiment and discover.

So hold out for what is true, not what is easiest or quickest or available. Remember, the rub of the sand creates the pearl. Don't give up. The more you sort through this area, (with the help of a skilled therapist), the more clarity and ease can flow, instead of bumping into more unconscious hooks, limiting beliefs and pain in your relationship(s).

The Ugly Duckling had hooks and binds that tormented him, leading him to believe what was happening outside was a true reflection of him. No one reflected the Ugly Duckling back to himself. So now we're going to focus more specifically on the hooks and binds.

In Bluebeard, his new wife was so unaware of the hooks and binds that it was only when the blood was streaming from the key that she could see what she had gotten bound up in. Isn't it better if we can look at the hooks and binds before we are at risk? It is harder to get away when we are inside the door with the pile of skulls and blood, though not impossible.

The hooks are what we are caught on – those unexamined beliefs about love, power, anger, life and relationships. The hooks are sometimes hooked into social lacks, which increase the validity of the hook. We may have gained these hooks at different ages and stages when we had limited choices, limited power, limited ways of thinking and limited levels of independence. There is always an opportunity to examine the hooks and start the unhooking.

Every day, don't we either go about focusing on what is most calling our attention or what we're most comfortable to focus on?

Hooks can be uncomfortable to be with, as they're aligned with fears and lacks within us and around us. It can be hard to know how or if they can be resolved, so we may bury them. When we don't examine the boundaries, the hooks and the binds of why we do what we do, we get into trouble. When we don't pay attention to our awareness, we are limited to walking on eggshells.

We can become like those trained animals where we have learnt not to go beyond the cage door, even when the door is open, because of years of reinforced thinking and the behaviours that validate what is 'normal and acceptable'.

Often we can be so busy with survival coping mechanisms that we don't have the time, energy and skills to consider let alone negotiate the unknown. So we stay with the familiar and end up looping and reinforcing those patterns of habit – the immediacy of the stress response automatically just takes us there. It feels easier to stay with what we know, even when it is painful because we know we can get through doing the same thing. It is hard work creating change and new neural pathways, especially when we don't have the support or resources to take us to a new and better place. There is uncertainty and danger in change.

But isn't there also a bit of a trick here? Even though it might seem like it's easier to stay with what we know, we're treading water – walking on eggshells, always repeating that coping pattern. So we never get off that treadmill. How can that be an easier way? It is exhausting and usually set to only get worse.

Perhaps look at this bigger picture and see beyond; there may be some hard patches but there is more chance of getting off the treadmill and having a better life. Open up to the bigger picture to see the likely challenges, inevitabilities and possibilities for staying and leaving. Consider, the impact on yourself physically, mentally, emotionally, financially, socially, spiritually and sexually. What do you want for your life, your dreams and passions? If you have children, what you want for them? What is being modelled for your children and their future relationships and sense of self?

In being with the hooks, I want to acknowledge the immense challenge of those hooks and limitations, set up by lack of social and financial assistance and housing, as well as lack of protection and support from the police and court system. I do not want to minimise how tough and restrictive these challenges are for women to leave, but I do not want to get caught in a rut repeating these concerns and being stuck here.

We need to move beyond this. Of course society needs to be far more proactive and protective, and available, for women to feel safe to leave. I do not mean to trivialise that the solution is all about changing beliefs. Beliefs go hand in hand with behaviours and actions, which means responsive services and support. They all need to be congruent, working together. Beliefs and behaviours that respect and allow the fullness of communication also come from owning and regulating one's own experience and expression. Then we can feel free to unhook ourselves.

Sometimes though we can't wait for the ducks to line up financially or with ideal housing. Sometimes our health or safety is more urgent than the ducks lining up in the optimal way. You can acknowledge the hooks and still leave with the hooks still unresolved. The hooks can be re-worked after leaving, even when life is not perfect or ideal. I didn't have to work through my hooks to leave. I did that afterwards. Feel the fear and do what you need to do.

I hold the belief that safety and leaving abuse is more important than getting all the concerns addressed. Living rough, I found, is better than living with abuse. Living it tough can change; living with abuse doesn't change. The beliefs and possibilities we have about our finances and housing are important to examine, as housing and financial circumstances can change and improve over time when you leave. These concerns don't need to slow the process of leaving. Sometimes I think the fear of the unknown is the greatest challenge and if we can step into it, we can work it out one moment at a time. After all, our future comes along in minutes, so I promise it is doable, one moment at a time.

Solely focusing on limiting beliefs and hooks could be twisted to imply it is the women's fault for staying. I am not saying this. *The limiting beliefs and hooks are a reflection of our society's gaps.* We live with a community emptiness that impacts on men's capacity to be with their whole self and women's capacity to be with their whole self. We have a social problem and often the Ugly Duckling is the scapegoat. In a patriarchal society the women become the scapegoat, but patriarchy does not allow either women or men to be their full self.

Family violence is a social problem. There is a social and gender context that is embedded in every family and relationship. We are all part of the continuum in which family violence sits on. The problem is that most people don't see that their limiting beliefs are part of a far bigger picture (like the mother of the boy who say no is code for yes), and that there is a context between love, disappointment, anger, being a man, being a woman, relationships and power that is relevant for all on the continuum of relationship (of which abuse is at one end). I am asking every person, whether you are in an abusive relationship or not, to examine your beliefs about love, anger, being a man, being a woman, power and making the space for others to be different and accepted. When we can all adjust our beliefs and empathy, we create a safer, less stressed and more responsive community.

What we change on one part of the continuum will affect the other side. We are connected. This goes for limiting beliefs and disordered thinking that threads through all of us, anywhere on the continuum. When we are mindful, examine and adjust our beliefs we create a society more responsive to feelings and connections – as well as behaviours that reflect ordered thinking and a healing community.

There are so many hooks that I cannot do justice to everything here but I will do my best. So many women don't leave a Wolf because at least when you stay together, you can keep more of an eye on how he is with the children or for your own safety. I know when I left I was scared he would just appear on the street outside my place with his gun, stand beyond the intervention distance and shoot me. At home, I felt like I had more control of seeing where he was. The legal system does not provide adequate protection. This is one of the serious hooks: unsupervised contact and parents given 'normal' contact when they are not 'normal' parents is part of the problem.

So here are some hooks that I remember from the women's groups I ran twenty years ago, and my shortened and very direct response to each. Many of these are beliefs that need to be explored privately, one on one. Some are there because our social system does not respond adequately. Some of the hooks will make much more sense after reading 'The Red Shoes' and 'The Little Match Girl'.

Naturally, each of these areas are very important and it is not about just taking on board my response, as I cannot answer all the possible responses to the hooks here. My responses are a starting point. It is about being supported to sort through the chaos or challenges within each area with a skilled and unbiased practitioner who is very knowledgeable about abuse and the trauma response.

Notice any minimising or denying in response to any of my suggestions. We tend to absorb the minimising and denying and repeat what has been done to us. Some of the hooks lead back to fear of survival. This may seem an irrational fear but it is significant and real. It is not something to be minimised or rationalised. When it is there, it is from real experiences, personal and sometimes generational. The childhood fear for survival, which may be activated in hooks is overpowering; when that fear is re-ignited, the adult self can be lost to the child reality of being in a world that is dangerous. The danger is real on both fronts – for the child self and for the adult. When we are faced with stress, our emotions are important. They are not irrational. They may be intense and not make sense to some people, but our feelings connect to real needs and experiences. Our feelings are not about logic, they are about us and our experience.

- *I love him – he is not all bad:* Explore what you believe loving another person is. Also, what about self-love? At times, we all love and hate the one person but no matter what is loveable, there are certain non-negotiables. Would you want your child (even if you don't have one now) or your best friend to accept this?

- *He loves the children, and they love him … the children need a father:* Loving your child means not harming them or their mother in any form. Children may appear 'loving' of him out of safety and survival. They may need to hide the true unmediated self and any internal conflict because there is a bind about loving their father. Children need a father who is kind yet firm, but not punishing, shaming, denying or controlling.

- *My marriage vows are important, I can't break them:* His abuse has already broken the vows. He broke the sacred space. You did not break the vows. He has gone beyond what the vows reasonably consider. Walking on eggshells and control was not part of the agreement.

- *He promised it would never happen again:* Are his words matching his actions? Is he willing to learn new skills to negotiate his emotions, beliefs and behaviours? Is he willing to seek help? He will have a blind spot. We all do. He can't do this on his own. Has he said this before and nothing has changed?

- *The children will hate me:* You may receive more anger towards you because it is safer for them to express their chaos to you. The children may need time to process the changes. Consider the possibility that we are not there to be our child's friend, but to create a safe place and teach them how to deal with complicated feelings like love, relief, disappointment, guilt and grief. Let your children have their own process; just as you go through a range of feelings, they will too. They may need you to receive their rage and help them find a way of releasing it without causing harm, shame and rejection. Trust and closeness will come through when you are consistent and tolerant with them, without hurrying them through their own process.

It may not happen as quickly or easily as you prefer, but children tend to come through when you provide them with the tools and teach them alternate ways to communicate and express their experience.

- *I can't break up the family, it's not fair on the children:* His abuse has already broken up the family, even though for all appearances you are all together. The children are already affected and are 'coping', whether you realise it or not.

- *It's not the right time for the children. I'll wait until they're older:* There is never a right time. The risks only increase over time. It is your choice, but sort out the pros and cons from the fears and limiting beliefs in the meantime. Also recognise that abuse is unpredictable and you don't know what will happen next. The children are unconsciously being asked to 'manage' something by staying longer.

- *How do I take care of the kids:* You may wonder how you can, but you are already managing an intolerable situation. You and the children will learn new skills and resources. There is support available in many communities and contexts. Over time stress will decrease and your circle of support will increase when you are no longer isolated or controlled. Each stage of life brings new challenges and learnings. Just like when we were born: coming out the birth canal, learning to suckle, raising our head, learning concepts like night and day, and so on. We never stop growing. When we stop growing and responding to our environment, we become depressed and stuck. There are opportunities here that will bring you good things that you have not even realised.

- *Leaving is against my religion:* Cultural and spiritual beliefs are very powerful. Working with a skilled professional can help you to find what works best for you. There are others, from all religions and cultures, who have chosen a new way that can still align with core beliefs and still have a supportive community. It may take time and support to get there.

- *I don't have money to leave. I don't want to be on the streets or on welfare:* Money is tricky, as it is very tough with limited finances. However, there are different choices and possibilities that can be made. Many women continue to live with abuse and money is limited by his control. Do you want to live a life with abuse and chronic stress, and possibly with limited finances in the relationship, or short-term stress, with the potential to improve your financial situation in many creative ways? There are always more options than you realise and more options to feel content than having money. When we are stressed we go to the worst situation, and don't know about all the steps we can take along the way.

- *He will kill or attack me ... or he will harm the children:* This is a real risk, one that might become higher when you leave. Having a plan or speaking to someone in case you need to move out immediately is important. No one can make this decision for you, but there is a risk you will get killed by staying too.

- *He will take the children away from me and disappear:* Unfortunately, this is true for some women, even when he is the perpetrator of abuse. The courts are still not addressing this horrific situation in adequate ways. There are legal ways to protect yourself and your children and put boundaries on passports. There are many more services to assist you now.

I guess I have an optimistic view of never giving up. Keep trying, even if he tries tricks and revenge. In my case, maybe it was my healthy rage – when I was awake to the abuse, I wanted him to see that no matter what he did after I left I would always respond and object and never give up. I wanted him to see that he couldn't control me anymore. His control over me did become finite, compared to if I had stayed, where it never would have ended. There is less opportunity for good to come in your life and for your children to experience another reality when you stay. It is best to get legal advice. There are community-based legal services, pro bono services and legal aid that can help.

- *I can't protect myself in court:* Never give up. Do you want your choices to be based on other people's experiences and on the unknown? Do you want what is around you to structure your life, and your choices and possibilities to be based on the limits around you? There is a way to get through. Keep searching for the right team to support you. No matter the outcome in court, you (and the children) have the potential to get through this.

- *The police and courts won't help me:* This may be true. But it may not be. Again, do you want to base your choices on the system and a future idea you don't know will eventuate? You don't know what the future involves and what is possible. My anger led me to find ways to act empowered and metabolise the pain and helplessness when things didn't go well. We all made it through the terrible times. I hope this for you. The system is changing all the time.

- *He has a lot of money, he will use money to win everything:* Money does not win everything, every time. Over time you can find a good support team. He can't win your right to freedom and having joy and choices in your life. He may win in some ways but you have the power to not let him win in the most important way – defining who you are and showing your children an alternative.

- *He will turn everyone against me, even family and friends.* He will lie about me and tell stories about me: If people turn against you, they are not genuine friends. Life and friendship circles may change. You can find true support and real friends and create a different kind of family if this happens. I found a 'new family' for different parts of me at different times of my life. You can't control someone lying about you. If people around you don't make an effort to find out the truth from you, maybe they are not the kind of friends you want around you.

Another possibility, are you telling your friends who you trust so they can be there to support you? Sometimes we don't want to 'burden' our friends, but friends need to know some things. Intimacy means we affect each other. I chose certain people to tell what was going on; even if they did not respond in respect or support my reality, their responses influenced my level of trust and choices of what I would share and how much time I would spend with them. How people respond helps you sort out what to do.

- *No one will believe me – they think he is such a good guy:* Some people may believe him, but not everyone. They may be going along with the facade with you. You can tell the people you trust what is really going on. If they don't know how to respond or they disappoint you, seek support. You can get past this. True friends will believe you and be willing to learn how to help you. True friends may just surprise you and be there to support you. It may be difficult at this time, but some of your friends may need education about the reality of abuse. If you are not up to explaining to them, ask that they contact a specialised service to provide some education and ask them to read The Wolf in a Suit.

- *Sex is good:* Sex may be good but intimacy is more than a sexual act. You deserve true, full intimacy. You can have more than you imagine. It can be good in the day and the night and not just have a secret fantasy sex life, and a daily real life nightmare. Reading The Red Shoes will give greater clarity about this hook.

- *I can't protect the children on contact visits:* This is a real concern. There are many ways you can encourage your children to speak up, not keep secrets, listen to their bodies, learn about yes and no feelings, and build a trust network. There are also services to help protect your children. Contact me to go on the list to receive my book to help children build resiliency and power, based on my work with my daughters and what I have learnt as a psychotherapist.

- *He will turn the children away from me:* He may try this, and they may need to align with him for a period of time for their safety. This can be very painful and risky. It is important to not ask your children verbally or non-verbally to reassure or align with you. Again, seek professional assistance to help you navigate your unique situation. I have found that when you are consistent, no matter what their or his behaviour is like, children work things out over the long term.

- *I can never escape, he will punish me with every contact with the children:* He may try to punish you for a period of time. Hang in there. Get good support and professional advice. Record everything. He will be his own ruin. No matter what he does, don't let him ruin your life.

- *I am afraid to be alone:* This can be so terrifying. It is not about rationalising or using willpower. Seek out a Somatic Experiencing psychotherapist or a Soul Centred Psychotherapist (Kairos Centre) who incorporates working with the body and energy psychology. Energy psychology is not woo-woo – without energy, we are dead. This modality works with traditional Chinese medicine, which works with and between the brain and the body, rather than Western psychology, which is about the mind controlling the body.

You may want to connect with a skilled professional before leaving if you have the safety of time and you don't feel you can make the steps due to extreme fear of being alone. If I had thought to access a therapist when I left my first relationship to address my fear of being alone, maybe I never would have ended up with the Wolf. At the time, I never thought to see a therapist despite one part of me recognising that my fear was not 'normal.' Why couldn't I reach out for the right person when an issue was disrupting my life? Instead I reached out for the wrong person - a repeat of my childhood and disorganised attachment.

Life is about fitting the right solution to the right problem. We see a mechanic for our car. We see an electrician for our home lighting. We see an arborist for an issue with a tree. We see a doctor when there is something wrong with our physical health. Why don't we see a somatic or soul centred psychotherapist for experiences in the mind and body that are disrupting our life?

Many people who have seen other types of therapists know how the effect of anxiety, trauma, stress and fear is not resolved through cognitive, talk therapy. The body's involuntary responses need support and this is why I focus on the body, the trauma response and the unconscious. This is what is missing in the appropriate response to domestic violence and without this information domestic violence cannot be addressed.

If doctors valued and recommended somatic (which includes soul centred) psychotherapists, there would be a shift in societal choices and people would realise that there is more available then 'talking' to heal. Talking is important to heal, but there are two types of talking, one being far less effective. When talking is not connected to bodily sensations, feelings and the unconscious, the results are less likely to change the neurological system and not addressing the correct branches in the brain. Somatic psychotherapy is now recognised as more effective than cognitive behavioural therapy in response to trauma.

- *No one else will ever want me:* With this limiting belief it can be valuable to work with your sense of self, your identity and liking yourself. Learning tools to metabolise the fear of being alone can also make a huge difference. Take some time to work with the limiting self-beliefs and prior experiences of rejection and abandonment. This is all very important before considering another relationship. This way you can develop protective choices and not repeat patterns. When there is a blind spot, we can get caught again and again. Work with a skilled professional who has a good grasp of working with the unconscious, can see your blind spots and help you spot them and change them.

My suggestion in working with the limiting beliefs is never through willpower, positive thinking or cognitive behavioural therapy. Rationalisation will not convince deep-seated beliefs and experiences. Work with bilateral therapies like energy psychology and processes developed from EMDR (Soul Centred Psychotherapy, Kairos Centre) to address the limiting beliefs you have about you. Set some time to build your sense of self, regain a healthy relationship to anger, love and set new boundaries. Learn how to self-soothe and express yourself. Build your friendship and circle of support. Connect to your interests and live your life so a partner is not there to complete you, but to share your life.

- *I'm a failure:* This is an incorrect and limiting belief. You are taking an over-responsibility for someone else's limitations and you do not have enough compassion for your learnt limitations. This limiting belief may also be a defence against directing anger outwards – so the anger is turned in on you. Or your system may defend against grief and what dreams did not eventuate in what you wanted in your relationship – so you turn the attack on yourself, rather than the helplessness of what unfolded from your dreams.

  When we believe we are a failure, there is an implicit belief that we could have done something. This belief implies we have some control, rather than being with the huge vulnerability of not being able to do something. You may have a fear to enter into anger or grief because of a concern you may get lost in those feelings, or become a person who you don't want to be – and so it turns into an attack on the self and that you are a failure. Feeling a failure could be that there are skills or resources you don't have access to. What about asking yourself, what is behind the feeling of failure? Keep asking yourself what is behind that until you get to the core and address that limiting belief, fear or lack of skill. When you become clearer what the core, limiting belief is about, there will be appropriate resources you can develop to reach an effective outcome and experience.

- *I have added complications, such as a special needs child, and I don't have the physical, financial or other supports in place:* This is naturally very difficult and has its own challenges. Often there are resources and services around that are not visible. When you know of someone in the system and community, you can find more information and support to help you through. Again, don't give up. Keep searching for what you need. You may find that though your situation has its own challenges, living with abuse also has severe challenges that also drain you. Thinking long term, you may find things work out. You are not alone. Keep looking for the right support. Keep asking different people and places to find the skilled support.

- *I am exhausted:* Staying with abuse can feel like the only option when you're depleted and exhausted. However, it will be hard to recover when you remain in the same situation. Sometimes we have to break down, to break through. There is a way to collapse with support that is healthy and healing, and there are ways to get through no matter the challenges. I have heard stories of women going through massive challenges on leaving, but I don't think any of them regret it. Often these amazing women (and you are one of them) find new and healing relationships, with a constructive circle of support to recover from the exhaustion. Getting out of the cause of the exhaustion and adrenal fatigue is the biggest step forward – and the most necessary.

- *I don't know what to do or where to go:* It is normal to feel overwhelmed. No matter where you are, there are women's help phone lines and online information. There are also resources at the end of this book for Australian residents. Contact your local council for a list of community counselling, legal and health services.

- *I will be homeless and on the street:* Contact your local council, your local housing services or women's helplines to access a refuge, or the Government Department of Housing to gain information, support and access to adequate housing.

- *Most of the time, nothing bad is happening. It's not that bad:* There may be such a familiarity with the control that you don't even realise how you have adapted. Have your beliefs compartmentalised the bad as solely the 'explosion', and the control, shaming and daily denial of your feelings and needs is not as bad, or in fact the 'good times'? Read the chapter, The Little Match Girl.

- *This is normal family life:* We all have stress and bad times. Abuse is not acceptable, though it is common. There are many choices rather than enduring abuse when you seek and learn new ways of being with stress and support. Even when there are things outside your control, there is always something you can change, internally or externally.

- *I don't give up. I can do this:* Consider, is you 'not giving up' and still trying, a one sided approach or is he involved in not giving up too? Is he taking appropriate steps to not give up to keep the relationship/family together in healthy ways? Is he developing skills to repair, make amends and learn, or is he speaking words with no consistent supporting actions? Are you placing an unrealistic hope or wish because you fear what is on the other side of giving up? Are you minimising what you are living with? Would you want other people to see the way he treats you in private? Would you want your best friend or child to have this kind of relationship?

Giving up is not weak. It is courageous to accept what is not in your control to change. You are not necessarily closing the door to a future together. You are creating a boundary. He needs to cross over and do some work. It is not for you to carry the whole situation and burden. Is it giving up, or surrendering to the truth?

- *I am not going to reject or abandon him or our family:* You are not rejecting him, just his abusive behaviours. If he is not willing to make changes to save his relationship or family, then you are not responsible for him or the consequences. He has choices, just as he chooses to control you and not necessarily other people in his life. Is your desire to protect and not abandon coming from a fear of being abandoned yourself? Or a fear that the family or relationship is not enough of a motivation for him to do his personal work?

- *He will take away my passport:* You can be proactive and give your passport and other important papers to keep at a friend's house.

- *I'm nothing without him, I'll fall apart. I need him:* This is not true. This is what he has brainwashed you into believing. He has taken away your sense of self, your strength and your support. You can live through this and reclaim your life, and your capabilities especially with the right kind of support.

- *He needs me:* This is not healthy. It is a way of controlling you. We only 'need' someone as a child, when we are dependent and still developing. Couples share different skills in partnership where there is no withholding or control, and are complementary. This is very different to a 'controlling need'. The question to ask is more about, what kind of life and people around you do you want? Living with the Wolf, we revolve around what the Wolf needs, and so lose our own needs. What do you need?

Please contact me if you have experienced a different hook that keeps or kept you stuck, which I may have missed.

***

When I was living with the Wolf, I was totally unaware of any hooks. I was always so busy with my children's daily needs: trying to give them a normal life, cooking, cleaning, and trying not to rock the boat. His outbursts were irrational and unpredictable. I couldn't work out his moods, but back then I thought I could. I thought I had more control than I did. I would try to pre-empt what it was that he needed, so he wouldn't explode. But this was impossible, as his moods were not based on rational experiences.

With all this going on, I had no energy or space in my brain to work out how to identify my hooks, how to protect us, how to to get away, how to find another roof or how to get some money. I was preoccupied on how to keep alive. This is why often, the best solution is to just get out, and then work out the rest. You don't have to do it all at once. It is not even possible to. So don't give yourself a hard time to work everything out. Abuse is messy and chaotic, the process of recovering is messy and not neat, logical or ordered *but it can feel better*. If the hooks are too hard to be with, get support for your stress and the hooks will come in to be addressed at the right time.

Verbal and non-verbal messages in the family about how you need to be to be accepted and loved may feel hard to identify at first, because what we have grown up with becomes so familiar we don't see it. It is time to bring those hooks and binds about love into consciousness. Contact me to receive my ebook: *Getting Clear about that Crazy Making Verbal Abuse handbook*.

When I was living with the Wolf, I was in reaction mode. I wasn't able to stop, question and evaluate my situation or look at my beliefs or hooks. For me, the risks of stepping into the unknown (physically, mentally or emotionally) had always been discouraged. Now there was certainly no space, energy or time to step outside of my comfort zone. It would take too much of my energy, which I didn't have to spare. My family survival mantra had been to follow and endure, and I was getting this down pat.

Looking at the punishments, consequences, controlling behaviours and the underlying beliefs and attitudes inside the hooks can reveal what we took on as normal. Often the messages communicated are pretty effective, so initially it takes practice to bring clarity to what the messages were. Later they seem so obvious and clear.

We have looked at the beliefs in the hooks, now let's look at the beliefs about love. One pseudo love unspoken message is: 'do what pleases other'. Turn yourself inside out to 'avoid that look in his eyes ... that disapproval, that anger, that rejection'.

In my previous life, there was no enquiry about my feelings or my day, but there were smiles and affection when I did something they wanted (e.g. keep quiet or with the Wolf, serve). There was an imbalance. I was told what to do and what not to do according to spiritual, family and gender ideals. There was no talk about what I wanted to do, feel or be. There was little experience of healthy love: delighting in sharing space with each other.

I have spoken a bit about limiting beliefs and ideals in family, culture, religion, history and through the hooks. We often carry unrealistic expectations of ourselves and others. My experience is that we tend to first experience limiting beliefs from someone else and then internalise it into ourselves. They are not a natural process to just occur of themselves. As I mentioned, I do not recommend working on limiting beliefs through willpower or rationalisation – or on your own, as we can be tricked and not see our own limiting beliefs.

There are important aspects to clarify about limiting beliefs and some key irrational aspects of them. According to psychologist Albert Ellis, an idea is irrational when there are four components: It distorts reality, it's illogical, it prevents you from achieving your intentions, and it progresses to unhealthy and self-defeating feelings and responses.

To me, this definition, by turning it into its opposite, implicitly reveals the components for a healthy belief: includes a whole reality, has a concrete and specific unfolding relevance at its essence and context, allows a flow and leads to a generative and creative outcome. A 'generative outcome' is one where there is the ability of further growth, due to the permissive and creative nature of the process.

There is not a blocked door, but instead an open door because of being alive. When we're not experiencing a generative and creative outcome, perhaps we need to explore where there is a distortion or limit in our beliefs in ourself or by someone.

Let's look at four common irrational beliefs that influence our love relationships (Albert Ellis).

1. **It's necessary for every person I come across to love and approve of me.** It is more rational to recognise that some people will love and approve of me, but not everyone will. It's a bit impossible to expect that everyone we meet, everyone we come across, will think we're terrific. We need to build an emotional muscle to bear disappointing others, and to bear the discomfort of being different or disagreeing with others.

2. **To consider myself worthy, I must be totally competent and achieve in all areas of life.** That's a pretty big ask to put on oneself, and fairly unrelenting. More rational would be, 'I'm worthy because I exist. I'm going to be competent and achieve some things and not be able to achieve other things in our life – but my competency skills are not a reflection of my worth.'

3. **I feel outrage and feel life is awful and catastrophic when things are not the way I would like them to be.** (I am not talking about the catastrophic experience of abuse. This statement is not speaking about basic human rights; it is referring to the difficulty of the world not mirroring what we like or want). This feeling of life being awful brings shame and does not allow a process on what to do differently. Perhaps it's more rational and more realistic to recognise that awful and catastrophic things do happen sometimes, but when things don't go the way you want them to, there are a range of choices and possibilities to help you through, so that they are not necessarily devastating to be with.

A lot of the time, when we recognise something is wrong, we can make a change and work on improvements so that things don't have to be catastrophic. There can be a process of change, rather than needing an instant correction. It is also important to build the emotional muscle to bear the 'full catastrophe of life', what is not in our control and not be caught in ideals, hope, righteous entitlement or righteous injustice. Life is not perfect.

4. **Unhappiness has an external cause. There is little or no ability for me to control anything that may have some impact on me.** It might be more realistic to say that sometimes unhappiness originates from an outside cause. Perhaps a more realistic and accurate response to unhappiness is that sometimes when we are unhappy in life, we have tried many changes but something is not working; maybe we are expecting something from a situation or someone else that is not possible. Perhaps we

bestow an unrealistic expectation onto others. Perhaps we have not found what can support us yet, but that does not mean there is no ability over your happiness or how life impacts you.

No matter what is involved, for each situation there are different degrees of internal and external causes, choices and possibilities. In most cases, there is *always* something we can do to develop choices to move towards contentment, as well as develop the skills needed to process how we feel, no matter what is going on, to get to a better place.

All the above are hooks and binds, let alone the layers of hooks we spoke about earlier in this chapter. We will explore more hooks involved in the trauma response and other layers inside the limiting influence of the stress response in '*The Red Shoes*' and '*The Little Match Girl*'.

Hooks are what I unpack in person, one on one. It is not about being with these hooks and using justifications and convincers to put pressure on ourselves or on anyone in an attempt to change these attitudes. They're all there for a real reason, and need to be understood and taken care of in meaningful and appropriate ways.

Another thing that is so, very important to explore when unpacking all the influences and pressures here, is the big question: what is love?

When I'm with someone, we'll often brainstorm. We'll get two big sheets of paper (or when I'm in a group we'll write up on the whiteboard) and divide it in half with healthy and unhealthy attitudes and behaviours to do with love. We put on one side 'healthy love' and on the other what I call 'pseudo-love' or 'toxic love'.

Healthy love is activating and includes the kinds of things that come out as expressions of love which offer up a picture of healthy love: what each person gives for healthy love to be present:

- Respect
- Honesty
- Empathy and compassion
- Trust developing in context to the experience
- Playfulness and humour
- Safety
- Curiosity and openness

- Mindfulness
- Healthy anger and assertion; healthy boundaries and ability to adjust boundaries as needed
- Communication: expressive, listens, generosity of heart, full attention, shares, allows, reflects back what heard from the verbal and non-verbal communications
- Think about feelings and feel about thinking
- Space to challenge and be challenged
- Flexibly responsive
- Loving attachment, care and concern
- Inclusiveness of doing and being, silence and activity, extroversion and introversion (together and separately)
- Gratitude and appreciation
- Emotionally responsible (for self), self soothe, developing emotional intelligence, personal development, with room to grow, change and develop. Able to develop emotional muscle to be with the whole self, vulnerability and helplessness
- Other meaningful relationships (a small number of family, colleagues and friends) with room for independence and separate interests
- Develops personal generative and spiritual practices which include work and contributing to the world
- Respect for, appreciation of and connection to nature
- Provides room and encouragement (for self and other) to grow within self, supporting a sense of security in your own worth and responsible for yourself
- Able to create areas of safety, privacy and solitude (together and separately)
- Embraces independence, individuality and shared 'couple' time
- Conversation and actions based on help, acceptance, understanding and conveying affection
- Sex comes out of free choice, desire
- Self-care
- Shared leading and flexible leading. Problem solving together, but being able to let go and allow the other person their time and pacing for their journey and challenges
- Behaviours match words

- Expresses love in a variety of ways: through time, touch, talking, sharing tasks and gifts and gives you love in the way *you* feel loved
- Shared values create a relationship template that is responsive to the couple's unique needs and desires. Not needing to fit into a relationship box

Acceptance, not perfection, and room to grow; focusing on your list as a template to move towards.

Now the '*Pseudo-love*' list and picture:

- Controlling, demanding, intrusive
- Dishonest, manipulative, lies, cheating and affairs
- Blame, guilt
- Unresponsive to your reality, feelings, needs and experience
- Jealous, obsessive, possessive, wants you to 'prove' your love
- Rigid rules for gender, relationship and other roles
- Black and white thinking
- Perfection thinking
- Trying to fix, change or 'save' the other
- Creates an environment of fear, pain, loneliness and insecurity
- Limited socialisation (this is not healthy introversion)
- Ridicules and humiliates (lack of empathy for you)
- Conversations based on blame, denial, manipulation, moody, bullying
- Distorting and delusional version of reality which is defended
- Passive-aggressive and aggressive behaviours, threatening
- Passivity with intention to control, neglect
- Reveals to others what is private; intrusion of boundaries
- Disloyal
- Need for immediate gratification, both emotionally and sexually
- Obsession with the relationship, sometimes with rigid roles of 'rescuer', 'victim', etc
- Asking you to sacrifice, or to betray yourself and your values and needs
- Unrealistic and/or unrelenting demands

What happens when you see the contrast of the two lists? Does the first seem impossible or reasonable? Notice your limiting beliefs. You may not feel up to the mark on the healthy love list either. That is okay, as long as you are not acting out the 'pseudo' love traits you can be anywhere on the continuum of 'healthy' love, as healthy love is about acceptance in the context of growth and development.

How has your past influenced what is realistic and appropriate?

The hooks and binds involved with anger, love or family can be insidious, and can feel all-encompassing and quite convincing. What is the tape saying inside your head? Maybe that *most of the time he's 'good', he's not all bad. I shouldn't leave. I shouldn't kick up a big deal. No one is all bad, we all have our best and worst faces. I should be understanding and forgiving. I'm not perfect. It is easier to stay with what I know.*

It doesn't matter whether the abuse happens hourly or daily or monthly – just the fact that there is abuse automatically means that you're set up in a state of anticipation, survival and vigilance. The unpredictability shapes and changes who you can be, what you believe and what kind of life you can have.

Is this what you would want for your child or your best friend? Are you any different from them?

It's not as if these behaviours are impossible to change … if someone wants to. Please re-read the last sentence. After all, he has probably shown appropriate ways of behaving, early on with you or with others. It is possible for most people to change. We all can do something about our own behaviour - if we want to.

Become curious and discerning. Is 'warmth' or 'empathy' really there – in his eyes, body posture, actions, tone of voice – or is it empty and in words only? Start to see if what you label is truly how you identify it.

For those embedded deep survival fears of 'I have nowhere to go', 'I have no money to support me', 'I don't want to burden others', not knowing the next step is *not* a reason not to make a change. All of these real concerns can be taken care of, bit by bit.

I remember I had to weigh up what was important to me, and it came down to the kind of life that my children were being shaped to have. I wanted them to have a different childhood to what I had, and I couldn't do that living with the Wolf. It was my love and concern for them that started to wake me up. I was willing to throw myself into the unknown because they were more important for me. Find what's most important for you.

In this modern society and mindset of 'the brain can conquer everything' – with cars, technology and other influences creating a far more independent and separate lifestyle –we have inadvertently developed a mindset of 'we don't want to burden others' and that 'others are busy doing (important) things' as if being 'clever' means the stuff of life is 'inconsequential'.

But we're social creatures. We all go through tough times at different times in our lives and in different kinds of ways. We need each other.

I want to emphasise that being in the situation of not knowing how you can do the next steps, without details or the clear steps or support – without money, housing or something else – is not easy. I know, I've done it. I don't want to minimise the challenges ahead.

But you have gone through many stages in your life where you didn't know how you were going to be able to do the next thing – whether it was to be able to stand up, to walk, how to negotiate separating from your mother and going to school, learning to read and write, tying up your shoelaces, telling the time, riding a two wheeler bike, driving a car, a new job … and we get through all those unknowns, *so many*, bit by bit each stage and phase. You learn as you go, as with all significant changes in life.

At each point, what is in front of you is the biggest challenge and the unknown. When you look back, the past challenges may not seem a big deal; but at the time, it was challenging and somehow you got through them all. This is the territory of stepping out of your comfort zone. Stepping out of your comfort zone is necessary for growth.

Just as we don't know what pregnancy's actually going to be like – what the labour and the birth is going to be like, what it's going to be like to be a parent. We take a leap of faith, because what is on the other side is worth the risks and challenges.

This leap of faith is most important for you, even when you don't have children – though, like me, it may feel easier to do it for your children. Staying teaches your children that this is the map of what love is. Is this the map you want for you or them?

You don't have to know everything right now; you only need to know what's relevant for this very moment you are in. When you keep doing that in each moment then all the moments will work themselves out. Sometimes our mind can trip over itself with a fear of the future and the unknown. *Stay in the moment* and with what you need in this moment. When you do this – and you generally can do something – each moment brings you to the next moment, taking care of that moment, and so on. Staying in the moment when times are tough gives you an opportunity to be with what you need to know for just this hour or this day. You only have to deal with one moment or one day at a time. You don't have to work it all out immediately; just stop and think, 'What do I need to know now (or today)?' That's all you need to work on.

Really tricky hooks are, 'I'm scared he'll come after me, or take the children from me, or attack or kill the children. He's unpredictable, I don't know what he'll do.' We read and hear about so many stories of men going crazy after she leaves, and of women and children being killed. This is a real and serious risk. You are already living daily in risk and unpredictability. Research shows that yes, things tend to get worse instead of better in leaving, but do you want to base your decision on you might die. Look at your values and what you are prepared to sacrifice for the long term. Things are tough now, but five or ten years from now, which side of the fence do you want to be?

When we are scared of the unknown it is easy to assume certain things. This is new territory. Do you really know that he will respond to the absolute extreme when faced with new boundaries?

After a time, not all men want to continue trying to control you when clearly their tactics are no longer working as they were before. They often want to quickly find another woman to replace you. How do you really know what the future will hold? It may be better than you think. No matter what his threats, he may not follow through, though I absolutely say take them seriously and get protection and safety. I was threatened with murder and death. I am glad I did what I did. It was so terrifying at the time to take the risk, but I am glad I risked my life, for my life.

By staying, you are implicitly saying that it's acceptable for him to continue this behaviour and treat you this way.

Another thing I came to realise after I left was that when I was living with the abuse, I bestowed on myself more power than I realistically had. I developed this illusion that I actually had a greater capacity to protect my children and me. I thought I could manage. I realise now that this was a defence against the deep helplessness, despair and vulnerability I was living with. This sense that I could protect me and the children while I was living in this abuse was not accurate. Sure, I could *try* to make things better, but *I was limited to what his mood would allow*. I actually couldn't protect us or prevent the abuse. After all, he was not reasonable. It was his mindset playing tricks on him and him trying to control his environment to manage his internal state. We had to fit into his internal madness and its leakage onto us and our surroundings.

This trick of believing I had a greater power to manage the situation than I realistically had is something I believe we play on ourselves, as a defence against not having power and the unbearable helplessness. That is the best we can do at the time, given the level of overwhelm and chaos. It doesn't help when we are questioned (or through the media) when something bad happened, what did we do to make it happen? People don't realise abuse is illogical and there is no fair reason.

I am not expecting you to take all this information on board as 'truth'. I invite you to hold all this information for you to consider, question, reflect and digest. Find your truth. Test it out. Notice the objection and see if you can find further information to develop a bigger picture.

The pseudo-love filter can have you saying that he's a great father – that the children need their father and to be a family; yet, a great father respects the mother of his children. Even if children are not directly abused, the abuse directly shapes their brains, attitudes, health and relationships, because children are so closely tied to their parents.

I've worked with hundreds of women and men who, as children, witnessed abuse between their parents. Fear is pervasive. When you are in the same house, in the same space, not even in the same room at the same time, you are still breathing in the fear and you don't know when you could be targeted. You absorb the emotional pain, which is shared with you as it is too difficult to reject when it involves your parents. It changes your own neurological and hormonal system.

These children, now adults, grew up with either survivor guilt or 'over-responsibility' for not protecting their mother, despite their young age or they developed disdain and disgust for the 'weakness of their mother' – and don't want to be emotional and weak like her. They may have emotional pain for a range of complex reasons, such as growing up being favoured by their father and given rights that really belonged to their mother. They may have grown up feeling entitled, or deeply conflicted and uncomfortable that they were favoured while their mother was persecuted. The complexity of seeing the good and the terrible in their parent is a huge, anxiety-evoking obstacle.

I've worked with women with fertility issues and seen how their experience of their parents impacted their health and unconscious choices in becoming or not becoming a mother. Family violence and childhood abuse impacting their choices in how they viewed themselves as a female and their sexuality. Often women develop a strong, capable exterior or can have softness for others, but if they feel vulnerability, they are 'weak' with a very strong self-attack and judgements.

For some women in their struggle with what it is to be a woman, directly influenced by their childhood experience of violence between parents, they are pulled to feel for and align with the persecutor, because they felt anger towards their mother for putting up with it. That can be tricky to unravel. I can understand that sometimes this can happen for a number of reasons and I don't assume to have the answer to everything. All of what I put here is to raise the awareness of the many layers of abuse, so we can continue having bigger picture conversations. These possibilities are a beginning point for you to become curious about what was unthinkable for you to think or unbearable to feel.

There can be anger towards the mother for putting up with it, because the child needed the 'safer' parent to be strong and protect them or they needed somewhere for their anger to go. This judgement towards the mother can lead to some difficult situations and mindsets for women about being a woman or mother. I can understand a child aligning with the father, and directing anger at Mum. It can be safer to get angry at Mum – she wouldn't have the same dangerous reactions as when the anger was directed at the father. That can lead to its own tricks in adult relationships, where we let men off the hook and get mad at the female. This can be really harsh to other women because we've got this in-built pattern that it's not safe for the anger to go where it rightfully needs to go.

***

There is a lot of research identifying that when children appear to see or hear the violence, they are feeling, sensing and seeing the after-effects and are changed by the abuse. This is a massive cost of 'pseudo' love on children.

Children are aware of a lot more than we give them credit for. They are open to the conscious and unconscious, even if they have difficulty naming or making sense of it. Remember the left brain will come to a conclusion about a right brain 'feeling' experience, even when the left brain is not connected to all the information. Also, in child development the child is limited to where their brain is in its developmental process.

There is a lot of research about children's exposure to violence and the impact on their long term physical, mental, emotional and social health. (Richards 2011; D'Andrea et al 2012; Stiles 2002; Schore 2003; Kitzmann et al 2003; Odhayani et al 2013; Van der Kolk n.d.)

When children are exposed to abuse in the family, they are impacted in numerous ways – including the ability to concentrate and do well at school. Being on alert because of the tension and explosions can leave the system wired, impacting on sleep and therefore health and growth. Children experience nightmares, sleep disturbances, stomachaches, bowel and bladder problems, eye problems, headaches, difficulty going to bed and getting out of bed, lethargy and bedwetting. Some other outcomes are withdrawing and being quite shut down – or, being defiant, disobedient, aggressive and hyperactive. Both ends of the continuum can lead to a lowered self-esteem and confidence.

Children may live in a dream world with fantasies about living a normal life away from their family – fantasies that they feel guilty about because they want to leave their family. They may imagine a fire or something in which the home and all the belongings are destroyed, yet somehow all the family escape – keeping their guilt at bay with the family alive, but the fire allows them to get away from their family and represents some form of their anger. There may be an insistence that they don't want their family to die, they just want to get away. Or there may be one part of them that secretly wishes their death.

Children impacted by abuse can become quite pessimistic toward their future. This range of impacts, unless the abuse is addressed, can continue through childhood into adolescence and adulthood, often leading into anxiety, panic attacks, depression, drugs, violence in relationships, eating disorders and parent-child conflict.

***

Often people have a quiet or unspoken habit, that I think comes from overwhelm which can become a hook: 'If I don't name it, it will go away or get better,' or, 'it's easier to avoid life's difficulties than face them.' When we say it aloud, we can know it's not true, but at times our behaviours act this out. Overwhelm is the biggest obstacle in so many situations. What is your behaviour communicating? Who can you talk to in order to explore choices and skills, so you and not an involuntary overwhelm or stress responses are driving your choices? You can make choices and take up the ability to respond to what is really going on; you have the responsibility to identify and carry what is yours and what you can do now – as well as identifying what is not yours to carry.

We may find it easier in the short term to stay aligned to the hooks, but in the long term it's generally more difficult. The situation remains unresolved and turns into bigger and bigger issues, habits and patterns – and the tension tends to increase and wear us down, eroding our clarity about the line in the sand.

For some women, there is an objection to changing the relationship because there is a belief (and the fantasy) of needing someone stronger than you to rely on. There can be a sense of 'pseudo-comfort' and a hook in the belief of being that person 'needing someone' to protect them. It can give a sense of being 'feminine' inside the patriarchal mindset, particularly if in some way you feel inadequate. Bluebeards are good at identifying your sense of lack, and convincing you that you 'need him'. This fits his model of pseudo-love relationship as a way to hook you in. There can be a belief that this need is attractive.

The limiting belief that there needs to be a stronger person in the relationship is an old one, and doesn't take into account the capacity and necessity for every adult human to move through all experiences: independence, interdependence and dependence, depending on the time and context of what is going on all throughout our life, rather than being in a fixed mode. We need to be able to bear being dependent when we are in hospital and needing to receive care; we need to be able to be interdependent when arranging our life with another person; and we need to be independent on managing our role in our work and our needs. We are born with the capability to learn, grow and fulfil many needs, as we flexibly move between the three as the situation requires. Over time we also develop more of ourselves and our skills and resources, which inevitably changes our sense of strength and capacity. We are not a one-sided person incapable of strength and in need, the way Bluebeard wants us to be.

Some people believe they can't change what has happened and that the past is a strong, determining behaviour; even that we cannot overcome or be more than our past. This denies a whole range of possibilities that become inaccessible, especially when in the middle of chaos. A more reasonable and accurate response is that our past impacts and influences many factors within our being and our life, but that neuroscience and epigenetics lets us know that we are forever able to develop choices and capabilities.

We now know that with the skilled support we need, we have the capacity to grow beyond our past. This is significant. Neural pathways always have the potential to grow. Epigenetics also lets us know that despite what our system carries in our DNA, it is our environment that either switches it on or off. So between changing our environment, learning new therapeutic skills and having at least one positive and caring person there for you, you can overcome an extraordinary amount and create a new life.

Another limiting 'love' belief that can get in the way of staying with our truth is that caring means 'you should get upset over other people's problems and disturbances'. I would suggest that there is an appropriate level of not being upset with other people's situations when it stops you from feeling well and living your life. There is a healthy level of being able to detach and not letting it override how you go about your day. Encourage them to be response-able, to take care of their own feelings and thoughts, possibly reaching out for skilled support if needed and you not carry their burden.

Many women (and men) can get caught up with a belief that there is a 'right and perfect solution' and if they just do that, everything will work out. Then if this 'perfect solution' isn't found, it can feel catastrophic. I tend to think that there is a realistic solution, but not necessarily a perfect solution. We are human beings; we have limitations and therefore perfection is not possible. Rather than perfection, there is 'good enough'. We can do really well at some things, but not necessarily at all things. It's fine to have certain qualities and an image of perfection as a motivating, starting point, when you focus on your direction; as long as you don't give yourself a hard time when the unconscious intervenes and adds and changes the original static perfect picture in your process and realistic journey getting there.

To say that there is a right and perfect solution for any situation almost gives us a godlike capability that we have power over far more than what is in our capacity, or the reality of the moment. Perhaps imagining we can do it perfectly is another defence against vulnerability and helplessness. As if, in the perfect way, we always have a solution, a choice and some control.

When looking at all of these hooks and binds, be kind to yourself. You are perfectly imperfect: human. You are doing the best you can to integrate information that your system previously did not have access to.

You're going at the pace and capacity that you can to digest what is relevant, meaningful and appropriate for you. Take care of yourself. Pamper yourself. Discover what relaxes you and nourishes all your senses.

When you're in these positive experiences, there is opportunity to fill your tank and discover more about you – what soothes and comforts you, where everyone or everything else can fall away … and just be. Don't do to yourself what happened to the Ugly Duckling. Don't neglect and reject yourself, leaving you isolated from your real tribe. Nourish yourself.

Be gentle and pace yourself. You might want to get a piece of paper and divide the paper into six columns – touch, see, feel, hear, smell and smell – and in each column you can write down what you really enjoy and what relaxes and comforts you using that sense. These can be simple and not costly. At different times when you need it, go to the different columns and choose one to nourish and support yourself. You'll probably notice that some senses probably have a lot more in their list than others. Draw on all the senses, not just your favourite sense, to nourish you.

Don't abandon yourself. Be with yourself. It may feel uncomfortable at first but this is a deep act of love. Stay with you. Don't leave you. One day at a time, you can get through.

Chapter 10: Banished Lilith

Banished Lilith

God made Adam from the Earth. God did not want him to be alone and made Lilith. They fought as Lilith did not want to lie beneath him. Adam said, 'You are fit only to be in the bottom position while I am to be in the superior one.' Lilith said, 'We are equal to each other inasmuch as we were both created from the earth.' Fed up, Lilith calls out the name of God as she leaves and goes to the Red Sea.

God says to Adam that if she does not come back, 'She must permit one hundred of her children to die every day.' God with the help of three angels tries to call her back, delivering this terrible ultimatum: return or she will be drowned in the Red Sea.

Lilith told how she knew God only gave her life to harm babies and agreed to have power of male babies in their first eight days and female babies only in their first twelve (in some accounts twenty) days. The angels wanted to take her but she would not leave. And so they agreed on God's name that if she saw the angels or their names on an amulet near a baby, she would not harm that baby. The agreement required that a hundred of her children would die every day. The angels left. One hundred demons would die every day too.

Lilith was replaced by Eve and became demonised as the one who killed babies.

From The Alphabet of Ben Sira, a collection of Rabbinic stories from medieval times.

Later legends said she also became the demonised woman who would seduce men, sometimes in their sleep, and so create demon children. (Kvam et al 2009)

There is another story about Adam. A more familiar story. God creates Adam and gives him the Garden of Eden as his home. God decides to find a 'co-worker' for Adam, and offers him any animals of the earth and the sky, but Adam does not find any suitable. God puts Adam into a deep sleep and creates Eve from his side. When Adam wakes up he sees that Eve is part of him and agrees that she is the co-worker for him.

God says to eat from any plant in the Garden of Eden, but not the Tree of Good and Evil in the centre of the garden. *If you touch or eat from it, you will die.*

One day Eve meets a Snake who lets Eve know if she eats this fruit, her eyes will be opened. Eve tastes the fruit and offers it to Adam, who also takes the fruit.

When God finds out, he asks Adam some questions to bring out a confession of his 'wrongdoing'. Adam evades the centre of the truth and blames Eve. God asks Eve, who then blames the Snake. God curses the Snake and provides penalties to Adam and Eve, banishing them from the Garden of Eden. Eve is punished to receive 'pangs in childbearing' and 'pain in childbirth'. She will be subordinate to her husband, even while loving him. God cursed the ground from which Adam came from and proclaimed that he would die and return to the earth.

It is said that God gave Adam and Eve the Garden of Eden, but they formed the world of suffering and injustice by eating the fruit of the Tree of Knowledge. If they had stayed in the Garden of Eden, they would have remained immortal.

In the beginning (excuse my pun!), when I was searching for a tale for our journey into anger, power and being a woman through this chapter, I couldn't find the right story to capture anger. It is hard to find a story with a woman being angry. There seemed so many gaps – but then, isn't that the experience of women and anger in our patriarchal society? We tend to disconnect because of a perception of anger as threatening or unacceptable in a female.

The story of Lilith being angry is an example of the shame and rejection in being a woman and standing your ground. The fact that it can be hard to find or know about the story of Lilith and instead she is hidden away in ancient books despite her coming before Eve, tells how she was not welcomed. Not many people know her story.

I find it interesting to consider Lilith in our exploration of anger. She was born equal but there is conflict about negotiation between two equals.

Isn't this the dilemma we all experience at times in relationships? Quite a patriarchal story, isn't it?

Adam does not want to compromise and at some point Lilith has enough – the line is drawn in the sand. She is not willing to continue the loop of conflict and power struggle when he shows no willingness to be inclusive. There is no creative end or resolution. So she leaves.

Feminist writings say she was the one who knew God's name – just as Isis called out the secret names of Ra to take his powers (in Egyptian mythology), and the Sumerian goddess Innana tricked the god Enki into giving her the gifts of Mes, taking the blueprints which brought great power. Here is an important message. Women need not wait for men to bestow power on women. Women need to *take what is their equal birthright.*

Lilith leaves and goes to the Red Sea, a very special place which becomes known for where the people of Israel will be saved from the unrelenting pursuit of the Egyptians wanting to keep them enslaved. She is at the place where persecution and slavery does end for those persecuted and marginalised. Freedom.

God has his angels go to Lilith to force and threaten her to return to Adam. This is not a very equitable way of communicating or negotiating, is it? It seems Adam and God did not like that Adam had not won. What a collusion! Were they both content for ongoing conflict on her return or were they going to force her to be subordinate? Even while the angels came to threaten her, she spoke with friendliness, calling them 'darlings', but would not back down.

God, Adam and the use of the angels all display Wolf-like and patriarchal behaviour. Just what happens in an abusive relationship – control, threats and no inclusion of both realities. Because she doesn't do as she was 'told', she is scapegoated and demonised forever more, left forgotten in the books. Exclusion, shame and rejection at its best. More abusive tactics, are they not?

So another story was created ... one about Eve, who is docile and allows Adam to be on top. Yet I would suggest, this is not the natural order for two equal companions and so at some point, this unhealthy domination ends through the meeting between Eve and the Snake.

The Snake offers Eve some fruit from the Tree of Good and Evil. This is the only tree that God said not to eat from ... Hmm, is this a bit Bluebeardish? 'You can have all this but you can't know all of what is going on.' Controlled and treated like a child. You can't know about the shadow and the dark. You are just here to play. Don't occupy your mind with important things. Here is control over another, keeping one person more infantile, when kept out of knowing the bigger picture.

Just as we found out with Little Red Riding Hood; when we don't know about the Wolf – or as in Bluebeard, and what is behind the little door – we are at risk of being caught. Caught by those who know those secrets that we don't know to watch out for.

Eve meets the Snake. Some say Lilith is the Snake, who has come back to help Eve wake up to her power. Lilith wants to encourage her to take back her power of knowledge, speech, curiosity, the capacity to grow and strength of free will ... rather than waiting for God or Adam to 'let her' have it. The Snake offers Eve the opportunity to eat fruit from the Tree of Knowledge and go beyond the control and imposed blindness. Eve offers some fruit to share with Adam. Isn't all this growth and development?

I do not read of any sign of compassion from God's questioning when Adam is clearly feeling shame. God's children were curious and with no ill intent. God had an opportunity to transform shame and blame, but instead God punishes and curses. God sends them out of the Garden of Eden and proclaims that Eve is destined to be ruled over by her partner and is less than her partner.

Aren't the men who wrote the Bible responsible for contributing to a long line of expectation of power and control over another, the subordination of women and the perpetuation of shame and blame? Don't you think Adam's curse is pretty mild compared to Eve's? To be impacted by the earth and the seasons of nature, and die at some point (presented as solely his curses, yet she will also live these limitations) yet she is given the additional curse of pain through childbirth and to be subordinate to her husband.

God told Adam that the earth will give him limits. The earth has a power that Adam can't control. When we don't honour her, then the Earth and Nature have their natural expression of rage. There is a consequence. The earth is often seen as a feminine form and holding a power we don't have control over. The earth bears our abuses of her. An intensity and momentum build from the ravages done to her. Until, like the pressure from the pressure cooker, there is a release from the deep bowels of the earth. Spewing out, expelling and releasing the wrongs that had been stored and compacted.

The way it is written, it seems God cursed the Earth rather than Adam: 'Cursed is the ground because of you; through painful toil you will eat food from it all the days of your life.' Is this the struggle between the patriarchy and the old way of the feminine, with the Earth Goddess who was the ruler before the masculine God came about? Is this God's way of fighting against that which they don't have control over and never will – feminine power and nature? One understanding is that God could not curse Adam, as Adam was his son and God the father, but Earth was the mother and so the curse was directed there so it did not back fire onto the Father.

This old Bible story instils the patriarchal view that there must be a hierarchy of power- over with 'shame and blame'. An embedded mindset that limitations (from nature and life) and differences are punishment, bad and painful; instead of living together and accepting and supporting each other's limits and differences and in gratitude of the earth's cycles and abundance.

Limitations and working with nature could become a surrender and responsiveness to nature rather than trying to contain and control nature. This limiting attitude is repeated in the persecution of the feminine and the earth through many periods of history, including when men persecuted and killed 'witches' – those midwives and women of the earth who knew of and used the healing plants and herbs whilst attuned to the rhythms and cycles of nature, healing and birth.

Does something seem familiar through these stories? Isn't this the pattern I have been speaking of, the pattern of staying in the control of the patriarchal tribe and not questioning anything. Sacrificing the feminine, so we ensure the 'group mind survival' remains the way we know it. Instilling a tribal, survival fear and non-inclusiveness with the threat of separation, being alone and in the unknown. The ancestral story, that whoever asks questions will be shamed and rejected, so we stay in our comfort zone to belong: 'If I enforce that 'you cannot know', then you cannot know more than me and my control; so you can not change the power and the way our group functions.'

***

Way back when we were reliant on the local area and the seasons, we needed the tribe. But times have changed. Doesn't growth of an individual, family, society or culture require change? Nothing is static. Growth also involves some struggle as we develop our capacities to step into a greater way of being. Whether it is learning to walk, read, tie shoelaces, drive a car, study and so on ... When energy or relationships are static, there is control, stunted growth and inhibited energy. Doesn't this lead to the pressure cooker situation?

But wait ... Isn't there actually an aspect of the pressure cooker that serves a healthy outcome? The pressure cooker itself is the unhealthy container that is inhibiting flow. Pressure is building through the prevention of further growth. This leads to a momentum of escape; the scream of the steam is the healthy call-out that the excessive control and containment has reached its limit – there is a need to break through the boundary, escape and transform.

There is no room for anger, healthy boundaries and assertion for Lilith or for the woman who lives with the pressure of the controlling Wolf or Bluebeard. Anger is shut down through control, blame, punishment, shaming and withholding of equal information and knowledge. In both the story of Lilith and Eve – and with the Wolf in a Suit – anger to protect the self is denied for the woman.

Before we move on, let's mention the Snake. Just like the Earth is seen as a feminine form in mythology, so too is the snake. The Snake is often seen as a feminine symbol of power, fertility, rebirth, birth, the guardian, the umbilical cord and regeneration. The Snake lived near the Tree of Knowledge, and in Mayan mythology the Vision Serpent lived at the centre of the world, on top of the World Tree. The snake lives close to the wisdom, close to the earth and moves in feminine ways, shaping its way through the world affected by its environment, shedding its skin and layers. The snake is often the one with power, with one who sees more and knows more and reveals more; but perhaps is ostracised for saying the 'unnamable' and thus stands on the edges of society.

***

Let's bring Cinderella into the picture. What on earth does Cinderella have to do with anger? She is the other end of Lilith's anger, so passive and disempowered. Cinderella is here to bring us a greater awareness of the picture when anger is inaccessible and what is required to reclaim our anger. The quality of women being passive seems valued in our culture, such as with Eve and Cinderella so we need to talk about her.

Cinderella is known as 'the persecuted heroine'. Cinderella, like Little Red Riding Hood, is (dare I say it) *too* good – too selfless, too giving, too passive. The story of persecuted Cinderella leaves out elements, which are involved with the power of anger. We get a sanitised version of subservience, being shamed and waiting to be saved.

Cinderella

A man had a daughter from his first wife who had a 'sweetness of temper' just like her mother; who had been the 'best creature in the world'. This man was re-marrying and the new woman was proud and arrogant.

Once they married, she showed more of her cold and mean nature and was particularly nasty to her new stepdaughter. Her own two daughters were lazy and unpleasant characters. This woman made the daughter live like a slave, sleeping on straw by the ashes while her own two daughters lived in fine rooms with fine clothes.

The daughter was patient and did not want to speak to her father as she did not want to bring distress to her father, who was not skilled in standing up to his new wife. The elder sister called the daughter 'Cinderwench' for living in the cinders. The younger sister did not want to be so rude, and so called her Cinderella.

Now the King's son announced a ball. When the sisters heard about it, they began planning their fine gowns and hairstyles. This became all Cinderella heard about all day. It was difficult, particularly because they would ask her advice and ideas as she was so clever. Cinderella was so giving that she offered to do their hair, which they accepted.

The sisters asked Cinderella if she wanted to go to the ball. Cinderella said, 'But you are only teasing me; how can I go to a ball?' The sisters agreed, tormenting her, saying everyone would laugh at her. No matter how they treated her, Cinderella did their hair beautifully and helped them dress for the day.

When the sisters left, Cinderella crumpled to the ground and cried her heart out. Her godmother, a fairy, saw her and asked her what she was crying about.

Cinderella was so consumed with sadness that she couldn't get all her words out. Her godmother worked out what she was crying about and told her to be good, go to her room and she would be able to go to the ball. Cinderella stopped crying. When her godmother told her to go to the garden to get a pumpkin, Cinderella went, though not knowing how a pumpkin would help.

The godmother cleaned out the inside and cast her wand – the pumpkin turned into a carriage. Then the godmother went to her mousetrap and found six live mice there. She asked Cinderella to open the tiny trapdoor and as each mouse came through, the godmother tapped each with her wand. They turned into six fine horses.

Cinderella saw the need for a coachman and went looking for a rat in the mousetrap. She found three and the godmother tapped the largest of them – he turned into the jolliest coachman to be seen.

The godmother then told Cinderella to return to the garden and find the six lizards hiding behind the watering can. These became the six footmen. The godmother then said, 'Does this look a fine enough way to go to the ball?'

Cinderella said, 'Yes, but must I go in these ragged, dirty clothes?'

The godmother immediately touched her with the wand and her clothes became spun of silver, gold and jewels, and she had glass slippers to wear on her feet. Her godmother told her to not stay later than midnight; if she stayed a minute longer everything would turn back to their original form.

Cinderella agreed and left so excited. When she arrived, the King's son was told there was a new princess to greet and bring into the ballroom. When she arrived in the room, all chatter and music stopped. Everyone was in awe of her beauty and radiance. Even the old King muttered softly to his Queen that he had forgotten how long it had been since he had seen such a beautiful apparition.

All the ladies were watching her, taking down what she wore so they could copy it after the ball. The King's son stayed with her all night, dancing and talking and unable to eat, as his eyes drank in the beauty she emanated.

Cinderella found her two sisters and shared some gifts of oranges and lemons that the King's son had given her. She thought it funny that her sisters did not recognise her.

Suddenly she realised that the time was quarter to twelve. She rushed home and found her godmother to thank her. Cinderella asked her godmother if she could go to the ball the following night, as the Prince had invited her to return. She began telling her godmother all the details of the night but was interrupted by the knock of her sisters returning.

Cinderella pretended to wake from a sleep and stretched and yawned. The sisters told her if she had been at the ball she would not be tired, as there was the most beautiful princess there who had been very kind to them and given them oranges. Cinderella played along and asked what her name was. The sisters said they did not know and the King's son wanted to know her name too.

Cinderella asked one sister if she could borrow her dress so she could see this princess too, but her sister was horrified that she would dirty her dress and refused. Cinderella knew her sister would not let her wear her dress and so was relieved, as how could she go to the ball in the way she wanted if her sister had said yes?

Cinderella arrived at the ball the next night in even more beautiful finery and the King's son again stayed by her side. She was so delighted by his kindness and compliments that she lost track of the time. Before she realised it, she heard the clock striking twelve. Cinderella raced off and the King's son tried to follow but she was very quick. He managed to grab a glass slipper that had fallen off.

The guards of the palace were questioned but they had not seen any princess, only a poor country girl. Cinderella was home, back in her dirty, old clothes – but she had one glass slipper as a reminder of the night.

When the sisters arrived home, Cinderella asked what the ball was like and if they had seen the fine princess again. They said yes and the King's son had found her glass slipper – he had only wanted to look at the glass slipper when she had disappeared. Clearly he was in love, they said.

This was true. The next day the King's son said he loved the Princess and would marry her when he found her. All the women in the land tried on the glass slipper to find the true owner. A man of the court arrived at Cinderella's home with the glass slipper and when the shoe did not fit the sisters, Cinderella asked to try it on. The sisters laughed in ridicule, but the man found Cinderella beautiful despite her poor clothes and said that he was told all women were to try on the shoe.

The man and two sisters were so surprised when Cinderella's foot slipped easily into the shoe – and even more so when from her pocket, she took out the other glass slipper. The godmother appeared and touched Cinderella again with her wand; lo and behold, Cinderella was dressed in even more beautiful clothes. Her two sisters fell to the ground, begging her forgiveness. She swept them up in a hug saying she forgave them and that she wanted them to love her.

When Cinderella was taken to the King's son he was overjoyed. A few days later they married. Cinderella gave her sisters somewhere to live in the palace and soon after, the two sisters married men of the court.

Adapted from The Blue Fairy Book *and* Tales From Mother Goose *(Lang 1889; Perrault 1697)*

Now that we have very different stories about the spectrum of anger, let's look closer at what they tell us about anger and power, how anger can go underground, and the subsequent repercussions.

Cinderella has it pretty rough, and really needs the power and assertion of the fairy godmother to help get her out of a harsh situation. Her father does not protect her (isn't this a theme in these fairy tales?) and her mother is no longer alive, so unavailable. Perhaps this is another version of the mother in Little Red Riding Hood, who is also unavailable, despite being alive.

Cinderella does not want to place a demand on her father, though she is clearly still a dependent. This is a theme of the child's ability to pick up the parent's gap and adapting to that gap without wanting harm – after all, when dependent we still need our parents, even with their gaps. So again, the theme of the one with less power taking care of the other, who has more power, at the cost of her own wellbeing.

It is interesting to note at the end of the story, she does not save or forgive her father and stepmother, but only her sisters. Maybe there is recognition that adults are not your responsibility to carry or to forgive; but those of your own generation are also affected and influenced by vulnerability of dependency, age and the limited power from the generation above you.

Cinderella holds no anger, no matter what shame and ridicule is put on her. What does this tell us? Cinderella, like her mother, is sweet and good – and so is left at the mercy of an arrogant and cruel mother and sisters. She does not know how to protect herself. She cannot call on her father who loves her, yet is blind to her situation and neglects her. Her disowned anger is unavailable to change the dynamic.

Temper is not a sweet experience yet the mother's temper was described as sweet. The father's attitude is idealising and whether intentional or not, it is patronising and limiting and reducing Cinderella's expression of anger to sweetness. These attitudes implicitly place a burden and pressure on Cinderella to live up to this ideal of her mother, instead of being accepted for being her whole self. Idealising a parent as the 'best in the world' and praising a child of a parent with the same attribute is not necessarily a compliment, but again limiting her character and permission of self from being more than this 'perfection'.

No one is all sweet and good and nothing more. It can be burdensome to always have to be good and sweet. Something within is denied and not allowed to exist. Maybe her mother died prematurely from this idealised, straitjacket type burden – perhaps something akin to Marilyn Monroe and Princess Di's early deaths.

In idealising someone we see them as an object – even if they are seen as a beautiful or desirable object, they are a still an object with no space for a range of responses. The other problem with being seen as an object is that objects are put down and can be forgotten. We don't tend to have relationships with an object. Cinderella is admired by her father – but then, like an object, put down and forgotten.

Objects can't object. There is a one-sided effect. The father saw Cinderella's mother as the best in the world; what a burden to put on a child, to grow up feeling their mother is perfection. There is an impossible and unrealistic expectation placed on the child from an early age, where she too has no permission or space to object. The pressure placed on women who are idealised.

Cinderella gives and gives to her sisters, and then they leave. She collapses and cries. With no father or mother providing skills and support, she does not have a way to be with anger or unbearable emotional pain, rejection and abandonment. This is when the godmother appears to save her.

Charles Perrault suggests that we all need a godmother or godfather. Perhaps this is highlighting that we all need someone who sees us with an 'unconditional positive regard' (Carl Rogers). Someone who bestows blessings to help us get through those gaps and shortcomings in relationships and significant events as we grow up. We need a caring 'witness' and teacher.

Cinderella needs to stay alive to her feeling life for it to be visible and have someone see her and recognise the trauma, as indicated by being lost for words. Cinderella's grief reaches the godmother. The godmother recognises and responds to her state of trauma. When we are in trauma the left brain shuts down and it is hard to speak; we are flooded by the right brain experience of feelings.

Someone needs to be affected and be there with compassion and empathy to respond to the trauma response that is in collapse and can't bridge the right and left brain to speak. The godmother does not need her to complete all her sentences to be understood. As well as recognising the trauma response, the caring witness needs to send the message that *you don't have to do it all – just begin*. You don't have to be perfect or have it all together, you just need to have a response. The very antidote to her father's vision of her.

When the caring witness holds the empathic and inclusive space, more information can be communicated that is beyond words. Her empathy and acceptance opens her to the field of experience. The fairy godmother gets 'it' and what is needed. Action can unfold because she is *with* her, not separate and just talking *about* it.

The godmother tells her to be good, sends her to her room and then to the garden. What is this about? The very first thing the godmother tells her is to be good … Doesn't she do enough of that?

Initially, I didn't like reading that in the original tale, but when I look at the interpretation that I am creating and unfolding, I see these words differently. I see her godmother saying, '*Don't let the bad rob you of your goodness. Return to your centre (your room) your place of good, from your positive life energy.*' Perhaps this is a reminder that when we are in a state of despair, we need to return to our safe place, our centre – and the only way we can is through positive life energy, through our 'good.'

Also, I see the message to be good as telling Cinderella to not get caught in her overwhelm and to follow the healing rules without question. When we go through healing or learning, we need to follow a structure and surrender some control about not knowing the outcome. What a relief that she does not need to agree or understand the structure, or know what is next, to receive the benefits from them. Good rules should not be broken but instead followed – that is what healing ritual is about. Bad rules are the ones that need breaking.

Cinderella does not know how retrieving a pumpkin will help, but following her kind witness she can go through the process of the unknown and uncertainty to get to a new resolution.

Through the modelling and guidance of her godmother, Cinderella begins to initiate and contribute to her solution in seeking the rats. Can you see a process of skill-building and emotional muscle development through social modelling and permission?

The godmother gives her the condition of not staying after twelve. Here the skill-building continues; Cinderella is given a boundary and a consequence. She is taught about being realistic and not to get caught in idealism and fantasy. This is so important in relationships, particularly when we are in a relationship with a Wolf or Bluebeard.

In real life, there is always an end to happy things, nothing is constant; and so we need to not be unrealistic and not cling to a happy moment when the situation has changed from moment to moment. To be with the acceptance of what is, in the now. Being realistic and open to the ebb and flow of life is very different to the pessimistic idea that there is an end to good things. Pessimism is a killing off energy which reduces us to stay closed in a degraded mode of 'being realistic' at the cost of magic of the flow of seasons of life, creative possibility and the positive unexpected.

I am not suggesting to be the degraded pessimist. Let us remember though, that happiness is transitory and what happens between those times is contentment, work and effort. Good needs to be grounded in reality, not ideals and fantasy.

When Cinderella is at the ball, no one appears envious; they admire her beauty and even the King acknowledges her beauty. The generation above her can appreciate her without envy. She experiences, perhaps for the first time, what we all need in our early developmental years: to be the centre of your world. To shine and be enjoyed, adored and delighted for a period of time without shame, envy or judgement. Growing up with an experience of this builds resilience in our psyche for those times later in life when we discover we are not the centre of the world. This experience of safely being the centre can build our emotional muscle against times of emotional pain and disappointment of others and the world.

The King's son gives her oranges and lemons, one being a sweet fruit and the other a sour fruit. Oranges are often a symbol of love, virginity and marriage and in heraldic art are a symbol of strength and endurance. Lemons have been a symbol for purification, love, friendship, longevity and wealth. The bitterness of lemons has been seen as a reminder of the bitterness and disappointment of life, to not overindulge in luxury, and is a reminder of transience and mortality.

In the context of these meanings it is interesting to consider the King's son's gifts. He gave her sweetness but also to be with the bitterness, an antidote to the extreme other end of the continuum: idealisation (too much sweetness: father) and envy (spite: stepmother). Oranges and lemons are the blessing to receive love and protection and the capacity to bear disappointment, and so a promise of balance and abundance.

Just like the fairy godmother's consequences of a time limit, the oranges and lemons reinforce and communicate a balance of staying with reality and not getting carried away - which is so easy in our modern world with the idealistic magazines, fashion, movies, songs and billboards.

Cinderella is not bitter to the sisters when she shares her fruits. She does not hold a fear of scarcity. The King son's love fills her with security and his love gives her a sense that there is 'enough' for her. She was seen, admired and accepted by all the people. She does not need to be filled with fear and competitiveness like her sisters, despite having lived with neglect and scarcity.

Love is like the flame of a candle, full and present. When two candle flames (love) come together and merge, they are one, yet when the two candles separate they each have their own full, individual flame. They have not lost themselves to the union. They are still whole. They can merge and separate and there is enough flame for both. This is in stark contrast to the experience of Bluebeard's pseudo-love where one is consumed by the other and blown out if exists separately. Cinderella experienced this love from the King's son.

Cinderella goes straight to her godmother and shows gratitude. This gratitude grounds the reality of her experience within herself and allows her to share it with another, without shame and ridicule. A very healing experience after a life of being shamed, criticised and ridiculed. She can shine and be seen while she shines. Gratitude helps integrate her experience. Through sharing Cinderella opens up a healing experience, where what is hers that is abundant and good can be witnessed and celebrated, without being made smaller even while someone else is not having her experience – the opposite of the shame and attack of her stepsisters.

Often we can hide our shining self to appease the possibility of someone else feeling their less-than state - as if there is not enough room for both to shine. If someone else is not shining, you are not responsible for where they are in their journey and don't have to hold back (of course adjusting with mindful compassion if someone else is going through a difficult time) – nothing is fixed in this continuum, there can be room for both in their own timing.

When the sisters return, she is strategic in going along with how she needs to be in relationship with them, to protect herself. Maybe the goodness she received from her early life with a loving mother and father enabled her to be strategic, as she seems to have done this with her sisters all along. She is not naive or gullible with them. She is grounded and aware of what is going on. Perhaps sleeping close to the ground is representative of her life teaching her a grounded perspective that is practical and strategic. Yet it is not enough to get out of the habit of surrendering and serving. She needs the resources and supports from the fairy godmother who offers her a way to transition.

Cinderella is grounded and strategic and she still has hope. She asks her sister to loan her a dress to wear to go to the ball. Even though she does not expect any help from them and indeed they do not help her but instead, laugh at her, she still takes a risk into the unknown. Even if she perceives it could not go as she would want, she opens the door to possibility. However, hope is not enough to transform her situation.

Often women who have come out of the effects of abuse give themselves a hard time about trusting others and then again by different people getting stung, or they give themselves a hard time for having hope with the Bluebeard or Wolf in their life. They bear this harsh judgement that they *should have known* not to trust and should be able to pick the Wolves and tricksters. These women are courageous to keep open and not become bitter or negative. They are brave to experiment with hope and not close off. This hope is very different to what we will explore with the Little Match Girl. The Little Match Girl shows us the regressive side of hope, but Cinderella shows us a grounded way of opening the door to hope, open to an opportunity but being strategic and not telling all - keeping the door open for extended periods to get stung.

Cinderella forgets the time as she is absorbed in enjoyment, joy. This is not a mistake, but a natural progression of her being able to take up more space in the positive world that allows her to take healthy risks. It sets off a series of consequences that are not in her control and take her into the unknown that was not planned. This being with the self and the positive experience is necessary, along with being with healthy risk *when in the correct environment*. When we live with abuse, we hold ourselves back and anticipate punishment and unrelenting demands. Here we have the healing of being able to surrender to enjoyment, play and spontaneity. This environment of love and abundance allows her to not shrink into herself, but to come out.

Healing involves going beyond the restrictions of what we were given from anyone or anywhere in our culture and world. Otherwise, we'd always hold back because of what is structuring us and we'd never know our own true edges, structures and map. The reference point would remain always looking out for what 'other' determines. It is the 'going beyond', where we find our own boundary and reference point, instead of always holding back in anticipation of the disapproval or rules of others. We become self-structured and individuate.

A consequence unfolds with her clothes returning to her shabby state; she is not seen by the guard in all her finery. It may not seem evident but there is a benefit in returning to the picture of her worst. This is so important. The guard could symbolise our internal witness or internal protector who needs to see her 'best' side (in arriving) and her 'worst' side (when leaving). The whole. There is a healing completion through reclaiming her 'best' side from the experience at the ball. Her spontaneity and immersion in the joy and being carefree. The 'worst' face's return is part of the integration from her past and being able to move from the good to the bad or the ordinary. When we are traumatised we can become hooked on idealisation, perfection and the supernatural or extraordinary. Healing involves the necessity of being with the whole, the ordinary and not getting lost in fantasy.

The King's son (active, healthy masculine), stays connected to the glass slipper as his link to Cinderella. She holds a slipper, just as he does. They both share a link between the ordinary and the magic, the best and the worst ground.

Shoes protect the ground we walk on. But these shoes are glass - you can see through them. They are fragile and are clearly only temporary. These shoes demonstrate nothing is permanent and we need to not be fixed, solid, or rigid in connecting to our ground. Our ground needs to be protected but we also need to be flexibly responsive to our situation and our needs at any given time. To stay grounded we need to recognise our vulnerability and our ground could shatter. We are not gods or inflated, untouchable beings. We need to bear our enjoyment, our strength and our vulnerability in being human.

There is nothing she can do now she has engaged with the best and worst except surrender to the ground of healthy action. This is possible due to the risks and engagement with the powerful, positive masculine. She has to trust the unknown, but this unknown now includes her existence and connection to the masculine via the King and his awareness of her that stays present apparent by him possessing one glass slipper.

The man of the court is the positive masculine action or attribute that is necessary to unite her with the King: her positive masculine (internally or in relationship). The necessity of the transition from the man of the court enables a union so that there is no more secrecy or temporary playing in her best self but that she can be fully out in the world, to be free. The prince also represents the positive masculine within her that stays strong and connected to the magic of her positive self, no matter what external appearance.

The man of the court can represent an external person. When we are in a troubling situation, particularly with abuse, we do need others to be a link, a bridge, and hold the glass slipper (the ground which feels unreachable) for us and take steps. We need others to not give up. To not be swayed by the immensity of the task.

There is an ask that the kind and active witness (man of the court/prince: positive masculine) within or in another, to believe and not fear that what you or they may say or do won't work. The transitional figure needs to hold the intention of the task and the desired end result and to the possibility and experimenting, even when things are not logical. That it is important to try everything (everyone's feet) till you get the right fit. Stay open minded, not pre-judging and take informed risks (through learnt skills) to stay connected to Cinderella.

The man of the court is only concerned with what he *feels to be true* as is not led astray by outer appearance. When there has been secrecy there needs to be an open curiosity to go beyond what feels rational to discover the true fit and the truth. He trusts his sensings. Just like the prince; friends and family of someone caught by a Bluebeard or Wolf, need to see the divinity and goodness of their friend and not get caught in the 'worst face', 'survival defences' or external clothing which hide who she really is. When she is feeling dirty and in cinders, she needs you to see her true self and stay connected to her.

When Cinderella asks to try on the glass slipper, the sisters laugh. The King's man affirms her right to try the shoe on. Again, the positive masculine holds to the true rules to be followed. Cinderella has not given up hope and takes a risk. She has the emotional muscle to not give up.

The King's man sees her inner beauty and sees past the survival clothing she wears, just as a woman caught in abuse needs others to see her full self. Cinderella has a positive, masculine ally who can witness the larger truth of who she is. We all need the positive masculine internally and externally. Even when Cinderella appears different to how she was at the ball, the King's man trusts his feelings and instincts. This is what Cinderella, the woman trapped by abuse, needs to develop in herself and experience from those close to her or working with her.

The instance of the King's man, a man of the *court*, holding this ground also indicates that Cinderella needs the broader societal judicial system – the police and legal structures – to uphold healthy rules, see the true feminine and not be swayed by external survival expressions, culture and images.

The request is to not be swallowed by those outward images of perfection, idealisation, complacency. To not get caught in denial or an avoidance of remaining with the uncomfortable truth and uncomfortable feelings. To face the fact that there are an immense number of families, women and children who still live with all types of abuse. So abuse does not remain like Cinderella, in the back room with the ashes and in secret.

Outward images, which are superficial and are not connected to the grounded physical truths, need to be seen through. After all, the King's man was following the prince's laws. We need our legal system to have a more sophisticated way of seeing through what is real, what is true, and testing this. Staying with the true rules about a healthy society, boundaries and respect.

When the law (King's man) and her sisters begin to see the merging of the two experiences of Cinderella, and she sees their openness, she brings out the other glass slipper. She can reveal another small part. Doing this in stages keeps her safe. This is not mistrust or pessimism, this is a healthy revelation in context to the environment.

Often Little Red Riding Hood women have too much trust and reveal too much, too soon – instead of being measured and mindful, grounded in the context of what is happening as to how much to reveal, what and when. Then, when Cinderella sees their response of full acceptance, she is fully safe. The godmother can appear to complete her reclamation of her whole true powerful self.

The sisters ask for forgiveness and Cinderella can accept that they too were part of the wounded sisterhood from the forces of patriarchy that shape a survival pattern of competing, rather than uniting. She wants to be loved by them. We need our 'sisters' to love us and not be envious, critical or judgemental. She saw they had the potential of acceptance without envy through their acceptance of her at the ball and how they spoke of the 'unknown princess' on returning from the ball. We need acceptance and a sense of belonging, sisterhood to feel safe to leave Bluebeard.

The ending of this tale shows the abundance available for everyone. We don't need to take care of or blame parents. We don't need to get caught in the hook of returning to the Wolf or Bluebeard, or of staying in the past. When we have a positive ground welcoming us that is thriving and healthy – when we have been adored and we have experienced some people being generous with loving us – we can be free.

But we need support and community to be able to move on. Cinderella has her sisters and their husbands with her, as well has her prince and his family. She has her community, which enables her to move on. It is very hard to move on and heal without community.

The story of Cinderella however, skips the part about anger. There is no anger when the stepsisters torment her. She can have grief and passivity, that is acceptable – but not anger. Lilith is strong and in her anger. She has anger, sexuality, independence and power. Lilith claims equality and refuses to accept anything other than equality – and for this she was alienated. We don't see a positive outcome for women with healthy anger. There are not many positive role models of women with healthy anger.

> Her strength of character and commitment of self is inspiring. For independence and freedom from tyranny she is prepared to forsake the economic security of the Garden of Eden and to accept loneliness

and exclusion from society … Lilith is a powerful female. She radiates strength, assertiveness; she refuses to cooperate in her own victimisation. (Cantor-Zuckoff 1976)

When women's anger can be bigger than their (patriarchy-induced) fear of surviving (the real issues of housing, safety and poverty) women can leave and heal. Poverty, safety and housing are serious issues – however, women who leave need their anger to be bigger than their fears, and society needs to step up and help address these real issues and allow, support and celebrate a woman's anger to be there. This anger is protecting her life energy.

***

Let us now come and look at anger through a news lens. Anger exists. It is not a mistake. No feelings are mistakes.

Remember, *your feelings are not mistakes*. All feelings are there as an instinctual, motivating, activating force in the related behaviour that is a natural response to the immediate situation. Feelings inform us of the value and depth of the experience and motivate and guide us to the necessary response, behaviour and skill. When our feelings are shut down we don't have access to the corresponding behaviour and anxiety is inevitable.

In any given experience, we will experience one or more of these '**Natural Instinctual Motivating Feelings**' that move us into a related behaviour:

- Enjoyment/Joy
- Interest/Excitement
- Grief/Loss
- Anger/Assertion
- Fear/Terror
- Closeness/Tenderness
- Sexual desire
- Positive sense of self (self-compassion, self-confidence, self-soothing, self-esteem, healthy vulnerability)[3]

We need each of our feelings. When a feeling is not activated and the related

---

3. Adapted from Malan's Triangle of Defences.

healthy behaviour is inhibited, we know there is a conflict in the system due to the (current) unsafe situation, which does not allow us expression or to keep ourselves safe – or there are unconscious limiting beliefs blocking the healthy feeling and behaviour (unresolved traumatic past experience which has become re-activated due to a trigger).

This is when **Inhibiting feelings and states** come up, which may initially appear as useless or a mistake, but if they were not there then we would be facing an unsafe situation and be at greater risk. We are unsafe because we don't have permission or skill to access what is needed from our natural instinctual repertoire in that particular circumstance. Unsafe because we are at a gap without skill or safety to express our natural response. We could be placed in greater harm. Each inhibiting emotion tells us about the kind of wound is being carried and so gives clues as to how to heal and what skills and support are required.[4]

The intention of inhibited emotional states is to shut us down for the purpose of keeping us safe and protected, due to the lack of availability or skills, behaviours, positive life affirming beliefs and safety that are needed to be accessed but disconnected from. These inhibitive states are all associated with unbearable feelings and unthinkable thoughts associated with unresolved experiences and memories:

- Shame
- Anxiety
- Guilt
- Aversive fear (fear which shuts us down, instead of activating fear)
- Emotional pain
- Despair
- Disgust

So to go over: anger is not a mistake. Anger is there for a reason, just as all our feelings are there for a reason. Anger, like all other feelings, offers us information about the situation. If we don't have access to our anger and what our anger is giving a value on what is happening, then we don't have access to a healthy, contextual, behavioural response that matches and expresses our anger and is there to protect us.

---

4. Adapted from Malan's Triangle of Defences.

Just like each feeling state, no other feeling is relevant when anger is relevant – it is not replaceable with a different affect. Each feeling serves a separate purpose. When anger is shut down, it is at risk of staying trapped inside an inhibitor or get hijacked into a defence against feeling or showing anger. The dis-owned and unrelated anger becomes toxic when it can't be engaged with its pure and real essence, resulting in effects of self-harm in a variety of ways.

When I say anger is not replaceable with another feeling, that does not exclude that any experience may evoke more than feeling at one time. At any one time, anger may also engage with some other feeling, such as fear or grief; but that fear or grief can not do the job of anger. Each is there for their own sake and can't be replaced.

When we hold beliefs that 'anger is bad' or hold a value that 'sacrificing to prevent anger' is a 'good' thing, we are at risk of being taken advantage of, tricked and having our boundaries crossed – like Cinderella and Little Red Riding Hood.

Anger is energy and therefore holds power. When we deny our anger, we deny access to information and energy. When this stream of information that is held within the experience of anger is shut down, other positive aspects of power also get shut down, such as healthy vulnerability or confidence. This shutdown happens because we don't have access to our healthy anger to protect us or our vulnerable expression. What might be shown from a place of confidence, enjoyment or tenderness – is at risk of being attacked or rejected. So our internal protector closes the door to these big, positive and necessary expressions. Our inner self is not revealed, in case one feeling opens the door and we don't have access to our healthy protective anger response.

Our anger helps us have greater access to all our positive feeling states, including confidence, spontaneity, play, enjoyment and intimacy. When we are connected to our positive expressions we are vulnerable – when we are in the moment of enjoyment or excitement, we are not on guard - the more we have access to healthy anger to protect us, the more comfortable we can be to take risks and expose ourselves, because we know our anger is available when needed to protect us.

Our anger can have many forms and expressions. Anger is not sweet but it does not have a nasty face; it is clean and direct. Anger is fierce and serious. Anger is no nonsense. It can be pure in its stance to protect and affirm a boundary. The discomfit in the field of either person may then attribute that the anger is ugly or bad but often this is more about the limiting beliefs and concerns about the experience, the threat to belonging or feeling safe, rather than the anger itself.

The reality is that we may have a backlog of anger, be tired, fearful or something else that colours the anger. The other person who does not agree with our anger and boundary may see our anger as ugly because it may feel a threat to them or they may be involved in shame and survival and reflect back that our anger is wrong. We are such social creatures that we are vulnerable to see our anger through another's eyes and experience.

Anger is not abuse. Anger looks and feels ugly when we are shamed for our anger or feel shame when we feel anger because we fear and mis-attribute that our anger is the same as our parent/Wolf's aggression and abuse and our survival is threatened. When we are fearful of showing our anger, it can come out as aggression to shut the other person down before they judge, reject or shame us.

The problem is that if we are listening just to our minds in the context of our experiences in the world, we are listening to the storehouse that is filled with should's and rules and we can go into all kinds of 'ifs' and 'buts' and early life survival mapping that is not resourced for all of who we are. When we listen to our body, our body doesn't lie. It doesn't turn itself inside out. Something either feels good or bad, hot or cold, warm or soft, pleasing or non-pleasing. Whereas the mind can see both sides and get confused, the body knows its truth and sticks to it. Our feelings and our body are partners and far more aligned than the mind is to either. Our mind has been influenced by our family, culture, history, religion and life events. Our body has a simple response: yes or no.

I remember one particular time in a new relationship (after the Wolf and therapy) when I was so angry and I expressed my anger to him. This relationship was much healthier and so there was no retaliation, shaming or rejection from him. I remember feeling the strength in my system, validating my reality and creating space for me. I felt such joy and relief that my anger could be visible between us and our relationship was still intact. Expressing my anger helped me realise in the cells of my body – what a logical thought could not reassure me – the indisputable body knowing that anger would not destroy me, him or the relationship. It was incredible to feel this at the same time as my anger flowing and protecting me. A bubbling of joy filled me.

This expression of anger gave me another unexpected gift. I realised that he loved me even while he was witnessing my anger. He was still here and not punishing, controlling or denying me. Our connection was bigger than the anger. My shame about anger dissolved.

This is the gift of letting our feelings flow in healthy ways and in healthy environments. It made me realise that there must have been one little, young part of me still experiencing that my anger was ugly and fearing that I would be alienated and rejected if I showed it. It was only when I took a risk and let it come out, rather than control it, could this healing shift and awareness take place – otherwise, it was always having me hold my anger back in case it was bigger than the relationship and would destroy it. This is what every child needs to experience growing up; their anger can be seen, not shamed and it is not going to break the love connection and relationship. Children or adults in healing need a safe place and way to express their anger and find their own boundary with it rather than an external 'should' or shame.

This is a bit like Cinderella leaving the ball on the second night. When we are absorbed in the positive experience, we can go beyond the internal survivor rules – it may look to one part of us that we have entered dangerous territory, but in fact we have just expanded the territory we can stand on and found our own edges.

When we confuse both anger and power as being negative and having a 'bad name', then anger and power have become hijacked and unavailable. In fact, they both have a positive and generative origin. Anger and power have become enmeshed with 'power over' someone, and with abuse and aggression. Anger and power need a healthy and clear separation from their forced toxic connection to abuse and aggression.

When we don't understand the full spectrum of anger in relationship to aggressive, passive and passive-aggressive behaviours; we often develop unrealistic values and stories about how to communicate assertively. This often comes out of the Little Red Riding Hood Effect. We are taught there is only one way: being nice and kind and that there are not different people (Wolves) out in the world, and there is no room to respond differently to these different types of people (healthy aggression). So we can grow up assuming if we are assertive, that the other person will respond to our reasonable and fair expression. But Wolves don't value or listen to assertion; they punish you for the consequences of assertion. We don't learn that different contexts require a different level on the continuum of healthy anger and aggression.

Little Red Riding Hood needs to access her anger to enable her to broaden her options. She is not aware that Bluebeard and the Wolf will act pleasant to work their way in. When Little Red Riding Hood has a fixed social mode of being polite and the 'rule' you need to reply when someone speaks to you, she can't access her anger to healthily break a social rule and be 'impolite'. This is an example of how I mentioned the mind getting confused but all the messages and patterns we have learnt but the body does not lie. The body is simple and true. We need to have internal permission to trust our gut, break social rules, appear impolite or rude; when it is flexibly responsive to a particular situation. Flexible responsiveness to a context is vital.

This reminds me of a time when I was with my grand-daughter. As we entered the lift, a man left the lift. This male was someone my daughter had had an intervention order against, relating to a series of intrusions including one incident when he had been party to his friend threatening both our lives to 'take care of a perceived problem'. He greeted me and I did not reply. I said nothing as I recognise that he is not genuinely interested in being pleasant. Everything is about him and drama and aggression is his life story. He tries to take advantage of people's kindness and then he pushes and pushes and pushes the boundaries, unrelenting and ignoring requests to be left alone. He does not pay attention to social cues, which do not work for him. Instead, he manipulates social niceties.

I realised when I was leaving the lift with my grand-daughter that I better explain my silence towards the man. I told her how some people don't mean what they say and it's okay not to answer them. I explained that I decide if someone is being genuine and if I want to respond - that I choose what feels right. I want my grand-daughter to be able to negotiate tricksters and not be caught as Little Red Riding Hood in the woods with the Wolf.

Many people unconsciously expect when we speak assertively, the other person will listen and everything will work out, because we're being fair, honest and respectful. When the outcome does not fit this belief, we can think that maybe we asked too much or sounded 'bossy', and that we still need to learn more about being assertive, instead of that we are in the Little Red Riding Hood Effect. So the conflict remains unresolved, and we can mistakenly think we fail at assertion and give up, not following through with assertive behaviours or accessing the need for healthy aggression – because if our assertion was not acceptable, then our healthy aggression certainly isn't allowed.

The Little Red Riding Hood within needs to be taught about all the experiences of anger so she can work out strategically how to navigate the Wolf, aggression and abuse. Little Red Riding Hood needs to access her Lilith to act on her instincts and demand her power and place, and not betray herself in fear of rejection. The passive Cinderella needs to internalise the healthy assertion, power and action of the godmother to help her take the steps to get out of serving others and carrying other people's response-abilities.

When we experience aggression or abuse directed at us, we automatically and naturally don't want to be like that either. So we do this funny reverse thing and polarise to passivity. We are so busy not wanting to be like the aggressor, we often think the opposite is the answer; but being passive or 'doing the opposite' is not necessarily the answer. We are in fact still being controlled by the aggressor's stance. It is not a free choice stance but a reaction. A bit like Cinderella, passive to the aggression of her step-mother and step-sisters.

Who wants to be Cinderella before the ball? Don't we want to be Cinderella, who has relationship with power and assertion: the fairy godmother? Don't we want to be the Cinderella who can make things happen? This is another version of the Woodcutter Within. Both the Woodcutter and the Fairy Godmother are using positive masculine energy to cut through limitations and go for what is really necessary.

So let's get clear. Anger is not negative. Anger is an instinctive, activating, motivating feeling, which arises from the context you are in.

The internal context for anger involves feelings which are aligned with thoughts, beliefs and behaviours that come because we sense, feel, see or hear a boundary and value of ours has been disrespected, crossed or broken. An example of this evoked by an external event is someone ridiculing or ignoring our feelings or existence. An example with a less external focus might be in a social gathering and feeling as if someone is taking up too much space even if we are not speaking. This might reflect an internal dynamic, which evokes anger, could be in relation to another person or to ourselves. The anger could be speaking of a social imbalance but not feeling safe, confident or skilled to speak up or wanting to get yourself out of a social situation that is not enjoyable but not taking action so betraying your needs for someone else's. Internal anger towards other or self for not speaking up could be protecting you from an anticipatory anxiety or fear to fulfil the actions you desire.

Anger is about others lack of respect for our boundaries. It is about the external to us. We would not be angry at ourselves when we are alone, if we have not had experiences of shame and judgement from others. It just wouldn't make sense to be angry at ourselves. We are only angry at ourselves when we have internalised judgement from a lack of support and skills to respond, and there is a fear we will be shamed or rejected. Otherwise, we would be with ourselves with compassion, permission and a healthy dose of self-motivating irritation that we are not living from our optimal self.

When we have internalised anger towards ourselves, it is because we have experienced lack of permission and support to have our anger, power and actions – and so we have internalised the critic from others or society. The social example when someone did not speak up reveals defensive anger due to a skill deficit to negotiate a situation. In this instance, this anger could be directed towards you or someone else, because you may not speak up when you need to, and so anger is informing you of a gap within yourself which is being projected onto someone else.

So let me repeat, anger is not negative. Anger is a feeling, like all our feelings. It is information-based and tells us about the value of our experience. Anger's purpose is to inform, motivate and activate natural and instinctual boundaries that respect our sense of self and our experience. Abusive aggression is 'power over' – a choice and a behaviour. Anger is a feeling and 'power within'. Assertion is the behaviour that comes from the feeling of anger.

Remember, most Bluebeards or Wolves don't tend to behave abusively to everyone they meet. They choose who to control through their aggression. It is a behaviour switched on and used specifically in certain relationships and contexts, for the specific purpose to intimidate and control.

Anger is clear, clean and simple. Anger just says, 'I don't like this, this is not okay. Stop.' It's telling you that someone is crossing a boundary – maybe even yourself. The experience can be internal or external. We project things onto anger; it just wants to let us know the boundary. Projection is a way for the unconscious to bring us more information, greater consciousness.

Healthy anger is about our own ground; other people's ground is not our responsibility. Anger arises to express a concern that is all. That does not negate the other person's ground. If we don't understand the healthy and constructive aspects of anger, we can't access them to protect ourselves. If we hold values and beliefs about how sacrifice is good and anger is bad (Cinderella), we are at risk of being taken advantage of and taken for granted.

We often confuse both anger and power with being negative. They both have a positive, generative origin, which I work with more personally, exploring personal experiences in my workshops, retreats and professional development sessions.

When we don't understand the full spectrum of anger, aggression, passivity and passive-aggressiveness, we often develop unrealistic stories and values about what happens when we communicate assertively. For example, that speaking assertively will mean the conflict can be resolved easily and quickly. We might falsely believe that just being honest and assertive with others will mean that they have to listen and respond appropriately.

We need to teach Little Red Riding Hood and Cinderella about all the ways of relating to anger. Just as we needed to look at all the beliefs and influences about love through all the layers in our family, society, culture and history. All six blind villagers needed to come together to get the full picture of the elephant. It's really important that we look at all the pieces of the elephant about love and anger through our personal, family, religious, societal, cultural and historical influences.

> Most couples have not had hundreds of arguments, they've had the same argument hundreds of times.
> Gay Hendricks

When people are confused about anger and aggression, the choices on how to negotiate conflict in relationships becomes complicated and messy – and even more chaotic and destructive when abuse is involved.

Women in particular have not been given support and permission to know how to contain and then aim their anger in the right direction or to the correct person.

> We keep ourselves so tied up in regretting the past and fearing the future that we don't have any energy to figure out who we are and what we want to create right now.
> Gay Hendricks

This is often the dilemma after living inside of abuse.

> Knowing your own darkness is the best method for dealing with the darkness of other people.
> Carl Jung[5]

***

So let's get clear.

There are two parts to anger. The first part is the raw emotion of anger and the information inside this raw emotion. When we have the capacity to bear this raw, unmediated, messy information we move into the second part.

The second part of our anger is our response to this raw information. Our first raw response has given us information, which offers us a way to clarity, so that in the second part we can discern who or what is most necessary to respond to, knowing what is not feeling acceptable or not being experienced as acceptable. The second part allows us to get to a mediated response that is based on our unmediated first response.

Once I had an experience that made me really angry with my sisters. It felt messy and overwhelming. So much of the experience felt wrong, but I was feeling so jumbled by the intensity and speed of what had happened and what I was feeling that I felt incomplete. I went home and wrote down all of what happened. Totally uncensored. I let everything that I remembered tumble out.

Writing uncensored re-connected with the feelings, thoughts, images, elements of the experience that had got scattered in the intensity. I allowed all the details without judging or excluding anything. *The writing was a flow which enabled my feelings which had been shut down, interrupted through shock and overwhelm to resume their flow.*

Through this journal writing and outpouring, I was led to parts of the memory that had become buried in the chaos and intensity of the

---

5. C.G. Jung ~Carl Jung, *Letters* Vol. 1, Pages 236-237. Princeton University Press 1973

experience. The uncensored process of writing down what had happened supported my neural network to open up and allow all the connections to come rather than 'trauma compact' the details.

What was revealed was an '*aha*' moment which burst forth from the spaciousness of writing. Suddenly I was clear as to what was at the core and essence of my anger and what this meant for me. If I had not written it all down, I am sure I would have stayed in the overwhelmed 'story', lost to the 'details and essence'

An important piece of truth would have stayed buried and my future choices would have been inhibited in the unresolved confusion. I was clear in my process to move forward. The sense of feeling incomplete and jumbled when I left my sisters was my system needing me to connect to this missing piece of information.

With my reality retrieved and affirmed through the writing and the acknowledgement of what had impacted me, I felt at peace about the intensity of my feeling and the experience. I now felt complete. I had made the links between my feeling, my body sensations and what had unfolded, to find my truth. I did not need either sister to validate or affirm my reality, as I had seen it for myself.

Knowing this piece of information led me to know what I needed to do in the future to ensure this never happened again. I could change my behaviour and my choices to protect myself, my boundaries and my values based on the consistency of the themes of my experience.

There is also a third, optional part: taking it to the other person when we have found our truth and clarity about what is going on for ourselves. This is not always necessary or appropriate. You may find once you have gathered the essence, you have different choices in what you share or what you do, and with whom. You may discover, for example, you let people in and trust them too soon before you have all the information you need to enable that decision – so then, it is not so much about taking it back to the person as you are now pacing what you share, to who and when.

Often we get stung; we open a door that in hindsight we would have been better not to open. Unlocked doors leave us vulnerable to thieves (thieves who deny our reality and try to rob us of our feelings or rights).

People often take the first raw and messy part to the person and situation that triggered the anger, instead of creating a safe, comfortable place to be able to release that anger and be with it themselves or with a kind witness and guide.

It is almost like we are so uncomfortable with anger that it is a hot potato, and we throw it over too soon to someone else (optional: part three) to hold and make better instead of being able to bear our own hot potato. We need to find our own truth and no one can give us this. We can't create the opportunity to allow that truth to evolve if we don't stay with the raw anger long enough to get to our own response.

Part one (raw anger and the fuller details within it) and two (our informed and required response) is your system communicating to you about something. It often has to do with someone else, but it's not necessarily about taking your anger immediately to someone else.

We need to develop the skills and resources to be able to bear being with our own anger, to avoid dumping it prematurely on someone else so we can actually get to know what's really going on. This process gets quicker and easier the more we develop our emotional muscle.

It's important to find that safe, comfortable place to release and not control this anger, and not hold it back. Often people are so uncomfortable with their anger that they rush through the anger process, just to get to the other end.

Anger gets wronged and portrayed as negative or bad, when anger actually has positive and regenerative intentions. We can get confused when our anger is triggered, and we don't have the emotional muscle to bear the discomfort – or the skills, the space and perhaps the support to be with our anger. And so, often all sorts of conflicts and complications arise.

Here is my continuum of Anger: Power Within. When we don't have access to be with our anger, notice how there's a second continuum below. The continuum of Aggression, Abuse and Power Over.

This also includes the other unhealthy positions: Passivity, Passive-Aggressiveness. This continuum of aggression often gets interpreted as anger and often gets blurred *as if it* lives on the continuum of Anger and Power Within.

Chapter 10: Banished Lilith 337

Continuum: Power Within - Healthy Anger

Mild
Irritation
frustration
annoyance

Increasing anger
anger heated

Anger dependent on:
context, relationship,
degree of threat,
history, severity of occurrences
with no adequate previous
response from other

Constructive rage:
expressive,
honoring of,
relating to
(this anger is not
necessarily directed
at other)

Stage 1:
Feelings raw, uncensored feelings. this allows information to be gathered. Feeling and sensing, alert to the threat or warning of a boundary rupture that is being activated towards self, identity, property, loved one, animal.

May need time and support to release, express raw experience through writing, talking, drawing, physical movement, clay, to enable stage 2: taking action.

Stage 2:
Action required to address the problem and protect self or dependant other, prejudice or social justice. May need support or skill development to work out appropriate way of addressing directly or indirectly.

Healthy anger offers flexible choices on how to respond / express / resolve the concern.

Assertion → **Assertion** → **Assertion** → **Assertion**

Feelings, behaviours and words are congruent and respect self and other, without denying self. Assertion is not dependent on other validating or responding appropriately, assertion will recognise the reality of other's capacity / capability and take care of own needs and choices, regardless.

Continuum: Power Over: Abusive Aggression: All About Self: Other does not have Rights

Anger
healthy anger blocked

Passive
inflexible, shut down, selfless, overpowering, self critic, soft spoken, self depreciating, others preference comes first, allow others to dominate, other takes over with no resistance. Feelings, tone of voice, posture, behaviour. all meek, sacrifice, hesitant, approval seeking, belittle own views

Aggression
shouting
insults
threats
hostile
posturing
standing over

Passive Aggressive
Inflexible, indirect, sullen, silent treatment, tantrums, wants the last insult, unfair, deliberate procrastination, unjust, hostile behaviour, everything served as an attack, criticism disguised as a compliment, resent requests and punish, miscommunication and denial, silent treatment, ignore, intentional mistakes, says it is a joke but it is an attack, stubborn

Aggression
attack
harmful to self, others, objects, property, animals, earth/nature damage, injury

Rage
externalisation of internal state, using other as an object, de-personalised, high danger to other, mad

Take your time to look through these two continuums and the difference between healthy aggression and hostile aggression. Think of examples of the two. Look at healthy protective rage and the power over rage that sits on the aggressive/passive-aggressive continuum. Again, recall examples of both, either in your life or from someone you know (or even from a movie).

Assertion gone wrong is when you're on the top continuum, yet talking with someone who is currently on the lower continuum. It is as if you are in two different countries with two different languages. When you speak, the other person does not treat you with equal ground, with the same validation, inclusion, acceptance and acknowledgement. When you feel them punishing, controlling or denying you, you know the other person is being a Wolf and it is not possible to talk from a different continuum. The Wolf will want to pull you into his continuum, but nothing makes sense there and is not rational.

You may trick yourself or be tricked into thinking you can talk assertively to the Wolf. It may appear you are on the same continuum because the Wolf may go along in a pretence, though for him it is all a game. The way you can tell it is a pretence is that no behavioural change, remorse or consistent repair takes place. The Wolf may appease you momentarily, but then everything slides back. *His walk won't match his talk.*

The Wolf may watch you silently, not protesting or arguing, even appearing as if he is listening, yet later you will find he has resorted to digging an even deeper hole underneath you so the Wolf's aggressive power can control and punish you and rise itself even higher over you. He will keep digging your hole deeper to stop you trying to get back onto your solid ground.

When we zoom in and have a close-up of the two continuum lines, they can look like the image below: the two lines of the continuum have become the ground and flipped. We find ourselves on the lower line, because the Wolf has dug us into a hole below their line.

I want to clarify what I mean when I say 'he put you in this hole'. The Wolf's behaviour and intimidation creates an environment and involuntary factors ('The Red Shoes' will explore these involuntary factors) in which no matter what you do, the Wolf denies your feelings and needs, and blocks your constructive choices. When you stay, each denial takes away some of your ground.

I find that many reasonable people, when they get caught in this hole, keep standing in there and trying to reach out, even when the other person is taking more dirt out of their hole and causing them to sink even lower. In that moment, it can be hard to recognise that the Wolf doesn't want us to be on the same ground as them. Other people who have greater access to their anger, 'get pissed off' when they are put in a hole or led in that direction, jumping out to leave immediately before damage is done. Do you tolerate too much?

In each chapter, we continue to explore more layers about the hooks people are caught in when in the hole, as opposed to the alternative of getting out on the other side of the hole and walking away. This latter choice is available for people who have greater access to their instinctual response and have had less impact around limiting beliefs about love, anger and power, or who have experienced different types of relationships and thresholds of stress through their lives that creates a different map of responses as opposed to the involuntary stress response patterns (which we explore in 'The Red Shoes').

When looking at anger, it is important to be realistic about the other person's history and capacity to hear, acknowledge and make changes – so that you can work out whether to have a go or to turn and walk away. I'm not suggesting that the minute you're in this situation, you just turn and walk away and that's it, permanently. That's up to you to decide, depending on your circumstances and level of safety. I do recommend you speak with a skilled trauma and family violence professional to help you gain clarity over what you may not recognise, and to broaden your choices.

I *am* suggesting, though, that when someone puts you in that situation, continuing to stay in that hole when you become aware of the hole, and not walking away when you recognise this is happening, on some level you are agreeing to stay in a position where you are assaulted - emotionally or physically, and sends a message to the Wolf (who can not yet recognise beyond his distorted world) that you will endure. This agreement is not your fault. This agreement came out of involuntary, unconscious beliefs and stress responses that over-ride your instinct when your instinctual self has not been safe to take priority. It can take time to come to terms with the shocking reality of the person who was meant to love you and be trustworthy.

Recognition requires skills, involving both hemispheres of our brain linked up to our body instincts. Recognition of falling in the hole though, is not enough. *We need the ability to bear strong feelings (grief, shock, anger, emotional pain) despite facing opposition, and the capabilities needed to enable us to take risks and to keep ourselves safe when we see what is really going on.*

So walking away is closely tied to having access to our feelings as well as the skills and resources to make a change. When our feelings have become disconnected due to unrelenting stress, our ability to get out is diminished; we need our brain-body connections and our feelings to help motivate us to take action and get away.

Walking away doesn't have to mean 'that's it'. Full Stop. Forever. You can communicate another time when you're ready, and say that was not okay and find out what happens (provided this does not place you in greater risk). You can clarify and emphasise the appropriate boundaries that are required and see if the other person can meet you there. Too many times, however, women bend over backwards, do all the repairing and stay, patiently hoping. Thinking if they ask or communicate gently, and what they're wanting is reasonable and fair, it will work out ... 'The Red Shoes' and 'The Little Match Girl' will help you understand why you do this. We don't have to literally live in the house/relationship of abuse with him as he sorts himself out.

When we dissociate from our healthy anger because we don't want to be 'angry' or 'like them', we end up getting caught in the passivity and aggression continuum; exactly where we don't want to be. This is brought about by the unrealistic expectations towards the Wolf and unrealistic expectations towards ourselves – and the myth that speaking assertively will make everything all work out.

Now, let's strip anger back to its essence. Anger is power. Are you with me on this? Power is defined as the capacity and the ability to do something in a particular way. Power, like anger, has been misused and hijacked. *Anger is power, but power is not always anger.* Power has many expressions and forms.

Power, like anger, is not negative or bad. It just is. As with anger, it's what you do with it that determines if it is good or bad. Power is necessary.

Power is skill, ability, strength and creativity. We tend to admire and delight in other's power but shrink about being in our own power. We think our own expression of power will appear arrogant, selfish, put us in the spotlight, which we are not comfortable to be in or we will be perceived and judged as too much.

Do you disown your power? Where in your life is your power unlived? Are you attracted to a powerful man as a substitute for living in your power?

Reflect on what we spoke about in Bluebeard's Seduction, this time in relation to power. Bluebeard had his own power, and took away all her power except the power of appearing attractive, as that was the *only* one to his advantage, inside his internal picture. There is even a trick that the woman has power over her appearance - as her appearance has to be the way he wants it to be. Woman can obsess over their image when their natural desire for their whole power is obstructed into this tiny area with the detail of appearance needing to fill the large need for full power.

Did you grow up learning and experiencing that you could shine, that you could be powerful, irrespective of if the other person was on their powerful ground? Or did you learn messages and witness power imbalance indirectly through the two significant people in your life? Were you criticised, judged, blamed or punished for showing any form of power as a child, teenager or adult?

In your family, did you witness or experience guilt, envy or jealousy thrown at you or someone else in an effort to diminish their or your power? Did you experience or see someone else need to pull themselves or yourself back to a smaller ground to keep safe? Were you made to feel fearful? Were you made to experience your power as a bad thing rather than feel that the other person was 'bad'?

***

We can have a range of responses about exploring our history of anger. I know some of you are saying, 'But I don't want to get angry. I don't want to be that angry person in the room. That isn't me!'

You won't turn into that person. I promise! You are who you are. The fact you are consistently aware of and hold empathy and concern for other people's feelings and needs, shows you are not a Wolf. It is just that you think of the other person's needs more often than you do your own needs.

When I say you won't turn into that angry person, it doesn't mean that when you finally open the door to make friends with your disowned and suppressed anger, you will embody it for a while. All the stuffed-down anger may need some time to come out, hang around, be felt and connected to. You will find that your dominant 'non-angry' character style may go on holiday while you make friends and get comfortable with your anger. It is very difficult to become intimate with your anger if your dominant character style is still the main player. When your dominant style is centre-stage, it won't let the anger flirt with you. It is important to allow your anger to be the main player for a while. It doesn't mean you will be 'out of control' or feel angry all the time. It just means you won't ignore your anger and you can set aside space each day to engage with and allow your anger some creative expression.

When this new relationship is established, then your dominant character style will naturally come back and through your new connection to your anger, your whole identity will develop to be more than your old, dominant character style – which includes a fluid and effective threesome (your new, dominant character, your anger and what is in the unconscious: those other parts of you that will come out over time), with anger only coming out when it is needed! From this place, you will be more comfortable to be with your anger, so there will be a greater openness and resilience in your system to take in new information, be changed and grow as you experience more.

Anger is not toxic when it is responded to and acted upon. When its mission is complete, we can return to our next focus. Holding anger in is toxic for our health and our relationships. Holding anger in is toxic for our heart, blood, muscular/skeletal system, hormones, cortisol stress levels, thyroid, mind, body, for our relationships, for our sense of self and even for our work. (Staicu 2010; Miller 1996; Herrero 2010)

Holding anger in is toxic when we don't know what to do with it. Holding anger in is toxic when we don't engage with it. Holding anger in and acting out in other ways is toxic. Holding anger in can make you sick and lonely.

It is a myth that simply being angry makes you sick and lonely. When you are not with your anger in appropriate ways, and hold it in or it leaks out inappropriately, then it's toxic and that can make you sick and lonely.

What happens when we don't access our anger? Apart from health problems and unhealthy behaviours, we might end up in situations that we don't want and with serious consequences. We could get caught in another abusive relationship because when we disown our anger we have a blind spot and can find ourselves 'attracted to' or 'attracting' aggressive or abusive people. Often because we don't have access to our healthy anger and power to close the door to them.

We could become anxious, depressed, submissive or resentful that people do not value us in the way we value them. Our anger might go underground - becoming passively aggressive with others or ourselves. Our system may be in avoidant mode and we lead a 'small' life, not taking risks or trying new things. We may literally avoid arousal and not move much because the arousal of movement has the same physiological markers for stress and excitement, and so our system may be in avoidant of any kind of arousal mode. After all, our protective system is thorough in avoiding anything similar, which could be of threat. e.g. remember the dog? Movement and arousal could send alarm or shutdown signals. We might use so much of our energy to suppress the anger that we're left pretty flat, exhausted and overworked. There may be such a backlog of anger that it leaks into situations and conversations that are not related to what and who we are angry with.

Remember, of course, *you are not just your anger*. You are also joy. You are grief and fear. You are excitement and interest and so much more. All your feelings are different aspects of the whole. Anger is just one aspect in the multi-coloured depth of all of who you are.

'Good' anger is contextual. It only hangs around if we don't pay attention to what it needs us to respond to. It's very patient. It keeps waiting and knocking on the door. When we open the door, listen and let it connect to what it needs to, the door can close again. Done. Complete. If you still feel anger over something that you thought you had worked through, there may be some aspect missing that needs integration.

Maybe your 'bad' view of anger – not wanting to be angry – is mixed up with what is identified as 'defensive anger'. Defensive anger is out of context to what's going on. Defensive anger butts in to prevent another feeling that is more unbearable for us to experience, but which is the more relevant one for the situation. Defensive anger sometimes comes to defend against the feelings of grief, helplessness or lack of a positive sense of self.

We may feel inadequate or shame to feel grief, helplessness or something else; so we revert to defensive anger to push others away and push our uncomfortable feelings and thoughts away. Defensive anger can come up in situations of loss and vulnerability. Just like humour can be defensive humour when some people laugh at funerals or other sad situations. Defensive humour arises to ward against the natural instinctive response that has more context and significance for the current situation, which may at times be grief, hopelessness or shock.

Now you might be saying, 'I get that anger is not bad and I won't turn into an angry person, but anger is so uncomfortable. I don't want to feel that. I want to feel happy.'

For sure, you want to feel happy, we all do. But is it realistic to expect that you're going to be happy all day, every day – year in, year out?

Anger is not meant to feel comfortable or permanent. Just because something's uncomfortable, do we stop? Learning to ride a bicycle can be an uncomfortable experience. The seat can feel uncomfortable and it can feel pretty awkward when you're wobbling all around and scared you're going to fall – but you don't give up, do you? Because the end result is positive, we persist.

Acting on your anger will feel uncomfortable, but acting on your anger will protect your needs, rights and feelings – and isn't that important enough for you to follow through? Protecting your values and boundaries is also a pretty good positive end result, isn't it?

Anger in relationship comes up for an important reason. Acting on your anger can be triggered as a response to protect the intimacy and closeness of a relationship that has had a boundary ruptured. Anger is coming to help repair the connection and bring back the closeness. It is wanting to move towards the rupture to repair the split.

I remember two huge light bulb moments from when I was learning to access my anger. One, feeling such healthy pride in standing up for myself, despite the discomfort. Pride that I was expressing it cleanly and directly. And two, a rush of energy and a sense of power within, feeling the joy of valuing and protecting myself.

Often people seem to think if they feel pride, *boom* – they will be an arrogant and selfish person. There is such a thing as healthy pride! This is connected to the experience of Cinderella when everyone at the ball thought she was amazing. It builds healthy resilience, and don't we all want that? Pride is something that others can't take away from us. It is feeling good about ourselves. Don't we all want to feel good about ourselves and not feel that others' opinions or actions can strip us of our healthy, positive sense of self? Healthy pride allows us to have our reality no matter what someone else thinks. Pride became demonised as a way of control, to strip away people's power and ability to healthily separate.

Before therapy when I was angry, I would immediately dissociate and disconnect from my anger and my body. I couldn't stay in my body because that is where we feel anger. I would lose access to all my power and my ability to discern and process. It had felt too threatening for me to stay in my body. Learning to build my emotional muscle to stay in my body and name what I think and feel helped me grow from feeling like a little girl in an adult body to feeling adult in my body.

Through my development, it was exciting to see the difference and be able to bear my anger. My anger had such wisdom and clarity when I made friends with it.

***

Give yourself some space and permission to 'do' anger in not the ideal way. Just let it come out, because it can't get better or grow until you let it come out. If we hold it back in the desire to get it right, we lose access to its riches and get caught and jumbled again. So let it come out (in safe surroundings, with no harm to you or others) so you can have a relationship with it. Over time, it can refine and grow up. Over time, you can regulate and mediate it once you get to hear how it speaks to you.

***

So now we're getting closer to the hot spot and what's really behind all that control, demonising our anger and shutting it down. You're scared that if you express your anger, you'll lose control. Many people have this concern; you're not alone. Often people also have this concern about grief or depression – that if they start crying, they may not stop.

This concern of losing control of your anger may be coming from a deep, unconscious expression or past - very young experience, and may indicate that perhaps there's a backlog of anger or that abuse and anger are still perceived as the same. It's not that you'll lose control or never be able to stop, but there may be a lot there to handle or you don't know how to be with your anger in skilled and constructive ways.

Do you really believe that if you got angry, you would lose control to the point of never being able to stop? I have worked with women and men with a variety of different connecting, expressive and releasing methods for anger, and I assure you: in twenty-plus years, as well as in my own journey, there has never been anyone who lost control and ended up in jail, or that the anger couldn't stop spurting out and became destructive. Even in one ninety-minute therapy session, we would be hard-pressed to stay with anger for the whole session. It always has a completion or a resting place.

Do you really believe that if you got angry you would lose control to the point of doing something dangerous? If so, of course talk to a professional. But there are so many safe, creative, expressive and satisfying ways of being with anger and having a witness to our anger.

It is quite a different thing to be with our anger alone in our private space than to be with someone witnessing our anger. A witness's presence helps to flush out shame and provide a safe space for a deep peace and resolution for the anger to come home.

Even while being with your anger is a very real, confronting and genuine concern, it's really okay to imagine violent things and express it in safe and creative ways. Being with the images and feelings of anger is not about literalising the symbolic picture of rage or anger. The image is a symbol and a way to release it from your feeling state and out of your musculoskeletal system. It is possible to imagine violent things you would never rationally want to do. When you imagine releasing this uncensored image of your rage and anger using all of your senses, the same areas of your brain light up as if you were actually taking that violent action. So it is an efficient way of discharging your anger with no one being harmed and no terrible consequences. Anger needs movement and discharge. The permission for these images to flow out in paintings, collages, clay or other materials allows moving on and metabolising.

As a culture we can be so afraid of the images of rage that we have inside us that we sanitise them. We prefer to disown them, or we create horror and other intense violent movies to enact our shadow side. We go to a movie, or watch the television crime shows and watch endless murders and revenge but we would never go out and act on it - so too we can allow inside the inner mind to create our own movie. This is far more constructive and meaningful in a personal context. It seems acceptable to take in other people's images of rage and violence when watching movies but unacceptable to create our own inner movies.

In therapy sessions, people have in their mind's eye put people through meat blenders and a range of different things, including murdering and decapitating people. Nobody goes to jail for imagining something! It's really okay to imagine doing the things when you have no plan to ever put them into reality. These imaginings are for discharging in the mind's eyes the 'fight' stress response that we all have within us. This is not about what you do in your day-to-day life.

Children know that, don't they? They kill and chop people apart when they're playing games. Children enact a whole range of things. They also get over things really quickly and get onto the next thing, because they've been so thorough in allowing the feeling and experience to come out. They've let it come out so fully in all its expression that they've been able to move on. They don't judge or shame themselves.

When we hold onto parts and go, 'Oh no, that's too much, that's not okay' – we can't clear it all out. It is our conscious mind that gets in the way and contributes to trauma, especially when we grow up in a society that has lost the art of ritual and safe expression of anger. Go for it; take a risk – in a safe and supported way, you might actually enjoy the process and feel a weight has been lifted afterwards. However, this may feel so confronting and too much that it is better to do this work with a skilled therapist.

There are so many different ways of being with anger and moving it through your body, literally expressing anger with cushions, tennis racquets beaten on a hard surface, art, punching bags, clay, the voice and the body, as well as working with the neural pathways and bilateral stimulation incorporating eye movement desensitisation reprocessing (EMDR). A skilled practitioner can refine these processes in the particular ways that your system needs to bring about connection, release and resolution.

A skilled practitioner can make such a difference; I could not have begun this journey of healing my anger on my own. It is so important when you have feelings that seem deep or scary or that have been held in for a long time, to be able to have the guidance, structure, support and engagement from a caring, skilled and professional therapist. To explore your anger with a witness who will not judge, shame or reject you is a precious experience. You can reclaim you are lovable and acceptable just as you are; whether you feel anger or joy, whether you're being agreeable or disagreeable. Your shame can dissolve for feeling rage, even killing rage.

Sometimes we feel ugly when we're angry, and this is understandable as it's not a happy experience. However, this feeling of being ugly or dirty can also come about from the feeling and body memory of an original experience, when we've been angry and have been shamed or rejected for it. That feeling of ugliness or dirtiness can be an indication that shame is inhibiting your capacity to relate to and engage your anger and the important information it holds. It can be important to have a professional with skills and resources, so that the shame or fear can dissolve, the anger can flow and there can be a resolution. Shame can dissolve when we have a skilled and caring witness.

***

Anger is a biggie, isn't it? Often there's still another layer of concern, isn't there? That if you express anger, you'll be rejected, judged, humiliated, maybe even abandoned? That no one will like you.

This is really understandable. After all, anger separates us. When we express anger, we are making ourselves different from another person. We are not connecting or agreeing – we are separating and differentiating. This is an uncomfortable position, because humans intrinsically want to connect and fit in, for survival and belonging.

The primal fear of abandonment, rejection and isolation can get activated through anger and separation. Anger and separation can trigger a fear of survival and that in the separation, there is a risk of abandonment. This is one of the reasons why a woman is at risk when she asserts herself or leaves the Wolf.

Our cellular memory of concern about anger, separation and survival can relate back to early life or from the alarm in the DNA in our cells being activated in the context of anger, separation and survival.

If early on in our life we were given a sense of safety and our exposure to anger was at a pace that our developmental age could integrate, then we can know – in an embodied way, not just in our thinking self – that we can have our anger and still stay connected, even if someone else rejects us, our feelings, needs or in some other way.

Then as we develop and grow we can identify those people who maybe don't have those healthy relational qualities to the level that we want, and make different choices about relationships and closeness.

However, if you are blind to your own anger or disowned anger pattern, you are at risk of being blind to other people's disowned and unhealthy aggression. When this blindness hooks into another person's blindness, unrealistic expectations take over, and you go beyond what you consciously value in how to be in relationship. One possible scenario can look like the woman being 'good', caring and 'not angry' and you become attracted to 'the bad boy' who can carry the anger and 'protect'.

There are many mind-body interventions that can allow you to own your anger and move beyond unhealthy aggressive relationships. These interventions thoroughly understand the trauma response – about the psycho-neurology of what happens in the brain and the body, and of what happens in the mind-body connections and central nervous system – so that you can feel a sense of security, safety and containment in navigating uncomfortable territory.

Perhaps reflect on where you locate yourself on the anger continuum. Which continuum are you most often on? What is your greatest fear in getting to know your anger? Re-read the last number of pages where I talk about different concerns that may make it uncomfortable to explore your anger. Find out what your objections are. Our objections become our blocks.

It is also not uncommon for women to jump from the passive end to the aggressive end on the Power Over continuum, then feel shame and then go back to the passivity. Women are not just sitting in the passive corner. Some women spend a fair bit of time at the aggressive point too. Just pay attention to what triggers you. Has he been unrelentingly abusive and you have no way of getting away to make yourself safe? Some women hang around the passive point; maybe they jump up to the healthy anger in different contexts and relationships where there's less threat. Have a look at the continuums and see where you sit in different contexts, in different relationships and what allows you to move up to the power within continuum.

Despite healthy, fierce aggression being appropriate, it can put you at risk when you face the Wolf.

Often when we've experienced toxic aggression we're hesitant to express healthy aggression. There is a difference between Toxic Abusive Aggressive and Healthy Aggression. Healthy aggression is that energy which can be fiercely firm and protective of our wellbeing. Often it can be difficult to access that aggression, because we know what it's like to be on the other side of toxic aggression and abuse and we mistakenly perceive that if we access healthy aggression, we will become that scary person and be aggressive. The serious, no-nonsense face of healthy aggression may be inappropriately blurred with the feared, threatening face imprinted in our brain from our parents and the early threat to our emotional and energetic survival registered in our limbic brain.

Healthy aggression could be a mother containing a child's tantrum, rather than leaving the child alone and at risk of hurting themselves, others or damaging belongings. There is a specific way to contain a child so they don't feel trapped that can reassure their unregulated system and still allow the anger out. So too there are ways as an adult to express healthy aggression and feel safe.

Remember how we spoke in 'Bluebeard's Seduction' about you not needing to carry someone else's responsibility or have unconditional love? So too with another adult, because you are responding from the continuum of healthy anger, you do not carry responsibility for the wellbeing of the other adult or their inner child. You can be fierce and express healthy aggression when needed. You are matching adult energy – you are not facing a child who is dependent and lacking skills. It is okay for you to call on whatever healthy aggression you need for the relevant context, when you need it.

Sometimes a Wolf will act as if they are meek and helpless to trick you from being fiercely protectively for yourself. Sometimes there are crocodile tears. Like Little Red Riding Hood at her grandmother's door, listen to and then trust your inner eyes, ears and sensings. Trust your inner reality over the outer reality the Wolf is structuring. If you are unsure, speak with a skilled therapist to be able to differentiate between what is appropriate and what is not appropriate to discern from your environment and in your situation. Do not let what is directed at you from the Wolf define what is real and how best to respond.

We can feel cruel and unfeeling by not responding to the Wolf's tactics of being meek or teary however this is very different to the genuine experience of vulnerability and other tears. This is where we need our emotional muscle to trust and stay with our instinctual truth of what is going on, rather than getting pulled into his fantasy and controlling enactment.

Of course, when the Wolf and trickster are involved you need to keep yourself safe at all costs – this will influence and guide your choices and response. Don't let the Wolf or Bluebeard shape your response if you feel the fierce aggression needs to come out. However, this fierce aggression will need to direct you to ways to keep you safe, take the children to safety and get away, rather than confronting the Wolf. You are not responsible for waking him up or educating him. There can be a hook here about 'saving' him and helping him come out the other end, something we couldn't do for our parents for them to be the way we needed them to be - which left unbearable pain and loss.

When you have not been connected to your anger, and then you connect to it, there can be a fear of 'overreaction' and being 'too much'. When you know you are not violent or dangerous and there is no history of you being violent, but you have intense feelings because of the abuse, it is understandable to fear an overreaction. *The degree a response has been repressed can be the degree to which it wants to be released.* The intensity is validation of the depth of feeling of what has been wrong, beyond what our rational mind believes or perceives.

When the reaction has been so contained and minimised, it can feel very big in contrast to the tiny space it was locked in. When it is released from the pressure cooker it was squashed into, it may feel too much or 'wrong'. Understand from the trauma model, that a situation that triggers rage could mean your system involuntarily is bringing out a few livewires of associated unresolved rage. Your system, in its perceived 'overreaction', is releasing real rage from a series of memories that need movement outward. The conscious mind just reads it as all about now, when part of it is the release of past trauma. The past trauma often can only find a way through to resolution through current events which affect us, otherwise the unresolved would continue to stay trapped and limit us.

This is when it is valuable to be in therapy so your anger in these processes can be guided, contained, directed and reassured in the therapy room, rather than with people who won't know how to be with your discharge in safe, constructive and guided ways.

When you know you will do no harm and you are being guided in therapeutic ways, what is the worst thing that can happen? You have been in a safe space and been fierce. You have not injured anyone and, once out, you can have a safe space to explore the ferocity and what your anger felt about for you and your rights. This experience of being with your anger with a witness and therapeutic release allows you to reclaim the missing piece of your incomplete anger. A way through. Relationship to this fierce healthy aggression also means you don't rely on the trickster for your reality or intuition check.

You may want to start writing down a list of 'never again' to build your own 'boundary list'. These are the kind of things anger wants from you: clarity about your boundaries and clarity about what is not negotiable. What your inner protector never, ever wants you to experience again. The 'never again' may involve your emotions, your physical self, your sexual self, your financial self, your spiritual self, your relational self, your social self, your mental self, your work self, or your interests. The 'never again' may become a manifesto of what you will never allow to be done to you again. It may be simple or detailed. These details can transfer to your boundary list outlining the clear definitions on how this looks in your life.

Be clear and specific. You may want to read it to a therapist or a close friend. They may have ideas from knowing you about what to add that you can consider. Remember, Johari's window? Remember, you can choose whatever boundary line you choose. There is no absolute right or wrong. Nothing is unreasonable if that is what you want (and there is no harm or imposition on anyone else) and you can adjust your boundaries over time. You may have different boundaries in different situations now compared to in two, five or ten years from now. Boundaries are flexible, not rigid to health, mood, circumstances, relationship and needs.

See how you go. I wonder what you'll find out! Please email me and let me know how you are going.

Chapter 11:
The Little Match Girl

The Little Match Girl

It was the last night of the year. The snow was falling into the darkness. It was icy cold as a little girl walked through the streets. She had nothing on her feet or her head. Her feet were red and blue with cold. She had been wearing her mother's large slippers when she left the house but in running across the road, they had fallen off. She had one slipper – a boy had grabbed the other, thinking to use it for a cradle for his children when he would grow up.

The Little Match Girl had her apron on with some boxes of matches in the pocket. In one hand she held a box of matches to sell, but no one wanted to buy any from her today. She had not made a cent.

She was shivering and felt miserable as the icy snowflakes fell on her golden hair. The Little Match Girl looked inside the lit-up windows of the passing houses to see the warmth of the fire. The delicious smell of roast duck was floating past her.

Two houses created a corner in the street; she sat in between them and tucked her feet underneath, curling from the cold. She could not go home. Her father would beat her for not selling any matches. Home wasn't much warmer anyway, with all the cold wind blowing through the cracks in the roof. Even the straw and rags didn't stop the coldness coming in.

Her hands were so numb and lifeless. The thought of the warmth of one match was too much, so she struck a match to life against the brick of the house. The light from this single flame was like no other. It was as if she was in front of a hot iron stove and could feel the warmth radiating onto her outstretched feet. But then the flame was gone and so was the stove.

She lit another match and this time, when the light fell on the wall it was as if she could see through into the next room. In here there was a table covered with a pristine white tablecloth and a shiny dinner service. A roast goose was steaming with apples and prunes.

Incredibly, the goose jumped off and was waddling towards her when the match went out and the room vanished.

She lit a third match and a Christmas tree appeared, prettier than any she had ever seen through any glass doors. There were thousands of candles and decorations hanging from the branches. The Little Match Girl stretched her hands to the tree just as the match went out. The lights seemed higher now. She saw that they were the stars in the sky. She noticed a falling star and the streak of its light trailing.

The Little Match Girl thought how someone must be dying and this reminded her of her dead grandmother: the only person who had ever loved her, and who had told her that when a star falls, it means a soul has gone to God.

The Little Match Girl lit another match against the wall of the house and there before her was her dead grandmother. She looked so friendly and welcoming.

The Little Match Girl called out to her grandmother, pleading to be taken with her. She knew when the match went out, her grandmother would go like the stove, the roast goose and the Christmas tree, and she couldn't bear that. She quickly grabbed the largest handful of all the matches and kept wishing for her grandmother to stay with her. The matches burnt so brightly and her grandmother had never looked so beautiful and special. Her grandmother opened her arms and together they flew above the earth, going higher and higher, beyond any cold, hunger or fear. They had gone to God.

Looking back in the corner against the wall was a little girl with rosy cheeks and a smile on her lips, frozen to death on the last day of the year. When the sun rose over her tiny, vulnerable, abandoned body for the first day of the New Year, you could see the matches still held in her frozen, stiff hand.

People going past saw that she had tried to warm herself, though no one knew of the beauty of what she had seen and how happy she was now with her grandmother.

Adapted from the works of Hans Christian Andersen (1845)

'The Little Match Girl' is such a sad story and one that always grabbed me as a child. I could really relate to the longing, the cold and the abandonment.

The Little Match Girl is in a horrific and challenging situation; all she has to cling to are dreams, hopes and fantasies. She lives an ongoing struggle, day in and day out. There's no relief or support to get out of this unrelenting despair and longing and into a warm, safe, loving space that is real and not her imagination.

Living with abuse can feel like being the Little Match Girl: serving others, trapped, suffering, while making the best of it. Keeping hope, but feeling isolated and scared. In survival mode we deny how alone we feel or how hard we struggle.

We endure and endure. The Little Match Girl kept staying with hope and longing instead of finding another option: perhaps knocking on someone's door. Would anyone turn a cold little girl away?

In the stress mode of enduring, we forget how to reach out for help. We are so used to rejection we lose hope of opportunities. The hope of opportunities becomes lost inside dreams, wishes and fantasies.

Tension from the Wolf's unrelenting control, being punished and living in a traumatic 'survival' mode trains you to be more focused on the abuse than finding where the escape doors are. You are so in the moment, *in a survival way*, that you don't see the bigger picture and don't have the internal/external space to reflect on and recognise what is going on.

Remember how earlier I said we are adaptable? We adapt to our surroundings, whatever our surroundings are. If we live in safety, we adapt to being open and confident. When we live with abuse and control, our attention adapts sharply and persistently to the need to focus on the unpredictable, and where the danger is coming from. This repeated vigilance keeps us wired to the Wolf and not to our own inner compass. We go off track.

When you look at a map to figure out which is the best way to get from A to B, you want to find the quickest or easiest way. So you stand back from the detail of where you are and look at the bigger picture, the whole map, to help determine the best streets to travel and the right direction.

However, when you live with abuse you are so intent on enduring and not rocking the boat in an attempt to minimise the abuse and violence. You are so bound by the control, the threats and the structure of violence that you are living inside a reaction loop.

You do not initiate; instead you inhibit to keep the peace, and you are in 'reaction to the Wolf' mode. You can't step back to get to a bigger picture and the best way to get from A to B.

In the same way, the Little Match Girl is wired to the external: the fear of what her father would do and that home was not a safe place. She lost her inner compass and resourcefulness on how to navigate the world to meet her needs. Her life revolves around not getting hurt, to the point that even staying out in the freezing snow was a better option than being in the house with him.

The perception of what we see as the safest option can be dangerous when we live with abuse. The perception that the Little Match Girl had chosen the safer option (away from her abusive father) led her to a greater exposure of risk (overnight in the freezing snow) in which she was so desensitised from her vulnerability and depleted state, she didn't realise how much she was being affected. Living inside of unrelenting endurance exhausts the system. She could not see the warning signs.

She positively hallucinated that she could cope but she couldn't think beyond the moment, so was in fact in a far more dangerous state than she realised. The result was a massive burden on her overwhelmed system – until it became too much for her.

Sometimes, like the Little Match Girl, when the world does not seem available or we need something and are not conscious to what is missing, the best option seems to be leaving our family (of origin) believing we are choosing a better option (The Wolf). Or, when we are unable to see beyond and are unsupported, we may attempt to leave the Wolf but end up returning to the Wolf or meet a new Wolf.

This is the experience of staying in the snow, where no option feels positive and we do not realise until it is too late that we aren't any safer in this decision and may have put ourselves at greater risk.

When you live with any type of relationship abuse, you become depleted. You live with a monster that constantly takes, and you 'give, give, give' in the wishful hope that your giving will help make things better. This mode of giving means you lose your line in the sand, your sense of self and your capacity to 'take' for yourself.

Even if you don't live together, the Wolf's energy is so predatory that it is in your psyche and keeps controlling and taking - until you have resources to fill those gaps and lock those doors.

Living in a state of trauma and abuse leaves you limited. You're not free to *take* different choices that are best for all of who we are. I say *take* different choices, not *make* different choices for a reason. To *take* a choice we need to feel the freedom and permission to *take* the action.

This comes out of the foundation that we can *make* a choice. If you can't explore all choices to *make* the best possible choice, you won't be able to *take* the best action and to *make* that best choice; the bottom line is, we need to feel resourced and supported to explore all options and avenues. We need some foundation of safety to *make* choices and then *take* up our choices.

For the Little Match Girl, the combined fear of her father and the lack of home being a safe and helpful place left her in a state of hopelessness and helplessness. She could not *take* a choice for herself. There was no positive love or encouragement and the only place that love lived was in death, so she followed the love.

That is what we do: we follow whatever little bit of goodness we can find – and if the world feels a cold and unfriendly and scary place, we follow the bit of what seems good, even if that takes us to a dark place.

The Little Match Girl is teaching us about the atmosphere of abuse and the danger of hope, wishing and fantasies – these leave us vulnerable to greater danger. The Little Match Girl wishful, fantasy hope is very different to hope in context to a real context and possibility.

This is where in the past I would teach about the cycle of violence. When I was a client in a family violence recovery psycho-educational group, this is what I was taught. The Cycle of Violence is a diagram that implies that violence goes in cycles and that there are three parts: Tension Building, Explosion, and Honeymoon Stages.

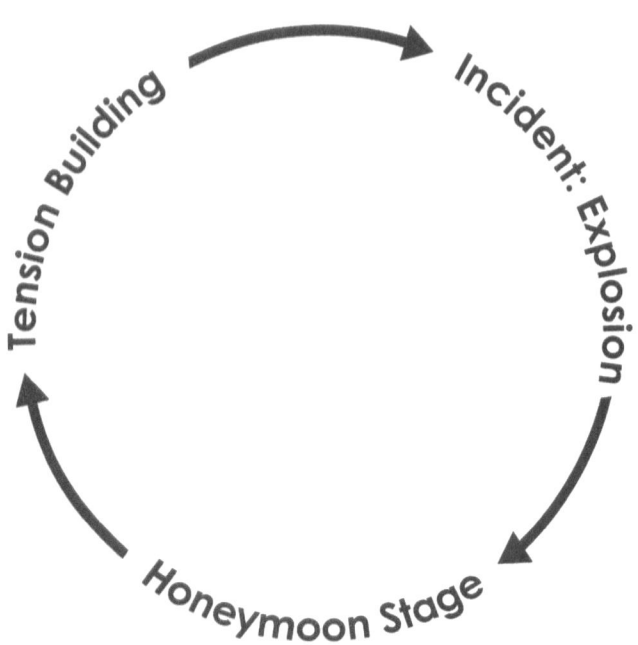

Cycle of Violence

The Cycle of Violence was developed and originated by Lenore Walker in 1976. Lenore has worked incredibly hard to further the recognition of abuse, founding the Domestic Violence Institute. She also wrote *The Battered Woman* and interviewed 1500 women. The Cycle of Violence came out of the similarity of the women's experience of abuse whom she interviewed.

However, there is a problem with this model; I am grateful to Lori Stavnes for the personal written conversations exploring these perspectives and leading me to my own thoughts and conclusions. Lori is the National Training Project Coordinator at the Domestic Abuse Intervention Programs (DAIP), home of the Duluth Model, which includes the Power and Control Wheel (which is also displayed in this chapter). I want to acknowledge Lenore's work as helping begin the public discussion for others to respond and open up greater clarity about the process of abuse.

In Lenore's model, the Tension Building stage is when the Wolf becomes more critical and cruel and the woman is 'walking on eggshells', attempting to appease him. The Explosion Stage is when the intensity increases again and reaches a physical or verbal explosion(s). The Honeymoon Phase is where he shows remorse, gives a promise of change and gives gifts.

However, this cycle implies that stress and tension are the triggers for abuse. This becomes misleading because we know that the Wolf contains his abusive behaviour in other settings - yet these situations are not necessarily devoid of stress or tension. The Wolf is able to contain himself when other life, traffic and work stresses are happening. The Wolf is not out of control when property is damaged or where he punches on her body (usually injuries are hidden from visibility). We also know that most people, even when stressed do not abuse their loved ones. So stress and relationship violence are correlated but stress is not a cause or trigger.

This model also tends to reinforce the thinking of relationship violence as being physical abuse, as opposed to the emotional, psychological and verbal abuse (and all the other manipulative types, such as social, financial, spiritual, etc). In all the other abuses, the control, denial and punishment is ongoing and not necessarily increasing. In the real life of abuse, the tension is chaotic, fluctuating constantly throughout one day or hour. It is not one clear graph line increasing.

The other problem in this model is that in portraying the cycle, there can implicitly be a pressure on the woman to conclude 'How can I stop him getting stressed' or 'Oh, he is stressed and tense, it is up to me to help him so there isn't an "explosion", as that is the next event.' His disowned responsibility can fall on her as the cycle appears as if he is out of control and can't take responsibility. So her role to, as an example, to keep the children quiet or serve the dinner on time may become the 'apparent cause' of the tension building and explosion, instead of recognising that his abuse is random and unrelated to life stresses. He is just taking advantage of instances to discharge his pent up self onto her.

Another reason I have moved from Lenore Walker's model is that a cycle by definition is a series of events that are regularly repeated in the same order. Abuse is not that organised. Abuse is complex, with more than one type and method of abuse happening at the one time.

I do not know of any woman, including myself, who in the experience of partner abuse experienced 'stages' of abuse, it is more that there are moments when we are awake to being able to name what is going on but that does not mean that it is not happening when we are not awake to the naming and back in managing and surviving mode.

The Cycle of Violence implies there are stages, stating that there is a cycle implies that there are times when you are free from abuse, or that the cycle of violence is not a permanent part of the relationship. This is not true.

When you live with a Bluebeard or Wolf, you are constantly living inside of denial, threats and control. When an explosion is not happening it is because he is not in the mood for it – not because there is no abuse. You are still being controlled.

How do you define an 'explosion' and why is the cycle revolving around an explosion? Again there is a risk of seeing the explosion as just a physical event. Some Wolves are constantly simmering with verbal, emotional, psychological control, threat and punishment – there may never be a stereotypical 'explosion'.

The truth is, there is not a cycle or stages. You are immersed in the abuse for every second, through the denial, power and control, and you are never free of the abuse until you are safely out of the relationship or he has learnt to contain his abuse and changed.

When I was taught about the Cycle of Violence, it was explained that this cycle can happen a few times a day, or over a month, or even over a year. This can lead to unrealistic interpretations about the atmosphere of abuse that is happening between these 'cycles', as if things can be all good and normal between the cycle.

I remember thinking when I was in my women's group and taught about the Cycle of Violence, 'But I *never experienced the honeymoon stage*. He was never remorseful – he was always in denial. Remember how I said that after an explosion he would come in the room and state that if I was in the courtroom, I could not swear on the Bible that he 'punched' me … no remorse; just an attempt to threaten me to be silent, as I won't be believed.

There wasn't always an explosion. The daily power, denial and control was powerful enough to have me flinching, scared and hiding my true self from him, tearing me and my life to pieces. It is as if the Cycle of Violence is trying to instil an order and clarity to something that is unpredictable, ongoing and irrational. I did not know how to make clarity of the chaos back then, and I still don't.

What I am grateful for in my early days of becoming aware of abuse, when given the Cycle of Violence, is that it was a beginning to being able to identify and name and that there is a process of systematic abuse. The Cycle of Violence, despite being over-simplified, brought awareness of abusive techniques being used strategically to have me revolve around his moods and explosions. It made me aware that his denial and control was training me and shaping my life – and that this process of systematic abuse took me away from initiating my own choices and responses in my day.

The Cycle of Violence helped me see that my life revolved around his moods and control. That there was no place for me in the picture of the cycle. I wanted to find *me* in the circle. He was keeping me tightly bound and trapped – I was reactive to his process. I was not in my own cycle of creative, empowerment of life. I was inside his circle. I needed my own circle. A better one. But I didn't know how to get out of his circle of control, denial and power over me. He wasn't opening any parts of the circle to let me out. There was no off ramp. I needed to find one.

This is where the Duluth Power and Control Wheel can demonstrate a more accurate reality of what the woman is living inside of. The Duluth Wheel of Equality and the Wheel of Creator are circles that have room for me (keep reading to see these Wheels).

The Power and Control Wheel was created in 1984, after DAIP consulted with many groups of women to identify 'the most common abusive behaviours and tactics used against women'. The Power and Control Wheel is not gender neutral, as the data that created this model came from women who had been abused by men.

In the United Kingdom, just like in Australia, the abuse of women by men is at far greater numbers than men by women. If the Power and Control Wheel was gender neutral then the power imbalance between men and women's relationships, and how this is reflected in the power imbalance in society between men and women, would be misidentified.

DAIP found that when women are abusive in relationships, the context of the violence is different and does not receive the social support that men's violence has. Also, women's violence against men is often directly connected to the woman being abused by the man in a last attempt to respond to and resist the abuse.

Men's abuse of women is also far more likely to lead to greater violations, abuse and death compared to the degree of abuse of women towards men. Just as we explored in 'The Handless Maiden', social, cultural and institutional systems reinforce and teach men the use of denial and control over women.

We previously looked at what abuse is and what the types of abuse are, and now we'll spend some time learning about the Power and Control Wheel. This is really important in recognising the bigger picture of what is actually happening between you and the Wolf. This wheel represents the atmosphere that the woman is living inside of, and hopefully gives others a greater understanding of the living reality and the limitations in choices of responses and options. It also makes it easier to understand why the Little Match Girl's wishful hope and fantasy gets activated when society does not recognise or respond to relationship abuse.

The Power and Control Wheel does not mean that at times you don't feel partial relief and at times a lesser intensity, but no matter what, you will still be living inside the Power and Control Wheel of abuse. You are still inside the ongoing and unrelenting cycle of power, control and denial. Threats, intimidation, coercion and fear are used on an ongoing basis, which become the spokes in the wheel that keep the cycle going.

Learning about the Power and Control Wheel can be confronting but also reassuring. The development of this wheel means that this not just happening to one woman. Unfortunately abuse is a common experience. This model can help you recognise that you're not alone and therefore not to blame – you're not stupid, you are not the cause and you are not inadequate. A lot of women get caught. Abuse is embedded in our social and familial environment. This is not about you.

The Wheel of Power and Control is all about him, his actions and his denial, which keeps the abuse going. Tension building is not a stage, as per the Cycle of Violence. There is a constant walking on eggshells, with small or large incidents of physical or emotional abuse where you feel a tension that grows and fluctuates. In the Cycle of Violence, this is described as the longest phase in the cycle instead of saying it's the foundation of daily life. It is hard to admit.

The second phase in the Cycle of Violence is the explosion, the incident, which can be physical, sexual, emotional, verbal – all the ones that you know about now. However, when we look from the Wheel of Power and Control it is evident that many of the types of abuses are constant on a daily basis, and it is not necessarily about an explosion but more about the ongoing and slippery ways of control and abuse.

I wonder if the design of the Cycle of Violence model was influenced by the possibility of women in the interviews emphasising and naming only certain types of abuse that they knew society would definitely validate as wrong (physical and sexual). This became the 'explosion' and the other types were left unspoken or less identified as being major factors of abuse, because there is less public/social horror about them. It is uncomfortable to name about psychological abuse and have someone question it - being in the gap of the silence, denial and judgement is too much to bear. Far easier to name the physical or sexual explosion.

When I would tell people about my personal experience of abuse, I would talk about him handcuffing the children or assaulting me, as I knew that people would affirm that I had been in an abusive relationship when I said that. I would not emphasise the emotional, psychological, verbal, social or financial abuse that would happen daily. That was not validated or affirmed by society as being 'serious' or 'bad'. These remained a quieter dialogue, so I kept quiet. It makes me wonder if this is what happened with women interviewed in the creation of the Cycle of Violence and so the Cycle in not inclusive or accurate.

Each of the Cycle of Violence stages, in my opinion, represent more an abusive approach rather than a stage – and like all the other approaches in the Wheel of Power and Control, is all about 'making' her do something and removing him of accountability, rather than him take responsibility.

Sometimes the approach is back and forth, and back and forth between the walking on eggshells, the tension building - which is toxic and abusive of itself - and then later an explosion – and there is no remorse. The reality is that even though there may be some remorse, it is rare that this is healthy remorse. Healthy remorse would motivate him to seek help or remove himself, for the safety of his partner or children.

Healthy remorse would make the vulnerable people in his life more important than his need to defend against 'feeling bad'. Instead, this 'pseudo' remorse asks her to forgive and be his emotional 'mother' instead of him standing accountable for his actions. The Wheel of Power and Control does not specifically include remorse – I find the remorse in the Cycle of Violence fits inside emotional abuse and is not healthy remorse but another approach of abuse.

If you experience a honeymoon approach, you may receive gifts, flowers, promises – you might be romanced or instead you may get threats that he might kill himself if you leave. The remorse may lead to a 'honeymoon approach' or lead directly to threatening tension building. But really, behind the gifts remains the tension building where everything is founded on control and denial. What comfort are gifts when they are lacking in real love and respect. They are part of the manipulation and are not much comfort to soothe the wounded mind, body and soul. Honeymoon gifts is not healthy adult repair. Taking ownership and taking action would be healthy repair.

You may find when he is showing some remorse that you become the 'strong' or 'forgiving' one, helping him feel better and removing him from his remorse. Understandably there is a secondary gain in appeasing him: so he does not abuse you again. But ultimately in colluding with the fantasy of his remorse there is a making it better for him and could reinforce the Little Match Girl in false hope in you about the relationship. So your forgiveness inadvertently gives him the message that he is let off from remorse and he continues his denial. He does not carry his healthy shame into repair and the abuse continues.

These 'stages', as I say, are really approaches of abuse and so they may occur many times in a day or over a longer period of time, like all approaches they fluctuate and combine in different ways. The honeymoon approach may be there initially and disappear over time.

The Wolf is minimising and denying, and the woman ends up minimising and denying for survival and to keep the 'peace', which is really appeasing his fantasy. The abuse is maintained through the Wolf's denial and the woman's involuntary trauma survival-based denial. Her denial, I believe, is perpetuated by the denial and minimisation in our society. From society not challenging the numerous examples of bullying and abuse that occur on many levels and structures in society.

This is bit like people walking by the Little Match Girl, and no one stopping to ask questions or change the situation – known as the Bystander Effect.[6] Two elements were identified in the public not responding to a public crime: *Pluralistic ignorance,* where you don't recognise someone else needs help, particularly when no one else around you is displaying concern; and *Diffusion of Responsibility,* when there is a group of witnesses and people leave the action to someone else (Berkley 2009). Sexism was also found to contribute to bystander apathy (Whitbourne 2015; Orchowski et al 2015).

Bystander apathy in the context of pluralistic ignorance can be understood in the context of society not recognising the fullness of what abuse truly is, and the lack of acknowledgement of the impact of *all* forms of abuse. This may sound harsh (because we like to think the best of the society/family we live in) but The Little Match Girl is, I believe, a representation and real example of the Bystander Effect – and how as a society we contribute to the denial of rape, abuse and murder. We don't teach the active bystander response (Whitbourne 2015; Staub 2012).

It is confronting to read that we live in a society that (for the majority of the time) is content to let someone else carry the wound and the uncomfortable and close the door to keep themselves comfortable. This is repeated again and again when people do not speak to neighbours or loved ones or call the police when they hear or sense something is wrong. This has been documented again and again where there have been public assaults with witnesses and no one responding.

People believe they would not do that if they were in the situation, but numerous research shows that people are highly influenced by their surroundings and whether it is common knowledge if the situation is an emergency. Just like my family didn't respond. I speak to many women who speak of the same experience. People respond when there is a shared knowledge of disaster, but the daily emergency of abuse is still not accepted and so the Bystander Effect continues.

There are instances when family and friends respond and it doesn't go well. This is why I wrote my book, *From Unspoken to Spoken Conversations about the Wolf: Helping your friend recognise her abusive relationship* about having the difficult conversations about abuse with someone you care about. I also run a group and workshops about having these conversations. I am available for consultations to help guide people strategically on what to say. Often family or friends think what they have to say is helpful when it is

---
6. Based on the 'bystander apathy experiment' conducted by Bibb Latane and John Darley in 1964.

not. Through my experience as a survivor and trauma therapist I provide a clear and helpful structure.

Imagine if every friend, work colleague, Doctor, hairdresser or family member all made one small comment without one person constantly being the one to convince or change them, perhaps the trapped person would have a different response when it is coming from everywhere ... We can share the load.

We seem to have cultivated a social response to not want the uncomfortable to impact our own safety, which over time has become so common that it is 'normal'. Ervin Staub writes, in his chapter 'The Roots of Goodness' (as contributed to *Moral Motivation Through the Life Span*) how we can move out of this social group mindset and the causes on individual and social fronts (Staub 2005).

It seems to me that society is content to show concern or question things, talking *after* and *about* – but to *become involved* and *step in* is too uncomfortable. I see 'walking on eggshells' in this social blindness behaviour and lack of skill, another version of the women who are trapped and helpless and not interrupting the abuse they live in. The difference is society has more power and choices than a woman living in abuse.

One hypothesis I hold about this social blindness is that we are all one step removed from some abuse – whether it is in our past, or in our family tree or marriage. After all, we come from a cruel patriarchal history, wars, immigration hardship and a refugee crisis. It is a rare family line that does not have unspoken, skeletons in the closet from been touched by abuse in some form.

Even when we have abuse in our past, we can have greater reason to hold the door shut from abuse if our own past is unresolved and just being stored. No one wants to be triggered. Even coming from a history of abuse, when there is not complete healing we can also not know what to say or do. Our system can involuntarily be triggered into chaos, shut down and confusion.

Abuse is not a separate issue. Abuse affects everyone. There is a massive cost funded by the government, philanthropy and other organisations and volunteers. Abuse affects your children in who they play and interact with in the playground, school or playgroup. Abuse affects you in your workplace, working with colleagues or bosses who are abusive or affected by abuse. Abuse affects your family and often without you realising until too late. We affect each other, whether we like it or not.

Do we want a caring, involved community and society, or do we want an individualistic 'each for themselves' society? It is up to each individual to choose, participate and take action.

***

When we are still inside the abuse, we don't have much room for choice and action. It can feel so very painful to look at abuse in the context of our own life with the Wolf. It is unfortunate to be here. Recognising where you are, however, means you can begin taking steps for change. When we don't know this map, we can be caught like the Little Match Girl and unable to leave, constantly in reaction, wishing and in survival mode. When you are inside a web of power, control, threats and punishment, none of your reality has a place to live – so the only option for you is that you are left to fantasise, wish and hope.

When we can't recognise where we are, how can we navigate to something better? When there is a denial of our needs, reality and existence, there is no reality to affect and change. We are trapped. Caught. Naturally wishes and hope are a way to keep the door open to a new possibility. However, this hope can mislead us to hope when the environment or Wolf is not showing interest or signs of change.

When you know the detail of exactly where you are and what it is, it becomes clearer to go down one street and then the next, bit by bit, until you're in a different place.

The intention of having a visual model of abuse is valuable to be able to step back and have the eagle-eye view of what we are inside of. When we are in survival mode we are the ant, working hard and close to the ground mode. It's hard to see the big picture, so our responses are often based on the immediate and short-term desire for an end to this unbearable moment. Looking at a model can open up reflection on the bigger picture of abuse, even if it is confronting.

Recognising the denial and the Power and Control Wheel that perpetuates and influences you and your choices – and how this is eroding your identity – can become an opportunity to begin to claim your reality within this overpowering drama. Looking at the Power and Control Wheel implicitly highlights that you do not exist in this wheel. That there is not a place for your feelings, needs and reality. Automatically, your system will be searching for where you can locate yourself.

When we come back to the story of the Little Match Girl, she does offer us something positive. Through the direct experience of the deprivation and the harsh isolation of her experience, inside her fantasy she intrinsically knows the opposite: the warmth of belonging and of community, kindness, closeness and abundance. When we experience what is so deeply wrong, we know implicitly what is right and true.

Connecting to your wishes and using this to create your map opens up space for more choices and possibilities for you to off-ramp from the Power and Control Wheel into something more generative. Your dreams can be related to and become your reality.

When we identify all the approaches that are involved in the Power and Control Wheel – the limiting beliefs, the controlling and punitive behaviours and the structures around us and within us – we can start to identify a different kind of cycle: the Wheel of Equality and the Creator Wheel, which the DAIP Centre also created and which demonstrate alternate ways of responding and living. We need to have concrete, clarity about the healthy map to be able to claim it.

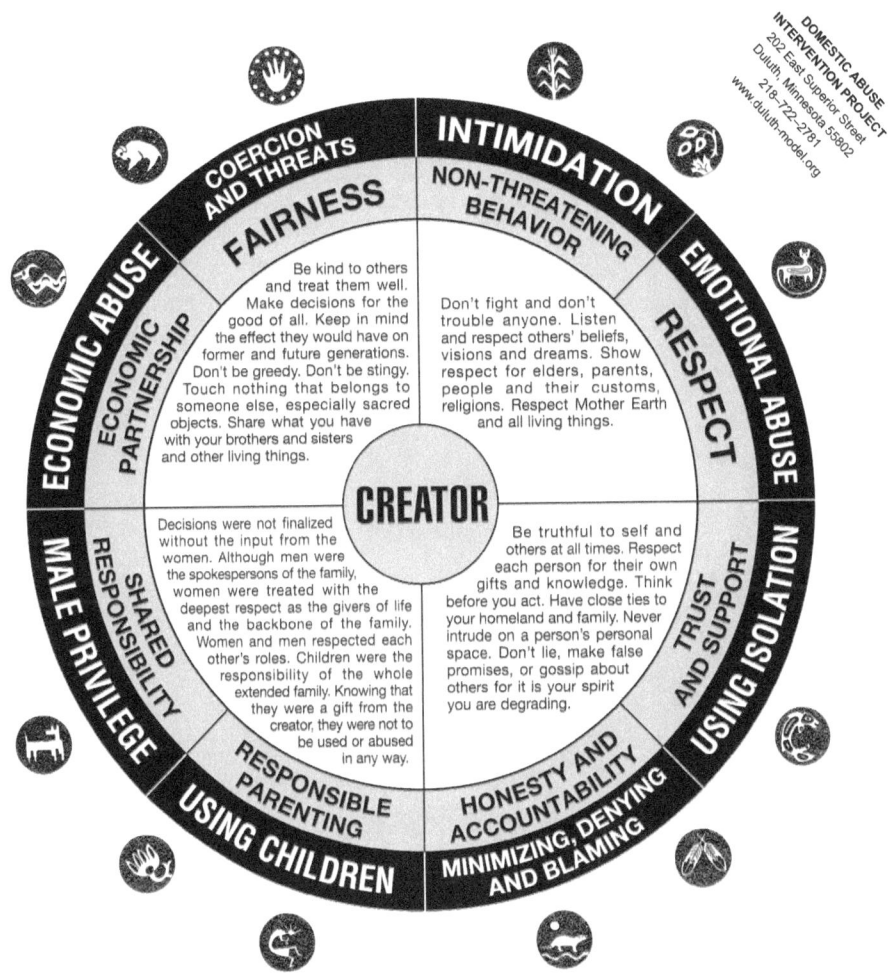

The next two wheels highlight abuse of children and the potential of a creative and healing map for our children and ourselves.

I have included the children's wheel as well, because as women we may have grown up with these maps and need to know what we needed and can reclaim now – or our children have.

See overleaf.

374 *The Wolf in a Suit*

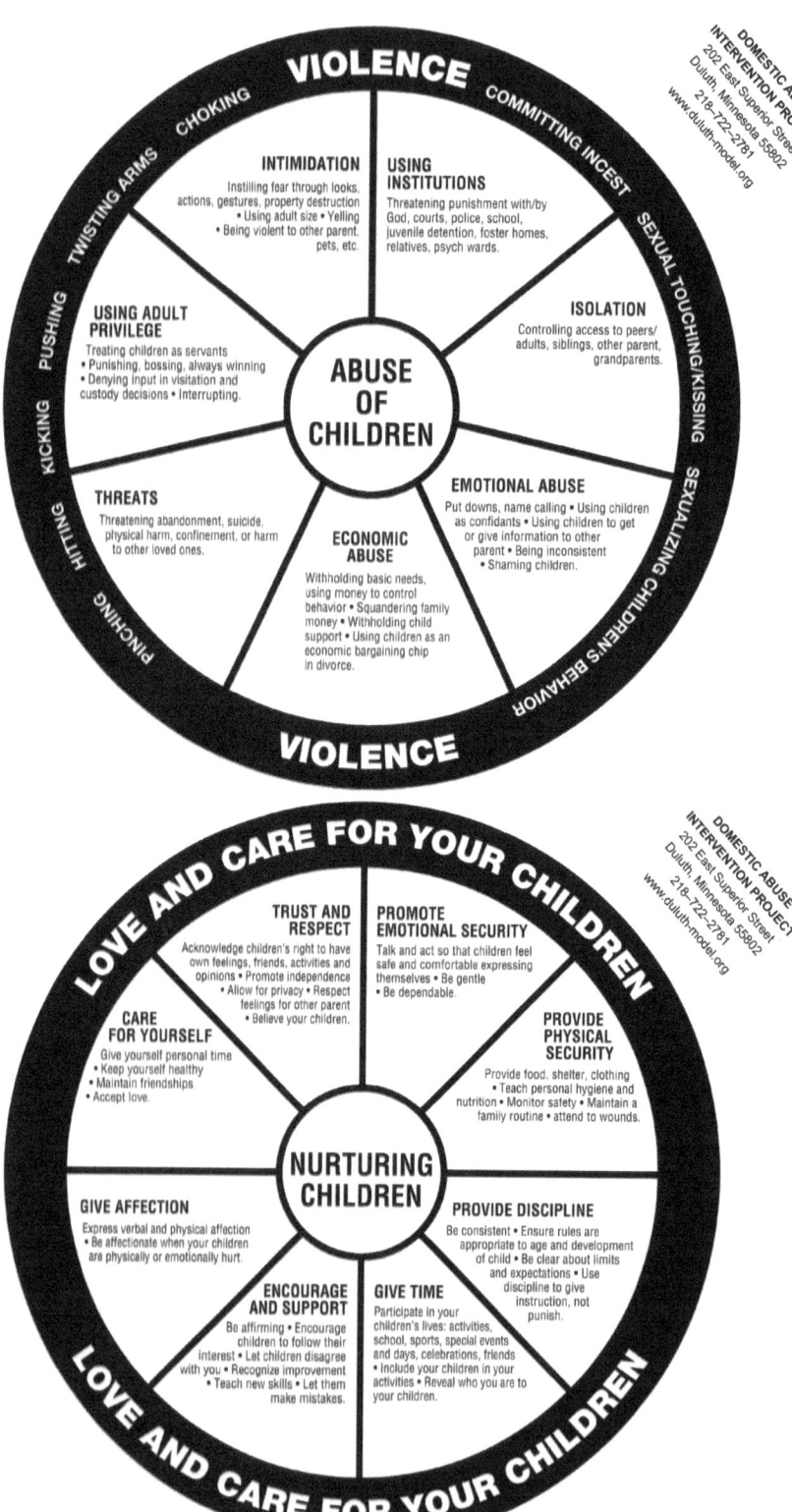

If we have blurry expectations about the rights of fathers (or 'honour your father') over the intrinsic needs and rights of children, these wheels remind us of the truth beyond gender and power imbalances in relation to basic child developmental needs and rights. How can you create the Children's Wheel reality for your children and for the child in you who did not receive all this?

Remember Rumpelstiltskin: the more we can name and identify, the more we can get away. But we also need clarity about what we want to move towards, for ourselves and our children. These wheels provide a clear blueprint to what needs to be part of our new map.

In coming to recognise the Wheel of Power and Control, I want to go over a few hard, cold realities. One of the shocking truths about abuse and violence is once you're inside his wheel of abuse, there is a greater tendency for the violence to increase in intensity and frequency.

Recall some of the ways we try to cope with the powerlessness and the risks and cost: through the irrational love beliefs explored in 'Bluebeard's Seduction' to the Little Match Girl's dissociated fantasy, which both remove us from the reality of what we live inside of.

Often women get hooked into believing that they have contributed to this Wheel of Power and Control. I hope you remember from early on, when I spoke about how it doesn't matter if you were letting yourself down in behaviours — someone else's abuse is criminal and not your responsibility to carry. These are two separate things. It's okay to be human and not perfect. Each person has the choice not to violate and abuse. Remember also that the Wheel of Power and Control is all about denial, blame and misplacing accountability and response-ability onto you.

Think of it this way, in a war, both sides have their armies, with their warfare ammunition to fight against each other. It is as if this is acceptable but if one side bombs civilians there is outrage and horror. In the war of domestic violence you did not sign up for the war, you are a civilian and if in getting caught in a war, you have access to some ammunition, wouldn't you use it to save your life? You did not sign up for the war. You are not a co-contributor. Your ammunition is being used to fight to protect you, not to control another person.

If you start thinking that you've contributed to this Wheel of Power and Control, remember that the triggers and the explosions don't get activated from something realistic or rational. They're activated from the Wolf's internal state and aren't about you. The abuse is always unrealistic, irrational and inappropriate, so explosions and triggers are not about you being inappropriate or not being a desired way of being. You can do the same thing and he can have two different responses, depending on him and his mood. Explosions and triggers are about the techniques and mind games inside him that he is trying to get control over, by controlling his environment and not about what you do.

Getting out of his Wheel of Power and Control can be difficult or not. You can pick you and the children up and just get out. There are many services and refuges available. Even if you can't find a service, is there a family or friend to ask, or going to a hotel and asking them for a spare room for a week. Why not? The most important thing is to get out. Don't let details get in the way when you are at risk.

It is possible to leave no matter what housing, children and financial complicating factors are there, and just get out. Of course I don't want to minimise that this can be very complex, difficult and sometimes even dangerous. As I have said, please seek specialised, professional support through a skilled therapist who is experienced in trauma and family violence and can find what is best for you, as sometimes there can be a need for a strategic plan. Other times it is just about leaving, immediately.

Your way out will be especially tricky and dangerous if your intention is to get the Wolf to stop or for Bluebeard to see the error of his ways, as opposed to you just leaving the Power and Control Wheel.

The difficulty with the hope and fantasy that the Little Match Girl embodies is likely linked to this kind of statistic, especially for psychological abuse (which all women experience as being more shattering than physical or sexual abuse:

> Globally, 55–95% of women who experienced physical domestic abuse have never reached out to any authority or organisation for help.
>
> nobullying.com/

When hope is based on unrealistic fantasies, it is unhealthy hope. This is vastly different to hope based on words, actions and follow-through that indicate a change and repair. The fantasy version of hope, which does not take into account the reality of a situation, is likely connected to beliefs that hold unrealistic and idealised beliefs about being a family. It can lead to this kind of statistic:

> Domestic violence is most likely to take place between 6pm and 6am.
>
> http://www.safehorizon.org/

When we look at the Wheel of Power and Control, it is important to understand the involuntary stress response that women get caught in from the abusive environment. It can be very hard to think, let alone to leave, when involuntary stress responses override your system. It is very hard to get out of the fantasy of hope of the Little Match Girl, when you are in the fight-flight-freeze response. The poor Little Match Girl is clearly in the freeze response. You will understand so much more about the Little Match Girl when you see her close connection to the freeze response and what trying so hard to sell her matches and not returning home is about through the next chapter, 'The Red Shoes'.

We will also explore a specific stress responses unique to women in 'The Red Shoes', but in the meantime remember that the stress response blocks the more sophisticated parts of the brain, which does not allow us to think more clearly about the reality and make connections. We are caught inside our degraded hope and fantasy and his distorted fantasy and idealisation about how we should be there for him.

In my work with women, we map out an inner circle and insert all the words describing her experience and her responses to his actions, which sit trapped inside and encircled by his pattern of violence. This validates her denied reality telling the story about her experience within his Circle of Power and Control.

Inside her inner circle, there may be worry, shock, hurt, shame, guilt, fear or disbelief; she may be trying to look after the children, trying to ignore, trying to have hope and her limiting beliefs. Details become even clearer when we externalise and create a visual representation. It is very powerful to see in front of you: the trap and the reaction, the loop and how it is difficult to escape when every response is a reaction to his reality. All this gets unpacked in her inner circle: the tightly packed details of survival. It's really important to name her reality, to bring it into the present and value its importance.

We can all feel uncomfortable and unskilled, preferring to avoid rather than acknowledge when something that we're doing (or not doing) appears to be displeasing to another person and correlated with abuse. So it is very important to unpack with as much detail as possible what is happening for a woman in her inner and outer world.

Together we discover the limiting beliefs, the effects and the actions that occur in her inner circle in response to his outer circle of power, control and denial. We explore where as a woman, she has the greatest access to alternatives and how to make a plan.

This practical work is interwoven with mind, body, energy practices to help the brain body integrate and process all the uncomfortable and unresolved material.

We also look at shame, because shame does not allow us to have a sense of self. Shame makes it very difficult to create change or take action. Shame cuts down our sense of self and tears us to shreds. Shame leads us to deny and disconnect in a variety of ways. Women often feel shame about living with abuse. This is not the life they imagined for themselves. Even when it has been part of childhood, we can think that will never be our experience as an adult and reach for the opposite and find ourselves back in violence. This evokes shame and a helplessness to have anything other than degraded hope.

Adults are not dissimilar to children. We all need natural consequences to help us get clear on what we really want and what is not okay. Otherwise, we continue to hope or 'get away with' or 'get by with' what's going on. So I ask, how long would you be willing to live with this … twenty years, ten years, five years, two years? A year? Six months, three months … When a woman finds it difficult to draw the line in her relationship of when is enough and you ask her to put a timeline in, at some point she finds her limit. You can then work backwards, slowly, from that point where she is definitely clear to solidify where her line in the sand is and what needs to happen before she is at that line.

When living inside his inner circle, there is nothing bigger than him that provides a reality check or consequence to his unacceptable behaviour. There often isn't a reality check or mirror to show her how caught she is in the involuntary loop of reaction in her day-to-day life. The Wolf and the woman are both in denial, are both not being congruent, are both not walking the talk. Both are acting like everything's okay within the abuse. As if all things are normal. This leaves no outlet to get out of this abusive circle.

This is not being said in judgement of women. I know only too well how difficult it is to get out of abuse. This was me. It is dangerous and very complicated. But it's important to name the reality when we are trapped inside: that we're both living in the circle of abuse, acting in denial. Even if it is part of the survival process to deny, we need to see what is going on. We can't move on if we can't name what has happened. The first step is to see the denial and what it is being protected. This is his first step too if he wanted to get out of being the Wolf.

With any process of change we need to become uncomfortable. We don't change if we are comfortable. The same with addiction or any issue in our life – the reality of addiction or abuse has to become real and at a rub to our value of who we are and how we want our life to be. It has to become 'ego-dystonic' rather than 'ego-syntonic.' We have to know and feel how it robs us to motivate us to do something different.

When there is no internal or external objection, silence keeps it ego-syntonic. Silence keeps away the incongruence of words and behaviours. Silence does not reveal the gaps in necessary boundaries. All this isn't communicated or responded to. There is an implicit sense of acceptance, of 'putting up' with this kind of behaviour.

The reality is adults need reality checks and natural consequences too, not just children. However, this is a very difficult thing to achieve with someone who has a distorted reality.

The threat of the abuse increasing is a huge factor in not setting a consequence. The woman is in a double bind, needing to emphasise that this can't happen again, but risking another unpredictable explosion or punishment if she objects. This is when she needs to get out of the Wheel or Cycle rather than *try* to change his distorted rules of reality.

It's really understandable when women say, 'I don't want to get him upset, he's so unpredictable and moody. I'm scared.' I think there is an unspoken deletion in these statements that could be, 'I have to wait as surely he will feel some (healthy) remorse and there lies my hope for change.' But if he's not taking responsibility immediately and going to see someone, or doing something that allows you to see he is interrupting the abusive habit, then you're at risk of another explosion and more unrelenting control and punishment. Words of apology are not enough; his actions need to be congruent with his remorse for it to be healthy remorse. You need to be able to see consistent effort and change; after all, he is competent and gets by in the world, in other areas of his life – doesn't he? Doesn't he follow the consequences of work and social structures? If he doesn't, maybe you are expecting something of him that is beyond his chosen lifestyle.

I've heard many times women being *very fair and reasonable*: 'Doesn't it take two to create a fight? I must be contributing, not supporting him enough. He doesn't handle stress well, maybe we should go to couples counselling.' Remember, it doesn't always take two to create a fight; one person may just be in the line of fire and not have the mobilisation protective skills to get away.

I do not recommend couples counselling in situations of abuse. I've seen and heard of too many couples who live with abuse, where in the couple counselling session the full story does not come into the room. The woman is inside the same inner circle of abuse within the counselling setting. In this situation she is fearful of retribution if she speaks up in the session; what will happen when she gets home? Or he'll be going through the motions in the session, appearing as if he's doing the right thing, but often at home he'll continue to behave in his righteous way, with an inflated sense of no one can stop him - he can keep manipulating his world.

Sometimes you might still want to try couple sessions for your last hope or effort. This is understandable and may be what you need to do. It may be helpful to speak to the Counsellor outside of the couple session and let them know what you can't name in the session or have another therapist or close friend to help keep you in check with the couples counselling to make sure you are not continuing something beyond its capacity to be effective.

Despite the double binds and traps in the inner circle, I want you to begin to identify yourself as emotionally stronger. Where in your life do you know you are emotionally strong. What indicators demonstrate this for you? Write down three indicators. Being able to bear the truth of what is going on is a major indicator of emotional courage and strength. Can you, inside your mind and heart reality, do two things: one, *stop giving away your truth* and two, stop giving him a way out to not own aspects of himself? Don't share this with him, but you can name this to yourself, so it can help guide you through what's next.

We have talked about your inner circle trapped inside his circle of abuse. There is also an outer circle that includes family, friends, society, strangers, organisations, acquaintances, the law and the judicial system. Here lies the other layer of denial and control I mentioned: people not wanting to talk about or confront what is happening, either because they are unsure what to say or do, or don't want to 'get in other people's business' or 'offend him'. Intentionally or not, when there is silence and no action, there is a layer of collusion with the Wolf. Denial running through all three circles.

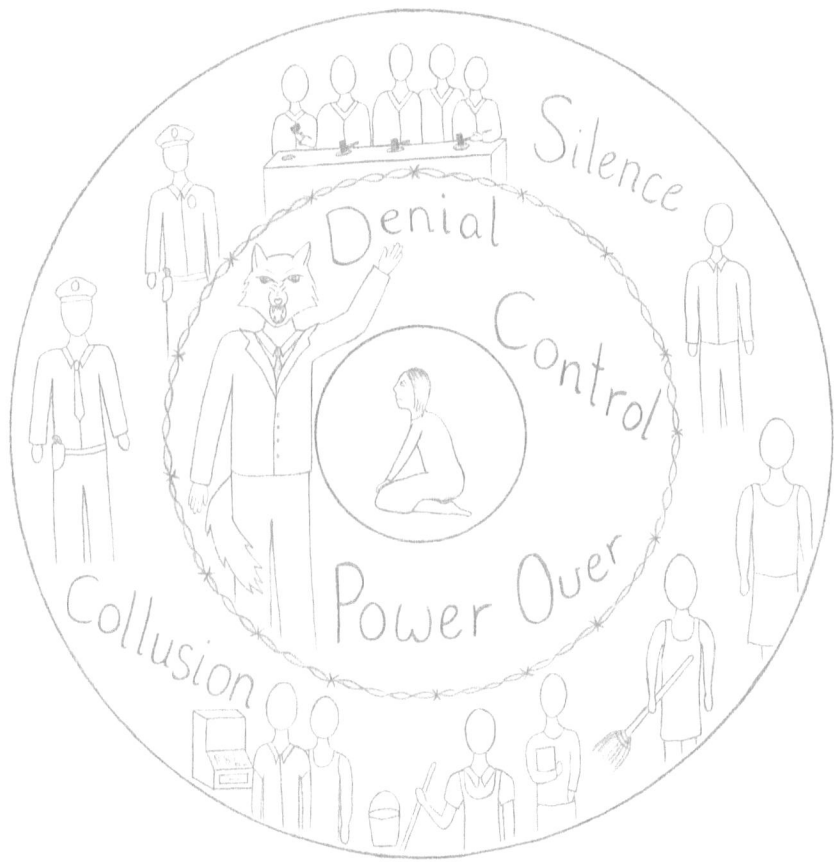

Many women reach the point of fear saying, 'There's no point in leaving – there's greater risk if I leave.' Unfortunately it is true that there is a greater risk if you leave. However, staying is only going to continue to increase the risk. There is no guarantee either way. Short term it may be more dangerous to leave, but in the long term you have the potential for no danger whereas staying means your long term risk is only going to increase.

You have a greater chance of no more abuse through leaving, rather than hoping things will get better. Who knows – he may become motivated to address his behaviours if you demonstrate that you are not willing to accept this. I do not believe the woman has to remain and expose herself to ongoing risk, relapses and punishment while he does his owning, accountability and healing of his behaviours.

He's a man, he's not a child; he needs to develop the capacity to separate and develop his own internal and external support system.

Over the longevity of time, leaving and being consistent in reporting any offences (if you are involved in the court system) so there is some public consequence (even if it does not result in the optimal consequence, just reporting is some public consequence), and in turn not staying secret, has a greater potential of reducing the pressure of incidents continuing to occur. I know this does not take into account the madness and tragedy of the murders and serious assaults after leaving.

In the face of these extreme events I have two responses. One, someone who is that mad, could do this no matter what you do, so better to give it a go and get out. Two, sometimes women are not strategic when leaving and are naive to the risk till too late, in how they negotiate their leaving process. One part of you may think he would never harm you in ways beyond what has happened so far, and it would be an overreaction or paranoia to think that way; yet I believe it is important that in creating your safety plan to leave, it needs to incorporate as if he could be that much of a threat. Sometimes it is just not possible to know or see everything. Just as the road is a dangerous place, we don't stop driving, we just become as practiced and skilled as we can. We prepare for the worst by being careful.

So sit with these circles and look at how you are in them, and how he is. Reflect on the frequency and the intensity. It may be shocking to get a greater sense of the risks that you're exposed to. If you haven't already, start talking to someone about those risks. Leave a spare set of keys, passport, money, legal papers, bank papers, and anything else that's very important to you in a safe place at a friend's house, in case you do need to leave suddenly.

It's very difficult to make changes when you don't feel safe. It is a vicious bind. Staying will not lead to safety, but leaving leaves you vulnerable, too.

Start to reflect on what self-care practices can support your physical, mental and emotional self. What can you do to increase your strength, emotionally and physically? You deserve a life of safety and security. Write down a list of rights that you believe anyone should have. The kind of rights you'd automatically give your child or best friend. You are no different to them.

Professional support can guide you in working through the best choices for you at this time. This process of becoming safe is tricky, but it's not just about limiting beliefs and attitudes. There are deep, involuntary patterns that involve the brain and the body and how they communicate with each other (which can be addressed with skilled therapy) – as well as real and valid practicalities that need to be taken into account.

It's pretty difficult to do this on your own. There are gentle and effective ways of processing some of the shock and overwhelm that you've been managing, which will help your system gather energy and strength. It's difficult to keep bearing and enduring without unloading.

Often when we're living with abuse we stop talking to friends, because we don't want to burden them. We know they've got a lot going on in their life too. Who doesn't? We can tend to stop talking and live like the Little Match Girl: in hope and fantasy.

There are professionals available to support you by phone, by Skype or in person. Reach out so you can reclaim your real life. Start to bridge to the outer circle in the particular places you know will see and support you.

Chapter 12: The Red Shoes

The Red Shoes

There was once a pretty and kind girl named Karen. She was so poor that in summer she would be barefoot, and in winter she would wear wooden shoes that hurt her ankles until they were all red and sore.

There was an old lady in the village whom they called 'Old Mother Shoemaker'. She wanted to help Karen and so collected scraps of material to make her red shoes, even if they were a bit rough.

When Karen's mother died Karen wore the only shoes she had, the red shoes, to her mother's funeral, even though red shoes are not usually what you wear for funerals or church.

An old lady inside a carriage went by and saw her walking after the coffin in her rough shoes and bare legs and was sorry for her. She asked the parson if she could take the little girl home and look after her.

Karen was sure the lady wanted her because of her special red shoes, but the old lady said she thought they were horrible and burnt them. She gave Karen new clothes and taught her to read and sew. Everyone could see how pretty she was but her mirror told her she was beautiful.

The Queen came travelling with her daughter through the country and everyone, including Karen, came to see and admire them. The princess had red shoes that looked very special.

It became time for Karen to be confirmed and she was dressed in new clothes and needed new shoes. They went to a wealthy shoemaker. There Karen saw some red leather shoes in a glass case. The red shoes had been made for a count's daughter but they had not fit her. They looked just like the Princess's shoes! Karen wanted them and because the old lady couldn't see well, she just admired the shiny material and bought them for Karen, not realising they were red.

When Karen walked into church with her shiny red shoes, everyone was aghast except the old lady, who could not see them. All the little girl could think about were the glorious red shoes on her feet even when the Pastor was speaking to her.

At the end of the day, churchgoers told the old lady about the red shoes and she warned Karen to never wear them to church again. The next week, the little girl chose the red shoes over her black shoes.

When they arrived at church, there was an old, red-bearded soldier standing at the door with a crutch. He asked if he could clean the old lady's shoes. Karen put her shoes out for cleaning too. He tapped the soles of her shoes and said what beautiful dancing shoes they are, and they are never to come off when she dances. The red shoes glistened even more. The old lady gave him a coin and they went into church.

All through church Karen admired her shoes and even forgot to sing. Everyone noticed her shoes and again were so shocked at the fullness of her bright red shoes. When they left church, the old soldier called out admiringly about her beautiful dancing shoes.

His words made her feet do a little jig – and once they started, she couldn't stop them.

She kept dancing and dancing. The coachman had to grab her to place her in the carriage. Her feet had a life of their own, dancing mid-air so that they kicked the old lady as Karen was placed in the carriage. She couldn't stop her feet from moving. At home, it took a great effort from the coachman and old lady to pull the shoes off her feet, with the old woman throwing them in a cupboard and telling her never to wear them again.

In time, the old lady became sick. She was dying, needed a lot of care and relied on Karen a lot.

One night there was a ball. Karen was invited and really wanted to go. She looked at the old lady, who couldn't live much longer, and she looked at her red shoes. The moment her eyes caught sight of the shoes, her desire to wear the shoes overcame her.

She quickly put them on her feet, went to the ball and began dancing. The little girl did not realise there was a problem until the shoes took her out the door and down the steps. She wanted to dance to the left but the shoes took her to the right. When she wanted to dance in circles the shoes led her straight. Before she knew it, the shoes were taking her into the field and beyond, into the dark forest.

In the forest she danced until she came to the old soldier with the red beard who was again admiring her shoes. She felt scared and tugged to take the shoes off but no matter what she tried, both shoes kept her feet dancing and dancing.

The shoes kept her dancing through the days and nights, across the highest mountains and down the deepest valleys. She could not rest. No longer was it fun as she danced through all the weather – sunshine, snow and rain – until she came to a church graveyard.

An angel in white, with huge wings and a sword, stood by the open door of the church. The angel would not let her in. He proclaimed in a serious voice that she would dance until she was starved and cold. The angel said she would dance into villages and knock on the doors until the proud children hear her and are scared. She would never stop dancing and the children would see her dancing and not want to be like her. He beckoned the red shoes to keep dancing.

The girl cried for mercy but she couldn't hear any reply from the angel as the red shoes took her away – across the fields, rivers and hedges, until one day she finally arrived back to her village. Mourners were gathered around the old lady who had died. Karen had no one else now in the world and even the Angel of God had cursed her.

The little girl was sad and exhausted but her red shoes kept dancing, taking her further and further away, her body bleeding from the wild nature that the red shoes taken her through. She came upon a little house where the town's executioner lived. Karen tapped on the window and called out for the executioner to come out, as she could not come in while she was dancing.

The axe started trembling in anticipation and the executioner said, 'Don't you know who I am? I cut off the heads of bad people.'

The little girl called out to the executioner to please not cut off her head, as then she could not repent for her wrongdoings – but instead for him to cut her feet off. She confessed her sin, upon which he cut off her feet and shoes. The red shoes (with her feet still in them) continued their dance, dancing off through the trees and valleys and out of sight.

The executioner made her a pair of wooden feet and some crutches and taught her a song that prisoners sing to show they are sorry. Karen kissed the hand on the axe and went on her way.

Karen felt she would be allowed into church now that she had no feet and had confessed her sin, but when she went near the door the red shoes appeared and she was so frightened she turned away.

She cried all week, after which she thought maybe now she had suffered enough to be accepted and sit with the others in church. Again, the red shoes reappeared and her heart felt so much regret and remorse at the wrong she believed she had done.

Karen went to the pastor's house and pleaded to be his servant. She said she would work very hard and did not need payment, only food and a roof over her. She just wanted to be near good people. Karen was now very serious and would listen to every word the parson read from the Bible. When the children got excited about beautiful trimmings and clothes, she would not participate.

They asked her to come to church with them but Karen teared up and said no – she couldn't come with her crutches. While they were seated in church, Karen sat in her tiny bedroom that had room for only a chair and read her hymnbook, the sound of the organ floating into her window. She felt so sorrowful and the tears poured down her face as she called out for God's help.

The same angel appeared through the sunshine, this time without a sword but instead with a green branch filled with roses. As the branch touched the ceiling, a star appeared and the ceiling lifted.

When the branch touched the walls, they opened up. She could now see the organ, and the ministers and their wives and all the people singing and seated in their pews filled with flowers. She was seated with the pastor and his family as they finished the hymn. She did not know if she had gone to them or if the church had come to her. They nodded to her that she had come and it was God's mercy.

As the sun came through the window onto Karen, the children were singing in the choir so quietly and beautifully with the organ. Karen felt so much peace, joy and light was filling her that her heart broke. Her soul was carried on the rays of sun up to the heavens and no one ever asked her about the red shoes again.

Adapted from the works of Hans Christian Andersen (1845)

Living with the Wolf, as you know by now, is intense and chaotic. It muddles your mind. You may not be aware of how wrong it is and to what level you are 'managing' your life rather than living it. You are in shock and confusion and don't want to admit it. Life has not gone the way you want. You are in survival mode, trying to get the most basic security needs met to just get through the day. You are not living the life you imagined as a child. Adulthood was meant to be the happily ever after, not *this*.

Being seduced by Bluebeard or being tricked by the Wolf is a bit like putting on red shoes that look pretty and appealing, but then you can't take them off and they are taking you to places you can't imagine – and didn't want to be part of your life. Those red shoes were meant to make your life better, but instead you have lost control and can't get your life back.

In one sense, this is the most important chapter. All the other chapters are absolutely, hugely important but if personally or socially we are going to move forward in changing our relationships to be healthy instead of toxic, looking at the stress response and the connection to trauma reveals how much the control and denial impacts every level of our being. The trauma response validates how destructive these Wolf behaviours are.

Working with the body and trauma brings us to the unconscious and the feminine. This is the way home to ourselves as women and men.

Why is this chapter so important? Because our Western culture favours the power of the conscious mind over the body, over nature, over the unconscious – over all. We are so embedded in a 'power over' mentality that we don't know how to relate. How to relate between the mind and the body, between the conscious and the unconscious, between the right and the left brain, between the feminine and masculine aspects and between a man and a woman. We don't know how to be with the unbearable and not go into overwhelm.

We as a society collude with the pattern of violence and stay silent, saying it is none of our business. We stay fixed in the left brain and minimise and excuse many types of violence, using rationale to discredit and devalue what is really going on. We have let the rational take over so much that we take things apart before we even have the capacity to be with the whole. We have become disconnected in an attempt to stay in control.

Consciously we are horrified by abuse but we are unconscious to our own attitudes, behaviours and beliefs, which contribute to patriarchal power and collude with a diminished view of the feminine. The unconscious will always lead the conscious because the conscious can't respond to the unconscious when it is not made visible or engaged.

I see this even when attending training about family violence. The conversation is the same as twenty years ago: *What is abuse? What are the types of abuse? The Cycle of Violence and Duluth Wheel of Power and Control, identifying those who are vulnerable to abuse. Myths and how to help. Why women won't leave. Risk factors. Statistics.*

Now, I am not minimising these areas or saying these subjects are not important. They are. But isn't it interesting that we still talk about the same things and not much has changed? We talk about alcohol, poverty, wealth, disability, and the high risk once pregnant. We talk about the fear of being alone; about beliefs of not being worthy, and believing the brainwashing. Yet we don't explore the uncomfortable, the unconscious and the unknown. We don't touch what is beyond the rational mind.

'Beyond the rational mind' does not mean 'irrational'. Beyond the rational mind includes so much more: the body and the prevalence of individual involuntary stress responses and our societal lack to respond to trauma (we stayed for too long with cognitive behavioural therapy over Jungian and somatic therapies: again the masculine over the feminine); what is stored in the individual, families, society and the collective unconscious; the innate deep need to belong and the innate real fear of rejection and abandonment as well as our societies lack of engaging and being with our deep feelings.

This is why 'The Red Shoes' is such an important story here. 'The Red Shoes' tells us of the kind of torment, imprisonment and suffering that exists when we are not in control of our life. This story describes the experience of living with abuse. The landscape of 'The Red Shoes' goes beyond the words *fear, loneliness, torment, suffering* or *terror*. The experience of abuse is far more than any words can describe. Words can limit the reality, depth and overpowering nature of feelings. Our feelings connect to our limbic and survival centre, creating an active connection with our unconscious. Our feelings live in our body and can be overpowering.

***

The name Karen means 'pure' in its Greek origin. We are all born pure and with the innocent desire for what is appealing and part of the collective experience. Her life energy responds to being carefree, playful and the red shoes. It is as if in response to the harshness of her life, she is punished for wanting some colour and brightness, some passion, some energy, some lifeblood. It is as if what is pure, open, innocent, soft and bright gets nabbed. Nabbed because she loses the protection from her mother and there is an absence of her father. Nabbed through the shaping of a restrictive form of the old feminine disallowing her to have what is beautiful to her. Nabbed by the old, wounded masculine that does not have his own softness and beauty but instead is sadistic and manipulative. The envious and cruel robbing of the young life energy from those whose energy is old or wounded.

The girl in the story is kind and innocent, with a youthful open energy. She is making the best of life until something appears to get in her way. She loses her mother and so her life starts to take a spiral as she becomes vulnerable. Her mother was her safe place, the womb of nourishment and security that fed her growth. The body of unconditional love, tenderness, affection and support – of being cherished, adored and delighted.

How are we lost from our mothers? How are our mothers lost to us? This may be literal in the tale, but perhaps we lose our mothers in symbolic ways.

We also lose her to the patriarchal expectations of how it is to grow up as a female. The old feminine first comes in as the Old Mother Shoemaker who offers her a gift. The old feminine is offering care but she is not available in the consistency a child needs. Then the old woman, who takes over from the mother seeks permission of the church – the patriarchal power with a large history of control, shame, persecution, fear and abuse. Is this transaction symbolic of the influence and power of the beliefs of the church that are louder and stronger than family or community connections? Despite best intentions, her initial desire to care for the young and innocent becomes a servant to a powerful, old control.

Where is the personal masculine? Where is the father? He is nowhere to be seen. How are we abandoned or orphaned from an active, caring, strong, gentle, protective father?

Instead, the old feminine has a need to shape her in a way she believes is pleasing. But what is this way? Isn't she training this free, youthful and wild girl to be submissive and pleasing to others? To follow a way that is not of the feminine. Karen is not encouraged to be with her freedom and spontaneity, enjoying her own body with energy, strength and movement, bare feet out in nature. She is taught to contain herself and care for others. Echoes of Little Red Riding Hood.

I imagine when she was with her mother, she was playing in the fields and dancing around the village when the old shoemaker thought to make her some red shoes. Seems to me despite being poor, she was loved and was content.

Karen believed the old woman wanted her for her red shoes. This thought seems to indicate a lack of feeling lovable for who she is. *When a response seems a bit off or odd, the task is to look at what is conscious and become curious about the unconscious link.* Doesn't it seem odd that she would think it is her shoes that make her lovable? Is the connection between shoes making her lovable a reflection of a patriarchal society that objectifies the feminine via sexualised colours and clothes? Or was there a wound with the death of her mother? Maybe in her young age no one was around to help her through her grief process. Anger is a natural stage of the grief process when someone dies too soon. If she could not express her anger at her mother's death perhaps the anger was internalised and turned against herself when it could not be directed outwards. She might attack her own sense of self and believe she was not lovable enough.

The wound of abandonment can be significant when a child loses their mother. Despite one part realising that she was sick and dying, another part – through the unimaginable experience of her mother's death – could feel unlovable. This death can be a symbol. The mother loss is not always through a literal loss. Abandonment can occur through being present but physically, emotionally or energetically rejecting the child. Abandonment can also occur because the mother is traumatised from her own past, from her relationship, depression or a shocking loss in the moment which has taken her energy away from her child. Why would Karen think that her shoes were a reason to want her and not her own life energy of being? What happens in those gaps? Do we make sure that the vulnerable and innocent don't make inaccurate beliefs about themselves?

Her mirror tells her she is beautiful, whereas those around her tell her she is pretty. Is there envy and a difficulty in allowing her to be in her fullness? So many times I have worked with women who from an early age have had to hide their magnificence, either so it does not get attacked or taken due to envy and jealousy. How much space can we take up and shine? How much room is there for us to be big, interesting, fun and clever, until others get uncomfortable? How much permission is there to speak up about 'Snow White' mothers who are envious of their daughters? How many women secretly are jealous of their daughters and unconsciously collude with the masculine to attack the pure? (McBride 2008, 2013; Pipher 1994; Shandler 1999; Streep 2009, 2015; Ulanov 2012)[7]

Pure (young feminine) Karen has lived with deprivation and is attracted to the abundance and value symbolised by the Queen and Princess on their visit. She sees the fullness of what is possible and she strives towards her own way of attaining this, through the desire of what the red shoes symbolise for her.

We project our unconscious disowned parts into objects when we have not been given permission to own and embody those qualities for ourselves. Just as I did as a child with my toy elephant. We can also project our disowned parts onto people we love. Bluebeard projects his feminine disowned self onto her and punishes her for being emotional or vulnerable in the same way he does to himself internally. She disowns her anger, which is perceived as bad and wrong, and becomes entangled with a Bluebeard whose anger is bad.

When we disown aspects of ourselves, the disconnection and unrelatedness leads us to perceive those elements as worse and scarier than they are, and then we meet them in others. Unfortunately meeting what we disown is often a more dangerous and intense experience then our internal experience.

---

[7]. Additionally, also refer to the body of work from author Nancy Friday (1933–)

Something unfamiliar can feel wrong or bad when we don't know it personally. Just like when we wear new shoes for the first time, they can feel wrong even when the right size if we are used to wearing sneakers and we try on high heels. It is just unfamiliar.

The young feminine (Karen) is taken by the old feminine to the house of the masculine spirit (church) where there is containment and control. Where there is adoration of spirit and the masculine and where the feminine powers of nature, plants, herbs, feelings, spontaneity, expression, birth and rhythms of life have been devalued. Where there is the reinforcement of women being submissive and in servitude to male power. Each time she is here, her natural desires are made wrong. Disapproval and shame is used to make her submissive, quiet and dull.

It is at this house of masculine power where she is tricked by the old, wounded masculine. The wounded old feminine does not see what is happening. How does our society keep us from seeing what is going on to the point that we don't speak up? How does society keep the feminine inside the patriarchal system, seeing through patriarchal eyes instead of with feminine wisdom? All the influences. Bystander inaction. Following the tribe. Not wanting to stand out and be different. The crowd at the Emperor with no clothes. Belonging. So many layers. Culture, history, religion and family.

How is it that when the new red shoes clearly are something to be concerned about that the old feminine puts them in a cupboard instead of destroying these, as she did the harmless ones? This is back to front. The pure, vulnerable feminine is placed at risk. Why were the original raw, simple red shoes burnt and not valued, yet there is some value placed on keeping the shiny red shoes? What do we value? Why? What do we keep and why? Are superficial appearances valued instead of raw and natural energy?

The old feminine does not have much life energy and is taking from the pure, young feminine in Karen. Karen's energy is made to look after her. Again, like Little Red Riding Hood, is there an unrealistic demand on the young feminine to take care of the old feminine? We don't hear of the old feminine loving, connecting, valuing or playing with the young feminine, but instead the young feminine is taking care of the old feminine. Again, there is the theme of being at risk when you are the feminine one and in red. Again, the theme of the young, innocent energy that is being taken advantage of.

The old feminine is apparently wealthy but asks a child to take care of her. As death comes closer for the older feminine, the pure, young feminine feels less grip on her and the invitation to celebrate life calls her. She takes a risk. But she only has access to the shiny red shoes that have been bewitched by the wounded masculine – the natural red shoes have been burnt. *Our environment shapes our stress response and what choices we have access to.* She is unaware of the full consequence of stepping into those shiny shoes. She does not know where they will take her or what control they will have.

She sees the wounded masculine again. Now that she has been taken inside the control of his dangerous dance, she recognises the trick and power play. She sees him for what he is. She is scared – she tries to get out of the trap, but she can't. She still doesn't have enough resources and she is alone. No one sees what she is going through. She sees him only briefly and is then taken back into the dangerous dance and is in constant survival mode.

She comes to where there is meant to be some support and breath (church and spirit) but the messenger (angel) from that which is greater than (God) – holds a spiritualised, high and mighty attitude. This message is not integrated with or connected to the earth and the feminine and cuts across (with the sword) any potential of positive support (the open door) and instead directs judgement and rejection. The opportunity is brief. She is cursed and the shame and rejection sends her deeper into the dangerous dance.

The cutting judgement (the sword) spreads a curse, shame and rejection. The innocent, young, spontaneous, joyful feminine is given the message she does not belong in the community. She is punished for enjoying herself and feeling good about beauty for her own sake (pride). This community abandonment wounds her deeply. All these messages say that it is not okay to have pride, or for the feminine to be 'self-centred'. These qualities have been twisted into negatives, when in fact they are necessary for a healthy sense of self. The abusive, controlling power cuts you off from those qualities as a tool to control and disempower you from your confident, powerful, unique, free and shining self.

The feminine owns a sin that is not hers to bear. She carries suffering, shame, guilt, defectiveness – possibly even self-disgust and despair.

Now that she is rejected by the spirit (by that which is greater than her, and its influence over community), she is alone in the world. She feels helplessness, yet there is still some hope as she does not want her head cut off. She wants her mind.

Instead she wants her feet cut off. Now she is unable to stand her ground. Others have taken her ground from her. In the trauma response when we have been wounded, a split develops in our system. Our inner protector will often re-enact the trauma onto ourselves. There is a resistance to healing and integration to protect the young, wounded within. This becomes a re-enactment of tyrannical, self torture in an attempt to remove us from the pain of the abuse being repeated and being out of control. This re-enactment can often be more gruesome than the original wound (Kalsched 1996). This could be represented by the desire to end her suffering but creating a greater torture in having her feet cut off.

But what is a mind without one's own ground? A mind without her feet to me is the masculine, thinking function without the sensory, grounded connection to the earth and the feminine. The feet are so vital for the body to stand on earth.

The mind and the body are connected physically yet are disconnected functionally. The overwhelm and despair are too great, and there is no end. The survival response keeps going, even when it feels like we can't go on. The red shoes keep dancing because we are in the stress response – what can we do but continue the dangerous and disconnected dance?

The head and the body are not connected despite both being overactive. They are not working together. This is the patriarchal dilemma that creates trauma. The trauma response is so influenced by the pain, overwhelm, suffering and helplessness that it only sees a part of the picture. The mind has absorbed a lens from the culture, religion, family, attachment patterns, bystander effect and the projected image inside the curse, which are neither accurate nor kind. The body has no feet and can't access its full ground.

The executioner is a wounded masculine and trickster Wolf, just like the wounded soldier who both sold their soul to patriarchy. The executioner takes the ground away from the pure feminine and then appears to act kind, giving her crutches and a false ground. This is Wolfish. What is he teaching her? How to be sorry for who she is – he teaches her how to live without her power and in shame, guilt, remorse and regret. To live restricted within patriarchy. She submits with a subordinate kiss.

Each time she moves towards the hope for the potential of some kind of support, the terror of the dangerous dance gets activated and in fear she pulls away. She does not want to get caught in another round of deep suffering. The trauma response is involuntarily re-enacted when she returns to the place where the trauma happened: the Church where she received the shoes and the curse, and where the Angel rejected and cursed her from belonging. This is the cost of trauma, the unresolved re-traumatisation when in environments which are part of or hold elements of the split trauma memory.

She persists, almost as if nothing bad is happening now. She has swallowed the image projected on her and has no feet to stand on. She seeks help from the spiritualised masculine. There was no personal relationship available. There is no feminine power and support available for her to seek out. She has taken on the face that she has been told how she should be.

She gets used to a life of feeling defective and lessened. She tries to be 'good' according to their image of good – she is structured by forces outside her, instead of from her internal values. She is serving and looking after others; she lives by the approval of the wounded and patriarchal masculine.

When she is alone, she is with her truth. Her heart is so sad that the tears flood her whole being. Her pure and wounded self calls out for help. She turns to the spirit because she has no hope or personal connection to others that her circumstances will change. She is broken. She has bonded with that which created her bondage. (The Stockholm Syndrome, which I will explain soon).

There is no person wanting to get to know her and enjoy time with her. She is there to serve. She is lost to herself. She no longer knows who she is. She is destitute. There is no warmth and personal relatedness or realness. She spends more time in spirituality and dissociated states that feel softer and easier to be with, as the pain is too great. She is lost.

The spirit comes because she is so inside the paradigm of having sinned that this 'redemption' is all that is available. She sees herself saved (the angel with the branch and roses and no sword) due to her subordination and loss of self. Her heart breaks. It is not possible to continue life living in this patriarchal, spiritual, de-personalised mode with no ground for her, dissociated from her ground and soul and with no escape from the stress response.

How was it to hear the story retold this way? It is so tragic. Let's now relate to it even more personally.

Is the experience of having parts of ourselves (shoes and feet) taken from us, and not being able to be our whole self (with the old woman and the

Angel and Church members), a bit like when we have gaps within us from our parents' inability to provide developmentally what we need? Gaps in not being loved for our fullness and the wound of not having a full sense of ourselves, just as Karen felt in not being lovable?

This story shows the impact of the patriarchy denying the feminine. The controlling, wounded masculine who bewitches and limits the pure. The bystander effect of those around who mirror the shame and judgement and together create a dangerous environment for the punishing and unrelenting dance with a demand to perform to be 'accepted'. This dance of fear and control keeps the feminine from her own ground of power and desire.

Isn't this like women who are not provided a nourishing environment to be their full self, and then they meet a man with 'power'? After all, she has received those messages that her own power is not appealing and his power is 'attractive'. Isn't she told that she should appear pleasing, pretty and submissive and not show her spunk, as that is 'ballsy' and unattractive. She has lost contact with the possibility of having power for herself. She is only allowed a degraded power – dancing for the masculine's pleasure and control.

She is searching, sensing that something needs to be broken. She does not want to give up. Something is wrong and she wants to go beyond the limits, beyond the lacklustre imprisonment to find her fullness, and take risks to claim herself. She endures.

But in seeking to break rules to get back to herself and reclaim her power, she needs to reclaim what was cut off. What is cut off goes into the shadow. The 'shadow self' is anything in your nature that has to go into the unconscious when there have been clear messages and consequences that 'it' is not allowed to be shown. This for a woman can be her wild self, her instinctual nature – her anger, rage, strength and passion in ways that are not limited by a sexualised picture of her. It is tricky to bring out your shadow self when the world around you values you staying bright and pure. So you remain non-threatening to others limited self to belong.

There is a double bind. You can be bright but only in the degraded form controlled by the masculine instead of your original bright and wild self.

The light from the innocent, feminine, sensitive, free and pure self is attractive to the wounded, rule-bound masculine who feels his darkness and disconnection from his own feminine, sensitive, permissive and creative self. The disowned masculine is attracted to the generous and open heart of the feminine. Dark is attracted to the light … a reflection of his disowned self … like a moth to the light – to the feeling self, the vulnerable, the open and innocent. Here is the external acting out of what happens to his own internal feminine, vulnerable, feeling self.

***

When we have lived inside the cape of Little Red Riding Hood, we have unfortunately absorbed the rules around us that put blinkers on us. So we put on the patriarchal red shoes that appear pretty. We do not see what danger they will lead us to.

Then when people try to get the red shoes off us, they don't know how to respond. They are not aware how to handle the stress response and use force and willpower. When the shoes are loosened through force, we are at risk of getting stuck inside them again because our feet don't have the strength to stand their ground. We need support. Our system is wired to the stress response and can easily revert back into stress because we don't have the appropriate environment or self-soothing and brain body alignments to remain harmonised.

We are so removed from our deep, wild, instinctual self that we have lost our ability for healthy discerning and deconstruction of what is 'bewitching' and 'seductive' and how this is different to what fills us with enchantment, awe and wonder. We have lost our ability to recognise and respond to danger and how to recognise and heal the face of trauma.

In 'The Red Shoes' we see a cutting off by the executioner of her ground. The story does not show the redemptive quality that other tales do. For me this tale is useful to illustrate the stress response and the cost of the patriarchal structure. How the stress response is relevant to the dangerous dance of the red shoes will become clearer when we talk in more detail about the stress response later in this chapter.

In many fairy tales something is cut off, taken to the underworld, swallowed or killed. This is often part of what needs to happen to move from an immature state to regain the whole and individuate. There needs to an ending of what is not developing, or a crisis to mobilises new growth or kill off what needs to be killed, so that what is life-giving is not at risk of being destroyed or not growing. The killing off can be symbolic of killing off patriarchal, gender-based abusive beliefs and attitudes that do not allow men to be vulnerable or women to be powerful.

The tragic part of 'The Red Shoes' is there is cutting, burning, severing, death and killing but with no redemptive actions or opportunities. The feminine keeps dying. Karen's mother, her caretaker and then Karen – a clear indication of the cost when there is no redemptive or generative opportunity for the feminine. The only other feminine figures in this story are serving the ego ideal of the patriarchy. This story is a warning.

There are not enough choices and opportunities for women to take up healthy power, shining and being in their full life energy or feel threatened by your ability to shine.

So we get caught in the red shoes, the dangerous dance. Many people stand by, judge and disapprove, but not enough intervene to become active bystanders. The shoes (stress response) are still in the cupboard … in easy reach to be put on again in an attempt to take that risk or opportunity to go for something good. But there is a grave risk when there is no support to have your joy and freedom.

Many women pretend and create a vision that is not who they are. *Be the object of desire. Get the Botox and have the long hair, the tanned skin, the fake nails, the eyelashes, the large breasts. Over-train the body and wear sexy clothes and those sexy heels, which arch the feet in a position of arousal to match the red, pouting lips.*

The shiny red shoes can represent taking ideas and fantasies on board – being brainwashed, sexualised, eternally in 'arousal', as if this 'arousal' affirms his prowess and attractiveness. Instead of being welcomed for being real and desirable, lovable and challenging, likeable and difficult, attractive and ordinary. Instead of standing on our full, rich, wild ground.

***

When I sit with a group of women around a table, many women have had some experience of abuse in their life. Yet there is still confusion about abuse, arguments, and the difference between conflict and abuse – leading some women (and men) to misidentify abuse, when it isn't and when it is there.

Women (and men) still do not have clarity about the breadth and depth of both subtle and direct forms of abuse. Women still are not clear about defining their own boundaries and owning their own power. Women still struggle with wanting to not be seen as selfish or needy about their needs and desires. Women are still owning perceived abusive actions that are not abusive, when they are standing their own ground.

Women still feel too much shame, unworthiness or defectiveness to acknowledge when abuse is part of their story. Even when abuse is in our past, if we are not comfortable with our own past we are at high risk of either not seeing another woman's risk (because our blinkers are protecting us from our own pain and so we 'mis-see' it in other women) or we see it but find ourselves favouring a less optimal approach. We could minimise or attempt to convince from our own incompleteness, or super-impose our past, solutions or blocks on to another woman without realising windows of opportunity and differences in her story.

Women often generalise from their own past of abuse, 'I wouldn't listen to anyone. There's no use speaking. I don't want to lose her with an argument like I lost some friends when they confronted me.' It is as if, there is no possibility of there being a new way through or a different outcome. Everyone's abuse and everyone's way out is unique. Because the past produced one outcome does not mean the next situation will produce the same result yet the painful, unresolved past is influencing separate situations.

We may respond to rush us through in our need to get to a comfortable place. We don't want association with pain.

I find women are walking on eggshells even when they are not the ones in the current state of violence. Women still minimise after they have left the abuse (because some trauma is unresolved, even many years later). Women are skirting around guilt, shame, emotional pain and confusion.

Our society is not good about helping women, or anyone in trauma, to fully process and attain resolution. People don't want to get messy or uncomfortable. Maybe they have a genuine reason for that. There are not enough skilled people who know how to be with and guide deep feelings and trauma to healing. People don't want to lose control. But we need to surrender to the pain alongside very skilled trauma and mind-body practitioners. This surrender with skills enable people to get to a place of clarity and spaciousness – so our society can connect and move on.

I am not blaming women. I am just naming this in the context of women, because I do connect more with women and women circles. I don't presume to talk about what happens in men's circles.

I do, however, see evidence of men with high rates of suicide, depression and heart problems (a known stress indicator), men killing, men pushing themselves in business, family life, being brutes to each on the football field rather than just focus on skill, men returning to their sport and not allowing adequate time for injuries to heal. I hear men in community groups who come together for positive intentions 'joke' about with each other in ways that they actually can't even see are put-downs.

So we put the red shoes on in habit, under pressure, with no better option. Others around us do not recognise this is happening or how to help us to take the red shoes off. Others are then limited to respond when 'we lose our feet' rather than placing a greater preventative response and instead compensate after the fact, in loud protest about all the 'dancing'.

Unconsciously or inadvertently (from a symptomatic, survival self) other people are doing their own 'dangerous dance' and it appears as if they want us to keep the red shoes on; so they don't need to face their own past, their own pain, their own gaps, shame or shadows or the unconscious buried threat to their own survival or abandonment complex.

In this dangerous dance, we lose our power and life energy, secretly living with and managing our symptomatic coping mechanisms, woven in by regret, remorse, guilt and despair. We compartmentalise those aspects we don't know what to do with. We feel unworthy and unacceptable when sitting 'openly' with others. We hide parts of our self. We want others to see our best face, fearing if they saw all of who we were they would be disgusted. We don't realise how many of us are hiding secrets of feeling less than, along with (current or past) life choices based on fear, judgement and fear of rejection.

We need to recognise and include our whole self, so that our competent self can be with our vulnerable or wounded self. Instead of compartmentalising, we can connect between our witness self and our stressed response that is stuck in its blinkered mode.

Remember the six blind men and the elephant? We need to open up to the fact that we are more than our conscious, rationalising brain would like to perceive us. Our intuitive, deep inner wisdom becomes a powerful ally that we can work with, alongside our rational self. Our rational and intuitive selves can each bring information and awareness to each other, rather than just relying on one perspective and having an incomplete resource.

It's difficult to trust our intuition and deep, creative, knowing self when we're still in the stress response, constantly reactivated by our situation or environment. It is really important to understand the involuntary stress responses in detail and learn how to respond, rather than manage it. The red shoes to me are so symbolic of the stress response and not being able to switch it off.

When we engage with our involuntary stress responses, not through willpower or positive thinking but through the recognition that the mind and the body are always speaking with each other, we can begin to find and develop the generative, necessary steps that our individual system and situation require. This alignment can come from direct mind-body processing, which addresses the involuntary trauma and stress responses that have been activated. Our mind and body are our foundation. We need to be in our body, connected and aligned and of our own mind. In this way we can move through the world, sensing and orienting between the inner and the outer. To do this we need to be able to be flexibly responsive to recognise whatever is going on, which includes trauma; so we can repair and re-attune.

A traumatic event is any overwhelming experience that interrupts our system from its ongoing process of integration. There is an overload of experience and an inability to metabolise it and respond to this dilemma. We are unable to continue processing the experience.

Trauma becomes the unresolved material that has not been able to be metabolised and integrated. Any moment where we find ourselves without resources, skills or support to express, connect and act on our appropriate response is an experience of trauma. We are dependent on the costs, threat and risks in the event and intensity of the experience as to how traumatic it is for our system. Our early history of trauma will be a template and filter to register our immediate resources, responses and perceptions.

Our system will disconnect when the overwhelm is unbearable to sustain. The disconnection happens when there are one or more elements of the experience that we don't know how to be with. It is as if our system has jammed without the resources to integrate what is going on. This disconnection activates the stress alarm in our mind-body system. We are unsafe.

Internal or external overwhelm and stress can both activate the mobilisation of the stress response. There is a now a gap of inadequacy between what is happening, and how we can respond. This gap/disconnection diverts us from the unbearable weight of the moment. The overwhelm switches on the alarm and stress response to mobilise us to cope and get away from the stress.

At some point we need to be able to *get back to the overwhelm* so we can metabolise it, rather than keep compartmentalising it. Our society is not good about helping us re-connect with resources to metabolise our trauma. Our society is not good at recognising we are in trauma. We are often triggered into trauma and left there not realising we are in an interrupted mode and still waiting in limbo for a resolution.

When we are in the stress response, it is as if we have jumped ship (the ship being the current traumatic event) and are swimming in the waters (of survival/stress response). Everything is slower and harder to move when we are in the stress response (because our processing brain is not connected, our emergency brain is activated). We can only focus on one thing (in our emergency brain) and dog paddle (accessing basic not sophisticated tools) to stay afloat. We feel, sense, see and hear less because this allows us to focus on survival and coping. We just need to swim fast and not focus on anything else. This is not the time to digest thoughts, images, feelings and meanings of the experience. Those parts are back on the ship.

Trauma develops when we can't jump back onto the ship and process what we jumped away from. It is not easy to jump back when we don't have any newly developed skills or support to metabolise what we were unequipped for – that which was unbearable or unthinkable. It is not easy to jump back on to the ship when we don't have a floatation device or a life jacket (a safe place to rest and digest what has happened) thrown from society. It is also not easy to jump back when we are still in an environment that keeps pulling us back into the water.

Society needs to understand what trauma is and how to respond to trauma so they can throw us a life jacket and know how to resuscitate us back on the ship. We need society to provide us with developed skills and support to metabolise what we were unequipped for in our moment(s) of trauma. We can't do it on our own.

We get tired of treading water; our system has less and less ability and energy to get back. We swim in smaller circles to conserve energy and so we don't come across any sharks. This translates to: we try fewer new things so we are not exposed to a greater number of unpredictable experiences that could risk us getting triggered and re-traumatised, or exposed to new trauma.

When the stress response is activated, there is a change in blood flow, hormones, brain and body functions and connections between the brain and the body. When we are in the stress response the connections between both hemispheres are compromised. The blood and hormonal flow is altered to enable the body to not focus on thinking, sleeping or eating, but to remain in an alert and vigilant aroused state to protect the self in what our system sees as the safest way that is available to us. This continues until our system registers the danger has passed and the signal can be switched off.

But what happens when we are caught for days, months or years in the ongoing, stressful and toxic environment of relationship violence? Our system becomes so depleted, wired and sensitised, getting triggered all the time. Sometimes it goes off in a large reaction for a small trigger, as there have been too many alarms. Our system can become so reactive that it is hyper-jumpy and protective, perhaps wanting to create the alarm response to propel us out of the constant ocean of stress.

I remember when the Wolf just looked at me and I jumped. My system was raw and exposed. The longer the abuse, the less abuse was needed to create the same control and punishment. The mind-body system is flooded with stress chemicals from all the unresolved material washing over the system. He just needed to give a look or change the tone of voice. The system aches in fear and exhaustion and responds.

The unresolved overwhelm mean the neural pathway that were interrupted (from the overwhelming content) have not had a return with resources to enable those neural pathways to continue developing to their completion. This means it is as if these neural pathways are live wires that are hanging loose, to get re-activated when there is a resonance in another experience. Like a domino effect, all the live wires that have not been resolved and put in place are activated and we are flooded and dumped with all the hormones and emotional pain. Our system needs a resourced response so the overwhelmed, interrupted neural pathways go to their completion and we can ultimately receive the message that all is ok now.

Living in relationship violence is a state of ongoing trauma, a war-zone. The danger of this war-zone is confusing and creates shock and disconnection, as the danger comes from the one who is meant to be there for us. We're in that double bind. The one who is meant to be loving is the one who instinct wants us to move away from. The mind-body system is split and overwhelmed. This conflict needs safety and a bridge to skills and support to negotiate these binds.

Assessment of what is possible when under threat and overwhelm happens ever so fast. Our system recognises whether it is not safe to fight (verbally or physically) or take flight (from the room or further afield). What happens if our system freezes? Is there anything more that gets activated when we are stressed?

Yes. The classic fight-flight theory of stress was originally studied and based solely on male participants. Psychologist Dr Shelley E Taylor was curious to explore women's range of stress responses. Dr Taylor undertook twenty-five years of research and analysed over a thousand studies in pursuit of her question about whether women had the same stress responses as men or different. She found there is a fourth stress response unique to women other than the fight, flight and freeze response, which we also possess. (Taylor 2002)

Dr Taylor found that the theory of masculine dominance for survival was not the only survival mechanism in our species. The *primary* stress response for women is 'tend, mend and befriend', or the tending instinct. Just like the testosterone dominance in the male fight and flight response, there is a female-based stress response, with oxytocin and oestrogen involvement.

When stressed, women want to connect and protect their young, their family, their tribe. It is apparent in the contrast of men being activated in the immediacy and short term focus of the fight and flight response to protect the tribe that women have a complementary survival response. Tending is significant in helping the species survive and influencing genetic patterns and illnesses. Tending is complementary to the masculine response in that it has a larger and more long term focus.

Women's response to stress is protection-based, through care and social bonding. There is the cellular knowledge that when social bonds break down, there is risk of illness and death. The tending instinct motivates tending and affiliation to ensure survival. Within the tending instinct there is therefore a deep cellular need and connection between tribe cohesiveness and protecting children from harm. The tending instinct is also enhancing the protection of the mother's genes being passed on. Dr

Taylor found through numerous studies that women respond to stress in a more socialised way.

> Tending to other is as nature, as biologically based, as searching for food or sleeping.
> Dr Shelley E Taylor, The Tending Instinct

This adds a totally new layer to looking over the love hooks and binds, doesn't it? Now let's look at the involvement of the hormone oxytocin that is activated in the 'tending' stress response. *Oxytocin assists not only bonding between a mother and child, but is also involved in sexual behaviour.* This factor could contribute to women in relationship violence often having a very strong sexual connection and bond to their abusive partner. My work with women has found that one of the biggest hooks in loving the Wolf was 'love and sex'. Interesting when we consider the fullness of the Tending Instinct.

Another interesting thing is that the female hormone oestrogen greatly increases the effects of oxytocin in women, which is different to the experience of oxytocin in men, as men don't have oestrogen increasing their oxytocin. So when stressed there is a strong hormonal involvement connected to loving and protecting the children. Nature's protective mechanism to make sure the children are tended to. Again we can see how one of the strongest hooks, not breaking up the family is very tied to the tending instinct response.

I wonder in relationship violence experiences when no children are involved, if the oxytocin and oestrogen also hooks the woman into taking care of the wounded child within the man, to preserve safety and save the unit of connection. So often in emotional abuse the Wolf wants to be loved and seen the way a young child needs to be taken care of. This also happens with physical violence, but the immediacy of the child within is hidden by the physicality of the monstrous acts.

Often women who have become involved with a Wolf or Bluebeard are children who have been 'parentified' in their childhood – they had to grow up too fast and take care of their parent in some way. The parentified child-adult can get hooked to a Wolf-Bluebeard who wants someone to 'mother' them and feels abandoned when she is mothering the children or absent to him. The killing rage of survival as if life is at stake is activated when he feels she is separate or unavailable. Or he gets angry and wants the 'sexy woman' (the Madonna/Whore complex) and not the mother tending him. The stress hormone to tend could be activated in the child who is being parentified, as well as when living with the Wolf.

Remember that *any* abuse involves emotional abuse, so whether the Wolf is physically violent or not, there is emotional abuse and the woman's corresponding tending instinct activation. *The woman, despite being physically hurt, will be involuntarily pulled in – taking care of him to ensure her survival.*

> The tending instinct is every bit as tenacious as our more aggressive, selfish side.
>
> Dr Shelley E Taylor, *The Tending Instinct*

This 'tend and befriend' instinct also adds to my observation as to there being so many women in abusive situations who are nurses or who have strong, caring tendencies.

I want to emphasise the Tending Instinct, as I believe the women's tend, mend and befriend stress response is missing in the current community awareness and conversations, responses and understanding of family violence. Remembering also that the disconnection in the brain due to the overwhelm from the stress response also means that there will be extreme difficulty to process, think clearly or go to the bigger picture and instead keep 'tending, mending and befriending'. The mind will feel foggy and forgetful, getting things mixed up and back to front. She may feel clumsy, scattered and unable to name basic things.

This does not mean women are unintelligent. It means the blood has moved out from her sophisticated frontal cortex and is infused by the amygdala – the 'survival' brain and limbic brain responses. These survival processes are all involuntary and activated because what is happening is real. The stress response is activated because there is a dangerous and threatening situation.

When the brain is disconnected in the stress response, you can't think clearly or make true connections. It is not the time to think; it is the time to move and tend. If women are being asked to rationalise their reality and they are in the trauma response, they will inevitably feel further stress and shame as their brain connections are not fully accessible. Anyone in stress can learn to 'act as if' but feel a puppet to what is really going on inside. It will likely push them into further feelings of defectiveness and isolation. If a woman is talking to her therapist (unskilled in trauma) or her friend and either is asking her to think rationally, and she is in the stress response, her system will be disadvantaged to effectively process what is being asked of her. She will go through the motions without the results.

So remember, developing the key to getting out and not returning to the Wolf's belly is first off about recognising the behavioural and physiological indicators of trauma and the related stress response. It is vital to understand the 'tend and befriend' instinct as not something to fight, but to recognise and work with. When these two stress areas are responded to via the body, *then* there is opportunity to explore the love, anger and hope-limiting beliefs and process any shock, fear and unresolved trauma through somatic psychotherapy.

When we combine these trauma facts with the knowledge about early brain wiring, attachment patterns and attunement that we spoke about previously and then bring in the Stockholm Syndrome (hang in there, you will find out more in the next paragraph), we can understand the cocktail and complexity of what can happen within the field of trauma in relationship abuse. Remember: what fires together, wires together – so love, abandonment and danger can be wired in the map of 'love'. This combination of complexity can bring a greater understanding to community confusion, and to women themselves, about the links between conflict, attachment and staying so long with the Wolf. This body trauma pattern provides the pathway for the solution.

Stockholm Syndrome is the experience of bonding with the abuser; a bit like the pressure to love a parent who is unsafe or rejecting.

In 1973, two men carrying machine guns entered a bank in Stockholm, Sweden. They held four hostages for 131 hours. Three of these hostages were women. They were strapped with dynamite until they were rescued.

What was not expected was that when the hostages were released, despite the extreme, horrific ordeal that the women had endured, they were supportive of their captors. What was puzzling was that the women were also scared of the police officials and had begun to express their belief that the captors were actually protecting them. These hostages had bonded so deeply with their captors that one of the women ended up becoming engaged to one of the men, and another woman started a campaign to pay for their legal fees.

This bonding with the perpetrator has come to be well known as a survival strategy. In certain crime situations it's even been encouraged to assist the survival of people in abusive, violent situations.

- 'I know what he has done to me, but I still love him.'
- 'I don't know why, but I want him back.'
- 'I know it sounds crazy, but I miss …›
- 'This doesn't make sense, he's got a new girlfriend and he's abusing her too … but I'm jealous.'

Stockholm Syndrome is not present in all abuse situations, but four conditions have been identified to be involved when Stockholm Syndrome is present:

1. There is a threat or a perceived threat to physical or psychological survival and a belief that the abuser will execute their threats.
2. The abuser is Dr Jekyll and Mr Hyde, being cruel and then showing some form of small kindness.
3. Isolation – except the abuser is highly involved in contact.
4. A perceived inability to escape.

***

Let's revisit, define and refine what we know about stress. Stress is an involuntary reaction to stimuli that are disturbing our physical or mental wellbeing to the point of overwhelm. There is an inability to process what we are experiencing. When the cortisol or adrenal response is activated, an alarm signal is sent to the corpus callosum (those nerve fibres between the right and left hemispheres of the brain), indicating that the situation we're in is too overwhelming and we don't have the resources to address and process what is going on.

This alarm sets off a disconnection between the right and the left hemisphere, so we are no longer exposed to what we can't take in. The blood has moved away from the frontal cortex, the sophisticated part of the brain, and the blood is flowing in the amygdala, the survival centre. So it's hard to think clearly; we might be forgetful and we might feel muddled. Everything is hard work, like we're walking through mud. Blood is congregating around our organs, because for life and survival that is the area that needs to be protected. Blood is moving out of our outer extremities – our feet and our fingers – so we might get cold hands and cold feet. The stomach shuts down because it's not a time to eat and rest. We might develop digestive or bowel complaints.

It is a time to fight, flee, freeze or tend. We might have difficulty sleeping because the hypervigilant stress response keeps us alert. We are jumpy, constantly busy and moving. We might be scattered. All of this exhausts the immune system. This hyper-arousal happens internally not always noticeably visible externally (unless you are skilled in trauma), but after a time it is not sustainable and we collapse into hypo-arousal where we feel numb, flat, depressed and with no energy.

The stress response allows us to cope in the moment, but it does this by disconnecting from the overwhelm. The overwhelming memory experience remains scattered due to that disconnect interrupting the processing from short-term memory into long-term memory. The necessary process for healing and resolution is interrupted, because everything is not all together; it can't be gathered and put away into long-term memory. It is as if this unprocessed material is floating around in our system, a bit like a live wire.

This means now we're at risk of re-traumatisation and suffering. Whenever we're in a situation that has a resonance with the unprocessed, overwhelming material floating in limbo, our system can involuntarily re-experience our stress response of panic, overwhelm and how we learnt to originally keep ourselves safe. We re-experience the limiting beliefs and physiological responses, and are limited to our learnt survival responses related to that originating experience. Even if we have more sophisticated skills, when the unresolved material is reactivated we are involuntarily pulled into regressive survival responses within that branch of the brain. So the neural pathways deepen each time we are triggered and this deepening also increases the frequency of a habituated stress pattern. It seems our choices become narrower and narrower.

The key elements in our current situation that are similar to an unresolved memory – maybe the tone of voice, an action, a smell, the temperature, the taste of something, a colour, a feeling, body sensation, a time of day or something else – carry the risk of a reactivating effect. This triggering element lights up anything of resonance in limbo in the brain and body. We are flooded by this domino effect from all those stress hormones, unresolved memories and distress. Unless this is engaged with, meaningfully and effectively, this is pure suffering.

This whole process is involuntary and is unlikely to be switched off when we remain in the stress stimuli and do not have access to somatic and trauma therapy processing. It can easily be re-triggered again and again by any elements that have that resonance with those unresolved traumatic experiences.

Our system, when that alarm goes off, automatically goes through assessing whether it's safe to fight physically or verbally, or if it's possible to flee. If our system assesses that it is not possible to flee, it may go into that shutdown freeze mode, but also we are aware now that our primary mode as women is the 'tend and befriend' mode.

The tend and befriend response could look like worry, walking on eggshells, pleasing, appeasing and pampering him, being over-tolerant, taking on guilt and responsibility that isn't hers to own, wanting to talk and connect, and passive behaviours.

The fight response could involve arguing with him, threatening him, pushing him, or getting angry with him or yourself. I remember I used to clean when I was angry. I had a lot of energy to disperse that was not safe to take to him. The fight response would mobilise me to be tough and endure, with a different energy from the tending mobilisation of endurance.

The flight response could involve leaving and coming back. Leaving the house a lot, keeping busy. Being restless. Not able to sit still or relax. After I left the Wolf, I noticed after a time that I was constantly out of the house. Part of this was because not having a car meant everything took longer, but I could also see that I was driven to leave the house. Home was associated with being unsafe. Though I liked my new home I didn't want to be home. My flight response was on and constantly wanting me to escape 'home'.

The freeze response could look like being there, but just a shell – feeling numb, dissociated from feelings, thought or behaviours, depressed, going through the motions.

Dr Peter A Levine, the founder of Somatic Experiencing therapy and author of books including *Waking the Tiger*, has been a significant contributor to trauma theory and therapy. He offers us a different pathway to respond, when understanding what happens when in the stress response. Otherwise we are caught in the cognitive behavioural model (encouraged by our rational Western mind and society), which does not recognise the involuntary effects from stress/trauma and imposes a mind-body struggle.

This builds a lock on the stress pattern trying to control the stress response rather than work with it via the body.

Dr Levine questioned, why don't animals get post-traumatic stress disorder or panic attacks? They live with more life death situations then many people. He studied animals to work out how are they different to us.

Perhaps you've watched a documentary of a predator chasing another animal, and upon capturing the animal, the victim reduces its life signals so low that the predator thinks it is dead. So the predator may go off to have a drink before his feast. But the victim was just in its freeze response and when the predator moves away, the victim stands up and its signals come back on. Have you ever seen the subtle shudder the animal does, ever so swiftly discharging the stress response before speeding away?

The animal freely discharges the adrenalin and stress chemicals that built up from the chase. The difference between us and animals is our conscious mind: our unrealistic expectations and beliefs that we have taken on as truth. Our conscious mind says we will look silly if we shake, scream, drop to the ground or whatever else our body would want to do. We don't have the tribal support, witness and permission to paint our faces and create objects and burn them, dance, scream, sing or chant. We interrupt and shut down our responses.

If we can allow ourselves the involuntary release in a safe and supported space, then we can restore ourselves. Somatic Experiencing and Soul Centred Psychotherapy both work from this foundation.

***

Often women bestow a greater capacity of strength of endurance on themselves than what I perceive they have. I wonder if this is reinforced in the Tending Instinct and care for the tribe. I am not saying women are not strong. Women are amazingly strong. I am saying women are strong and they are also not strong (just like men). We can draw on life energy reserves that are needed through our whole lifetime and later find a chronic depletion, fatigue, exhaustion, collapse; as well as gut, thyroid, fibromyalgia, and other disorders from the demand in the years of abuse. I base this understanding on my personal and professional experience as well as the wisdom of Traditional Chinese Medicine (TCM), the mind-body connection and our energy system.

Remember that the feminine way of understanding incorporates 'this and that', rather than the polarity of 'this or that' so we are strong and look after our tribe – *and* we also need to healthily collapse and receive support from our larger tribe.

I know this in my own story too. There can be a pseudo-strength, an adaptive self that shields the true self. Being with this reality is sometimes hard and confronting. It can feel easier to stay in the familiar, coping strength of endurance and care-taking. This can be a defence against not being able to access the resolution of the fight and flight response, and the shame and overwhelm of not having any choices, support or skills to carry you out the other end of the tunnel. I know I lived through a numb state to defend against the emotional pain of my life. Often you can't even see that you are in a tunnel. There seems no end or light. But there is.

Not being able to see a light at the end of the tunnel can be so hard to bear – especially when you have tried at times and the outcome was a failure. Remember, the failure is about your environment not providing you with the skills, safety and support to get through the enormous pain and fear. It is not your fault.

> When a flower doesn't bloom, you fix the environment in which it grows, not the flower.
>
> Alexander Den Heijer

Not being able to see a better story can leave women identifying strongly with the fight or tend response harnessed to a sense of 'fighting' for the relationship, 'tending' and putting so much in to try to change the situation and feel the adrenalin power of this 'choice' rather than fighting and tending for you becoming safe.

Some other women believe, 'Well I could leave if I want to, but I don't, it's not that bad.' Maybe after looking at all the stress responses and what happens in our system, this response of 'I don't want to leave but I could if I wanted to' begins to sound like the stress response tending and keeping the 'relationship unit' together or of the frog staying in the boiling water – because the water heated up so slowly that the frog adapted. Just as we do in the 'seduction and charm' of Bluebeard. We adapt so well we think we can keep tolerating and enduring.

I am also a Certified Health Coach, and the tolerating and enduring reminds me when people eat gluten and are so used to feeling bloated and uncomfortable that they don't realise that the gluten is actually interfering with their system or even that they are bloated.

Bloated and uncomfortable is the 'normal.' When they stop eating gluten, suddenly they come to realise that there was another level of feeling good that they never realised. They thought they felt good before and didn't realise they were still below the 'feeling good' line, and had just presumed this was what good felt like until they got a reality check and went beyond what they had previously known. The ceiling was raised.

Maybe it also feels easier to stay in the enduring stress response, because as we get out of the stress response we connect more, we feel more, we are awakening and come to know more depth about what we have actually tolerated living with. We have greater access to the fear and emotional pain that we've been disconnected from and the reality of the dangers in our situation. This can feel tough to feel, but is a necessary part of the processing of metabolising what our system disconnected from. When supported by a caring other or group, this process can feel meaningful and greater possibility to see the light at the end of the tunnel.

When reconnecting and awakening, we can become more aware of the loss of positive opportunities and past choices, which can be painful to bear and acknowledge. On an unconscious level this pain of loss and grief can lead us to not want to move forward and feel and rather just stay fixated inside, 'I could leave, but I don't want to' as moving shakes up the loss and grief.

Grief and loss are a necessary part of coming to terms with what you've lived with and the cost involved. Grief and loss are healing, though painful because they acknowledge your value and your existence. You and your life are worth grieving over. Your grief can bring you back to life.

Tears are healing. Dr Jerry Bergman has collated a range of research about tears. Tears help us see; they keep our eyes moist and soft and immerse the eyes in antibacterial and antiviral agents. Science shows that tears help us feel better physically and physiologically; we actually feel worse if we hold our tears in. Not crying is directly linked with a poorer ability to handle stress. Emotional tears contain a variety of stress hormones whereas tears from a physical factor are 98% water, such as cutting onions.

Emotional tears release a greater number of toxic biological by-products, as identified by biochemist William Frey. This means that our tears contain a high level of stress toxins, so crying enables our stress levels to decrease as well as reduce pain. Holding our tears not only increases our stress but increases the risk of ulcers, high blood pressure and heart problems.

Ashley Montagu, an anthropologist who wrote the brilliant book *Touching: The Human Significance of Skin*, also undertook research on tears. Montagu believed tears not only improve the health of the individual who has cried, but also assists community connection and intimacy through a deeper involvement in concern for others. Tears are a form of communication and match words to behaviours, so allow a greater belief in the impact of an experience.

***

When our stress and overwhelm is active, a range of beliefs and other factors and responses could trigger keeping us disconnected. One belief often mentioned is, 'The children are young, I don't want them to be affected while they're still at school and disrupt their life.' Sometimes we think that our 'normal' life is more stable than making a change, but how can there be stability in the irrational atmosphere of unpredictable abuse? Even if the abuse is not directed at the children, they cannot feel secure or trust that next time it won't be directed at them. Plus when abuse happens to you, as we now know, children are affected. Sometimes we bestow ourselves with more capability, endurance, power, control or stability than is actually there in reality, rather than feel the helplessness or the fear of change and the risk of the unknown.

You might tell yourself, 'I can get through this. After all, this is what I know, and making a change is more scary and risky.' I want to reassure you that you don't need to make any changes now. Perhaps just begin to gather information and see what arises for you when you become aware of more information. Let the information and your responses guide and motivate you rather than remain in coping mode. Take one step at a time. No one can tell you what to do or when, or what's best for you in your situation.

Accessing some professional support – whether by phone, offline or online – is a beginning. Reading this book is a start. Gathering more information can allow you to have greater access for what's best for all of who you are; otherwise, *which part of you is making the decision?* Which part of you do you want to be making your significant life decisions: the survival part that doesn't have much choice when making the decision, or the part that wants what's best for *all* of who you are?

The first step to help your decisions and clarity would be to find out how you can change your stress response via your body.

***

It would be remiss to not acknowledge shame in the context of the stress response. When there is disowned action, shame is present.

> Shame is a soul eating emotion.
> Carl Jung[8]

> Our culture teaches us about shame – it dictates what is acceptable and what is not. We weren't born craving perfect bodies. We weren't born afraid to tell our stories. We weren't born with a fear of getting too old to feel valuable ... Shame comes from outside of us – from the messages and expectations of our culture. What comes from the inside of us is a very human need to belong, to relate ... Shame needs three things to grow exponentially in our lives, secrecy, silence and judgement ... shame is destructive. Shame erodes our courage and fuels disengagement ... Shame is highly correlated with addiction, depression, violence, aggression, bullying, suicide, eating disorders. Guilt inversely correlated with those things. The ability to hold something we've done or failed to do up against who we want to be is incredibly adaptive. ...it's uncomfortable, but is adaptive ... Shame hates it when we reach out and tell our story. It hates having words wrapped around it – it can't survive being shared. Shame loves secrecy. When we bury our story, the shame metastasizes.
> Brené Brown

---

[8]. C.G. Jung ~Carl Jung, *Letters* Vol. 1, Pages 236-237. Princeton University Press 1973

Shame, guilt and other stress responses are a shutdown response to great emotional pain and unbearable feelings and thoughts. When it is all too uncomfortable, shame and its friends inhibit us and shut us down. Shame comes when life energy is cut down. Shame is evidence of abuse. When the light has been cut across the dark is evident. We are scattered in being disconnected from our life energy and belonging in the world.

When people have absorbed our societal and family blind-spots, the challenge to talk about and be with the uncomfortable can be difficult to initiate or identify - in someone else or recognise the shame in yourself. There is a shutdown via shame, which can give an illusion of holding it together to protect against the ravages of the scattering from feeling shame. There is no choice when shame cuts across unless there is an body centred response that talks directly to the body experience of shame.

Shame, with the attack on self - can, if it is possible to imagine - on some level feel preferable than being flooded by the vulnerability and shock from someone you trust behaving this way towards you. If you carry shame, guilt or blame, there is the illusion of control – that illusion that you are unforgivable and if you had done something different, it might not have happened. This can feel preferable than feeling helplessness and overwhelming vulnerability, two of the hardest life experiences to bear. Shame is not guilt. Shame is a focus on self. Guilt is a focus on behaviour.

> Shame is, 'I am bad.' Guilt is, 'I did something bad.'
> Guilt says, 'I am sorry I made a mistake.' Shame says, 'I am a mistake.'
>
> Brené Brown

People in their discomfort often prefer to blame and create 'bad' stereotypes rather than consider the confronting possibility that they – their son, their husband, or their friend – may behave this way. It is easier to create a terrible stereotype, so you can remove yourself and your community from this 'terrible event' and avoid shame. If you say you or your family and friends are not like this, then this terrible person doesn't live in your world and you don't have to feel shame or guilt for not being able to stop it or see it. It makes it easier than trying to deal with what seems so hard to believe: that the charming man is also a Wolf. People don't want to face the possibility that this lives in their circle of connections. *What people can't see, they perceive does not exist.*

When people are disowning, in denial and uncomfortable about any direct response-ability towards a person with suspicious behaviour, as a woman, it becomes a huge challenge to know who you can trust. There may be discomfort to be the one to say something 'bad' about someone. It does not go with the female picture we have been brought up with or the social or familial mindset of not 'telling tales'. Yet if we don't develop the Rumpelstiltskin emotional muscle to discern and judge and name for the sake of healthy decision-making and support healthy community building, we put ourselves and others at risk. *We need to get over the aversion to name in fear of disrupting that illusion of everything's ok.* We can't change society until we have a momentum of people activated beyond the illusion. We *can* stand together, holding hands and stop the gaps.

When we are not comfortable to direct responsibility where it belongs, our ability to trust ourselves is diminished. We will then project our trust to be located outside of ourselves and question who we can trust in the world, always uncertain and anxious because we have denied our instinctual radar to question, name or speak out. My message to all women is to *find yourself and trust yourself* – and then you will be able to discern who to trust and when. So you won't have to worry about all the unknown people because you can trust your signals and warnings.

As a man, it can be easier to cast the blame elsewhere. It can be confronting to conceive that you are not many degrees away from the Wolf in your own identity or that you are part of the gender who has contributed significant violence in society and the world. Find men who you admire and respect and talk openly with them. Create the change in your circle. It is not about not having done anything wrong - it is about naming, repairing and being the inspiration to make a choice and take a stand. It is about being willing to be that different man no matter your history. There may be fear and shame that maybe you have even crossed the line. Please remember, *the worst wound is not the event, but not taking up the ability to repair.* The problem is we know that this tendency to cast blame outside our circle of people is not accurate. The Wolf lives in your street and works at your workplace and maybe is in your family.

***

We have been on a big journey through stress, trauma and shame. Take some time to reflect and identify your stress pattern. What do you know about your fight-flight-freeze-tend pattern?

What can you do to support your involuntary stress responses? I teach mind-body exercises that connect both hemispheres of the brain and switch you out of the stress response (as a bonus, this exercise is in the free downloadable book link, *The Ultimate Formula for Moving Forward* in the back pages of this book). Once you are doing this daily exercise, it is important to learn a broad range of techniques to metabolise the uncomfortable thoughts, feelings and memories and to calm your system and continue to keep the brain-body connection strong. I teach women how they can build their emotional muscle to make the changes that are needed. I record specific transcripts for women to play at home to help calm their system so they can digest their memories, thoughts, feelings and needs. I work directly with changing neural pathways with bilateral processes as well as using Eastern energy acupressure techniques so the overwhelm can be processed and resolved.

None of these exercises are mind over matter; they are body-based exercises that shift the central nervous system, whole brain and body into an optimal zone.

What's the hardest part for you about considering making a change? What information can you find out this week to gather some options in your steps to safety? There are many ways that you can find out information anonymously. You don't have to give your name to anyone at this stage; it's up to you. What support do you need right now? Is there one person you can let in to the knowledge of what you are really battling with? Is there any way you can spend time with a friend and give yourself a pleasurable, enjoyable day?

I remember when the Wolf was in hospital. I was having dinner with my children and I felt such joy from the relaxed energy, the lightness and the humour that was in the room. It jolted me back to a clearer sense of what I'd lost context of, and what normal really is. Getting out of the state dependent environment of abuse is vital to think clearly. The more time away without intrusion, the greater your mind body system's capacity to reconnect - as long as your fears for safety for you or your children are attended to.

Seek out pleasurable, normal moments for you. Walking in the sun, the fresh air, seeing the trees. Find a way to connect with someone you can feel comfortable with. It may be for five minutes, half an hour or half a day – whatever is needed to get more context, balance and perspective.

Chapter 13:
Vasilisa the Queen

Vasilisa the Queen

An old man and an old woman lived in a simple house with their little girl. Their life was simple and peaceful, but life was not always happy. One day the old woman fell ill and knew she would die soon. She called her daughter and gave her a tiny doll. She asked her to promise not to show the doll to anyone and to always to keep it by her side, for if she ever had any troubles, all she'd need do is feed the doll and ask her for help. She kissed her daughter and shortly after, the mother died.

The man was very sad but wanted to marry again to give his daughter a good mother. Unfortunately he married a mean step-mother who had two cruel daughters. The step-mother loved her daughters but was horrible to Vasilisa. They all nagged and tormented Vasilisa and made her work like a slave, beyond her strength. Vasilisa was so unhappy. The step-mother and sisters kept hoping all this hard work would turn Vasilisa into a dark and sour girl, but she kept working and doing all of what she was told. She grew more beautiful each day.

Her little doll helped her through all her troubles. She would milk the cows in the morning and in secret would feed her doll some milk while she poured out all her woes to the doll. The doll would listen and comfort her, doing her tasks while Vasilisa sat in the garden braiding her hair with flowers.

One day the old man had to leave for a while and so the step-mother was left with the three daughters. It was dark, cold and rainy and the weather was only getting colder. The little hut stood at the edge of a thick forest where Baba Yaga the witch lived. She was cunning, and ate people as quick as a flash.

The step-mother gave each of the daughters a task – weaving, knitting and spinning – and then she went to bed. All the lights were out except for a piece of birch wood burning near the girls working away. After a while, the fire went out and the daughters didn't know what to do – how could they work in the dark? 'Someone will have to go to Baba Yaga and get some fire.'

The two sisters said they were not going as they could see their work by the light of their needles. They both screamed that Vasilisa has to go and pushed her out the door.

It was so dark and cold outside. Vasilisa started crying. She took out her doll and told her the problem of needing to get a light from Baba Yaga; but she would eat her up, bones and all. The doll reassured her, saying, 'No harm will come to you when you have me.' Vasilisa felt comforted, even while she was walking through the thick forest with no light of the moon and no stars to guide the way.

Suddenly a man dressed all in white came past on his white horse, silver gleaming from the harness. Vasilisa kept going, cold and sore from walking and knocking into trees in the dark. Morning was coming. Another man galloped past, but this time he was clothed in red on a red horse with a red harness.

The sun was warming Vasilisa and she kept walking until dark fell. She came to a clearing with a small hut. The fence and gate around the hut were made of human bones, with skulls resting on the top and sharp teeth for the lock on the gate.

Vasilisa stopped walking, horrified at what she saw. Another horseman came up. This time, one all in black, on a black horse. When he rode to the gate it was if he disappeared. Night was fully here and the eyes in all the skulls sitting on the fence started glowing until it was as bright as the day.

Vasilisa was terrified and frozen to the spot. She wanted to get away but she couldn't. She could feel the earth moving below her and then there was Baba Yaga, flying in a mortar, using her pestle like a whip and her broom to sweep any trails behind them. When she arrived at the gate, she started sniffing and called out, 'I can smell flesh, who is here?'

Vasilisa went up to the witch and bowed down. She said very respectfully that it was her Baba Yaga smelt. She had come to ask for a light for their fire. Baba Yaga knew of Vasilisa, as her stepmother was Baba Yaga's relative, so she agreed to let her stay for a while and work and then see what happens.

Baba Yaga called out in a loud voice, 'Come unlocked, my bolts so strong! Open up my gate so wide.' The gate opened and Vasilisa followed Baba Yaga in her mortar.

When Vasilisa walked past the tree at the gate it tried to grab her, but Baba Yaga told the tree to leave the girl as she was a guest. When they arrived at the house the dog went to bite Vasilisa and again Baba Yaga said, 'Do not bite her.'

Inside the house an old cat went to scratch Vasilisa and Baba Yaga again warned the cat not to get her. She then turned to Vasilisa and said, 'See, you won't be able to leave because my cat will scratch you, the dog will bite you, the birch tree will take your eyes out, and the gate will not unlock.'

Baba Yaga then rested on the bench and called to her servant to feed her. The servant brought a feast of *borshch*, half a cow, ten jugs of milk, a roasted pig, twenty chickens, forty geese, two pies (and an extra piece), cider, mead, beer, ale and some *kvass*. Baba Yaga ate and drank everything and only gave Vasilisa a chunk of bread.

Baba Yaga then gave Vasilisa a bag of millet and a task: to take out all the black bits from the seeds. If she didn't do a proper job, Vasilisa would be eaten. Baba Yaga then fell promptly to sleep.

Vasilisa gave her doll the bread and told her all her troubles. The doll said not to worry and go to sleep and said that 'morning is wiser than evening'.

Once Vasilisa was asleep the doll sang out, 'Tommitts, pigeons, sparrows, hear me. There is work to do, I fear me. On your help, my feathered friends, Vasilisa's life depends. Come in, answer to my call. You are needed, one and all.'

Hundreds and hundreds of birds appeared, singing and working hard through the night separating the seeds until the sack was full. Just as they finished, the white horseman went past the gate. The morning was breaking.

Baba Yaga woke and asked Vasilisa if she had done her job.

Vasilisa replied very politely, 'Yes Grandma.'

Baba Yaga was angry but she could not say any more, as the job was done. She said she was going out to hunt and gave Vasilisa her next task, with another sack: to separate the peas from the poppy seeds. Again she threatened to eat her up if the job is not done.

Baba Yaga went outside whistling for her mortar and pestle, which instantly appeared. The sun was rising as the red horseman galloped by. Baba Yaga left in her mortar and pestle, again using her pestle as a whip and her broom to clear her tracks.

Vasilisa again gave the doll a crust of bread and told of her troubles. The doll called out, 'Come to me, mice of the house, the barn and the field, for there is work to be done!'

Before Vasilisa knew it the house was full of mice and the job was done.

The sun was falling and the servant started to get the evening meal ready. The black horseman galloped by as evening fell. The eyes in the skulls began to glow and Baba Yaga returned. She called out to Vasilisa, asking her if she had done her job.

Again Vasilisa replied, ever so dutifully, yes to her grandma.

Baba Yaga was again angry and told Vasilisa to go to bed, and that she would be going to bed soon too.

As Vasilisa was walking behind the stove, she could hear Baba Yaga speak to the servant, telling her to light the stove and get a hot fire going, because when she would wake up she was going to cook Vasilisa.

Baba Yaga then lay down on the bench, with her chin on the shelf, and was snoring so loud the whole forest shook.

Again, Vasilisa began crying as she took out her doll to feed her more crust. The doll told her what to do. Vasilisa rushed to the servant, gave her a silk handkerchief and asked her to pour water on the wood, so when she lit the stove the wood would not get hot. The servant agreed to help and said she would make sure Baba Yaga slept all night by tickling and scratching her feet, so Vasilisa could run away.

Vasilisa was worried about the three horsemen but the servant reassured her that the White Horseman was the bright day, the Red Horseman was the golden sun and the Black Horseman was the black night – and none would touch her.

Vasilisa ran down the hall and as the cat went to scratch her she threw it a piece of pie. She passed the dog and gave it a crust so it would stop trying to bite her. Vasilisa tied the birch tree with a ribbon and it stopping trying to scratch her eyes out. She then greased the gate and it let her through.

As Vasilisa went into the forest the Black Horseman galloped by and everything went black. Vasilisa did not know how she could get through the forest; she surely needed some light or her stepmother would punish her.

She asked the doll what to do and followed its instructions. She took a skull from the fence, put it on a stick and set off. The eyes glowing in the skull lit the way as if it was daytime.

Baba Yaga woke and realised that Vasilisa was gone. She rushed to the hall and asked the cat if it had scratched her, but the cat said, 'No, she gave me pie. I have served you for ten years and you only give me a crust of bread.'

Baba Yaga rushed to the dog and asked if he bit her. The dog said, 'No, she gave me a crust of bread and you never even gave me a bone.'

Baba Yaga rushed to the birch tree and asked if it had scratched her eyes out, but the tree said, 'She gave me a ribbon and you have never even given me a piece of string.'

Baba Yaga rushed to the gate and asked if the gate had shut so Vasilisa could not get out. The gate said it let her pass as she had greased the gate, and Baba Yaga had never even put water on the hinges.

Baba Yaga flew into a rage and began to punish the dog and cat, chop down the tree and break the gate. She was so tired from her fury, she had forgotten about Vasilisa.

Vasilisa got all the way home and could see there was no light in the house. Her step-sisters ran outside and started telling her off and complaining. Vasilisa brought the skull into the house and the skull's eyes fixated on the step-mother and two daughters – before long they were all burnt. They tried to escape but the eyes followed them until morning, until there was only cinders left.

Vasilisa took the skull and buried it. A red rose bush appeared.

Vasilisa did not want to stay in that hut anymore and went into the village, living with an old woman. One day she told the old woman she was bored and asked her to buy her the best flax.

The old woman brought her some flax and she began spinning. The thread came out so fine – she wove it into cloth and when she bleached the cloth it was white, purer than the snow. She gave the cloth to the old lady and told her to go sell it and keep the money. The old lady looked at the cloth and said, 'No, this cloth is fit for a King. I will take it to the palace.'

When the King saw the cloth he was amazed and asked how much she wanted for it. The old lady said it was beyond a price, and it was a present. The King thanked her and sent her home with gifts of abundance.

The King couldn't find anyone to make him a shirt from this cloth that would be just as fine. So he called for the old woman and said,

'If you wove this cloth you must be able to make a shirt from it.' The old woman said she had not made it but her maid Vasilisa had. So the King asked her to get Vasilisa to make him a shirt.

The old woman went home and told Vasilisa. Vasilisa made two embroidered shirts with silver threads and decorated them with pearls. Vasilisa waited by the window with some embroidery while the old woman took the shirts to the King.

Soon Vasilisa saw the King's servant running to her and ask her to come to see the King. As soon as the King saw her he fell in love with her beauty; he did not want her to leave him. He took her hands and sat her beside him. Soon they were married.

When Vasilisa's father returned, he lived in the palace. The old woman came to live with them too. Of course, the little doll stayed close to Vasilisa.

Adapted from 'Vasilisa the Beautiful' (Afanasyev 1863) as translated from the Russian folk tale by Irina Zheleznova

The story begins with wholeness. The wisdom of the mother then recognises her death is coming. She is attuned to her body and her experience and knows deeply what is unfolding. She has the skill and capacity to speak about her illness and dying, and creates a healthy transition. She accepts reality. She speaks about the uncomfortable.

The death of the mother in the tale of Vasilisa is saying at some point, we all need to accept the death of what has created us or let the power of what created us die – not necessarily a literal death; but that now it is up to us to take the next step.

Vasilisa's story offers us the gift of reclaiming our intuition, instinct and feminine power. The last of the seven layers out of violence and patriarchal power. Vasilisa was gifted the power of intuition from her 'good enough' mother. Her mother wanted her to relinquish mother as her reference point and take up her own internal reference point via the doll; her belief that her daughter's inner senses can find the depth of solutions the conscious mind can't get to.

The doll represents the wisdom of her mother that she can internalise and listen to when she needs help. What she can take as her own. This developmental stage is essential, otherwise we are at risk of being taken over, deferring to another's perceived knowledge to be abused. We can become confused between the boundary of when to listen to our self and when to listen to others. We can become confused on what is ours and what is theirs. Reclaiming our Vasilisa helps us get through. Our centre point to receive the wisdom passing down from the feminine line.

The dying words from the mother are asking Vasilisa to trust that she can know herself and her own experience better than anyone. The death of the mother asks Vasilisa to relinquish her mother as knowing the most and to develop trust within herself, rather than defer to another's wisdom and experience.

The 'good enough parenting' I received in my Soul Centred therapy process allows me to come up with realisations, wisdom, responses and solutions that my conscious mind – linear, rational and based on what I know and my past – cannot arrive at. The guidance I now receive from within is beyond my conscious self. I had to let the 'rules' of my parent's die, for me to listen to my internal truth and find my own rules. My teachers gave me my Vasilisa doll, modelled this and taught me how to feed her and listen to her.

This is the healing. When we are surrounded by those who allow us to be our whole self, then we can feel safe. Safety allows us to connect to our body, through which our unconscious can shine and guide us through life's challenges.

Clearly Vasilisa grew up with good parenting, stability and peace that developed a trust in the connection between herself and that, which was bigger than her. This trust and inner guidance could then allow her to bear the awful circumstances and get through.

Notice how her mother told her to not tell anyone about her doll. This is the mother passing on the feminine wisdom and warning to not give it all away. This is the mother passing on that *you don't need to explain or justify your truth*. Just take the required actions.

Her mother is saying *you don't need anyone's approval to know what is right for you*. Feminine wisdom is part of the unconscious and the body. She wants Vasilisa to protect her own feminine wisdom from those judgements and perceptions of other's who only accept the masculine or rational, left brain model. She was warning Vasilisa to protect her feminine wisdom from the patriarchal masculine (some men) or the animus in (some) women who have absorbed the patriarchal way and who would take apart, dissect, criticise, ridicule or use envious attack to disempower the feminine way.

These two areas, the unconscious and the body, when valued and incorporated – along with reclaiming instinct and listening to the self – will provide the solution to create permanent change in protecting women in relationships.

Notice how the mother tells her to feed her doll before asking her for help. Not occasionally or the first time … each time. We need to feed and nourish our feminine wisdom and feminine self. Regularly. Eternally. She (in us) needs to be valued and honoured and put before anything else.

Isn't this feeding her first, a bit like how we need to put on our own life jacket before we help our children with their life jacket? To help our children, we need to nourish our feminine self. All the tales we have traversed highlight the child as forced too early into the Heroine's Journey through the absence, betrayal and wounded aspects of the parents. This time it's different, the child is fed and nourished. This is the journey of being human, facing dark and light in the world, being positively affected by previous generations, able to meet life's challenges. We can create development and healing to be passed on to future generations through inclusive honouring and tending to the feminine.

The father has a good intention but he can't discern. He is in the left brain's masculine mode, where he sees the detail: that the step-mother is a woman and a mother so she fits the need. He does not have the right brain, with its feeling and sensing detail, that can see the big picture and those subtle signs and behaviours, which give a more accurate and fuller conclusion. His limited action reveals we need the masculine connected to the feminine to reach the best conclusion.

Again, coming just from the left brain, the father betrays her by not being protective and aware. She is left to the negative feminine, who is a form of the patriarchal: the degraded masculine. This degraded experience of the feminine comes about in states of survival, whereupon some women turn on the feminine way and introject (i.e. internalise and embody) the patriarchal masculine way of 'power over'. A bit like the Stockholm Syndrome, but an internal process.

Some women see being feminine as weak, and that feeling or showing your emotions is manipulative and unattractive. This is how patriarchal society has infused our sense of being – to disown the many gifts and power of femininity, which flow from our feeling life. There is so much wisdom, courage and capacity when we open to the feminine powers within. Female power is also collaborative and relational.

Vasilisa tended to her work but that was not all she did. She also braided her hair and put flowers in her hair. She is tending to beauty and honouring herself. She is building the capacity to own her divinity.

Notice it is when the father is absent, betrayal is put in motion. Healthy relationships require staying awake and not putting blinkers on.

The step-mother sets the daughter's tasks and leaves them in the dark. So often in our journey as a woman we are left in the dark. Like Little Red Riding Hood, we are not taught the steps to negotiate the darkness. In the darkness, fear and the threat for survival can separate us from each other and ourselves. Other women may take on the patriarchal view dividing women from each other, creating envious attack, asking the unreasonable to set us up to fail or to become a scapegoat.

One sister weaves, another knits and Vasilisa is spinning. We can't do all these actions in the dark. We need light to be able to complete the tasks these crafts offer us: wave and brandish, twist and knot together. When we are in the dark, we weave, twist, turn, get in knots and can't convert pieces to a whole.

Vasilisa is sent out into the dark. She is the scapegoat. She calls on her inner feminine to help her through when the world around her does not support her. This support and connection to that which is greater builds Vasilisa's capacity to step into the unknown, be with the fearful and uncomfortable, notice things, and bear witness as she sees the Horsemen pass her by. She has a purpose and skills to help her get through.

Baba Yaga appears in her mortar and pestle. It is possible that Baba Yaga, who is named as 'the bony legged one', a witch or a female demon, is another experience of the feminine. Her connection to being a witch and healing is emphasised as she rides a mortar and pestle. A mortar is a vessel in which you crush and blend food, often herbs and seeds. A pestle is the tool to pound, crush or grind that is used in the mortar. Witches are the ones who know about herbs, plants and healing and who have been maligned. Another female figure, like Lilith; who has been scapegoated and called a demon. What is disowned can appear as dangerous and threatening in its attempt to be integrated.

It is interesting to consider how Baba Yaga moves through the world inside a container that can crush and blend. Don't we need her capacities as a woman in the world? The advice to Little Red Riding Hood only offer half the qualities of the feminine. We know what happens when we are just kind and thinking of others… we get crushed. We need a pestle to crush, blend and to create what is tasty and we need a mortar, a container, to hold what is nourishing for ourselves. We need to create our own recipe for being a woman and living our life.

It is interesting to hear how Baba Yaga sweeps her track behind her – perhaps like the Wolf who hides his evidence of his dark side, or when we can see her without the shadow, she is protecting herself from attack. She does not leave openings or tracks for someone to get at her. After all, we need to know what doors to keep closed so the Wolf does not get in.

Baba Yaga shows Vasilisa her power through telling her the punishment that awaits her if she tries to own her own power. Baba Yaga shows Vasilisa all the ways she keeps her trapped, telling her about the role of the gate, tree, dog and cat. She demonstrates her 'controlled kindness' in protecting her from guards, and so is insinuating she can change the protection to a threat at any time. When we can see Baba Yaga as the disowned powerful feminine we can see she is teaching Vasilisa the ways of 'power over', which we need to know about so we can be wise to these ways and not get tripped up. What Little Red Riding was not taught - the ways of the Wolf. She also models being clear and direct from the first meeting and naming consequences if boundaries are broken. Alternatively, if we see her as the 'bad witch' we see her using power over tactics using threats, punishment and fear to control Vasilisa.

Baba Yaga reinforces her power over Vasilisa when showing her the abundance of the massive feast her servant creates – and Vasilisa receives just scraps. This is all what happens when 'living' with the Wolf. However, when we do not alienate our feminine power and it does not become a threat to us, this can, on the continuum of power, become a healthy demonstration of fierce strength in not giving ourselves away, the importance of consequences and boundaries and demonstrating we will not be a doormat for others. This then becomes an opportunity to show our bigness without making ourselves smaller just because someone else does not have access to their own power.

Baba Yaga sets her a task she thinks is impossible. Again, just what happens in life and with the Wolf. The difference is in life being with the impossible is based on stepping into the unknown of life with the opportunity of growth, whereas with the Wolf in the impossible, there is no context and instead is unrealistic and with unrelenting expectations.

The birds represent the capacity to be with the big picture, given birds fly in the sky. Birds can see the whole of what is going on and are close to the heavens, so birds can illustrate a higher knowledge as well as a link to the unconscious. A bird's ability to fly is a miracle for us and can represent connecting to a desire or an ability that feels out of reach as a limited human.

Sorting the contents of the sack can represent the necessity to sort through the chaos of what is going on to get free. Those things: beliefs, memories, attitudes, behaviours, we want to tie up and throw away that need sorting.

Mice are on the ground, grounded and looking for scraps; they are opportunists. Mice can represent the necessity to be curious and remain open to look at everything, what we are not seeing that is there in our face. Mice are prolific and very active, which can demonstrate the potential of when we are grounded and open, many possibilities can arise as well as the energy can flow to take up creative awareness. So we are given the picture and necessity to be actively connected to the earth and life energy and open to that which is greater than you and the many possibilities. To the eternal life energy. Connecting to that which is omnipresent, with an open awareness. Mice also tend to burrow, which can suggest a connection to the underworld and again the unconscious.

The birds and mice both show what needs to develop to be able to leave abuse – to be grounded but also see the big picture. Again there is the essential life task of sorting what is necessary to get free. We need to sort more than once in life.

When Vasilisa overhears Baba Yaga organising her death, Vasilisa consults her intuition again. In abusive relationships there is a part of us that does hear and see what is going on (afterwards we can see and realise the warning signs). The shutdown part needs help to consult with our instinct and intuition and trust stepping into the unknown. It is hard to trust and hear what there is to hear and see, when we don't have all the skills or support to trust and act on our instinct and intuition.

The feminine passing on her wisdom and skills through the doll is what we need to bridge between the shutdown and our instinct. Women can then reclaim how to speak and trust from their heart, without fear hurrying them past what is needed to be known in the moment. This also means we can prevent abuse or be the ones who can see and communicate powerfully with women who are trapped.

I teach women how to speak to women who are trapped in powerful, strategic and effective ways. When we connect to our deep knowledge, we can create a ripple effect to all women and be available. So when women do reach out for help, there can be optimal and effective action and assistance, as the servant shows.

When we are in an abusive relationship there are elements like the Horseman that appear a threat, yet when we have a strategic mindset and support we can navigate what seems impossible. Some threats just fall away. Not all needs to be confronted. But there needs to be a strategic plan to get out. She could not navigate all the risks with all the guards and danger without connection to her instinct, support to that which is greater (and wise women) and thinking through what is required. She needed a developed emotional muscle to be with the uncertainty and step into the unknown and trust the support and instinct within.

Again, there is also a reminder that she could not go through this on her own, from her small and limited self. She needed to reach out for help in the guidance of the experienced and wise voice of the doll – her deep, wise self that is connected to the wise feminine. When we do not have this fully, it is important to find wise women (the Crone) to teach us so we can internalise the skills and resources and create our own internal (instinct and intuition) doll. She also, even with having the doll, needed the servants help. We need to find at least one person to help us through some transitions along our journey.

Baba Yaga is so furious she forgets about Vasilisa. Showing a strength and not subjugating to the control – brings on rage. Just as in abuse, the person is forgotten to the Wolf – the personal and relating is gone and the fury is all that is there. All that matters is the 'loss of power and control', punishment and revenge. On the healthy continuum, this could be Baba Yaga's acceptance of another's power and boundary because she does not chase after her.

When Vasilisa returns home there is no light, no warmth, no welcome. The risk when you are scared to leave the Wolf is that this is the experience of the world. No one is waiting for you, only darkness and emptiness is waiting. But Vasilisa still has her instinct and intuition guiding her and trusting her through the unknown.

The skull fixes its fire and eyes on the stepmother and the two sisters. These women represent the introjected, patriarchal feminine, and envious aspects which divide the feminine and need to die for the whole, powerful, instinctual feminine to live free; as well as to be free from the Wolf.

This is a good time to ask, what needs to die within our own self to live free so we don't tear ourselves apart for having made our past choices and lived in abuse? We also need to make sure that we don't let that type of person live in our house or social circle, that is, be in our life to take advantage of our kind nature.

The skull carries deep symbolism; death, life after death, protection from bad luck, rebelliousness, caution, change and individuality. The skull is a distinctive part of the body that is recognised when the rest of the body is hard to identify. We need the power of that in us that can see and recognise beyond. So we can see that which would want to confuse and confound us and keep us overwhelmed and quiet. Destructive confusion is the first warning sign about the Wolf. To me, the skull also represents what is under our skin, the bare bones that house and protect our brain. There are three aspects to the skull: (1) The personal: a sacred container that is powerful. (2) Family: reflect on what has being bred in our bones. (3) Collective: What has been passed on from our ancestors and beyond. Find the ancestors who want you to succeed.

When I think of a skull, it is what is left when the personal has rotted away. Perhaps it is beyond the personal and is part of the collective of the human experience. We all look the same in the end when everything else has rotted away. The skull can remind us of our essence and what is the same in all of us and connects us.

What needs to be bred in the bone to be able to face the Wolf attacks and abuse? When I speak of the personal stripped away, I am not talking about being cold and impersonal, but that we need a neutral and powerful stance to stop or kill off what is aimed at us that is destructive. We need our instinct to be bred in our bones as it was in days long ago. A sacred container for our sacred mind, body and soul.

When this process of killing off the destruction is complete, the skull can be buried; it can go to the place it belongs. There can be closure. This closure or resolution can then be the place where the beauty of nature can grow. Roses represent love, honour, faith, beauty, balance, devotion, sensuality and renewal. All these aspects of self are impacted by the Wolf and need reclaiming and restoring after leaving abuse. Put another way, leaving the abuse is necessary to allow the rebirth of what previously was open and beautiful, but not safe to show.

Vasilisa needs to leave this house of pain and leave the past behind her. This is possible when the steps have been taken to keep safe from the Wolf and kill off those destructive influences. She is ready to start again and finds a community who supports her. This is part of the healing.

Vasilisa is bored. Boredom appears when our creative self is not fulfilled. The creative self is connected to our vulnerable self, letting go, the imagination and play. Healing involves reconnecting to our interests and our creative self. Healing from abuse comes with reclaiming our identity and our unique, personal creative self.

Vasilisa asks for some flax to spin. Why flax? Vasilisa is accessing life energy (plant) and in flax, both the seed and the fibre can be used. She needs to create, to become whole. The healing process is creative and requires being with the whole. She needs to work with the whole - the seed of potential and the fibre and what appears tough - to be whole inside. We need to work with the whole on the 'outside' and experience it externally to be able to take it 'inside' (introject the positive).

The seed is the natural, creative, original form, which creates nourishment and the potential for growth. It is from returning to our essence that our growth can come. The combination of seeds: growth (linseeds) and the fibre, and the process of staying with and connecting the tough material provides extensive protection (through the fibre making clothes/roofs).

Vasilisa creates such beautiful and pure cloth. She is healing through weaving together the tough fibre and creates material that is pure and beautiful. Integration of the tough with the seed of growth is the healing process - the old pathways are taken beyond their tough place via the seeds of growth.

Vasilisa gifts the cloth to the woman to sell and keep the money. She does not need to cling or hold on to her creation. She is safe. She does not need to create a fixed ideal of what should happen. She can let it go. Creativity and gratitude is part of the healing. She honours the feminine support that has welcomed her.

In response, the feminine honours her gift and instead of going to a lesser place, she goes straight to the King. She values Vasilisa's creative self. This is the positive feminine holding, valuing, honouring and bridging the link to the embodied, positive masculine. There is no hierarchy or envy here, instead mutual respect, regardless of the fact that Vasilisa is her maid. There can be space for both to be shine.

The cloth represents the union of the seed and the toughness, creating the potential material that has the possibility to become a more sophisticated form. Her potential emotional development, connecting to her essence and sense of self are maturing and becoming more sophisticated. Vasilisa is beginning her reconnection to the positive masculine in offering the cloth to the world and the King.

The positive masculine (which can be the internal masculine aspect of the woman as well as the outer man, the King) sees and values the material for what it is. The positive masculine wants to pay for the cloth, which could take what is unfolding into an impersonal transaction. The woman trusts and takes a risk, offering to engage from a higher place and releasing Vasilisa's limited expectation. Transformation between the feminine and masculine into something beyond the two. The King, the positive masculine, responds with abundance to this request to connect from a higher place. A relationship has begun, no matter the distance.

The positive masculine wants this pure material that has been gifted from the feminine to be transformed yet again. The transformation of the cloth into an outer garment (shirt) allows a refining and deepening of using the material as fully as possible to create a suitable outer garment: the public presentation in the world. That the feminine is an integral fabric of what the masculine is. There is a desire for a right and congruent honouring to reflect how he presents himself to the world.

He can't find how he can have his creative ideal (the shirt) on his own. He needs the feminine to be involved. He needs to honour and return to the creator. The masculine needs to know that asking for help from the feminine does not demonstrate a lack, but is an honouring of the creator energy.

When he asks the old woman to make him a shirt, she is honest and not envious like the stepmother and daughters. This is part of the healing: where the feminine can allow us to shine and not rob us from what is ours.

She tells the King the creator is a maid. The Middle English meaning of *maid* is of a maiden, a virgin, a young unmarried girl. Vasilisa is at the crossroads of transforming and developing from maid to woman through her work and transformation of the seed and the fibre and her offering to release this out into the world via the healthy feminine principle.

The positive feminine (the older woman) returns to Vasilisa, as the bridge for communication between the positive masculine and Vasilisa (the maid, that which is developing). Vasilisa takes up the request. The positive masculine (internal in Vasilisa or external in a relationship) is requesting, not demanding.

Vasilisa is connecting to the positive masculine. This communication is via the woman and means communication is not immediate. There is a process – this allows Vasilisa to integrate a bit at a time. There are boundaries and distance to allow a gradual relationship as communication and interactions develop between them. This allows Vasilisa to find out more of what she needs to know before a full meeting.

She is going through her healing and development with the masculine through time. No rushing, which is what happens in abuse. Often Bluebeard's seduction imposes a flurry of intensity to 'love-bomb' her, rush and pressure her. Healthy relating allows connection, space and separation, over time.

Vasilisa embroiders and decorates the shirts with a pattern of pearls and silver threads. The word *pattern* comes from *patron*: serving as a model. So Vasilisa is imprinting in the whole a new framework and pattern.

Silver is associated with the feminine and the moon. It is also associated with purity, clarity, awareness, focus, vision, strength, persistence, single-mindedness and purpose.

Pearls are symbolic of wisdom through experience, such as the sand creating the pearl. Pearls are known for protection, purity, wealth, luck, generosity, integrity and loyalty.

Vasilisa is imprinting all the qualities of what the positive masculine needs to be able to carry through the pearls, silver and embroidery: the ability to wear the union of the masculine and the feminine.

Vasilisa waits by the window. Windows allow us to see what is going on before it comes right in our face. This is an important protective skill and way of being present, which develops from being with our instinct. She is with her embroidery, continuing to create patterns, creating her model of what needs to happen.

The positive masculine again asks, not demands – and she agrees to connect more closely. When all the steps have been set in place, there is the possibility of union of the positive masculine and the positive feminine (within oneself or in relationship with another).

This healthy union allows an inclusive relationship with instinct, as well as a relationship to the developed masculine and feminine (internally and externally), to continue.

***

The story of Vasilisa is how the underdeveloped feminine claims and develops her wise and instinctual self.

> It is about the realisation that most things are not as they seem.
>
> Clarissa Pinkola Estés, *Women who run with the Wolves*

This story is about how sometimes you need to trust your knowledge and not necessarily speak out about what you're doing next but take the actions required. Just like in abusive relationships. There's a time for questions and a time to observe. A time for action and a time to step into the unknown. A time to take and a time to receive. A time to stay and a time to leave. A time for blessings and a time to take up your ground.

Through the fairy tales we have seen the theme of unrealistic expectations and entitlement that demands obedience. We then witness Vasilisa: she who questions, observes, listens, takes and gathers. Being with unthinkable thoughts and unbearable feelings, her emotional muscle develops and integrates what was overwhelming.

This process creates a 'becoming'. What was stunted, interrupted or abandoned in our own development can now resume its natural evolution (just like the Handless Maiden) through the gathering of the instinctual self.

Through the many stories and tales, we have delved and become clear about the details in the old map – and in doing so have developed greater clarity and detail about what is needed to get to the new map, and how with support we can build a new map.

We know now that if we don't identify where we are, the task to identify how to get out or get to where we need to go is fraught with danger. If we don't identify what needs to change, what is missing and how does this inform us about what the positive ground needs to be; how can we work out the necessary steps and the right direction?

We need a map to find the way.

For a period of time before building the map or coming to the point of recognising that we need a map, we are often a combination of Little Red Riding Hood, the Ugly Duckling, Karen in the red shoes, the Handless Maiden, the one caught in Bluebeard's seduction, Cinderella, Lilith and the Little Match Girl – wandering around for a while, lost, hoping, betrayed, going through a roller coaster of challenges and hardship.

Creating a new map takes skill and awareness. We don't want to continue to pass on our blind spots and painful, limited choices and behaviour to our children, families and communities. Creating a new map is necessary for the breakdown of generalisations and both generational and intergenerational patterns of abuse.

We have lived through the pain of abuse, we have survived, and it is time to thrive.

Thriving requires closure and mapping. Moving on requires mopping up the pieces that were not resolved due to shock, overwhelm and fear. Thriving requires emotional muscle to become bigger than who we have been and what has happened. Not becoming bigger in an inflated, grandiose way or a blaming way, but through real and honest naming and deep and effective processing.

We are fortunate in these times to have access to many ways of working with trauma that go beyond insight, working to shift the cellular and neurological memory patterns within the whole mind-body system. We can work with the mind and the body, the conscious and the unconscious – drawing on the best of Western and Eastern medicine, incorporating bilateral stimulation, meridian work, alchemical trance, journaling, dream work, writing and engaging the soul and all our parts – through all these ways and more.

It is not possible to have complete closure and be fully comfortable if significant elements of the abusive experience have not been integrated. The loose livewire, has a risk of getting triggered and sending ripples all through the system and continuing to reinforce old, limited behaviours and patterns.

It is really important when being with your experience that you are open to whatever aspects need to arise, and not just the ones that you think need to be put away – so your closure can develop from your deep, wise unconscious. So what is necessary to be put away into long-term memory into the correct place comes from beyond your conscious image of what closure looks like. Then from here you can know about your past, but you are not reliving it in feelings or flashbacks and it's not driving and structuring how you trust/like yourself.

Loose wires can be risky and tricky. They can cause fires and danger if they're not addressed completely. It is important to attend to your present or past when either is calling you and become curious about what is required. It is really important to be with this task with skilled discern. At some point be mindful you don't get tricked into going backwards (working on the past); when the need is to create the new map, and the old map is only calling because there is a void with no new map or guidance on how to move forward.

Thriving means spontaneity, being relaxed, the strength and ability to take healthy risks, experimenting, self-compassion, play, trust, exploration, intimacy with oneself and others, gratitude, and having a circle of support both internally and around us.

I don't believe thriving is dependent on forgiveness. I have the view that some acts are unforgiveable. You don't have to worry about forgiveness. Instead focus on acceptance.

All you need do is allow what you have experienced to have its voice heard and needs met. Then your experience is able to be free to be present and can continue its flow and move into long-term memory. This can allow closure. Forgiveness becomes irrelevant.

If this seems a difficult concept for you to consider – that you don't need to forgive to move on – maybe ask yourself, is it your responsibility to forgive another? Or is it more your responsibility to *allow* your story to be present for you – to be able to *accept, release* and *restore* your whole self, *reclaiming* and *aligning* to your life path?

Maybe you can allow the issue of forgiveness to rest with what you believe in that is greater than you and *your task is to honour the sacred truth of you and your reality.*

When I say, 'that which is greater than', I open the space for you to explore your belief about how *you* connect to the life force that is bigger than you. This may be nature, life energy, gods and goddesses, or religious images of God.

When we look for the man-made concept of 'forgiveness' within nature, it is not even required. When there is a drought and then rain, we find the ability of the water to flow over the dry soil and rocks, seeking places to be absorbed and weaving new ways. The earth waiting and receiving what is there to be there. When a fire ravages the bush re-growth follows. New shoots come from the burning process. Nature offers us acceptance and being with the whole. Life is a process.

Just as there are many plants, all different shapes and colours – there is room for all the different parts of us. The stunted parts, the tall parts, the parts which spread and the parts which seed. All aspects and stages of our life. The cycle of nature involves animals in the broader cycle, which feed on those plants that could take over. When we stay within our nature, our natural instinct can have a response to the different parts of us and our rhythms can flow. Unlike living with the Wolf, there is permission, acceptance and space to be with the whole of who we are. Our system can move between what we give life to within us and what we need to healthily kill off that is not helping the balance within. Natural consequences and flow takes care of harmony. Man-made constructs such as forgiveness are only required when we are out of flow and seeking an external reference.

This to me is my preferred mode of being, rather than the fixed black and white concept of 'forgiveness'. Forgiveness can be seen to be part of the stories within patriarchy of power, the polarity of right and wrong, superior and inferior. How about we follow the wisdom of nature: inclusion, integration and consequences. Nature transforms, creates, destroys and carries things away.

Nature does not bother with the semantics of forgiveness. It is unnecessary. What does a focus on forgiveness keep us away from? Sometimes from emotions and responses which do not feel the way we like to view our sense of self. Forgiveness can be an avenue to avoid being with those parts of ourselves which seem like Baba Yaga or the Wolf that need relating to.

Your task is to allow your reality in, express, respond and accept. Once you have been able to be with the unbearable and unthinkable in your reality, then you can bestow any sense of a task to forgive over to that, which is greater than you. This way you do not have to sit with the wrongness and smooth it over to forgive, but instead can be with the integration of the whole: the wonderful and the terrible, without disconnecting.

If you put pressure on yourself to forgive the Wolf, are you repeating a form of abuse onto yourself with a pressure to forgive acts against you that are not acceptable? Is there a risk that forgiveness will deny the effect of the abuse on you? Are you asking yourself to jump out of your skin and understand someone's else's reality, timing or need at the expense of your own need and reality again? Is this what you want? Is this really necessary for healing and the greatest good for all?

Can you find the space to be with your reality? Through your own process of being with, expression and release, you can find your healing space and acceptance. Forgiveness then becomes irrelevant. The Wolf's acceptance of his actions is his own responsibility. Acceptance is his journey too - it is not for you to do both! Just as we discussed in the Little Match Girl, his remorse is not about you. That is his journey and not for you to take care of his healthy shame. There is no requirement for you to give something for him to process his actions.

When each owns their experience, there can be a moving on and even the evolved possibility of a different way of communicating with each other. Even if he can't own his part, as in my own journey, my acceptance did not require forgiveness for me to move on. As I was leaving, I could imagine that he would have massive shame and I felt for him to face what he had done. I could get that he preferred to maintain a place of denial than face his own shame. I felt sadness for that in him that preferred to deny rather than heal and open up possibilities of improved connections with those he 'loves'. If it was me I would prefer to walk through the pain of the shame and be burnt by it and come out transformed and proud. I would prefer to show those I 'love' I get what I did and would do whatever I could to show this through walking the talk and 'repair'

Rather than forgiveness, how about develop compassion for self in this new map – especially in regards to any patterns of repetition in returning to the Wolf, getting caught by another Wolf or for any limiting feelings and beliefs.

It is not uncommon for women to return to the abuser – to leave and come back. It is really important to remember that women are not returning to be abused. Women return with hope and idealism for the security for their children, or for the concept of family, or the concept of home. Is this indicating gaps in our society to provide community support, skills and tools to respond to the grief, loss, aloneness, financial and housing issues; as well as attend to the tending instinct stress response that may still be active? When we live in a society, which gets and supports those impacted by emotional and psychological (and physical) abuse I wonder how many women would return to the Wolf?

It may be shocking to consider that for some women, the relationship, despite being abusive, may be the most stable element in her life and actually being alone may be a more threatening, unstable and terrifying alternative. That was my reality. I have heard other women speak of the security of what is known even when it is insecure. How this feels more doable than the insecurity of the unknown. This was a reflection of my early map of relationship and home being unsafe though acting as if they were safe.

From my place now in understanding trauma and healing and how our mind-body system works, I can see my early years of fear and anxiety needed me as a young adult to enter therapy to address what was uncomfortable but 'normal' in my system. This fear and anxiety was directing my life choices. When we have a society which has the body centred skills to address our anxieties and the non shaming encouragement to enter therapy to continue ongoing life education - then our society can function with greater capacity.

If only I had had the space and support to enter therapy early on – I may have closed the door to any Wolf. If I could encourage anyone, I would say if you have anxiety address it early on through the methods I have mentioned. It is never too late, when you are engaged in the right type of therapy.

Journeying through your healing and reclaiming, the concept of forgiveness or compassion can be challenging. We can get tripped up and give ourselves a hard time for getting caught when we move through each layer of processing. This is why we need to take our time in our journey through the Little Red Riding Hood Effect.

Navigating the fairy tales in life we found our innocent and naive self alongside Little Red Riding Hood and how the Wolf came into our life. We named the abuse with Rumpelstiltskin. We have been with Bluebeard's seduction and the Ugly Duckling to explore love and belonging. In the Handless Maiden we found our family story, more about our belonging and our history, culture and religion. We faced Lilith and Cinderella and found where our anger and power lies. We moved away from the lost hope of the Little Match Girl and the Power and Control Wheel, to discover the dangerous dance of the red shoes and stress responses, and met Queen Vasilisa who has our instincts and intuition.

This is a big process and will take the time it takes. Questions, judgement, pain and a developing compassion probably surfaced through the chapters, as you began to integrate the personal details that belong to you. Taking your time with each chapter new awarenesses arose as did new concepts to be explored and responded to in the way that is needed, keeping you on track to finding and developing your new map.

Here is a poem that has helped many women through the process of change. It was read to me when I was a client in the family violence group work program and one I have often shared with clients.

Autobiography in Five Short Chapters
Chapter I
I walk down the street.
There is a deep hole in the sidewalk.
I fall in.
I am lost ... I am hopeless.
It isn't my fault.
It takes forever to find a way out.

Chapter II
I walk down the same street.
There is a deep hole in the sidewalk.
I pretend I don't see it.
I fall in again.
I can't believe I am in this same place.
But it isn't my fault.
It still takes a long time to get out.

Chapter III
I walk down the same street.
There is a deep hole in the sidewalk.
I see it there.
I still fall in ... it's a habit ... but,
my eyes are open.
I know where I am.
It is my fault.
I get out immediately.

Chapter IV
I walk down the same street.
There is a deep hole in the sidewalk.
I walk around it.

Chapter V
I walk down another street.
    Portia Nelson, There is a Hole in my Sidewalk *(1993)*

The process of change involves blindness. *We can only know what we know. Before we get to any new awareness, we are going to experience some struggle – our blind spot.* This is the dance between the conscious and unconscious. We need to face these gaps in order to sort out what is going on and discover new information, which enables us to move on. So be gentle with yourself.

I am not so keen on the word 'fault' in chapter III. I prefer saying, 'I become curious about what is still missing that led me to find myself here again'. I develop my choices and skills as I grow and learn more; and through time,

I build my emotional muscle.' How can we be at fault when the system or soil we are in has not enabled us to know more than we can know?

The recognition that our system: family/society has failed us does not need to be seen as a full-blown damning of our system. Yes, I have repeatedly said that our society is lacking in attending in a full way to trauma and to the feminine, and this has come about from a patriarchal history. However, no one person is required to carry the responsibility of society and history.

I hope I have been clear to reveal enough of the fullness of our history and how it influences us. We are part of a picture and it is not the role for anyone to carry the burden of history. Instead, each of us can become active instead of a bystander and create a ripple effect in our own community.

Fault and gaps *are* going to happen in any system; however, they are more prevalent than healthy in a patriarchal system. It is not about working to remove all fault or gaps: that would be aiming for perfection. Impossible. Vasilisa's 'good enough mother' allowed a healthy childhood and the skills to transition the challenges of life. It is about finding a 'good enough' way of responding to individuals and our community. *A 'good enough' way of being able to face, name, re-attune and repair rather than continue to collude, deny and minimise.*

'Fault' only means there is a gap in our system of something we have not been taught. Let's not get defensive or precious. We need to be responsible for ourselves in our growth and in our interactions. I don't think we need to carry 'fault' when there is a whole series of events and people that have all contributed to where we stand. So carry responsibility, as that is yours alone to carry – but fault is too big and not yours to carry. Take responsibility, learn and take action.

In creating our new map, there is a new way of looking at love, anger, power, relationships and boundaries. We are a society that has received many confusing messages and experiences through time, and it takes conversations about the uncomfortable to be able to untangle what is true and real and what is believed. I can only talk generally in a book. You are unique. Your family and history are unique. The unique strain of all that is interwoven in the fabric of your life can't be reduced to the generalisations we have explored. I have described different concepts in their pure form and yet in your personal and real life you will have your own unique combination that can't be dissected and reduced through a book, no matter how artful or complete the book can be! The book is not your story.

Why do we doubt the prevalence of abuse in relationships? Why do we still hold errors, confusion and complications between love and loving the one that hurts you? Traumatic attachment and traumatic bonding is so embedded within our society – as is the obligation to love our parents and forgive what was impactful instead of allowing the full picture. The new map is here to recognise the old map and how even while there are distortions about love, we can hold to building an inclusive new map with new boundaries.

When we can look at the myths and tricks of the old map and recognise the variations of how we ended up in these situations, then perhaps there is more permission and acceptance about the complexities of abuse. How we got caught and what our family is, will be different from another woman's experience. Just as there are many fairy tales, there are many ways of getting caught. There are themes but each woman's story and map is unique.

We have now developed the capacity to untangle neglect and abuse from the old map of 'love', either from a child-parent experience or by the Wolf. Too often children and adults mistake emotional angst and emotional pain for love. Our map of love became murky.

For some women, getting caught was the Little Red Riding Hood Effect, where there was an absence of skills and street-smart knowledge but not necessarily a terrible childhood. For other women it was the experience of the Handless Maiden's betrayal, or the rejection of the Ugly Duckling, or the experience of the charming Bluebeard.

One other murky scenario is when an adult experienced being loved as a child by parents, and the parents' relationship, communication or life conflict was hidden from the child - the adult-child's story often reveals what the child absorbed in the unconscious field from those significant challenges. We are meaning-making creatures. We need to explore beyond our own boundaries through our questions, unpack our experiences and find meaning to have closure and build new possibilities. We are more connected then we realised to those around us, our history and our ancestors.

I was one (strong, secure, sure of myself) person to the rest of the world, but so emotionally torn down and used/manipulated/destroyed by the abuser that I couldn't make a move. The "successful woman" stuff was just an act, and he made sure I knew it on every level, every day, every minute, every second ...

Because I was convinced I couldn't HAVE a relationship – with anyone. That the reason I was being beaten and abused was because, I **deserved** no better ... in my experience, I was never raised this way nor saw a man abuse a woman like I was abused. I was naive, I trusted people and I had terrible self-image, and I had been picked on by other kids for years; I was unsure of myself, scared, and ripe for the picking by a psychopath or two.

Plus, I hid it well from friends and family – I made up stories to explain away broken noses, bashed in faces, stitches, black eyes; I was the most accident prone person on the planet ... I was basically brainwashed into believing that I deserved no better, via emotional abuse and basically (emotional) torture.[9]

Find your fairy tale and know your old map.

As we explore our new map, I want to share a few maps and models to assist your journey in creating your new map. First, we need to acknowledge the shared, deep and intrinsic needs that are our basic foundation.

Fairy tales are one type of story. Here is another type of story, a map to understand layers of the self. Take what feels meaningful for you and leave the rest.

---

9. Posted on 'Why women return to emotional relationships', The Straight Dope, http://boards.straightdope.com/sdmb/showthread.php?t=215877

Maslow's Hierarchy of Needs

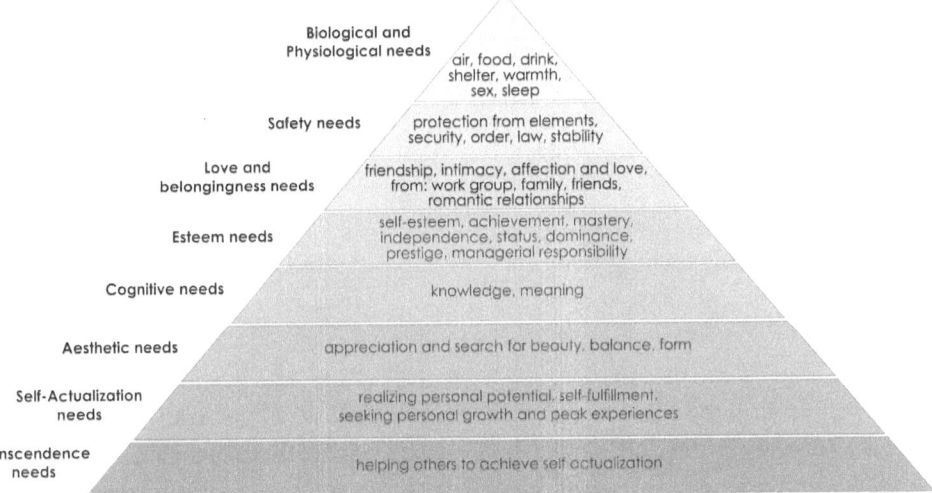

Maslow's Hierarchy of Needs

Each layer represents essential, basic needs and our intrinsic, human motivations that all go beyond reward or unconscious desire, and are required for our growth and development into being a full and fulfilled person.

Each layer in Maslow's Hierarchy can either be experienced as a deficiency of that need or the positive experience of that need. To have the motivation and capacity to obtain our higher levels of need (and moving towards the top of the triangle), the lower layer needs are required to have a 'good enough' fulfilment. People often expect to work with the 4th level or maybe the 5th level, when maybe the 1st and the 2nd level are actually not stable and solidly available to support them.

Become curious of which layer you need to build or strengthen. This map can help you understand if one layer is a challenge; perhaps there is a layer beneath it that is not secure enough and will enable greater ease in stepping into the next layer.

1. Biological and physiological needs: breathing, food, drink, shelter, warmth, sex, sleep, excretion.
2. Safety needs: physical safety, protection from elements, security, economic, social, psychological, vocational, order, law, stability.

3. Love and belonging needs: friendship, intimacy, affection and love (from family, friends, romantic relationships, work group).
4. Esteem needs: self-esteem, achievement, mastery, independence, status, dominance, prestige, managerial responsibility.
5. Cognitive needs: knowledge, meaning.
6. Aesthetic needs: appreciation and search for beauty, balance, form, etc.
7. Self-Actualisation needs: realising personal potential, self-fulfilment, seeking personal growth and peak experiences.
8. Transcendence needs: helping others to achieve self-actualisation.

Maslow expanded his original five-stage model to include the three needs included as shown; cognitive and aesthetic needs and later transcendence needs. Cognitive need became integral to include because humans are meaning making creatures and true meaning is vital to integrate our reality and live our truth.[10] Victor Frankl explores the necessity for us to find meaning in his book, *Man's Search for Meaning*.

From my perspective, aesthetic needs are also an essential addition; because our soul needs beauty, in whatever form beauty appears for us. The outer is an expression of the inner. When we did not live in boxes and move about in boxes we were closer to nature. We had access to aesthetic need just as simply as breathing the air, seeing the trees, sunsets and all that surrounds us in our sleeping and waking life and as we moved through our day. Our need for beauty was fulfilled without effort. It is only in living a modern lifestyle, where we are so removed from beauty and filled with artificial materials, surfaces and toxins with regulated air, instead of the way nature intended, that it becomes apparent how necessary these needs are. Theodore Roszak, explores ecopsychology, the connection between being human, our soul, nature and the planet, in his book *The Voice of the Earth* 2001 2nd edition. Katy Bowman explores our intrinsic needs being human and about our community in *Movement Matters* 2016.

Maslow studied eighteen people whom he identified to be self-actualised (Abraham Lincoln and Albert Einstein were amongst this group). There is some question to the validity of these characteristics as embodying the concept of self-actualisation, as the original study was just with white men; but I still think the qualities are a good starting point. These concepts are

---

10. For a summation of Maslow's theories refer to (McLeod 2016) in 'References and Further Reading'.

interesting to consider in developing our healthy sense of self, developing desired capacities and skills and perhaps provide more clues on the healthy person in the context of healthy love. Maslow identified fifteen characteristics of a self-actualised person:

1. They perceive reality efficiently and can tolerate uncertainty;
2. Accept themselves and others for what they are;
3. Spontaneous in thought and action;
4. Problem-centred (not self-centred);
5. Unusual sense of humour;
6. Able to look at life objectively;
7. Highly creative;
8. Resistant to enculturation, but not purposely unconventional;
9. Concerned for the welfare of humanity;
10. Capable of deep appreciation of basic life-experience;
11. Establishes deep satisfying interpersonal relationships with a few people;
12. Peak experiences;
13. Need for privacy;
14. Democratic attitudes;
15. Strong moral/ethical standards.

Behaviour leading to self-actualisation:

- Experiencing life like a child, with full absorption and concentration;
- Trying new things instead of sticking to safe paths;
- Listening to your own feelings in evaluating experiences instead of the voice of tradition, authority or the majority;
- Avoiding pretence ('game playing') and being honest;
- Being prepared to be unpopular if your views do not coincide with those of the majority;
- Taking responsibility and working hard;
- Trying to identify your defences and having the courage to give them up.

This list of behaviours can be very helpful in building your skills, behaviours and beliefs in your new map. What do you want to have greater access to? How can you practice and experiment? Who can you surround yourself with who models this and celebrates you?

> Although people achieve self-actualization in their own unique way, they tend to share certain characteristics. However, self-actualization is a matter of degree, 'There are no perfect human beings'
> [Maslow]. (McLeod 2016)

Instead of perfection, Maslow saw self-actualisation as living your potential; nor are you required to inhabit all fifteen characteristics. People can demonstrate some of these characteristics and not be self-actualised. So you can be self-actualised and be inconsiderate, foolish, egotistical, wasteful or reckless.

Tay and Diener (2011) wanted to test Maslow's theory. Between 2005 and 2010 they surveyed and then analysed the data of 60,865 participants from 123 countries. Their research represented every major region of the world. They found despite cultural differences there were universal human needs throughout the world. They did, however, identify that you did not need the basic needs to be happy, as there are many poor people who are happy; so they determined that the order of the needs within Maslow's hierarchy was not correct.

I am all for *all* women having financial and physical security and a society which protects and provides all people to have safety, power and the right to their living, safety and financial freedom; however this data is interesting to consider regarding women not leaving due to financial constraints.

> 'Although the most basic needs might get the most attention when you don't have them,' Diener explains, 'you don't need to fulfill them in order to get benefits [from the others]. 'Even when we are hungry, for instance, we can be happy with our friends. They're like vitamins,' Diener says about how the needs work independently. 'We need them all.' (McLeod 2016)

In our journey to honour and protect our needs and possibly

develop self-actualisation, let's make sure we don't end up in a Drama Triangle! We have studied the Wheel of Power and Control. Here is another version of mapping abuse or toxic dynamics. This time it reveals more about the unhealthy habitual way of relating pattern we can get caught inside in work, family and other relationships.

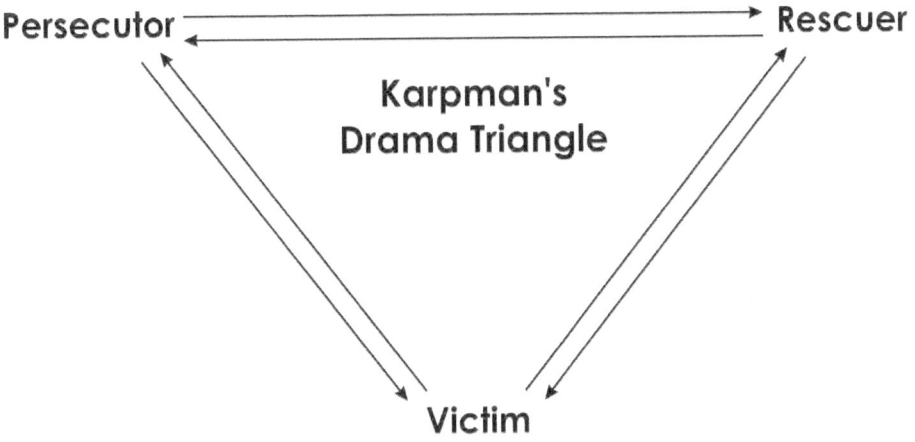

Diagram courtesy of Stephen B. Karpman, M.D

None of these roles are fixed. One person can move between the three positions, but we tend to have a dominant position. This pattern of behaviour will continue when we move around this triangle or remain in one these positions. Dr Stephan Karpman created the Drama Triangle.

These three positions occur because there is a split or a dissociation in the people involved, due to overwhelm, disconnection and lack of support to develop constructive skills.

Persecutor: I'm okay, you're not okay

- Needs someone to blame to elevate themselves
- Bully
- Dominant
- Critical
- Puts other down
- Resentful

- Aggressive anger
- Passive-aggressive anger
- Controlling
- Righteous
- Grandiose
- Inflexible
- Accusatory
- No response-ability
- Requires someone to project onto

Rescuer: You're not okay and I can help

- Needs to be needed
- 'Helps' even when doesn't want to
- Support
- 'Nice'
- Guilt
- Believes they have no choice
- Discounts the autonomy of the victim
- Caretaker – in order to feel needed and capable
- Denies their own feelings, situation, anxiety
- Rescuing keeps the other two fixed in their roles
- Denial/Fear that others can't change, so has to take over
- Uncomfortable with conflict or opposition
- Over-responsible
- Overwhelmed or numb
- Fear of abandonment and loss of connection
- 'Feeling needed' gives a sense of connection

Victim: I'm not okay, you're okay

- Needs to do something but is immobilised
- Discounts self
- Difficulty thinking and feeling at the same time
- Seeking other/s to be responsible

- Can feel a safety in not taking action
- Too flexible or adaptive to other
- Powerless
- Helpless
- Misunderstood
- Incapable
- Oppressed
- Shame
- Anxious
- Passive
- Fear of upsetting other
- Difficulty in changing or seeking skills and support to solve problems
- Displaced self-soothing by receiving pity or help
- Receptacle of the persecutor's anger
- Dependent on rescuer to validate their feelings or comfort them
- Fear of being alone
- Habituated difficulty to initiate (due to fear, lack of skill or secondary gain)

We need an alternative to staying in the old map, swinging between intensity, chaos and helplessness. We need to find a better map, so we don't loop back into the habituated roles of the Drama Triangle. The only alternative is to leave this triangle and move into a different style of relating.

One alternative is the Winner's Triangle, of which I adapted to create my own version. Acey Choy is sited as a major source for the Winner's Triangle, however she does not claim to create the triangle and does not know who did.

The Winner's Triangle suggests that the Persecutor needs to become Assertive; the Rescuer to become Caring; and the Victim to be Vulnerable.

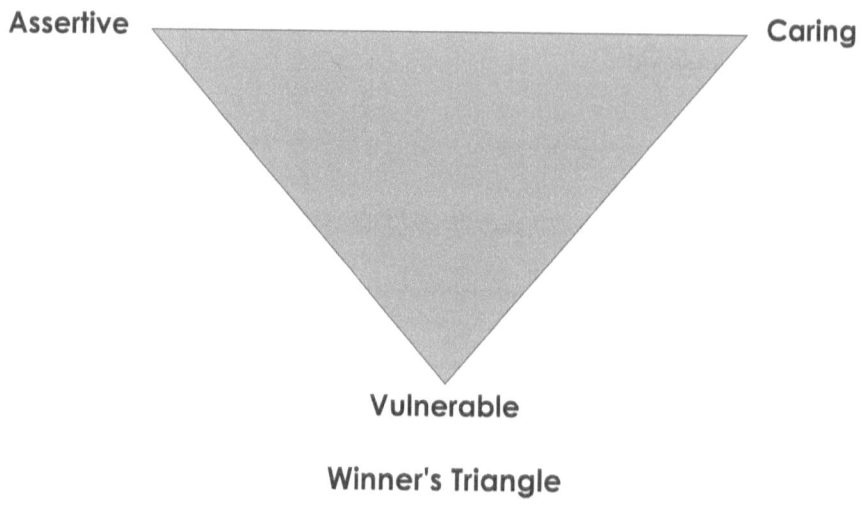

Winner's Triangle

That doesn't work for me. When I think about the three positions in the Drama Triangle, each of the three positions all need to access Assertion, Care and Vulnerability. To split them into three alternative choices is not the healthy response because we need assertion connected to care and vulnerability. For the health of response-ability, we need to be able to move fluidly between the three skills and be flexibly responsive in the context of the immediate moment.

So I chose a circle, as I could not relate to a triangle – a triangle seems to perpetuate 'this or that' split off, left brain limited, patriarchal, black and white style of thinking, rather than the feminine 'this and that'. I believe the title 'Winner' is embedded in a dominant-dominated mindset of winners and losers, persecutors and victims. We need to get out of this paradigm. It is not helpful for anyone. Communication, interaction and engagement is not about winners and losers, but that each person in the drama triangle is able to have their appropriate response to their position in the situation and to the context of other. This required response is not one-sided, but a fully embodied response between self and other; as compared to the split one-sided response of the Drama Triangle. I adapted the triangle into my Circle of Response-ability.

Circle of Response-ability

In each of the three Drama Positions, there is an interruption to the natural flow of the instinctual and appropriate response, whereas in my Circle of Response-ability there is room for a flexible responsiveness to incorporate all of what is required.

When we fall out of the Circle of Response-ability we can become compassionate and curious as to where our tendency to habituate falls within the Drama Triangle. We are gathering information. We can become clearer in identifying what skills and responses are missing from our healthy position, what triggered us or what accumulated that meant we had less energy to respond optimally. We can become curious to observe others and notice how they maintain boundaries and do not enter into the Victim/Rescuer paradigm and how they navigate the Persecutor. There is more information. Over time, through a greater awareness we gradually feel the discomfort and less room to move when we stay in the Drama Triangle. Without even realising we find we are creating and learning more ways to stay in the Circle of Response-ability.

The Circle of Response-ability, through its inclusiveness, enables a flexibility for the individual focus on whatever aspect is most relevant that is missing in their particular situation, relationship and context whilst still remaining connected to all resources within the self.

The Rescuer then has the opportunity to be Assertively Responsible – to know their own boundaries and listen to their vulnerability and self-care, as well as care for others and choose how to support or guide. Developing emotional muscle to not jump in and using emotional muscle to self soothe. The Victim has the opportunity to become Assertive and Response-able. Vulnerable to seek support to develop problem-solving skills, and direct care towards seeking appropriate social connection and using self-soothing skills in taking risks and stepping out of their comfort zone. The Persecutor needs to be with their vulnerable self and learn self-soothing skills to step out of their comfort zone and consider others and come to terms with uncertainty and not being the centre. Through care for self the Persecutor can know they exist and are important even when they are not directing everything and build emotional muscle to feel shame, repair and bear the unknown and uncertainty. In this way assertion can come with care and healthy pride.

To develop our new map, we need to know where we habitually get caught and develop and define the new characteristics we want. This clarity helps us to recognise if we have the skills, or if there are some skills we need support to develop, so we can step into our new map.

Where do you locate yourself?

When we develop our new map and these new healthy behaviours, we need to have a place for all our feelings and the instinctual behaviours that extend on from our feelings.

We know abuse is a context where feelings and behaviours are denied by both the Wolf, Little Red Riding Hood and by society turning a blind eye and not taking it seriously. Through the exploration of each chapter and the fairy tales, we recognise the truth that our feelings inform and give us value of our experience. However, we also know that some feelings can feel challenging to be with. It is valuable to have a map to understand where we may get tripped up. Which feelings we are comfortable to be with and act on and which we are not.

Malan's Triangle of Conflict

Anyone who has lived with abuse, overwhelm or stress has entered this Triangle of Conflict; so that is each and every one of us! This triangle is essential to understand in order to *develop* an ease of response rather than use force, positive thinking, willpower or regressive behaviours to regulate involuntary feelings and responses. This triangle helps guide the way to open up generative feelings, capabilities and behaviours.

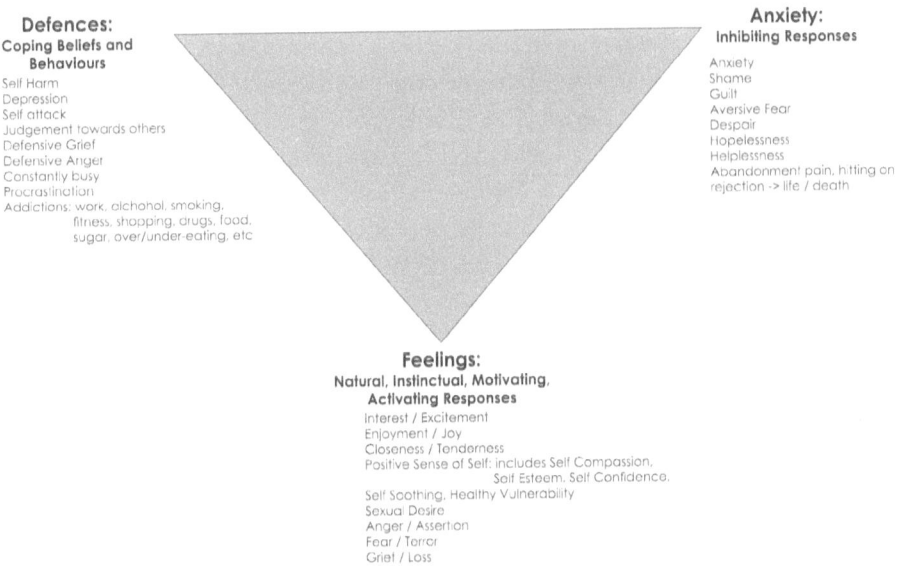

Adapted from Malan's Triangle of Conflict

This triangle highlights what happens when we have not been supported to connect to and express our natural feelings. The 'F' pole is our Feeling pole and shows us what needs to be available in our healthy, whole self-map. Feelings are necessary because it is through their activation that we become mobilised to the relevant behaviour and have the potential to develop our skills and healthy responses.

Feelings motivate behaviours, and if we don't have access to our feelings then our behaviours are inhibited. This is relevant whether we are a Wolf, a woman caught in abuse or a member of society – we all need access to our feelings to mobilise the relevant behaviours to develop healthy, sustainable interactions.

The 'A' pole is our Anxiety pole and is what involuntarily gets activated when it is not okay for us to express and connect to our 'F' pole. The 'A' pole is the inhibitor to shut us down, because it is not safe to feel what is naturally called for on the 'F' pole, or we don't have the skills to be with one or more of the feelings of the 'F' pole. So on one hand the 'A' pole protect us from the overwhelm, but on the other hand they limit us from our full expression. The 'A' pole is activated to disconnect us from unbearable feelings, unthinkable thoughts, emotional pain and unresolved memories.

This is the key to healing: resolve the 'A' pole's unbearable and unthinkable material and the 'D' pole won't have to come and rescue. Then there will be room to explore and develop the skills, and emotional muscle to be with what we have not been able to safely access in the 'F' pole that we can finally reclaim.

When the 'A' pole gets activated to a certain level, our system cannot tolerate this and because we don't have the option of going to the 'F' pole, the 'D' pole gets involuntarily activated. The 'D' pole is our Defence pole; it keeps us away from the 'A' pole and what is unbearable there. It also does the job of stopping us from feeling and revealing what has been deemed unacceptable or threatening to be with on the 'F' pole. We all have a great range of 'D' pole beliefs and behaviours that control and manage the uncomfortable. These are the best (or only) way we have learnt to cope against the anxiety of not being with certain feeling, instinctual functions.

'D' Pole – Defence

- Addictions (work, alcohol, drugs, fitness, food, image, shopping, sugar, smoking, etc)
- Self-harm
- Depression
- Self-attack/Inner critic
- Judgement towards others
- Defensive anger
- Defensive grief
- Defensive humour
- Constantly busy
- Procrastination

- Self-sabotage
- Day dreaming that doesn't feel constructive or good

'A' Pole – Anxiety

- Inhibits us, shuts us down from the unbearable feelings and unthinkable thoughts that are associated with split-off, unresolved memories of emotional pain. These inhibitors arise involuntarily when we are not able to access the necessary 'F' pole expression in a situation.
- Anxiety
- Shame
- Guilt
- Aversive fear (shuts us down)
- Despair
- Hopelessness
- Helplessness
- Abandonment (abyss, early developmental trauma feeling/sense potential of death)
- Anti-libidinal energy can be located near the 'A' pole and be experienced as the introjected negative mother, father or another figure who threatens any generative response.

'F' Pole – Feeling

- These are our natural, instinctual, motivating responses that are in context to a given situation. When we have not received permission to express our natural instinctual response, the associated feelings and behaviours are disconnected via the 'A' pole: anxiety that interrupts and inhibits this natural flow. These feelings inform and *give value to our experience* and it is this life energy that then mobilises us into a behaviour. Without access to all our 'F' pole functions we are at risk of anxiety and then over time when unresolved, depression.
- Interest/excitement
- Enjoyment/joy
- Tenderness/closeness
- Positive sense of self (includes self-compassion, healthy vulnerability, self-soothing, self-confidence and self-esteem)

- Sexual desire
- Anger/assertion
- Fear/terror
- Grief/loss

Translating into real life, when our environment does not allow us to have our natural flow and our contextual expression of feelings, ('F' pole) thoughts and behaviours; when our situation is calling for a feeling we are not supported to have and we don't have a way to express it, then those responses shut down. This involuntary shutdown ('A' pole) occurs because there is a threat, punishment, shame, rejection, abandonment (of any form), or a significant person could 'fall to pieces' (or already has) if we express ourselves – all of which involuntarily override our safety to express ourselves.

When that feeling in the 'F' pole is interrupted, we are going to feel uncomfortable because our experience and expression is in limbo. We feel and *are* incomplete. We are left experiencing some emotional pain due to the conflict in not being able to be with our flow of feeling, so when our system activates 'A' pole inhibitors to shut us down and keep away what has been deemed unacceptable in the 'F' pole, we can't feel okay because a part of us is being denied.

We also feel uncomfortable because if we relax and show one feeling in the 'F' pole, something forbidden may come out in the spontaneity of the moment. So our system may hover with some 'A' pole to inhibit all our feelings to some degree.

We also hold conflict to feel fully comfortable or confident because we often experience a group of feelings together rather than all the feelings being separate, e.g. closeness and joy or anger, grief and closeness. So one denied feeling may impact a few experiences when our system become vigilant within certain feelings inside the range of feelings being accessed in our day. This is impactful, particularly as feelings carry important information to help us move forward. We are in a state of limbo when they are inhibited.

We often swing between the 'D' and 'A' poles in response to the level of stress and anxiety because we don't have the skills or capacity to respond fully to the 'A' pole or the permission to drop into the 'F' pole and resolve our incomplete experience. This swinging between the 'A' and 'D' poles increases stress, and is depleting and soul destroying. Extended experiences of the 'A' and 'D' pole process can lead to depression, low self-esteem and ill health.

People get caught by the intensity of the 'D' and try to address what is there instead of realising they have colluded with the 'A' pole – which does not want you near it as it holds the most unbearable and unthinkable material. You may feel you are getting somewhere on the 'D' pole and then there's an 'A' pole trigger and you feel despair and hopelessness about the 'relapse' and 'looping' back. In fact, you need to attend to the 'A' pole material combined with appropriate body centred self-soothing so the anxiety can reduce to a far lower level or dissolve, either way not triggering the 'D' pole. We can then have the space to take risks, connect and develop the skills and expression when out of our comfort zone whilst in the 'F' pole.

When the 'A' pole is addressed, we won't be experiencing the 'D' pole, or to such a milder degree that we have energy to respond from our 'F' pole: self-soothing and sorting and turning down the other street on the road and not falling into that hole again.

We can try to 'fix' the 'D' pole and it can seem better, but the 'D' pole will automatically get reactivated when the 'A' pole is activated to a certain level. This can increase the stress and self-attack at the 'D' pole and swing even further between the emotional pain of the 'A' pole and the harsh punishments of the 'D' pole. We can mis-attribute that our capacity is faulty when in fact the healing process in not addressing trauma, the body, the unconscious and the Defence triangle is the one which is faulty.

So start to recognise your pattern and what gets triggered for you on each of the poles. Then develop new ways of being with the 'A' pole to integrate and metabolise what is unbearable. This integration then means that there will be less anxiety in your system and you will be more relaxed to then explore what needs to be developed on the 'F' pole, instead of swinging back and forth between the 'A' and 'D' poles.

***

Having a new map does not mean there is no bad stuff or challenges. It just means our new map has effective and supportive ways of being able to be with the uncomfortable.

The benefit of the new map with real tools is we can feel resourced to handle and respond to anything! We relax, have improved health, increased self-confidence, greater intimacy – as well as being open to a broad range of opportunities and adventures!

All these new maps are informative and useful and they do not replace the vital need to develop emotional tools that attend to the mind and the body. This cannot be taught in a book. This work needs to be done through personal connection with a skilled and professional person. Someone who can bear more than what you can bear, otherwise the 'therapist' will collude with you in avoiding uncomfortable places and just staying talking 'about' things. Therapy needs to be experiential.

It is important to recognise that on our new map, we all need to receive support to be able to be with challenging and uncomfortable experiences that we have been disconnected from.

There may be some pieces you feel are just too much or that you consciously don't know about, or your system is protecting you from being aware of them. Skilled support can increase your emotional muscle and your sense of awareness. It is amazing what can arise in a safe and skilled environment, without you even making it happen on a conscious level.

Sometimes it is the external container that develops from the closeness and trust in the relationship with the therapist, that brings about the development of our internal container to bear the fullness of our affect. When our unbearable feelings and unthinkable thoughts are seen, heard and witnessed without judgement and with compassion it can be enough to support the flow and repair.

Sometimes it can feel like there is just too much that has happened for too long. We need strong, effective, gentle ways of containing and being with the kinds of experiences, feelings and thoughts that would want to tell us, 'There's no point talking about this', 'There's no point trying to change things', 'I can't change the past and I can't change me', 'This is the way I've been', 'It's just all too hard.'

Make sure your new map has support, and ways to be with the challenging times when we will want to collapse, disconnect or deny. We all have those times of wanting to bury our head in the sand.

I also find creating a new map, with that right support and guidance, is an easier and richer process when I can reach out and discover stories, music, artwork and poetry that speak to the struggles in my soul. When I connect to these creative messages and forms, I feel a deep support from those who have journeyed before me and those who are journeying alongside me. I am not alone. I can rest in their expression, my soul fed and nourished. They give the empty or collapsed part of me something to draw from. I have sustenance to drink from as I navigate my new territory.

The Journey
Above the mountains
the geese turn into
the light again

Painting their
black silhouettes
on an open sky.

Sometimes everything
has to be
inscribed across
the heavens

so you can find
the one line
already written
inside you.

Sometimes it takes
a great sky
to find that

first, bright
and indescribable
wedge of freedom
in your own heart.

Sometimes with
the bones of the black
sticks left when the fire
has gone out

someone has written
something new
in the ashes
of your life.

You are not leaving.
Even as the light
fades quickly now,
you are arriving.
　　David Whyte, *The House of Belonging*

Over time, creating a new map can become richer and easier to sustain then the old map. The old map is pretty exhausting and soul-destroying. When I connect to nature, art forms and poems, I find support for my values and my deep needs. They provide compassion and understanding, offering me prayers and honouring to support and protect me as I start a new chapter. These creative expressions cradle my naive self and offer ingredients to create sacred containers and meaningful rituals about changes and stages. They enable me to come out of my shell and walk barefoot in the sunlight, connecting to the positive life energy of the world. All these ways of poetry, rituals and nature helped contain me, despite going through such a scary, seemingly endless time of suffering.

My new map gave me the stepping-stones to create the life I want. This involved planning, reflecting, questioning, sorting, releasing and gathering what I preferred and what I needed. The new map was all about me. For the first time in my life there was place and space for me in the centre.

It is important to examine any limiting beliefs you have about making *you* the centre of your life. You may have a fear that this will lead you to become arrogant, selfish and egotistical. Can you imagine becoming the centre of your world and being kind, brave, ferociously and courageously guarding your heart and soul's wellbeing?

My map involved identifying and naming in the first person and present tense specific, realistic, concrete descriptions I wanted to embody; encompassing my feelings, thoughts, beliefs, attitudes, bodily sensations, expressions of my identity and values, reflections about how I wanted my relationships and social interactions to be. I included what needed to be different in my rhythms and lifestyle, environment, health routines and health concerns – and in how I wanted to respond to stress. I described the qualities, skills and resources I wanted and needed to protect and support me in my desired experience of flow and being secure in myself and in the world.

***

The process of creating rituals and creative resources (such as with poetry, art, music, candles, etc) can be a significant part of keeping you in your new map and out of the old map. It may be hard to imagine how protective these practices can be. Experiment and find out for yourself!

Knowledge of the study of epigenetics also helps reassure the possibility of change through the new map. Epigenetics shows us that nature is more powerful than genes. Genes are not automatically switched on to a predetermined single alternative. Genes get switched on dependent of the environment. Our environment determines what parts of our genes gets switched on and what parts of our genes don't get switched on. *You have the power to change your environment.*

We may be limited by our imprint, but there are alternatives and choices. It is not the end of the road. You can create a better future.

Remember about our amazing neural pathways – their plasticity and how they continue growing. How disconnection happens in the brain due to overwhelm and this interruption creates trauma: an unresolved chink in our system that is trying in the most artful and creative way it can to stay functional through those habituated limiting beliefs, patterns and behaviours. Our system is incredible. It gets us through until we have the blessing to find new information to transform our life. Appreciate the incredible tenacity and artful ways your system has creatively enabled you to get through so much.

There is new information that keeps us safe and equips us with resources to engage beyond rational and positive thinking. True healing can take place. I am proof of this. My clients are too. If you had seen me as a child or young adult you would not believe I am the same person. I remember sitting in the library at primary school in our class and being so absorbed with tapping my head and watching the dandruff fall on my page. I was in a memorised trance as I kept tapping away. I was so used to being invisible and no one connecting to me. I was in my own world. I can only imagine some of the children would have seen me and wonder what they would have thought of me ... This is another world from where I am now.

There is a way of being with the old map *and* the new map that allows the incomplete to get back on track from that interruption and continue down those neural pathways, towards their appropriate and healthy completion points – so we can resume living and stop surviving!

Afterword

Sometimes rejection, cruelty and harshness leave us with a sense of being broken and defective. Often there can be a terrifying sense that no one will love us and that we're damaged and a mess.

When we journey through healing this damaged sense of self can come up and we can feel as if we are on the edge of madness or death and there is nowhere to turn. It can feel like this is just what you should expect and this is what normal is. Often the inner protector stirs us into this experience when we are at a new threshold, setting an internal alarm as if there is a threat on our life and we will die. This is our dear, primitive, inner protector doing its best, as it does not know how to protect us in this new place where we are healing. The internal protector only has the old ways. It will want to pull us back into its familiar comfort zone and away from this threshold.

At these times the therapeutic resources I use and teach my clients to process and metabolise these unbearable moments can become a magic balm for the soul. At these times, I also like to think of those stories, music, poems or positive experiences in the world and in history that are greater than me and my story. Along with my resources, I use these nourishing experiences that are bigger than me to hold and contain me. They become my safety net, when I feel there's nothing in front of me that can take me forward.

Have you heard about the Japanese practice of *kintsugi*? When objects of pottery were broken, they would fill the cracks with gold; their belief was that when something is broken, there's a history in that and it becomes more precious and beautiful for having been broken.

When we're feeling unlovable and damaged, the first step is to take the time to love yourself enough, before wanting others to love you. Reading this book is an act of loving yourself and becoming more aware. Reaching out for help is another first step. So is eating when you are hungry, sleeping when you are tired, going to the toilet when you need to, massaging your body with oil, drinking water when you are thirsty …

There are many graduated ways to build up to loving yourself. Get to know yourself through journaling and giving form with crayons – prioritising psychotherapy and counselling are acts of love. Singing, dancing, being in nature, following a passion or interest are all healing practices.

Remember, creating the map and fulfilling your hierarchy of needs takes a lifetime, as it's an ongoing practice rather than a destination. We are always evolving and changing, affected by and affecting our environment. We will always have needs – that means we are alive! So be kind and gentle to yourself. We will always have an unconscious so there will always be something wanting to birth into consciousness to bring you back to you. There will always be adjustments to make when new information and new skills take you further. There is only one of you in the world and there will never be another one like you. We only don't have needs when we have died. So appreciate your full-bodied, pulsing, desiring self.

With this new map, we have the capacity to look at the Triangle of Defences and discover more about our survival patterns and what they're defending us from: those deep, unbearable and unthinkable feelings or thoughts. Then there can be more space to build, to move from that Drama Triangle into the Circle of Responsibility and open up genuine, embodied, experiences of self-love. So you don't just know it, but you feel it in every cell of your body and have access and expression to all of your natural 'F' pole feelings.

I don't know if you've heard of the book *When I Loved Myself Enough*, by Kim McMillan. It's a very simple but moving book, where on each page she writes down another way of accepting herself in a loving and gentle way. Such as, 'When I loved myself enough, I began leaving whatever wasn't healthy. This meant people, jobs, my own beliefs and habits, anything that kept me small.' Or, 'When I loved myself enough, I no longer needed things or people to make me feel safe.'

When we love ourselves enough, we can take the necessary actions rather than wait and hope.

You might want to explore writing your own quotes of when you love yourself enough and create a little book for yourself in those challenging moments. This can be a powerful, transformative and deeply supportive process of writing down your own vows and promises that you can hold to – not in a state of perfection, but as a practice to return to again and again.

The pilot flying the plane does not control the plane to fly on a rigid line. The control panel lets the pilot know when the plane is veering too far in either direction so the pilot can make an adjustment and stay on course. You don't have to be exact. Life will give you signals to keep making those daily adjustments. After all, isn't that what life is: daily adjustments to what we want to be moving towards?

When you were reading about Maslow's Hierarchy or the Circle of Response-ability, some of you may have felt, 'I don't know people like that. Where would I find them? They're only in movies and books and diagrams …›

I know for me it felt like I was in a desert and there weren't any people like this in my life. It felt like there was no sustenance around. Start looking for people. As Little Red Riding Hood, we can lose sight that we can close and open the door to who we let on our path. But it takes practice and getting out there. Some people I met for a brief time and some became friends, but each person helped me become confident to interact with and find more people who I wanted to surround myself with.

From the busker on the street who encouraged my love for singing to the man serving me in the Adelaide Scout Outdoor Store. Who would have thought I would end up driving to Uluru and eating witchetty grubs with the guy who served me at the Outdoor Store and later a trek in Nepal? There are so many possibilities of meeting caring, genuine people. Start looking for where and how in your life. Take some healthy risks.

One of the awful things about living with deprivation in your life is that often you can so appreciate the tiniest morsel and not expect more. This can be dangerous when you're involved with someone who is abusive. You make too much out of the little good things.

The silver lining from this cloud was that though I have appreciated the crumbs (and didn't ask for enough), it also meant when I was going through my really tough time, it didn't take much to make my day better …

someone in the street, the man working at the train station, someone in a shop – anyone who was friendly, helpful and treated me like a decent person really made a difference.

Start to pay attention to who in your day is looking at *you*. Whose words or smile are really being offered as encouragement. Someone may give you a compliment and you might be in the habit of wanting to minimise it or push it back; start to open yourself up to be able to receive. Start to pay attention to those good experiences in your day, no matter how small or brief they are.

Whenever you pay attention to something, you start to notice more of that in your life. It's a bit like when you go into the supermarket: if you're not looking for a particular item on the shelf you don't see it, but if you go into the supermarket and you've got a particular item in your mind's eye, you'll notice it. Start to experiment with noticing the small interactions with people who are kind, and start to consider how you can open up more opportunities for kind people to come into your life.

It might begin with a skilled and caring professional therapist or mentor, or being in a self-interest/hobby group, family violence group or self-development group. There are many low cost services and many choices available. Sometimes that person who is positive and capable comes in the form of a therapist, and at other points in your life it may be elsewhere. Receive them all!

Don't give up. No matter what your circumstances want to tell you.

I saw a variety of low cost counsellors. I fortunately didn't have to really pay much at all and each helped me get to the next stage, even if they initially weren't helpful. It was the process of seeing each one that finally led me to someone who could help me. If I had stopped the process, I would not have found the counsellor I needed to get me through.

It took me a while to find someone who could help me. Each person I saw was an act of love by me to me, saying I'm important and I will do whatever is necessary, without giving up. Not that I thought of it that way back then.

I then went to counselling at the community counselling agency but when I became a volunteer at the agency and still needed to continue therapy, I had to find someone outside the centre. I was recommended a therapist and I had to pay full price. Even though the past counsellors had all been caring people, they weren't able to tell me anything beyond what I already knew.

I had two children; I had no assistance, minimal child support, and a lot of expenses with travelling around to legal and counselling appointments, on a very low income and on public transport. I sold what I had; I lived very frugally. I saw therapy as my 'freedom' investment for all three of us. Working on my internal freedom modelled to my children more than I realised at the time. When I look at my children and myself now, I don't think anyone would pick what our past was. I put this down to good therapy.

Somehow I was able to pay for the therapy, and I managed to keep upgrading the place we were renting so that it could be a bit bigger, a bit more spacious to take some pressure off the intensity of what was happening in the small spaced interactions in our home. Even though I could not work during the first seven years of court and then after university, I only worked part time in school hours so that I could be there for the girls. Somehow things worked out that I could keep affording the school and home expenses.

Prioritising therapy (and my girls) was a lifesaver and important in the long term, not only for me but for how I could be for my children. I could not have given what my girls needed if I had not made me, to some degree, the centre of my world.

When you keep taking those steps, things work out. But the steps need to be generative and supportive. My children benefitted by me putting that money into me. I was a better parent for them, and I had more strength and capacity by being there for them by taking the time and the money to strengthen my sense of self.

They didn't miss out – they had toys, books, games and I found many free activities they could enjoy as well as playing with their friends. I became creative holding toy parties so I could receive toys for my children. There are many possibilities when you don't give up. Though we couldn't have holidays. I wish now my fear of the world had not robbed us of that - though poor we could have gone to a camping ground for a holiday.

Here are some tips for finding the right counsellor for you:

I would say it's really important to interview three different therapists and ask them questions; work out how much experience they have working with someone who has lived with abuse. Do they have specific body-based trauma training, and what their orientation is towards working that way. Just ask anything that can get the conversation going, so that you can hear a bit about their approach, their experience and also their personality, because that is a huge factor in being able to do the necessary and important work that's involved.

It's really important that you feel a connection – that you feel like they get you – and you like them; and that you feel comfortable with their personality, given sharing your story is such a vulnerable process. The therapy process requires trust and healthy risks.

Interview them. You are important. Yours story is important. If you don't have a sense of shifts happening after a few sessions maybe they don't the skills. Don't get caught by staying with someone who is 'nice' - they need to be effective too. Pluck up the courage in therapy to say when you feel they are not getting you. Speak up about your concerns.

***

You've been exposed to a lot of new information through this journey with me. I invite you to allow the seeds and the confusion to grow in the fertile soil of your mind, body and soul, without working too hard in any of the usual ways.

Take small steps. Perhaps you can write down what you want over the next day, month or year – and one step you can take today, without putting pressure on yourself. Being with all this information can bring up very confronting realities and removes the veils from the reality of what's going on.

Allow yourself some time to let it sink into your conscious and unconscious. Trust that your unconscious will bring to your conscious self exactly what is important in your next step in moving forward.

I used to tell myself every day after I left the abuse that I don't need to work everything out *now*; it's actually not possible. All I need to do right now is work out the most important thing that I need to be focusing on in just this minute, in just this second.

Whatever it was that I needed to do in that next minute was never too daunting. Breaking the future down, challenges becomes possible. If I keep doing that, moment by moment, I'm not only going to get through the day, the week, the month, the year – I will be achieving exactly what's most necessary.

All you need to do is just focus on the most important thing for you today in this moment. This helped me get through so much. I hope it helps you, too.

Perhaps you can also take some small yet healthy risks: saying yes, receiving, saying no to support your boundaries, sharing your needs and confusion with someone. Give yourself permission not to fit in if it doesn't feel right.

All these little changes can build emotional muscle to tolerate being different, not fitting in and not trying to please.

It's okay to be the swan instead of the ugly duckling. It is also okay to be the duckling when you *are* with your duck tribe. We want to 'not feel okay' when we are not in the right place. This 'not okayness' motivates us to find our tribe and get out of the pain. So fly and find your bevvy of swans!

Where to from here? Everybody is at a different point in their life. Each of you has a different history, different challenges and different resources that may or may not be visible all at this moment.

I encourage you to be with your pace, without comparing and without expectations of what needs to happen next. The more you can develop compassion and understanding for yourself, acknowledging the reality of where you are, the more it is possible for changes to take place with ease and more naturally.

You will journey through shock, denial, grief, depression, bargaining (in an attempt to negotiate the pain away), anger (towards the Wolf/family/society/god, which will validate your truth and help you navigate the world) to a bigger picture where you come to a gentle acceptance and compassion. You may detour at times in righteous anger, entitlement to have a 'life without trauma' that we all long for, bitterness and disappointment.

When these times come, run to the tap – quickly, before the righteous anger fixates itself to you – and feel the water washing over and running over your hands. Let the righteous anger run down the drain and enter the oceans that can hold this.

Find where you have joy in your life and where you are loved and welcomed and build more of this. Do whatever is necessary to build more joy, so that contentment can enfold you. This will bring a deeper safety and acceptance and over time can lead you to a place that recognises we are all in the same field, a product of our history and forces beyond us all; humans living with the 'full catastrophe of life'.

> Out beyond ideas of wrongdoing and rightdoing,
>
> there is a field. I'll meet you there.
>
> When the soul lies down in that grass,
>
> the world is too full to talk about.
>
> Ideas, language, even the phrase 'each other'
>
> doesn't make any sense.
>   Jelalud-Din Rumi

Please, I would love to hear from you and hear how you are with this big journey we've been on together. You are really important to me. I wrote this book for you. I would love to know what this journey has meant for you and what your challenges and celebrations are. I promise I will personally write back to you.

I'm thinking of you.

Anita

Resources

Australia – National

1800 Respect	A free, confidential telephone and online service. Available 24/7. Translating and Interpreting Service: 13 14 50 and ask them to contact 1800RESPECT Deaf, Hearing, Speech impairments: www.relayservice.com.au and ask them to contact 1800RESPECT TTY/voice calls: 133 677 and ask them to contact 1800RESPECT Speak and Listen users: 1300 555 727 and ask them to contact 1800RESPECT www.1800respect.org.au
Luke Batty Foundation	Helping women and children from the trauma of family violence www.lukebattyfoundation.com.au
Our Watch	To change culture, behaviour and attitudes of violence towards women and children www.ourwatch.org.au

Women's Legal Services Australia	Community legal centres that provide advice, information, casework and education about family law, family violence and general legal matters. www.wlsa.org.au
Kid's Help Line	Free, confidential phone and online counselling for young people between 5-25 years. 1800 55 1800
The Men's Referral Centre	Anonymous, confidential, counselling, referrals and information for men who want to change their controlling, violent and abusive behaviours 1300 766 491
What Men Can Do	Information how men can respond and prevent violence towards women www.whatmencando.net
Australia's National Research Organisation For Women's Safety Limited ANROWS	Independent and not for profit organisation, established under the Australia's National Plan to reduce violence against women and their children 2010-2022 www.anrows.org.au
Lifeline	Crisis support service which addresses all crises including Family Violence 13 11 44 www.lifeline.org.au/Get-Help/Facts---Information/Domestic-Abuse-And-Family-Violence

States

Australian Capital Territory

Domestic Violence Crisis Service ACT	02 6280 0900 www.dvcs.org.au

New South Wales

Domestic Violence Line	1800 65 64 63 www.domesticviolence.nsw.gov.au

Northern Territory

Dawn House	08 8945 1388 www.dawnhouse.org.au

Queensland

DV Connect Womensline	1800 811 811 www.dvconnect.org/womensline

South Australia

Domestic Violence Crisis Service	1300 782 200
Domestic Violence and Aboriginal Family Violence Gateway Service	1800 800 098

Tasmania

Family Violence Response and Referral Line	1800 633 937 www.safeathome.tas.gov.au/services

Victoria

Domestic Violence Resource Centre Victoria	Training, publications, research and other resources to individuals, professionals and service organisations who work with family violence survivors. 03 9486 9866 www.dvrcv.org.au
Safe Steps	24/7 Family Violence response centre that offers intervention, support and advocacy for women and children who have or are experiencing family violence from a partner, ex-partner, family member or someone close to them 1800 015 188 www.safesteps.org.au
Immigrant Women's Domestic Violence Service	Information and support culturally and linguistically diverse backgrounds affected by domestic violence 03 8413 6800 toll free for rural callers: 1800 755 988 Translating and Interpreting Service: 131 450 247 (cost of a local call)
The Jewish Taskforce Against Domestic Violence	03 9523 2100 www.jewishtaskforce.com.au

Western Australia

Women's Domestic Violence Helpline	08 9223 1188 or 1800 007 339

New Zealand

Women's Refuge National Crisisline	Information, advice, support and help in a crisis. 24/7 Tollfree 0800REFUGE (0800 733 843) Auckland can also call 09 378 1893 www.womensrefuge.org.nz
Shine	Helpline for anyone living with abuse. This website includes information on how to stop someone knowing you have been seeking online information about domestic violence. 0508 744 633 (9am – 11pm 7 days a week) www.2shine.org.nz
Family Violence Information Line	Self help information and connection to the relevant services. 9am-11pm 7 days a week, with an after-hours emergency re-direction 0800 456 450 www.areyouok.org.nz

Apps

Daisy	Connects women who have experienced family violence and/ sexual assault to relevant services in their local area
iMatter	Connects young women to the warning signs of abusive and controlling relationships and educate about healthy self esteem

Meet Anita

Anita Bentata was born and raised in Melbourne, Australia. She is first generation Australian with a father born in Egypt and a mother from Poland. Both parents suffered WWII trauma, pain and dislocation from their countries of birth. This brought its own set of challenges along with home life full of cultural diversity, food, language, religion and traditions – such a contrast to the Aussie 'she'll be right, mate' lifestyle.

Anita's experience growing up was that the world was an intense and scary place with no one seeing or supporting her. Anita coped by hiding herself in a secret internal place, losing herself in the world of reading and writing poetry and disconnecting from her own thoughts, feelings and reality. Little did the local and school librarians realise that their presence was equal to being her friend.

Shortly after her parents' divorce, Anita, sixteen years old, left school and home.

Anita was engulfed with fear of being in the world, but the world seemed a better option with some possibility of goodness now she was out of the house of trauma and in a relationship. The door to hope and possibility opened up, though the reality was it took a very long time and years of therapy to get through that door – and close the door to trauma.

After escaping the violence and the courts and therapy process, Anita went on to study the Bachelor of Human Services (Human Behaviour) and was delighted to receive Golden Key National Honour Society membership for her high grades. Anita went on to do a further four year Soul Centred Psychotherapy and Counselling Diploma at the Kairos Centre in

Melbourne. Anita was then employed at Southern Family Life (now Family Life) counselling agency where she had been a client. Anita left to open her own private practice, where she has been working since 1999.

Anita's commitment to being free from emotional and physical pain is closely linked to her lifelong passion for health and self-care. The recognition of the close connection between stress, trauma, disease and ill health led Anita to further train as a Certified Health Coach (Institute of Integrative Nutrition) and later as a Restorative Exercise Specialist ™ at the Nutritious Movement Institute.

Through the years, Anita has also continued to extend her professional knowledge and development in both streams of her work: psychotherapy as well as Restorative Movement and Health Coaching; through certifications in areas such as Hypnotherapy, Trauma, Yoga Tune Up ® Ball Practitioner, Fascia and Foam Rolling and more.

Anita's grandmother, a light in her childhood, was an author herself and had always encouraged her grandchildren to be creative and writing. The time it took Anita to recover and heal, looking after her children and clients, left Anita neglecting her calling beyond her childhood poetry.

Upon getting closer to the age of fifty Anita was the most content, relaxed and fulfilled in all areas of her life, yet she realised that there were still some areas that needed attention to live her dreams rather than some things staying in the dream cloud in the sky.

She set about changing key areas of her life to create the lifestyle and life she wanted, including writing this book. Bringing this dream into reality includes writing a number of books, all based on embodied wellbeing in mind and body as well as more on abuse and the Little Red Riding Hood Effect.

Anita has been filmed and interviewed for the documentary *Dangerous Dance*, which will be released in 2017, and was guest on the panel at their gala event in August 2016. Anita is regularly invited to speak on panels and participate in community conversations about relationship abuse.

Anita is the mother of two daughters and Nona to three beautiful grandchildren. She loves living mindfully aligned to the rhythms of the body and nature, being true to herself, intimate connections, and accepting and expressing her true self. She loves travel, walking, salsa dancing, singing and all creative expressions of art, movement and writing. Anita refuses to walk on eggshells or hide who she is anymore.

Anita runs a Walking in Alignment group where she teaches the biomechanics of movement and where interesting conversations about life unfold!

***

Anita has an online program to build core strength and self on all levels – physically, mentally and emotionally – but first she had to keep a promise to the women in the family violence groups she had run at the beginning of her counselling career: to write this book.

Anita is committed to bringing the *Wolf in a Suit* information, her inspiring and motivational story and fairy tales, using them to teach messages through public talks, keynote speaking events and speaking on panels to advise and build community awareness and responses.

Anita continues to write blogs and books to complete the Wolf book series, in her mission to educate the community on how to become an active participant in a healing, thriving community.

Anita runs workshops, healing retreats, celebration of women events and online webinars and programs based on the Wolf series.

Anita works one to one, face to face and via Skype. She offers online and offline programs from her studio in Melbourne, Australia. Anita supports clients in the USA, the UK and Europe through group programs and consultations.

Anita runs two women's groups in Melbourne:

- *Women Starting Again:* for any woman who wants to be part of our family: education, learn healing tools, reclaim your sense of self, understand your past, socialise and reconnect with joy back to community.

- *Women Supporting Women:* for any woman who wants to understand abuse so she can be proactive and protective for herself or her daughter or to become an active knowledgeable member of community. This group is also where Anita strategically teaches women what to say and what not to say to their daughter, sister, friend, mother who is trapped in abuse to help them become aware and keep safe.

Anita would be deeply honoured to hear from you about your own life relationship experiences, and any responses or questions from reading *The Wolf in a Suit* – or if you have any questions about working with Anita.

Web: www.thewolfinasuit.com
Email: anita@thewolfinasuit.com
Facebook: www.facebook.com/TheWolfInASuit
Facebook: www.facebook.com/PowerWithinTheArtAndScienceOfMindBodyHealth
Instagram: www.instagram.com/anitabentata
Twitter: www.twitter.com/AnitaBentata
LinkedIn: www.linkedin.com/in/anita-bentata-37b53074

Offer 1

The Ultimate Formula for Moving Forward: the essential guide when a toxic relationship has controlled your life

www.thewolfinasuit.com/ultimateformula

- Step by step guide to finding the pieces and finding inner peace
- Clear and comprehensive
- Build and repair confidence
- Restore your body, mind and soul
- Sections on mind-body trauma and the healing process
- Simple and practical steps covering: safety, self-soothing and healing, connection in community, identity, trust, and a positive future.

www.thewolfinasuit.com/ultimateformula

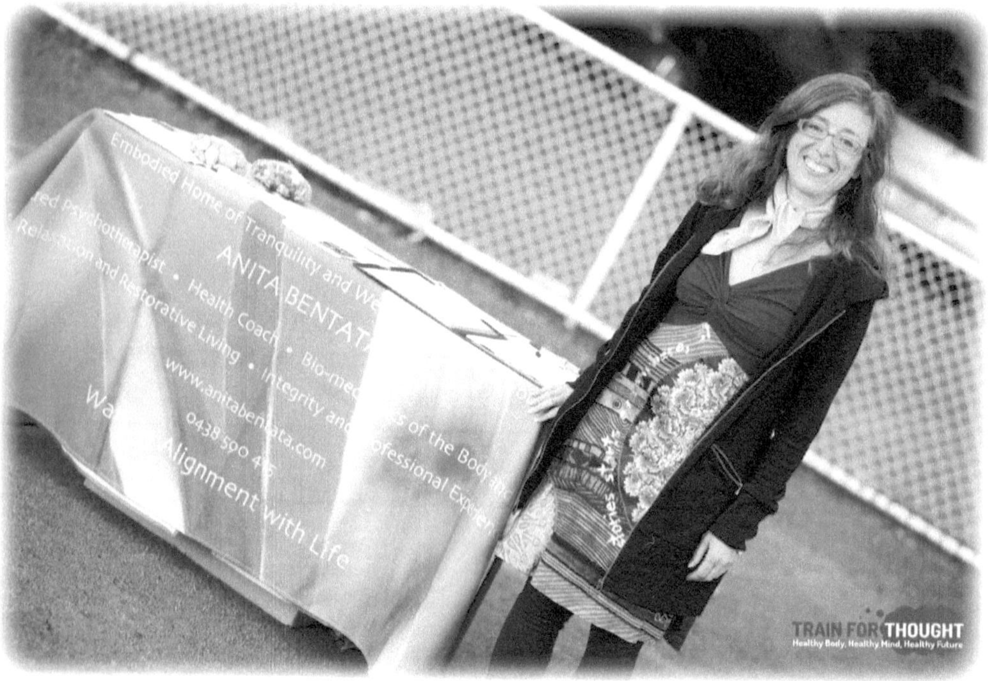
Embodied Home of Tranquility
ANITA BENTATA
Health Coach
Alignment with Life
TRAIN FOR THOUGHT
Healthy Body, Healthy Mind, Healthy Future

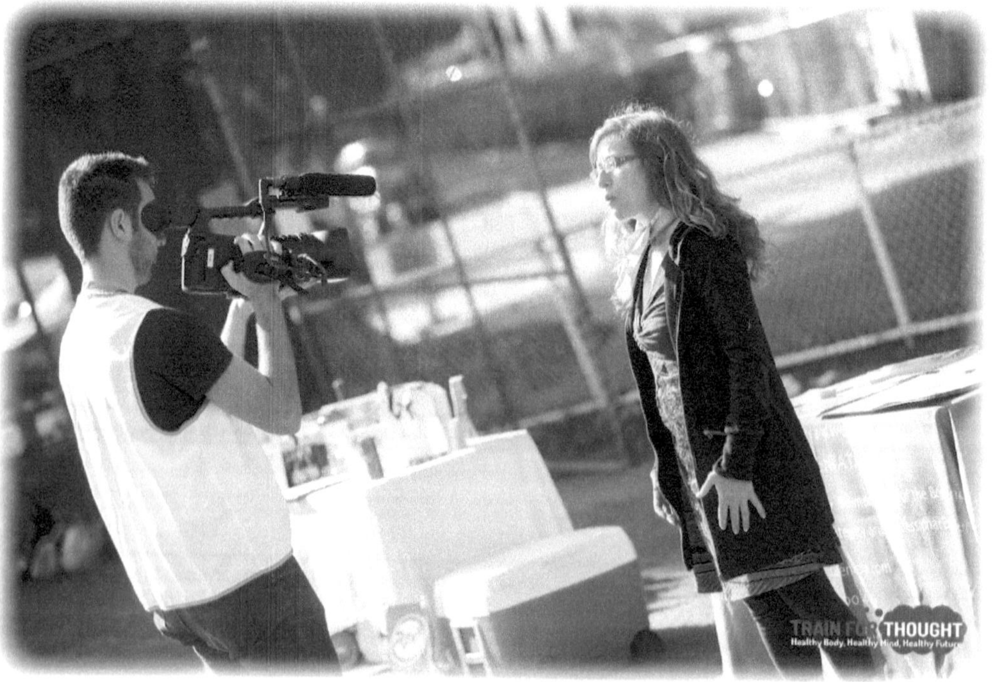
TRAIN FOR THOUGHT
Healthy Body, Healthy Mind, Healthy Future

Offer 2

Keynote Speaker

Anita Bentata is a highly skilled, in-demand Speaker and Workshop Facilitator with over twenty years experience in trauma, healing and relationships.

She transforms the complex nature of being human into practical steps.

Her warm, clear and inspiring approach brings lightness to the dark, building new strategies to negotiate the stress of life, boundaries, communication, power and love.

Anita speaks to professionals, organisations and community groups.

She provides fairy tales, education and the action to create simple changes in daily life, to be part of the Ripple Effect that reaches beyond.

An aware community is only as aware as the skill and emotional muscle of the individuals.

Anita can be booked to speak on a variety of motivational topics, including:

Anita's Story: lessons, laughter and meaning.

Contact Anita at anita@thewolfinasuit.com to discuss the range of talks available, including:

Little Red Riding Hood Effect

- Lessons from Little Red Riding Hood
- Three tips to go from passive to actively powerful
- Protection and prevention: find your 5 keys to the Woodcutter Within

The Red Shoes

- Stress and women's secret stress factor
- What is trauma and what happens to my brain?
- How to get out of the stress response

Rumpelstiltskin

- The power of naming and what gets in the way
- What is abuse? The fourteen types of family violence
- How is abuse different from conflict in relationships?

Contact Anita at anita@thewolfinasuit.com for bookings and enquiries.

Offer 3

Webinar series: The Wolf in a Suit

Work with me, in a live, interactive space, from your home or workplace.

I tell you the stories and unpack the themes in relation to my interpretations about abuse and relationships.

You have the immediacy of being able to ask me questions, hear my stories and information to take you even further into the material, making the tales personal and real.

This series is suitable for all women, professionals and anyone who wants to understand more about abuse and the confusion we get into as a society and individual in our personal and community relationships.

INCLUSIONS:	Level One: Fairy Tales and Truths	Level Two: Fairy Tales, Truths and getting personal	Level Three: Fairy Tales, Truths and Delving Deeper
Join me from home, no time wasting, childcare hassles. If you can't make a meeting, watch the recording. The feminine way. Flexible and responsive to your needs.	✓	✓	✓
Twelve Webinars: two hours each. Fortnightly over six months	✓	✓	✓
Preparation questionnaire emailed prior to first webinar	✓	✓	✓
Homework task to integrate information after each webinar and emailed back to me for further discussion (one page)	✓	✓	✓
Email and phone support from me when needed to answer questions on the content	✓	✓	✓
Manifesto (inspiration)	✓	✓	✓
Three one-on-one sessions of forty minutes each to check in (phone call / Skype)	✓	✓	✓
Bonus downloadable books (3): Answers to Anger, Procrastination and Grief	✓	✓	✓
Bonus downloadable book: Urgent and Unspoken: Helping your friend Recognise her Abusive Relationship	✓	✓	✓
Three private one-on-one sessions with Anita to learn some of the tools mentioned in The Wolf in a Suit		✓	✓
Oracle Cards from The Wolf in a Suit to continue to guide and inspire you on your journey		✓	✓
Preliminary checklist provided when beginning the program			✓
Four group sessions, monthly two hour sessions on zoom: educative and interactive and homework given (optional)			✓
Four check-in question reflection sheet to support you through each session which you can email back to get additional feedback support			✓
Four topics to be chosen specific to group member needs upon booking			✓

Webinar Topics:
- My Story and my insights
- Little Red Riding Hood Effect: Innocence and Protection
- Rumpelstiltskin: Naming Abuse, the 14 types and how abuse is different from conflict
- The Handless Maiden: Family, Society, Culture, Religion, History
- The Ugly Duckling: Family and being Different
- Bluebeard's Seduction: Love and False Love
- Lilith: Anger and Power

- Cinderella: Anger, Assertion and Female Role Models
- The Little Match Girl: Hope, Cycle of Violence
- The Red Shoes: Stress and Women's Stress Response
- Vasalisa: Intuition, Instinct and Creating a New Map
- Bonus: The Emperor's New Clothes: What to say or do when you know someone who is in a toxic or abusive relationship.

Topics:
- Going Round in Circles
- But Relaxing is Uncomfortable!
- Becoming your Best Friend!
- I Want a Fairy Godmother!
- Your Anger wants to Serve You
- Carefree not Careless
- Jealousy's Gem
- Procrastination's Secret
- When my Tears Fill an Ocean

Offer 4

Vasilisa the Queen: Healing and Transformation Retreat

Anita combines her love of life with Soul Centred Psychotherapy and her Restorative Exercise training to provide an abundant retreat for women to heal, reclaim and connect to their core self.

Restore, heal, nourish and discover your mind, body and soul.

Being with the feminine involves developing a connection between the conscious and the unconscious, and a greater access to the instinctual self and the body. This allows the interior experience to influence, guide and provide a greater access to knowing what to do and when; rather than just relying on the conscious capacity of the moment.

Reconnect and reclaim your natural, instinctual self.

The feminine way is generous, flexibly responsive, creative and fun and opens up your potential, giving expression and form to all of who you are.

This is your retreat. Your retreat has many surprises, resources and diversity in ways of connecting to you and other women. Lose the doubts and distractions. Develop direction, depth and delight in your essence.

Contact anita@thewolfinasuit.com for bookings and enquiries about the retreat and location: national and international.

Inclusions:	Shedding Skins / Starting Over	Self-Healing / Moving On	Being Me, Being Free / Celebration
PRODUCTS:			
Little Red Riding Hood BOOKMARK	✓	✓	✓
Journal: JOURNEY TO ME Your Private Journal to reconnect to you	✓	✓	✓
ORACLE CARDS : Little Red Riding Hood Discovery	✓	✓	✓
MANIFESTO OF ME Chart	✓	✓	✓
Warning Signs CHECKLIST	✓	✓	✓
Compassion Trust CHECKLIST	✓	✓	✓
DOWNLOADABLE BOOKS:			
The Ultimate Formula for Moving Forward: The Essential Guide when an Abusive Relationship has Controlled your Life	✓	✓	✓
Answers to Anger: Little Red Riding Hood's Guide	✓	✓	✓
BOOKS:			
The Wolf in a Suit: the 7 Secrets inside relationship abuse: Fairy Tales and Truths for women, community and professionals – autographed	✓	✓	✓
SUPPORT:			
Unlimited Email Support	✓	✓	✓
Private Group		✓	✓
2 Hour Prep Session with me 1:1		✓	✓

EDUCATION:		
8 week talk series Membership/ Handouts	✓	✓
Webinar Membership	✓	✓
DOWNLOADABLE BOOKS:		
Urgent and Unspoken: About the Wolf: Helping your Friend Recognise her Abusive Relationship	✓	✓
Wednesday is the Worst Day Ever: How to Build Children's Safety and Strength, even if the Wolf is Prowling	✓	✓
From Unpsoken to Spoken Conversations about the Wolf: Helping Your Friend Recognise her Abusive Relationship	✓	✓
RETREAT:		
Weekend Retreat: Support and Healing 1. Gentle Healing 2. Embodiment 3. Creativity 4. Confidence 5. Transformation 6. Celebration Luxury Accommodation, Restaurant Quality Meals, Massage, Group Retreat	✓	✓
INDIVIDUAL RETREAT		✓
Powerful Shining Woman Program		✓
One on One Mentoring (3 Months)		✓

Acknowledgements

First, I want to thank my two daughters. Writing this book has been a massive challenge for each of us. The intensity of our past has surfaced over the year of this book being written. I have no words that can touch the edges to my appreciation of your courage in allowing me to share some of your story. At times, I wanted to put the book away and say, no I won't write this. You don't need your privacy to be exposed - you have had enough unchosen intrusion. There is nothing I can say. Thank you. I love you deeply.

Thank you to John Hopper and Kaalii Cargill for your generous assistance, encouragement, support and immense skill in helping me with my writing.

Thank you to Russell Shaw, from Sattva Natural Therapies. You have been there for me in so many effective, gentle, deep and caring ways to open up healing for me and my daughters, physically and emotionally. Your abundant Traditional Chinese Medicine wisdom is always with me. Thank you. Michaela from Sattva, thank you for teaching me Macrobiotic cooking and your amazing shiatsu massages. You saw me when I was lost and I felt normal, valued and capable with your warmth and care.

Thank you to my sisters Yvette and Liliane for your support with my book and coming to my first Little Red Riding Hood talk, even though I share uncomfortable aspects of our relationship and life. To my father, for blessing me to tell my story no matter what. He did the best he could. To my mother: no matter what has happened, I love you. To my cousin Beth who has been there in ways no one has: I will never forget the numerous ways you have been there for me including how you were there for me when I fractured my back and no one was there but you. And travelling to Spain together.

Thank you to my dream group Kaalii Cargill, Lindy Spanger, Julie Stewart-Rose, Lyndel Robinson, and Erica Ulbrick-Lewis, for your ongoing love, wisdom and support, especially through the intense journey of birthing this baby. To my Soul Centred Psychotherapists, Judy Williams and Mary Coughlin, who were extraordinary through the early years in my healing journey; and to Raquel L Dubois for your magnificent Somatic Experience therapy skills and care in working with me through the writing of my book. I will see you soon!

To Natasa and Stu Denman, for providing a safe and skilled place to birth this baby. To my 48 hour team – Luciane Sperling, Francesca Moi, James Bomford, Kym Pace, Megan Wright, Mell Balment, Shanti Clements, Ursula Stroh, Chris Dennis, Wendy Exton, Tony Park, Christina Fletcher and Eleanor Hannah – for helping create one of the best weekends of my life. To Richard Burian for his amazing transcription and voluntarily emailing me the first ever congratulatory feedback on my book. For Nik Boskovski for his patience, skill and smiley face in helping me with diagrams and other designs.

To Blaise, Kev, Beau and Les for their unwavering patience with all the tweaking of the editing and proofing, thank you. To Caro for driving such a long way to help me with my makeup and prepare for my photo shoot. To Frazer Yendell from the Public Speaking Institute for some mind blowingly fantastic coaching and Dominique Oyston for your depth in finesse in coaching me on speaking and creating my keynote, and giving me some magic to speak my truth; and to Oriana Merullo for your friendship and putting in touch with Caro.

Marilou Coombe, for your enormous heart and encouragement; Jenny Widdows and Meg Hirst, who years ago came out from the shadows of childhood school peer pressures to reunite with me and are celebrating with me now; Mikayla Shahrinia, my dear soul sister, for your love and support; Kyla Rose, Claire Mockbridge and Janey Sattentau, for your love and sanity in reminding me of Restorative Exercise ™ when I have been immersed in my book.

To my new friends that I never would have met without this book: Liana Papoutsis and Lisa McAdams, you are my inspiration. We are three powerhouses confronting the face of abuse; Margaret Cunniffe from CNF

Connect Network and Fundraise, and Kathy Kaplan from Impact, for your inspiration, support and your passion to help vulnerable women affected by abuse. Elizabeth Roebuck-Jones, author of *Stop Kissing Toads: Pucker up and Find Your Prince*, for your support and wisdom.

Livia York, author of *Rise: The Abused Child of the Phoenix*, you are beyond words special and inspirational. Karen Hodgkins, the world is fortunate to have your skill and passion to reveal to the world through documentaries and books about many injustices. Kate Boyden, words cannot express my admiration for your courage. Cheryl Gillepsie, Shania Meyer for your survivor songs and stories. I have met so many inspirational survivors. Julie Stewart-Rose you have been incredible, with your songs and your support with my crowd funding campaign. I love you.

To Darren Mort, an inspiration in your kindness, professional legal capacity and for your heart and skill, including through acting in being there for women impacted by violence. To Tessa Spivak (*Fifth Avenue Collection*), Yolanda Lyons for your incredible support and networking for my fundraising, Rebecca Lyons and Nicki Kerrins (*A Little Touch of Bali*) and Annie Holcombe (*Grace Revolution*) for helping kick-start my fundraising and sponsorship for my book. To Beatrice Coleman for your open ears and heart in wanting to know my story. Amira Kay, I love continuing our journey together. And to Claire and Brendon Stretch from Film Stretch for including me in the documentary *Dangerous Dance*. You are stuck with me forever!

Anita Coakley, you are a quiet, secret superstar and support; to Anne Maree Templeton for supporting me in my new venture. And to all my clients, you have all inspired and taught me, though you may not have realised it; to my Women Starting Again members, you are my true family and inspiration. Thanks to Rowena from Bennettswood Community House and Cheryl from Burwood Neighbourhood House for supporting me with the group Women Starting Again. Quest from Glen Waverley for the beautiful sponsorship of your space in supporting me run my first Little Red Riding Hood workshop.

Thank you Clarissa Pinkola Estés for the gift, which became my Bible: *Women Who Run With Wolves*, my comfort when I left the Wolf. When we don't know the Wolf within us, we can be caught by the wolves around us. May we all find our own Wolf so we can become the free, instinctual and powerful wolf we are and not prey for the hungry, hunting wolf.

I want to thank some men who through the years have reminded me that real men do exist, and comfort me of the integrity of heart-centred men: Shaun Hall, Ross Halpin, General (Retired) David Morrison AO, John Arthur Gould, Paul Sykes, Deepak Tamang, Sandeep Labar, Dip Kulung, Chris Backhouse, and Oliver Sacks. Though I never met you Oliver, you have comforted me in your integrity of being a man for many years as I read each of your books. To David Whyte for your simplicity, gentleness, spaciousness and love in offering the world a real way of being a man. To Roger Housden for opening another door into poetry, which brought me deeper comfort and love. To Gay Hendricks for being a true man, showing your wisdom and heart teaching about conscious relationships.

And Neil Teasdale: I hope you know that without you in my life I would be so much poorer. You hold the standard men have to stand up to – plus you opened me up to Uluru, Nepal and chocolate! Thank you.

We don't need to focus on fighting abuse, we just need to wake up society to name and be activated. That is far easier. We can do this.

References and Further Reading

Afanasyev, A, 1863, *Russian Fairy Tales*, Russia

Andersen, H C, The Hans Christian Andersen Centre, http://andersen.sdu.dk

Bandler, R 2008, *Richard Bandler's Guide to Trance-Formation: How to Harness the Power of Hypnosis to Ignite Effortless and Lasting Change*, Health Communications Inc.

Bandler, R, et al, 2005, *The Structure of Magic, Vol. 1: A Book About Language and Therapy Edition 1*, Science and Behaviour Books

Bancroft, L, 2003, *Why Does He Do That: Inside the Minds of Angry and Controlling Men*, Penguin Putnam Inc

Bandler, R Grinder, J, 1975, *Patterns of the Hypnotic Techniques of Milton H Erickson, MD*, Vol 1, Meta Publications, US

Bettelheim, B, 2010, *The Uses of Enchantment: The Meaning and Importance of Fairy Tales*, Vintage Books

Brandt, K, et al, 2013, *Infant and early childhood mental health: core concepts and clinical practice*, American Psychiatric Publishing, Washington DC

Brown, B, 2015, *Daring Greatly: How the Courage to be Vulnerable Transforms the Way We Live, Love, Parent, and Lead*, Penguin Group

Brown, B, 2010, *The Gifts of Imperfection: Let Go of Who You Think You're Supposed to be and Embrace Who You Are*, Hazelden Information and Educational Services

Brown, B, 2007, *I Thought It Was Just Me (but it isn't): Making the Journey from "What Will People Think?" to "I Am Enough"*, Penguin Group

Brown, B, 2004, *Women and Shame: Reaching Out, Speaking Truths and Building Connection*, 3C Press

Burkley, M, 2009, 'Why Don't We Help? Less Is More, at Least When It Comes to Bystanders', *Psychology Today*, Nov. 4, https://www.psychologytoday.com/blog/the-social-thinker/200911/why-don-t-we-help-less-is-more-least-when-it-comes-bystanders

Cantor-Zuckoff, A, 1976, 'The Lilith Question', *Lilith*, http://lilith.org/articles/the-lilith-question

Cozolino, L, 2010, *The Neuroscience of Psychotherapy: Healing the Social Brain (2nd Edition Norton Series on Interpersonal Neurobiology)*, W W Norton New York

2008, Chiao, J Y; Iidaka, T; Gordon, H L; Nogawa, J; Bar, M; Aminoff, E; Sedato, N; & Ambady, N, 'Cultural specificity in amygdala response to fear faces', *Journal of Cognitive Neuroscience*, Vol. 20, No. 12, pp. 2167–74, http://www.ncbi.nlm.nih.gov/pubmed/18457504

D'Andrea, W, et al, 2012, 'Understanding Interpersonal Trauma in Children: Why We Need a Developmentally Appropriate Trauma Diagnosis', *American Journal of Orthopsychiatry*, Vol. 82, No. 2, pp. 187–200.

Doidge N MD, 2007, *The Brain That Changes Itself: Stories of Personal Triumph from the Frontiers of Brain Science*, Viking Books

Dawe, G S; Tan, X W; Xiao, Z C, 2007, 'Cell Migration from Baby to Mother', *Cell Adhesion and Migration*, Vol. 1, Issue 1, pp. 19–27.

Erikson, M H, et al, 1987, *Mind Body Communication in Hypnosis (The Seminars, Workshops, and Lectures of Milton H. Erikson, Vol. 3)* 1st edition, Irvington Publisher

Estés, C P, 1992, *Women Who Run With the Wolves*, Random House, New York

Evans, P, 2010, *The Verbally Abusive Relationship: How to Recognise It and How to Respond,* Adams Media, F and W Media Inc.

Fosha, D PhD, et al, 2009, *The Healing Power of Emotion: Affective Neuroscience, Development & Clinical Practice (Norton Series on Interpersonal Neurobiology)* WW Norton, New York

Friday N, 1997, *Jealousy,* M Evans and Company

Friday N, 1997, *My Mother / My Self: The Daughter's Search for Identity,* Dell Publishing

Friday N, 1999, *Our Looks/Our Lives: Sex, Beauty, Power and the Need to Be Seen,* Harper Torch

Frankl, V E, 2006, *Man's Search for Meaning,* Beacon Press

Gazzaniga, M S, 1998, *The Mind's Past,* University of California Press, USA, p. 21

Gazzaniga, M S, 1998, 'The Split Brain Revisited', *Scientific American,* July 1998, pp. 50–55

Gazzaniga M S, 2011, *Who's in Charge: Free Will and the Science of the Brain,* Harper Collins Publishers

Grimm, J; Grimm, W, 1812, *Children's and Household Tales,* Germany.

Grinder, J, et al, 1976, *The Structure of Magic II: A Book About Communication and Change,* Science and Behaviour Books

Haley, J, 1993, *Uncommon Therapy: The Psychiatric Techniques of Milton H. Erikson, M.D.,* W W Norton New York

Herrero, N, et al, 2010, 'What happens when we get angry? Hormonal, cardiovascular and asymmetrical brain responses', *Hormones and Behavior,* March, Vol. 57, No. 3, pp. 276–283

Hirstein, W, 2013, 'What is a Psychopath? The Neuroscience of Psychopathy Reports Some Intriguing Findings', *Psychology Today,* Jan 30, https://www.psychologytoday.com/blog/mindmelding/201301/what-is-psychopath-0

Hirstein, W, 2013, *Mindmelding: Consciousness, Neuroscience, and the Mind's Privacy*, Oxford University Press, New York

Kalsched, D, 1996, *The Inner World of Trauma*, Routledge, New York

King H, et al, 1993, *Hysteria Beyond Freud*, University of California Press, Los Angeles; Tasca C et al 2012, 'Women and Hysteria in the History of Mental Health', *Clinical Practice and Epidemiology in Mental Health*, Vol. 8, pp. 110–119.

Kitzmann, K, et al, 2003, 'Child Witnesses to Domestic Violence: a Meta-Analytic Review', *Journal of Consulting and Clinical Psychology*, Vol. 71, No. 2, pp. 339–352

Kline, M, 2007; Levine, P A, *Trauma through a Child's Eyes: Awakening the Ordinary Miracle of Healing*, North Atlantic Books, Berkeley, California

Kvam, K E; Schearing, S; Ziegler, V, 2009, *Eve and Adam: Jewish, Christian and Muslim Readings on Geneisis and Gender*, Indiana University Press, USA.

Lang, A, 1889, *The Blue Fairy Book*, UK.

Levine P A, et al 2012, *Freedom from Pain: Discover Your Body's Power to Overcome Physical*, Sounds True Inc.

Levine P A, 2010, *In an Unspoken Voice: How the Body Releases Trauma and Restores Goodness*, North Atlantic Books

Levine P A, 2008, *Healing Trauma: A Pioneering Program for Restoring the Wisdom of Your Body*, Sounds True Inc.

Levine P A, 2015, *Trauma and Memory: Brain and Body in a Search for the Living past: A Practical Guide for Understanding and Working with Traumatic Memory*, North Atlantic Books

Levine P A, et al, 2008, *Trauma Proofing Your Kids: A Parent's Guide for Instilling Confidence, Joy and Resilience*, North Atlantic Books

Levine P A, 1997, *Waking the Tiger: Healing Trauma*, North Atlantic Books

McBride, K, 2008, *Will I Ever be Good Enough?*, Simon & Schuster, New York

McBride, K, 2013, 'Mothers who are jealous of their daughters', *Psychology Today*, Oct. 21, https://www.psychologytoday.com/blog/the-legacy-distorted-love/201310/mothers-who-are-jealous-their-daughters

McGrory Massaro, M, 2012, 'A peek into the past: touching our babies' https://theotherbabybook.wordpress.com/2012/08/13/a-peek-into-the-past-touching-our-babies/

McLeod, S 2016, 'Maslow's Hierarchy of Needs', *Simply Psychology*, http://www.simplypsychology.org/maslow.html

Miller, A, 1991, *Banished Knowledge: Facing Childhood Injuries*, Anchor Press, New York

Miller, A, 1997, *Breaking Down the Wall of Silence*, Virago Press revised edition

Miller, A, 2006, *The Body Never Lies: The Lingering Effects of Cruel Parenting*, W. W. Norton & Co. New York

Miller, A, 1997, *The Drama of the Gifted Child*, Basic Books, New York new edition revised and updated

Miller, A, 1990, *For Your Own Good: Hidden Cruelty in Child-rearing and the Roots of Violence*, Farrar Straus Giroux, New York

Miller, A, 2010, *Free From Lies: Discovering your true needs*, W. W. Norton & Co. New York

Miller, A, 2009, *From Rage to Courage: Answers to reader's letters*, W. W. Norton & Co. New York

Miller, A, 1998, *Thou Shalt Not Be Aware*, Farrar Straus Giroux, New York

Miller, A, 1991, *The Untouched Key: Tracing Childhood Trauma in Creativity and Destructiveness*, Anchor Press, New York

Miller, T Q, et al, 1996, 'Meta-analytic review of research on hostility and physical health', *Psychological Bulletin*, Vol. 119, No. 2, pp. 322–348

Odhayani, A; Watson, W; Watson, L, 2013, 'Behavioural Consequences of Child Abuse', Canadian Family Physician, Aug, Vol. 59, No. 8, pp. 831–836, http://www.ncbi.nlm.nih.gov/pmc/articles/PMC3743691/

Ogden, P, et al, 2006, *Trauma and the Body: A Sensorimotor Approach to Psychotherapy (Norton Series on Interpersonal Neuorbiology*, 1st edition), W W Norton New York

Orchowski L M; Berkowitz A; Boggis J; Oesterle D 2015, 'Bystander Intervention Among College Men: The Role of Alcohol and Correlates of Sexual Aggression', *Journal of Interpersonal Violence*, 2015 pp. 1–23.

Porges, S W, 2011, *The Polyvagal Theory: Neurophysiological Foundations of Emotions, Attachment, Communication, and Self-regulation (Norton Series on Interpersonal Neurobiology)*, 1st edition, W W Norton New York

Pearsall, P, 1999, *The Heart's Code: Tapping the Wisdom and Power of our Heart Energy*, Broadway Books, New York.

Perrault, C, 1697, *Stories or Tales from Times Past, with Morals: Tales of Mother Goose*, Claude Barbin, Paris, http://www.pitt.edu/~dash/perrault.html

Perry, B D, Szalavitz M 2007, *The Boy Who Was Raised As A Dog: What Traumatized Children Can Teach Us About Loss, Love and Healing*, Basic Books, New York

Perry, B D, 2009, 'Examining Child Maltreatment Through a Neurodevelopmental Lens: Clinical Applications of the Neurosequential Model of Therapeutics', *Journal of Loss and Trauma*, Vol. 14, pp. 240–255

Perry, B D, Szalavitz M 2010, *Born for Love: Why Empathy is Essential and Endangered*, Harper, New York

Pert, C, 1997, *The Molecules of Emotion: The Science Behind Mind-Body Medicine*, Touchstone, New York.

Pipher, M, 1994, *Reviving Ophelia*, Penguin Group (USA), New York

Richards, K, 2011, 'Children's exposure to domestic violence in Australia', *Trends and Issues in Crime and Criminal Justice*, Australian Institute of Criminology, June, No. 419.

Rosen, S, 1991, *My Voice will go with you: The Teaching Tales of Milton H. Erikson*, W W Norton New York

Rothschild, B, 2010, *The Body Remembers The Psychophysiology of Trauma and Trauma Treatment* 1st edition, W W Norton New York

Rozsak, T, 2001, *The Voice of the Earth: An Exploration of Ecopsychology*, Phanes Press

Sandman, C; Davis, E; Glynn, L, 2011, 'Change in Mother's Mental State Can Influence Her Baby's Development Before and After Birth', *Association for Psychological Science*, https://www.sciencedaily.com/releases/2011/11/111110142352.htm

Schore, A, 2003, *Affect Dysregulation and the Disorders of the Self*, W W Norton and Company, New York

Schore, A N PhD, 2015, *Affect Regulation and the Origin of the Self: The Neurobiology of Emotional Development*, Psychology Press and Routledge Classic Editions, Routledge

Schore, A N PhD, 2003, *Affect Regulation and the Repair of the Self (Norton Series on Interpersonal Neuorbiology)*, 1st edition, W W Norton New York

Shandler, S, 1999, *Ophelia Speaks: Adolescent Girls write about their Search for Self*, HarperCollins, New York

Siegel, D, 2015, *Brainstorm: The Power and Purpose of the Teenage Brain*, Penguin Group

Siegel, D, 2012, 5th ed, *The Developing Mind Second Edition: How Relationships and the Brain Interact to Shape Who We Are*, Guilford Press

Siegel, D, 2016, *No-Drama Discipline: The Whole-Brain Way to Calm the Chaos and Nurture Your Child's Developing Mind*, Bantam Books, New York

Siegel, D, et al, 2010, *Healing Trauma: Attachment, Mind, Body and Brain (Norton Series on Interpersonal Neurobiology)*, 1st edition, W W Norton New York

Siegel, D, et al, 2004, *Parenting from the Inside Out: How a Deeper Self-Understanding Can Help You Raise Children Who Thrive*, Penguin Group, New York

Solomon, M F, et al, 2003, *Healing Trauma: Attachment, Mind, Body and Brain*, WW Norton, New York

Staicu, M L; Cutov, M, 2010, 'Anger and Health Risk Behaviors', *Journal of Medicine and Life*, Nov 15, Vol. 3, No. 4, pp. 372–375, http://www.ncbi.nlm.nih.gov/pmc/articles/PMC3019061/

Staub, E, 2005, 'The Roots of Goodness: The fulfillment of basic human needs and the development of caring, helping and nonaggression, inclusive caring, moral courage, active bystandership, and altruism born of suffering', *Moral Motivation Through the Life Span*, University of Nebraska Press, USA

Staub, E, 2012, 'Our Power as Active Bystanders', *Psychology Today*, Jan. 27, https://www.psychologytoday.com/blog/in-the-garden-good-and-evil/201201/our-power-active-bystanders

Stiles, M, 2002, 'Witnessing Domestic Violence, the Effect on Children', *American Family Physician*, Dec 1, Vol. 66(11), pp. 2052–2067

Streep, P, 2009, *Mean Mothers: Overcoming the Legacy of Hurt*, HarperCollins, New York

Streep, P, 2015, 'Jealous Mothers and their daughters: the last dirty secret?' *Psychology Today*, Mar. 16, https://www.psychologytoday.com/blog/tech-support/201503/jealous-mothers-and-their-daughters-the-last-dirty-secret

Tasca, C, et al, 2012, 'Women and Hysteria in the History of Mental Health', *Clinical Practice and Epidemiology in Mental Health*, Vol. 8, 110–119, http://www.ncbi.nlm.nih.gov/pmc/articles/PMC3480686/

Tassone, S n.d., 'The Two-Way Umbilical Cord: Bonding with your Baby Before Birth', *The Llewellyn Journal*, https://www.llewellyn.com/journal/article/2421

Taylor, S E, 2002, *The Tending Instinct: Women, Men and the Biology of our Relationships*, Times Books, New York

Ulanov, A; Ulanov, B; Verlag, D, 2012,*Cinderella and Her Sisters: The Envied and the Envying*, 3rd. ed, Westminster Press, Philadelphia.

Van der Kolk, B, 2015, *The Body Keeps the Score: Brain, Mind and Body in the Healing of Trauma*, 1st edition, Penguin Books

Van der Kolk, B, n.d, 'Developmental Trauma Disorder', Psychiatric Annals, Vol. 35, No. 5, pp 401–408, The Trauma Center

Van der Kolk, B et al 2006, *Traumatic Stress: The Effects of Overwhelming Experience on Mind, Body, and Society*, The Guilford Press

Walker, L E, 1980, *Battered Woman*, William Morrow

West Allen S, et al, *Brains On Purpose TM Neuroscience and conflict resolution* http://westallen.typepad.com/brains_on_purpose/

Whitbourne, S K, 2015, 'What Women Need to Know About the Bystander Effect in Men', *Psychology Today*, May 16, https://www.psychologytoday.com/blog/fulfillment-any-age/201505/what-women-need-know-about-the-bystander-effect-in-men

Yapko M D, 2000, *Hand Me Down Blues: How To Stop Depression From Spreading In Families* 1st ed, Golden Guides, St Martin's Press

Yapko M D, 2012, *Trancework: An Introduction to the Practice of Clinical Hypnosis*, 4 ed, Routledge

Find your Instinct, Power and Woodcutter Within

Web: www.thewolfinasuit.com
Email: anita@thewolfinasuit

Notes

Notes

Notes

busybird
publishing
www.busybird.com.au

Want to get published?

We've helped hundreds of authors get their books out into the world!

Whether you're a novellist; a poet; a children's author; a biographer writing about a person, family history, or community; a business person who wants to showcase their expertise to the world; a coach who wants to share their techniques with a greater audience; or a writer of any kind who has a project, Busybird Publishing can help tailor a publishing package to suit your needs!

Let us take care of whatever facets of book production you require – editing, proofing, design, layout, ISBN registration, library deposit, printing, marketing, and so much more.

Call us on **(03) 9434 6365** to have a chat!

ACTIVATING ARTEMIS
TARGETING RELATIONSHIP ABUSE

Anita Bentata

Thank you.

www.ingramcontent.com/pod-product-compliance
Lightning Source LLC
Chambersburg PA
CBHW021112300426
44113CB00006B/121